CONVEYANCING 2018

CONVEYANCING 2018

Kenneth G C Reid WS

Professor of Scots Law in the University of Edinburgh

and

George L Gretton WS

Lord President Reid Professor of Law Emeritus in the University of Edinburgh

with a contribution by Alan Barr of the University of Edinburgh
and Brodies LLP

Avizandum Publishing Ltd
Edinburgh
2019

Published by
Avizandum Publishing Ltd
25 Candlemaker Row
Edinburgh EH1 2QG

First published 2019

ISBN 978-1-904968-99-3

British Library Cataloguing in Publication Data
A catalogue record for this book is available from the British Library.

Typeset by Waverley Typesetters, Warham, Norfolk
Printed and bound by Bell & Bain Ltd, Glasgow

CONTENTS

PART III: OTHER MATERIAL

PART IV: COMMENTARY

PART V: TABLES

PREFACE

This is the twentieth annual update of new developments in the law of conveyancing. As in previous years, it is divided into five parts. There is, first, a brief description of all cases which have been reported, or appeared on the websites of the Scottish Courts (www.scotcourts.gov.uk) or of the Lands Tribunal for Scotland (www.lands-tribunal-scotland.org.uk/), or have otherwise come to our attention since *Conveyancing 2017*. A notable feature this year is the number of unreported cases which Professor Roderick Paisley has retrieved from the archives and passed on to us. We are grateful to him; the cases enrich this volume.

The next two parts summarise, respectively, statutory developments during 2018 and other material of interest to conveyancers. The fourth part is a detailed commentary on selected issues arising from the first three parts. Finally, in part V, there are two tables. A cumulative table of decisions, usually by the Lands Tribunal, on the variation or discharge of title conditions covers all decisions since the revised jurisdiction in part 9 of the Title Conditions (Scotland) Act 2003 came into effect. This is followed by a cumulative table of appeals, designed to facilitate moving from one annual volume to the next.

We do not seek to cover agricultural holdings, crofting, public sector tenancies (except the right-to-buy legislation), compulsory purchase or planning law. Otherwise our coverage is intended to be complete. It has been possible to include a small number of cases from England.

We gratefully acknowledge help received from Sir Crispin Agnew of Lochnaw QC, Alan Barr, Mike Blair, Ian Bowie, Malcolm Combe, Denis Garrity, James Lloyd, Rebecca MacLeod, Hector MacQueen, David McIndoe, Andrew Steven, and Neil Tainsh.

Kenneth G C Reid
George L Gretton
14 March 2019

TABLE OF STATUTES

TABLE OF ORDERS

TABLE OF CASES

PART I
CASES

CASES

MISSIVES OF SALE

(1) Law v Robertson Construction Eastern Ltd
[2018] CSIH 24, 2018 SC 428, 2018 SLT 377

On 2 May 2008 missives were concluded for the sale of commercial premises at 34, 36 and 47 South Esplanade West, Torry, Aberdeen, at a price of £475,000. Clause 8.1 of the offer provided that:

> In exchange for payment of the Purchase Price, there will be delivered (a) a validly executed Disposition of the Subjects in favour of the Purchaser ... and (b) the duly executed Overage Agreement (in duplicate to allow the parties hereto to retain one copy each).

A draft overage (or clawback) agreement was included in the schedule to the missives. It provided for further payment to be made to the seller in the event that the buyer obtained certain types of development consent.

In fact, no overage agreement was ever finalised or signed, and the transaction settled on the basis of payment of the price only. Settlement was on 9 May 2008. Just a little more than five years later, on 7 August 2013, the buyer applied for planning permission for development of the property as offices. The seller's claim for payment under the overage agreement was rejected by the buyer on the simple basis that no such agreement had ever been signed. Three years later, in October 2016, the seller raised the present action, seeking specific implement of the obligation in clause 8.1 to execute and deliver an overage agreement, which failing damages of £1,025,000.

But was clause 8.1 still enforceable, more than eight years after settlement? In most cases the answer would have been an emphatic 'no' because of the existence of a two-year supersession clause. But far from containing a supersession clause, the present missives contained a *non*-supersession clause:

> The terms and conditions of this offer and all that may follow hereon will remain in full force and effect and binding on both parties, in so far as not implemented, notwithstanding entry having been taken, delivery of the Disposition hereinbefore mentioned and payment of the Purchase Price.

The intention and effect were for missives to remain in force and enforceable. That disposed of an obvious and standard difficulty.

3

But a second difficulty remained. Contractual obligations normally prescribe after five years. The only relevant exception in a case such as the present was for obligations 'relating to land'. The question to be determined, therefore, was whether clause 8.1(b) was such an obligation. If so, it remained enforceable. If not, the buyer could keep all profits deriving from the grant of planning consent.

At first instance, the Lord Ordinary (Lord Doherty) held that the obligation to deliver an overage agreement was not an obligation relating to land. Consequently, it had been extinguished by the five-year negative prescription. See [2017] CSOH 70, 2017 SLT 577 (*Conveyancing 2017* Case (1)), under the name of *JAL Fish Ltd Small Self-Administered Pension Scheme Trs v Robertson Construction Eastern Ltd*. On appeal, the Second Division has now reached the same decision. As we covered the decision at first instance in some detail (*Conveyancing 2017* pp 113–18), our treatment here will be relatively brief.

It is not intuitively clear what is meant by an obligation 'relating to land'. But there has been a certain amount of case law including the decisions of the Inner House in *Barratt Scotland Ltd v Keith* 1993 SC 142 and *Smith v Stuart* [2010] CSIH 29, 2010 SC 490, and there is also a full and helpful discussion in David Johnston's book on *Prescription and Limitation* (2nd edn, 2012) paras 6.54–6.62. In the light of the case law, the Scottish Law Commission has recently concluded that the boundaries of the exception 'are now not significantly in doubt': see *Discussion Paper No 160 on Prescription* (2016) para 2.58. Some of that case law, however, is questioned, or at least explained away, in this new decision of the Second Division.

In the appeal, the seller did not seek to argue that clause 8.1(b), taken in isolation, was an obligation relating to land (para 37). Rather the argument depended on the context in which the clause was found. The core deal between the parties was said to be (i) payment of the purchase price, (ii) delivery of the disposition, and (iii) delivery of the overage agreement. And since the substance of this core deal was a contract relating to land, so its constituent elements, including therefore clause 8.1(b), must necessarily be obligations relating to land as well. 'Specifically, it was argued that, in substance if not in form, the obligation to deliver the executed overage agreement was to be deemed a part of the consideration in return for which the land was transferred: in its broadest sense, the land was sold in return for a cash price together with the separate payment obligations contained within the overage agreement' (para 33).

In putting forward this view, the seller relied in particular on two decisions of the Outer House: *Glasgow City Council v Morrison Developments Ltd* 2003 SLT 263 and *Clydeport Properties Ltd v Shell UK Ltd* [2007] CSOH 92, 2007 SLT 547. But those decisions, said the Second Division, could be explained in other ways. *Clydeport Properties* proceeded largely on concessions by counsel (para 32). As for *Glasgow City Council*, it was 'merely indicative of the fact that it will often be sufficient, in practical terms, to determine whether an obligation "relates to land" according to whether it forms a central part of a contract creating or transferring rights or interests in land: namely, the "typical" case of obligations relating to land conceived of in *Barratt Scotland*'.

The central question, said the Second Division, was not whether clause 8.1(b) was one of the central features of a land transaction but rather whether the clause, in its own terms, related to land (para 34). After all (para 28):

[a] particular obligation may not be a 'core obligation' of the deed or contract relating to land, of which it happens to form a part; nonetheless, it may amount to an obligation relating to land because it otherwise has land as its main object. Conversely, a particular obligation may be a 'core obligation' of such a deed or contract, yet it may not have land as its main object and therefore may not amount to an obligation relating to land.

That was not to say that context was irrelevant. The Second Division appeared to accept that the obligation to pay the price was an obligation which related to land (para 36). But context was not determinative, and in the present case clause 8.1(b), not having land as its main object, was not an obligation relating to land.

(2) Iftikhar v CIP Property (AIPT) Ltd
[2018] CSIH 44, 2019 SCLR 118

Property at 35 Argyll Street, Glasgow, was sold by CIP Property (AIPT) Ltd by roup at a price of £500,000. The buyer was Muhammad Iftikhar. In terms of the articles of roup, the buyer was taken bound to provide to the seller's solicitor KYC (ie 'Know Your own Client') information on or before 15 December 2016, otherwise the seller could rescind. The articles of roup further provided that:

'KYC information' means such information as the Vendor and the Vendor's Solicitors require in relation to the identity of the Purchaser and the source of funds utilised in respect of payment of the Balance of the Price and/or the deposit including, but not limited to, the verification certificate, and initial due diligence form aftermentioned.

CIP Property made two separate requests for KYC documentation. The first, dating from 12 December 2016, was complied with by the buyer's solicitors by email on 15 December – the deadline stipulated in the articles of roup – and, presumably, by hard copy shortly thereafter. This was concerned mainly with verifying the buyer's identity and involved a certified copy of his passport, a utility bill and the like. Four days later, on 19 December, CIP Property made a second requisition, this time seeking information as to how the buyer had come to acquire the funds being used for the purchase. Although the time limit specified in the articles of roup had expired, no new time limit was set. Nonetheless, on 22 December, and before the requisition was complied with, CIP Property rescinded the contract. This appears to have been because of increasing concerns, prompted partly by its own investigations, in respect of money-laundering compliance. The formal justification, however, was the buyer's alleged failure to meet the deadline of 15 December in respect of KYC documentation.

In this action, the buyer sought declarator that the seller was still bound by the contract and that the purported rescission was of no effect; and having failed at first instance – see [2017] CSOH 148, 2017 GWD 40-609, *Conveyancing 2017* Case (4) – he now appealed to the Inner House. The appeal was heard by the First Division, and the opinion of the court was given by the Lord President, Lord Carloway.

In his judgment Lord Carloway made a clear distinction between the two requisitions. The first, having been made before the deadline of 15 December, needed to be satisfied by that deadline; otherwise CIP Property would be entitled to rescind for breach of contract. Here a key issue between the parties was the meaning of the word 'require' in the clause quoted above. The buyer's argument was that it was for the seller to list the documents that it wished to see, and that it was not then entitled to anything else. For CIP Property it was argued that it was for the buyer to produce such documentation as was needed to satisfy the seller from the perspective of the Money Laundering Regulations 2007, SI 2007/2157 (since replaced by the Money Laundering, Terrorist Financing and Transfer of Funds (Information on the Payer) Regulations 2017, SI 2017/692). If the seller was not satisfied it could ask for more.

The Lord President had no hesitation in agreeing with the interpretation put forward by the buyer (para 29):

> The reasonable man, with the parties' background knowledge, would interpret those words to mean what they say; that the buyer has to supply the seller with such information in relation to the stipulated matters as the seller requires. In order for this article to operate, the seller has to make the requirement by stipulating what he wants. Although the buyer may be able to make an educated guess about what the seller may require, he cannot know what that might be.

It followed, therefore, that '[s]ubject to overall considerations of reasonableness in the timing of any request, had the defenders required certain information prior to 15 December and had that information not been provided by then, it may have been open to the defenders to resile from the bargain' (para 30). But in the event, the information requested *had* been provided, albeit by email. There were no grounds here for rescission of the contract.

As for the second requisition, the Lord President accepted that it was one which CIP Property was entitled to make, even although the deadline had passed, because the articles of roup conferred an overarching right to ask for KYC information. The Lord President continued (para 34):

> In that set of circumstances, the defenders [CIP Property] would have been entitled to fix a reasonable deadline for the production of the relevant information. That deadline could have been relatively short. That, however, was not what was done. The defenders had sought 'a brief explanation', but imposed no ultimatum in relation to when it had to be produced. They did not make the time for the production of the brief explanation (which was all that was asked for) an essential element in the bargain (see generally *East Dunbartonshire Council v Bett Homes* [2012] CSIH 1, LP (Gill) at para 27 et seq). In these circumstances, they were not entitled to rescind the bargain suddenly and without warning only three days later. Doing so without warning and on the stated basis, which concerned only the absence of the source of funds information, amounted to an unlawful repudiation of the contract.

Hence the buyer was entitled to the declarator sought.

A subsidiary issue was whether, if CIP Property was unable to satisfy itself as to money-laundering matters in respect of the purchase, it would have been unlawful under the Money Laundering Regulations 2007 for CIP Property to have proceeded with the transaction. The Lord President rejected the concern. In the first place, it was unclear why CIP Property, as a nominee company holding for a unit trust, should be regarded as a financial institution carrying out one of the defined activities which triggered the need for AML compliance; nor was the buyer a 'customer' of CIP Property or, indeed, of the unit trust. As the Lord President explained (para 37):

> The Regulations are designed to apply to persons who are the customers of, *inter alios*, financial institutions, accountants, solicitors and other similar persons. They are designed to strike at persons investing, or otherwise dealing as (using a similar term) clients of these institutions. The pursuer is neither a customer nor a client of the nominee company (the defenders) or their principals (the unit trust). He is simply an arms-length purchaser of a property owned by them; that is all.

In the second place, even if the Regulations did apply, they had been complied with by CIP Property (para 38):

> The defenders were able to carry out 'customer due diligence', as defined in regulation 5, by verifying the pursuer's identity on the basis of documents and information obtained from a reliable and independent source. They required to do no more than that. They had copies of the pursuer's passport and driving licence duly certified by a solicitor as true copies. They were entitled to rely on the solicitor's representation (reg 17). In these circumstances, proceeding with this transaction would not have amounted to a breach of the regulations and hence be deemed illegal. In short, the contract does not force the defenders to act unlawfully and the court is not requiring them to do so.

(3) Halvorson v Persimmon Homes Ltd
[2018] SC EDIN 40, 2018 GWD 25-325

The defender is a well-known housebuilder. In 2012 the pursuer bought a house from the defender in Whitehouse Way, Gorebridge, Midlothian. The terms of the contract were contained in a minute of agreement between the parties. There were a number of problems with the house but the present litigation was concerned only with the garden which, or so the pursuer averred, was waterlogged to the extent that it was unusable. This state of affairs was said to be caused by (i) a failure by the defender during the initial construction, and (ii) subsequent drainage work carried out by the defender two years after the sale, in 2014. The pursuer sought damages of £25,000.

The pursuer's case rested on both contract and delict. So far as the former was concerned, the minute of agreement contained a warranty that the property being acquired 'will be completed in accordance with the requirements of the NHBC'. Having investigated the flooding, however, the NHBC concluded that

NHBC standards had not been breached. That knocked out the warranty and with it any express term in the contract. The pursuer, however, argued that a term could be read into the contract to the effect that the garden ground would be conveyed to the pursuer in a condition that was fit for the purpose for which the garden ground would reasonably be used. The sheriff (Sheriff Peter Braid) had no difficulty in rejecting this argument. There was, as he pointed out (para 18), already an express warranty in respect of the physical condition of the property (albeit that the warranty had not been breached). By incorporating the NHBC standards, that warranty already made detailed provision for the state of the garden. This left no room for an additional implied term.

The pursuer's case in delict related both to (i) the flooding problems arising from the initial construction, and (ii) the flooding problems said to be caused by the drainage work carried out in 2014. The sheriff rejected the first part of the case as being a claim for pure economic loss which did not fall within one of the grounds on which such loss could be recovered (para 9):

> The determining factor, it seems to me, is that the purchaser of a new-build house does not rely upon the expertise of the builder, in the sense that reliance is used in cases such as *Hedley Byrne & Co Ltd v Heller and Partners Ltd* [1964] AC 465 or *Henderson v Merrit Syndicates Ltd* [1995] 2 AC 145. In the latter category of case, the claimant relied upon something that was said, in deciding to do something or pursuing a certain course of action. However, that is not the sense in which the pursuer says that she relied upon the skill and expertise of the defender. She may have had an expectation that the defender would have, and exercise, skill and expertise in their performance of the contract but that is not the same. In a sense, whenever one contracts with a third party to provide goods, or services, one can be said to be relying on that party to provide satisfactory goods or services. However that is different from receiving advice or information and acting in reliance upon it.

As for the second part of the case in delict, the sheriff accepted (para 11) that there was a distinction between property being acquired already damaged (ie the first part of the case) and property which suffered damage after it had been acquired (ie the second part). Proof would be allowed in respect of the second of these on the basis that the loss was derivative rather than pure economic loss.

The position, however, was complicated by an exclusion clause in the missives. In the event of the defender being required to carry out work on the property, the purchaser was to have 'no right of compensation arising from the carrying out of such work or the need for the same'. On the question of whether this clause might apply to the 2014 drainage project the sheriff ordered a proof before answer (para 47). A proof was also needed on the question of whether, if the clause did apply, it was struck down by s 16 of the Unfair Contract Terms Act 1977 as unfair and unreasonable. A further complication was that, by s 15(2)(e) of the Act, s 16 did not apply to a contract relating to a grant of 'an estate or interest' in land; but, as the sheriff pointed out, the present contract was a composite one, being both a contract for the sale of land and also for the provision of building services. At least in respect of the second element, there was no reason why s 16 should not apply (para 33).

A final question was whether recourse to the contract was prevented by the two-year non-supersession clause, or rather clauses because, bafflingly, there were two such clauses, expressed in slightly different terms. The main issue here was whether the non-supersession clauses, being terms of a consumer contract, were capable of being struck down by s 17 of the Unfair Contract Terms Act 1977 as unfair or unreasonable. Again a proof was allowed.

A related argument was less successful. Regulation 5 of the Unfair Contract Terms in Consumer Contracts Regulations 1999, SI 1999/2083, provided that:

> A contractual term which has not been individually negotiated shall be regarded as unfair if, contrary to the requirement of good faith, it causes a significant imbalance in the parties' rights and obligations arising under the contract, to the detriment of the consumer.

But here the pursuer's averments concerned only an alleged imbalance in the parties' rights and said nothing about good faith. Accordingly, they were not admitted to probation. It might be added that the two provisions last mentioned have now been subsumed into Part 2 of the Consumer Rights Act 2015.

(4) Anwar v Britton
[2018] SC FAL 31, 2018 GWD 20-251 affd [2018] SAC (Civ) 27, 2019 SLT (Sh Ct) 23

This was an action by purchasers of property, in Strathblane, Stirlingshire, following the discovery that a river running through the property had flooded the previous year, for (i) reduction of both missives and disposition, (ii) repetition of the purchase price, and (iii) damages. The basis of the action was not a term of the missives, but rather the representation made by the sellers in issuing a qualified acceptance which incorporated cl 2.1.3 of the Scottish Standard Clauses. Clause 2.1.3 read:

> So far as the Seller is aware (but declaring that the Seller has made no enquiry or investigation into such matters) the Property (including in respect of Clauses 2.1.3 and 2.1.4 the Building, if appropriate) is not affected by ... flooding from any river or watercourse which has taken place within the last 5 years.

The sellers had various defences, but they were all repelled by the sheriff and then, on appeal, by the Sheriff Appeal Court. See **Commentary** p 133.

(5) Deveron Country Club Ltd v Grampian Housing Association Ltd
2 July 1987, Aberdeen Sheriff Court

This decision from 1987, on the interpretation of a variation of concluded missives, has only recently come to our attention. The original missives were initiated by an offer dated 4 July 1986 from Grampian Housing Association Ltd ('GHA') to buy from Deveron Country Club Ltd ('Deveron') property known as Panton House in

Fife Street, Turiff, Aberdeenshire. The offer was conditional on GHA obtaining planning permission (condition 3), and consent of the Housing Corporation (condition 4), for a development of flats. Deveron's qualified acceptance, of 11 July, provided that:

3. Your condition 3 shall be amended to the extent that your clients shall have until 30 September 1986 to satisfy themselves as to the matters contained therein after which time the condition shall be held as purified.
4. Your condition 4 shall be satisfied before 30 September 1986 failing which it shall be deleted.

Naturally, this was not acceptable to GHA as it would have had the effect of locking GHA into the bargain whether the necessary consents were obtained or not. Hence GHA countered on 16 July with the following further qualification:

With regard to your qualification 3 in the event of our clients not being able to obtain planning permission in outline and consent of the Housing Corporation by 30 September 1986, the bargain will be held to be null and void.

A final letter concluded the bargain.

In the event the requisite consents were not obtained by 30 September. Accordingly, in terms of the letter of 16 July the whole contract was 'null and void'. Deveron, however, sought to revive it by a letter sent on the next day (1 October). This included the following provision:

Our qualification number 3 [of the letter of 11 July] is amended to the extent that your clients shall have until 31 October 1986 to satisfy themselves as to the matters contained in your condition 3 of your said offer. Our qualification number 4 shall be amended to the extent that your clients shall have until 31 October 1986 to satisfy themselves as to the matters contained in condition 4 of your said offer.

This letter of revival was accepted by GHA without qualification. But there was a problem, for while the letter changed the dates in Deveron's earlier letter of 11 July, it failed to make a corresponding change to GHA's further letter of 16 July. This would not have mattered if the required consents had been obtained by the revised deadline of 31 October. But they were not obtained. Could GHA walk away from the bargain or, as Deveron now argued, was GHA bound to proceed with the purchase even without the required consents?

In the sheriff's view, GHA was bound to proceed with the purchase. The only provision which could have avoided that result – the provision in GHA's letter of 16 July – had expired on 30 September and was not revived by Deveron's letter of 1 October:

In my opinion it is clear that, up until midnight on 30 September 1986, clause 1 of the letter of 16 July was in full force. The consent of the Housing Corporation had not been obtained by that time; in terms of the clause the defenders [GHA] were therefore entitled to have the contract 'held to be null and void'. This being so, they could have ignored the pursuers' letter of 1 October and taken the matter no further.

They chose, however, not to do so but accepted the contents of the letter of 1 October as 'a modification to the missives'. I can read this only as being a clear indication by the defenders that they were departing from their stipulation that the contract was 'null and void'.

The sheriff indicated, without explaining why, that the position might have been 'very different' if Deveron's letter had been written earlier than 1 October, at a time when the contract was still alive.

The sheriff accepted that it was 'open to question' whether this interpretation 'truly represents what the parties had in mind'. But 'it is of course trite law that, where a contract has been reduced to writing, the court is entitled to look only at the writing and cannot go behind it to ascertain what the parties may actually have intended'. These words were written in 1986. It may be doubted whether any court today would adopt so literalist an interpretation of missives. Compare, for example, the more contextualist approach taken in *Anwar v Britton* (Case (4) above). And a contextualist approach, especially one which appealed to business common-sense, might well have changed the result in *Deveron Country Club*.

(6) Cooper v Skene
2 March 2016, Aberdeen Sheriff Court

The defender built a house on his land, in Dyce, Aberdeen, and sold it to the pursuers for £435,000. Missives were concluded on 13 November 2014; entry was to be on 28 November. The missives incorporated the Aberdeen and Aberdeenshire Standard Clauses (2013 Edition) but with modifications.

The pursuers took entry on the agreed date but, for reasons which are unclear, paid only a notional £1,000 of the price. They did not remain in the house for long because, or so the pursuers averred, the house turned out to have no water supply. After moving out the pursuers stayed in hotels and then in rented accommodation before eventually buying a new and more expensive house. They then raised this action for damages for £70,000 on the basis of (i) breach of contract, and (ii) fraudulent representation. At a debate on relevancy the focus of the discussion was on the first of these.

The sheriff (Sheriff W H Summers) was critical of both the missives and also (paras 70 and 71) the pursuers' pleadings. In respect of the former, the Standard Clauses were, he said, hardly suitable for the sale of a new house. Moreover, and unaccountably, two clauses which related to services (including water), and hence would have been of use to the pursuers, were removed 'without demur' during the course of negotiations and did not form part of the final contract (para 66). As a result, the pursuers were forced to rely on other clauses in the missives 'which, on any view, were not clearly intended to deal with the situation that has presented' (para 67).

A principal focus of the debate was on clause 7 of the Standard Clauses. This was in the following terms:

7. Construction and Alterations

(a) If there has been any addition or alteration to the property within 15 years of the Date of Entry, requiring Planning Permission, Change of Use, Building Warrant, Completion Certificate, Pavement Access Consent, or Listed Building Consent, these will be exhibited prior to, and delivered at settlement. Any work carried out to the Property after 1st May 2005 (other than work carried out in terms of a building warrant granted prior to 1st May 2005) complies with the terms of the Building (Scotland) Act 2003 and the Scottish Building Standards.

(b) The Seller warrants (i) that any building work carried out to the Property has been in a state of substantial completion for a period of not less than 12 weeks prior to the date of conclusion of Missives; and (ii) that no valid objection to the work was made at any time by any person with title and interest to do so under a real burden.

(c) If any works have been carried out on or to the Property requiring consent of any other party in terms of the Title Deeds such consent will be exhibited prior to and delivered at settlement.

(d) There are no planning conditions of a continuing nature which restrict the current use of or adversely affect the Property.

A preliminary issue was whether clause 7 had been excluded by modification 8 of the defender's qualified acceptance:

> With reference to your Standard Clause 7, we enclose herewith Planning Permission reference G/APP/2011/1490, Building Warrant reference G/BW/2011/4971 and Completion Certificate dated 29 January 2013. No further planning documents will be exhibited or delivered.

The sheriff held, surely correctly, that clause 7 was not excluded (paras 85–91). Apart from anything else, the documents mentioned in modification 8 related only to para (a) of clause 7, and indeed only to the first sentence of that paragraph.

But even although clause 7 applied, it was, said the sheriff, of only limited help to the pursuers. Paragraph (a) of clause 7 was, quite simply, inapplicable (para 92). The 'Property' was defined in missives to mean the property 'situated at and known as The Bungalow, Parkhill, Dyce, Aberdeen'. In the sheriff's view – though another view is certainly possible – this referred to the building itself, ie to the new house; and since the house was being built rather than added to or altered, this necessarily excluded clause 7(a).

The sheriff was more sympathetic to the potential applicability of clause 7(b) (para 105): see **Commentary** p 139.

Of the other points touched on in the debate, one deserves mention here. Of the £70,000 claimed by the pursuers in damages, some £30,000 related to the costs involved in purchasing a replacement, and more expensive, house: Keir Heights. The sheriff was unpersuaded as to the merits of the claim. His reasoning (para 100) gives helpful guidance as to how loss should be calculated, and justified, in a claim for damages:

> It seems to me that the pursuers' averments in Article 4 of the condescendence in relation to the purchase of the property at Keir Heights are irrelevant. The averments

do not come close to entitling the pursuers to recover the sum of £30,000 in relation to the sums supposedly lost in that transaction. It is not apparent from those averments that by virtue of purchasing a different property, the pursuers have actually sustained any loss. At its highest what is currently pled on behalf of the pursuers is that they purchased a more expensive property. The difference between the price of the property the pursuers intended to buy and a more expensive property is not a loss that they are entitled to recover from the defender. The situation might have been different if the pursuers had averments, for example to the effect that the two properties were identical in terms of style, specification and quality, were in areas where prices were the same but the property had become more expensive in the period between conclusion of missives for the property and the conclusion of missives for Keir Heights. That might or might not have been sufficient to render the averments relevant. The averments are not relevant as they currently stand and they should not be admitted to probation.

(7) Smith v Jack
22 December 2004, Aberdeen Sheriff Court

This decision from 2004 has only recently come to our attention. On 31 August 2001 Mr and Mrs Smith concluded missives to sell their house at 10 Midmar View, Kingswells, Aberdeen, to Mr and Mrs Jack. The price was £120,000, and entry was to be on 21 September 2001. The qualified acceptance deleted a clause in the offer concerned with the absence of development and with local authority letters and provided instead that:

> The usual Property Clearance Certificate from Aberdeen City Council will be exhibited prior to settlement and if this discloses any matter which to a material degree adversely affects the subjects of sale then the Purchasers' sole remedy shall be to resile from the bargain to follow hereon, without penalty provided intimation of such intention to resile is made to us in writing within three working days of your receipt of the Certificate.

In the event, the property clearance certificate issued by Aberdeen City Council disclosed two matters which adversely affected the subjects of sale, whereupon Mr and Mrs Jack resiled. The question was whether they were entitled to do so, ie whether the matters adversely affected the subjects 'to a material degree'. The form of the action was one for damages by the sellers, Mr and Mrs Smith, for breach of contract.

The first matter disclosed by the clearance certificate was in the following terms:

> A site at the rear – Gillahill, Kingswells is currently the subject of two separate outline planning applications for the same site for the erection of 200 houses and associated works.

As was pointed out for Mr and Mrs Smith, these were merely applications, and no planning permission – not even outline permission – had been granted.

Nonetheless, the sheriff (Sheriff Graham K Buchanan) found that (finding-in-fact 34):

> The defenders were justifiably concerned about the possibility of having a substantial housing development constructed at the rear of their property. They did not want the noise, dirt and mess which would be associated with that. They were concerned that during the building phase there would be disruption, dust, mud and noise and after the building was completed there would be 200 houses of unknown quality at the back of their property.

This, said the sheriff, was an adverse effect 'to a material degree'. Hence Mr and Mrs Jack were entitled to resile from the contract.

Furthermore, said the sheriff, they were equally entitled to resile in respect of another matter disclosed by the clearance certificate:

> It has been reported that mechanical ventilation may not have been installed in the bathroom and the en-suite bathroom on the first floor of the above subjects. When the new building regulations came into force on 1 April 1991, it was a requirement for mechanical ventilation to be installed in all bathrooms. Therefore as the alteration works to install the bathrooms were approved late 1991, if mechanical ventilation has not already been installed it will require to be.

Alive to the risk of losing the sale, Mr and Mrs Smith responded to this entry in the certificate by proceeding at once to fit mechanical ventilation in the bathrooms. Nonetheless, said the sheriff, Mr and Mrs Jack were still entitled to resile, not least because of concerns about possible wet rot in the roof timbers caused by the lack of ventilation hitherto.

As the buyers had won, the question of damages did not arise. The sheriff, however, offered some thoughts on quantum. Mr and Mrs Smith sought damages for the period beginning with the contractual date of entry (21 September 2001) and ending with the date on which the house was resold (2 April 2002). The heads of damage were, in respect of the unsold house, for (i) mortgage interest; (ii) insurance premiums; (iii) council tax; (iv) energy bills; and (v) additional conveyancing fees for the resale. The total was then reduced by the profit which was made on the resale. On this whole topic, see para 5–17 of G L Gretton and K G C Reid, *Conveyancing* (5th edn, 2018). While not questioning the heads of damage, the sheriff thought that the period in respect of which damages were claimed should not begin until November 2001, being the point at which Mr and Mrs Smith moved into their new house and so had to finance the maintenance of two properties.

(8) Krajciova v Feroz
17 May 2013, Aberdeen Sheriff Court, affd 2014 GWD 27-536

This case was noted in *Conveyancing 2014* Case (44), but at that time we had access only to the brief judgment of Sheriff Principal Derek Pyle, affirming the decision of Sheriff Peter Hammond. We have now seen a copy of Sheriff Hammond's judgment, and the case has sufficient interest – factual more than legal – to be worth returning to.

Sultan Feroz was the owner of 53 Kirk Brae, Cults, Aberdeen. In December 2005 he was sequestrated. In August/September 2007 the trustee sold the property for £210,000 to Tatiana Krajciova. Mr Feroz was still residing at the property, and he continued to do so after the sale to Ms Krajciova. The essential question of the litigation was whether he did so (i) as tenant of Ms Krajciova, as she maintained, or (ii) as purchaser from her in terms of an oral contract. That there could be any doubt about the matter seems hardly credible, but so it was. Mr Feroz was paying Ms Krajciova £1,076 per month, but they disagreed about what this money was for. She said it was rent. He said it was towards the purchase of the property, and specifically was to cover the mortgage payments that Ms Krajciova was making. In 2010 Mr Feroz stopped paying, whereupon Ms Krajciova raised the present action for removing Mr Feroz from the property, and for recovery of arrears of rent, while he counterclaimed for declarator that there was a binding contract of sale.

Ms Krajciova produced a contract of lease, which she said had been signed in Starbucks by Mr Feroz, and she produced three witnesses to that effect. Mr Feroz initially denied signing it, but eventually said (para 10 of the sheriff's note) that 'he signed a bit of paper folded in two in Mr Mouti's car in Golden Square'. (Khalid Mouti was Ms Krajciova's husband.) He denied knowing that it was a lease and said that he had been told (paras 10 and 44) that the paper was 'for council tax purposes'.

Mr Feroz produced no documentation of his own, saying that the agreement between him and Ms Krajciova had been oral. That fact was potentially fatal to his case, for a contract for the sale of heritable property must be in writing: s 1 of the Requirements of Writing (Scotland) Act 1995. But that section contains an exception where an oral agreement (or a written but unsigned agreement) has been backed up by part performance: this is commonly called (though not in the section itself) 'statutory personal bar'. The monthly payments amounted to such part performance, Mr Feroz said. Moreover he claimed that on the same occasion that he had signed the bit of paper he had handed over to Mr Mouti £30,000 in an envelope. (Evidence was conflicting as to whether the envelope was brown or yellow.) Presumably Mr Mouti was being considered as Ms Krajciova's representative for the purpose of receiving the money. This alleged payment was the alleged deposit for the alleged purchase. Ms Krajciova denied ever receiving such a sum. Mr Feroz was able to lead evidence from Ali Gharni, Behros Hamedi and Hassan Nazer that they had each given him loans of £10,000.

Other witnesses were also called in an attempt to cast at least some faint light on the 'opaque' (para 52) dealings between the parties. In the end the sheriff held that, on balance of probabilities, the position was as stated by Ms Krajciova, and accordingly granted decree in her favour, at the same time assoilzieing her from the counterclaim. Mr Feroz appealed but, as already mentioned, in a brief judgment the sheriff principal affirmed the decision of the sheriff.

We end with the reflection that a reader of this case is left deeply unsure of what really happened between the parties. At the same time, on the evidence that was before the court, a decision in favour of Ms Krajciova was probably inevitable.

COMMON PROPERTY

(9) Bruce v Bruce
24 April 1997, Aberdeen Sheriff Court

In raising an action of division and sale of common property, does the pursuer require a completed title or is it sufficient if the pursuer holds on a delivered but unregistered (or unrecorded) disposition? In K G C Reid, *The Law of Property in Scotland* (1996) para 33 it is stated that 'the pursuer probably need not be infeft provided that he holds under a delivered conveyance' but, as the qualifier 'probably' indicates, no authority can be found for the statement. *Bruce v Bruce*, a decision from 1997 which has only recently come to our attention, provides some authority.

The pursuer and defender in this action of division and sale were brothers who had inherited a farm at Midmar, Aberdeenshire known as 'Backhill of Bandoddle' from their late father. A disposition had been granted by their father's executor but, at the time of raising the action, had not yet been recorded in the Register of Sasines. The defender challenged the pursuer's title to sue. It was held that the delivery of the disposition gave the pursuer sufficient title.

The reasoning, however, was suspect. The defender relied on a passage from Erskine's *Institutes* to the effect that a charter not perfected by seisin (and hence, today, by registration as its equivalent) is a right merely personal which does not transfer the property. (The reference given, III.23.48, is incorrect and it has not been possible to trace the passage. Erskine says something similar at II.3.48 but the wording is not the same.) The pursuer founded on certain *obiter* remarks by Lord President Emslie in *Gibson v Hunter Home Designs Ltd* 1976 SC 23 at 27:

> In the law of Scotland no right of property vests in a purchaser until there has been delivered to him the relevant disposition. On delivery of the disposition the purchaser becomes vested in a personal right to the subjects in question and his acquisition of a real right to the subjects is dependent upon recording the disposition in the appropriate Register of Sasines. Putting the matter in another way the seller of subjects under missives is not, in a question with the purchaser, divested of any part of his right of property in the subjects of sale until, in implement of his contractual obligation to do so, he delivers to the purchaser the appropriate disposition.

The sheriff (Sheriff Graeme Warner) thought that 'it would be a brave sheriff' who would prefer a passage from Erskine to a *dictum* of Lord Emslie – a statement which seems to us to be exactly the wrong way round. He continued (p 17 of the transcript):

Accordingly, I think it is beyond peradventure to say that the parties were, therefore, 'owners' of the heritage in question as at the date of warranting of the Initial Writ herein. It is true to say that the right remained purely personal in any dispute between either one or both of them, on the one hand, and the executor, on the other, and would not become perfected as a real right until the delivered disposition was recorded in the Register of Sasines. Nevertheless, they were owners and should anyone have sought to claim otherwise, they could have produced the duly executed disposition in their favour to support that claim.

In the light of the decisions and reasoning in the celebrated cases of *Sharp v Thomson* 1997 SC (HL) 66 and *Burnett's Tr v Grainger* [2004] UKHL 8, 2004 SC (HL) 19, no one today would claim that a disponee holding on a delivered but unregistered disposition was the 'owner' of the property in question. So to that extent the decision in *Bruce v Bruce* must be approached with caution. In fact it is odd that the decision took no account of *Sharp*. The case was argued over two days, on 27 January and 7 April 1997. The decision of the First Division in *Sharp*, in which Lord President Hope said of the passage from *Gibson* relied on in *Bruce* that it was 'not entirely accurate' (1995 SC 455 at 470), had been handed down almost two years earlier; and by the time of the second day of debate (7 April 1997), the House of Lords had delivered its opinion in the same case (27 February 1997).

The reason why the debate was split over two days was to allow the pursuer to register the disposition from the executor. This, one might have thought, would have disposed of the defender's arguments. But when the debate resumed on 7 April 1997 the solicitor for the pursuer stated that, while the disposition had been presented for recording, it had not yet been recorded as this took up to six months to complete. Hence 'the factual and legal positions had not really changed' (p 6 of the transcript). This view, however, overlooks the rule that registration in the Register of Sasines is back-dated to the date on which the initial entry is made in the minute book: see Titles to Land Consolidation (Scotland) Act 1868 s 142.

TENEMENTS AND OTHER DEVELOPMENTS

(10) Mackay v Dickinson
28 March 2018, Lands Tribunal

A vennel and patio were held to serve both flats in a tenement in Musselburgh, East Lothian, and hence, in the absence of any relevant provision in the titles, to be the common property of the proprietors of both flats under s 3(4) of the Tenements (Scotland) Act 2004. See **Commentary** p 181.

(11) Cullochgold Services Ltd v Blair
6 July 2018, Perth Sheriff Court

In order to be allowed to do business, a property factor in a residential development must first register in the Register of Property Factors, which was set up by the Property Factors (Scotland) Act 2011. But what is a 'property factor' for these purposes? Section 2 of the Act gives two main instances. One is 'a person who, in the course of that person's business, manages the common parts of land owned by two or more other persons and used to any extent for residential purposes'. The other is 'a person who, in the course of that person's business, manages or maintains land which is available for use by the owners of any two or more adjoining or neighbouring residential properties (but only where the owners of those properties are required by the terms of the title deeds relating to the properties to pay for the cost of the management or maintenance of that land)'. In the first or normal case the factor manages other people's property. In the second case he manages what is usually his own property but on the basis that neighbours pay and have a right of use.

Cullochgold Services Ltd v Blair potentially concerned the second of these cases. The claimant owned and operated a private sewerage system at Murthly, Perthshire. The respondent owned one of the houses served by the system and, under the deed of conditions, had to pay a service charge for the privilege. Was the claimant a property factor and so bound, as the respondent contended, to register under the Act? The sheriff thought not, on the basis that the homeowners (including the respondent) could not be said to have a right to use the sewerage works – as opposed to a right to benefit from the service which the works provided. See **Commentary** p 223.

[Another aspect of this case is digested as Case (14) below.]

(12) Procurator Fiscal, Oban v Melfort Pier Holidays Ltd
13 September 2017, Oban Sheriff Court

Like the previous case, this case too concerns the second of the instances of 'property factor' given in s 2 of the Property Factors (Scotland) Act 2011, ie 'a person who, in the course of that person's business, manages or maintains land which is available for use by the owners of any two or more adjoining or neighbouring residential properties (but only where the owners of those properties are required by the terms of the title deeds relating to the properties to pay for the cost of the management or maintenance of that land)'. Unlike the previous case, however, the point at issue was whether the person managing property was doing so 'in the course of that person's business'.

Melfort Pier Holidays Ltd ('MPH') had created a development centred around Melfort pier and harbour at Kilmelford, near Oban, Argyll. As part of that development, 18 houses were built. MPH retained ownership of 13 of the houses and let them out as holiday homes. The remaining five were sold. The development was subject to a deed of conditions. Among other topics, the deed contained provisions about a recreational area. Everyone was entitled to use the area, and everyone was bound to contribute to the cost of its maintenance. A management structure was put in place, and MPH was the first manager. A management fee could be levied but MPH had not so far done so.

A summary complaint was made against MPH by the procurator fiscal at Oban for failure to register as a property factor under the 2011 Act. MPH challenged the competency and relevancy of the complaint. In particular, MPH argued that MPH could not be a property factor in the sense of s 2(1)(c) of the Act because the statutory requirement that the management function be carried out 'in the course of that person's business' must be understood as meaning 'in the course of that person's business *as a property factor*'. MPH's business was the letting of holiday cottages.

The sheriff (Sheriff Patrick Hughes) rejected this argument. The definition was intended to distinguish between those for whom factoring was a business (even if not the only part of the business) and those who factored on an amateur basis and without remuneration. As MPH fell into the first and not the second category, registration under the Act was required. See **Commentary** p 221.

(13) Speirs Gumley Property Management v Lafferty
2018 Hous LR 78

Spiers Gumley were factors for a development in Paisley, Renfrewshire. They carried out repairs to individual balconies in the building and billed everyone as a common repair. As there was no mention of balconies in the deed of conditions, there was said to be uncertainty as to whether they were commonly owned and hence included within the common-repairs regime. We would comment that the uncertainty is puzzling, given the existence of default provisions as to ownership in s 3 of the Tenements (Scotland) Act 2004. (For a 2018 case in which s 3 was applied, see *Mackay v Dickinson* ((Case 10) above).)

Mr Lafferty, a house-owner in the development, challenged the factors' bill, not by refusing to pay, but by applying to the First-tier Tribunal (the Housing and Property Chamber) under s 17 of the Property Factors (Scotland) Act 2011 in respect of Speirs Gumley's conduct. The First-tier Tribunal decided, in terms of s 19 of the Act, that Speirs Gumley (i) had failed to carry out the property factor's duties (defined in s 17(5) to mean duties in relation to the management of the common parts), and in addition (ii) had failed to comply with s 2.5 of the Code of Conduct for property factors. Section 2.5 provides that:

> You must respond to enquiries and complaints received by letter or email within prompt timescales. Overall your aim should be to deal with enquiries and complaints as quickly and as fully as possible, and to keep homeowners informed if you require additional time to respond. Your response times should be confirmed in the written statement.

Accordingly, the Tribunal made an enforcement order against Speirs Gumley. As part of this determination the Tribunal found that the balconies were not common property.

Speirs Gumley appealed to the Upper Tribunal, but without success. Much of the argument was as to whether an arbitration clause in the deed of conditions had ousted the jurisdiction of the First-tier Tribunal. Leaving open the question of whether such ousting would have been competent, the Upper Tribunal concluded that the wording of the clause did not have that effect.

Another jurisdictional argument was that the First-tier Tribunal could only deal with matters concerning common parts, among which balconies, it turned out, were not included. This argument too the Upper Tribunal rejected:

> The Code deals largely with service to homeowners. It is not restricted to dealings in relation to common parts. If that were so it would make a nonsense of the Code. Section 2.1 states that the property factor must not provide information which is misleading or false. Section 2.5 deals with response to enquiries. There will be many situations where there might well be an overlap between common property and private property. Section 3 states that transparency is important and homeowners should know what it is they are paying for, how the charges are calculated, and that no improper payment requests are involved. Where a payment request is improperly made because it relates to private property rather than common property, standing the provisions of Section 3, it cannot be the case that a property factor can say he is not bound by the Code. The Code is made in terms of Section 14 of the Act. The Code is not a Code dealing with common parts. It is a Code for registered property factors in their dealings with homeowners.

The Upper Tribunal accepted that Speirs Gumley had been 'perhaps in an unenviable position'. Due to problems with water ingress the balconies were in urgent need of repair. The factors had had to decide whether this was a common repair. Whatever view they took on this matter was open to challenge, as indeed events proved. The Upper Tribunal continued:

> I imagine there will be extreme cases where at one end of the scale the First-tier Tribunal might for example have little difficulty in finding that an unscrupulous factor that regularly and deliberately invoices homeowners for private property work will be in breach of their factoring duties and/or the Code of Conduct. At the other end of the scale perhaps, where a factor, genuinely unsure of what is and what is not a Common Part has to make a decision one way or the other, the First-tier Tribunal might have more difficulty in finding that the factor was in breach of its factoring duties and/or the Code of Conduct. Much might depend on how the factor reached its decision and how it communicated its decision making process to the homeowners. All of that would be for the First-tier Tribunal to consider.

In the present case, Mr Lafferty had been entitled to apply to the First-tier Tribunal, and the Tribunal was entitled to reach the determination that it had reached.

REAL BURDENS

(14) Cullochgold Services Ltd v Blair
6 July 2018, Perth Sheriff Court

Must a property manager or factor account for expenditure before seeking to collect service charges? The answer, almost always, is yes. This is because (i) property factors require to be registered under the Property Factors (Scotland) Act 2011; (ii) as registered property factors they are, by s 14(5) of that Act, bound

to comply with a Code of Conduct prepared by the Scottish Government; and
(iii) by s 3.3 of the Code of Conduct, a property factor:

> must provide to homeowners, in writing at least once a year (whether as part of billing
> arrangements or otherwise) a detailed financial breakdown of charges made and a
> description of the activities and works carried out which are charged for. In response
> to reasonable requests, you must also supply supporting documentation and invoices
> or other appropriate documentation for inspection or copying.

But what if, for whatever reason, the person seeking to collect a service charge
is not a registered property factor? The question of whether the charge requires
to be justified and vouched for will then turn on the terms of the real burden
by virtue of which the money is due. Here there are, broadly, two possibilities.
One is that the burden imposes an obligation to pay a stipulated share of certain
costs, such as the costs of maintaining shared parts of the development. The
other possibility, much less common in practice, is that the burden imposes
an obligation to pay a fixed sum of money. In the first case, the amount due
depends on the costs incurred, making it unavoidable that details of those
costs are produced and vouched for. In the second case, there is no necessary
connection between actual costs and sums claimed. It was the second case which
was litigated in *Cullochgold Services Ltd v Blair.*

The dispute concerned money said to be due in respect of the provision
of private sewerage facilities. The facilities were owned and provided by the
claimant; the respondent owned one of the houses in the development. In terms
clause (ninth) of the deed of conditions, which dated from 1988:

> Until such time as the development of the Whole Area is complete, of which the
> Superiors will be the sole judges, the proprietor of each dwelling house shall pay to
> the Superiors as a contribution towards the maintenance of the roadways, footpaths
> and street lighting referred to in clause Seventh (b) hereof, all sewers, drains, and
> pipes connecting the Whole Area within the sewage works erected on the subjects
> hereinbefore described (Third) or the public sewage as the case may be, the said
> sewage works, the machinery and plant contained therein, the sewers, drains, pipes
> and out fall discharging from the said sewage works …

The amount due from each proprietor was set at £40 per month, but with a
mechanism for increasing this amount in the future.

The original developer, and feudal superior, was Druids Park Ltd, but the
claimant was now owner of the sewage plant (as well as of an area of grassland
forming part of the development). Insofar as clause (ninth) was a feudal
burden, it had of course been extinguished, with the feudal system itself, on
28 November 2004: see Abolition of Feudal Tenure etc (Scotland) Act 2000 s 17.
But it was accepted by both parties that the burden was now a facility burden
(private sewerage being one of the examples of a 'facility' given by s 122(3) of
the Title Conditions (Scotland) Act 2003), that it had survived feudal abolition
by virtue of s 56(1) of the 2003 Act, and that in terms of s 56 it was enforceable
by the claimant against the respondent. Nonetheless, the respondent disputed

that the sum sued for (£1,105.35, being the accumulated arrears of service charge since the respondent became an owner) was due.

The respondent had three main defences (para 40). (i) The claimant must justify the sum claimed by reference to the service provided. (ii) Insofar as the sum exceeded what had been expended by the claimant, it was an unlawful periodical payment under s 2 of the Land Tenure Reform (Scotland) Act 1974 and could not be recovered. (iii) The claimant was required to register as a property factor under the Property Factors (Scotland) Act 2011; having failed to do so, and to comply with the transparency requirements of that Act, the claimant could not recover the sum sued for. The last of these arguments is explored at p 223 below and only the first and second arguments will be dealt with here.

The first argument raised an important issue of fairness. As summarised by the sheriff (at para 43) this was that:

> before an obligation to pay arose there was a duty to account to contributors for sums already contributed and a duty to satisfy those who were subject to the burden that the funds were being expended appropriately. If that were not the case exorbitant amounts could be charged without any form of redress available to those so burdened.

The sheriff (Sheriff Gillian A Wade QC) was unpersuaded. The real burden placed an obligation on each proprietor to pay £40 per month for the private sewerage system. In deciding to become owner the respondent must be taken to have accepted this obligation (para 82). If that turned out to be bad bargain – if, in other words, the cost of providing the service was less or much less than the sums which were being collected (as the respondent believed to be the case) – that was not an arrangement which the court was at liberty to disturb.

As a second argument, the respondent relied on s 2 of the Land Tenure Reform (Scotland) Act 1974. Among other matters this prohibits the imposition by deed of an obligation to make a 'periodical payment'. For the most part, ss 1 and 2 of the Act were designed to prevent the imposition of new quasi-feuduties and quasi-groundannuals, but s 2 applies more widely to any periodical payment imposed under a title condition, subject to three exceptions. As it could hardly be disputed that an obligation to pay £40 per month was a periodical payment due under a title condition, the only question to be determined was whether clause (ninth) fell within one of the three exceptions. These were:

> [1] a payment in respect of a lease, liferent or other right of occupancy, [2] a payment in defrayal of or contribution towards some continuing cost related to land, or [3] a payment under a heritable security.

Only the second of these exceptions was of potential relevance. As the monthly payment of £40 was to pay for the private sewerage system, so it could plausibly be regarded as 'a payment in defrayal of or contribution towards some continuing cost related to land'. But, said the respondent, that could only be so if the amount claimed was actually spent on maintaining the sewerage system. Insofar as the monthly payments exceeded the sums spent, s 2 prevented them from being recovered.

This is an ingenious and attractive argument. The sheriff, however, thought otherwise (para 69):

> If, as has been conceded, the burden is a facility burden then it is difficult to see how section 2 of the 1974 Act applies as that is concerned with feudal burdens which have been abolished. Facility burdens are a creation of statute under the 2003 Act. The respondent has failed to satisfy me that there is any duty to account to those who are obliged in terms of their title deeds to pay a certain amount by way of a facility burden.

The sheriff's point of departure – that s 2 'is concerned with feudal burdens which have been abolished' – is unfortunately not correct, and that error vitiates the rest of the passage. This is not to say that the respondent would necessarily have succeeded in his argument; but the argument was worthy of more serious consideration than it received.

[Another aspect of this case is digested as Case (11) above.]

(15) Sheltered Housing Management Ltd v Bield Housing & Care
30 August 2018, Dundee Sheriff Court

The deed of conditions of a sheltered housing development imposed on the proprietors of the individual flats 'the burden of upholding in good condition and repair' certain parts of the building. As well as parts owned by the proprietors in common this also referred to other parts – the warden's office, a plant room for the lift, and a toilet – ownership of which was held by Sheltered Housing Management Ltd, the one-time manager of the development. A dispute arose as to the right of the proprietors to make use of these other parts. The evidence was that the proprietors made use of the toilet (which was adjacent to the communal sitting room). Furthermore, the replacement manager, acting on the proprietors' behalf, occupied the office every weekday morning and also made some use of the plant room which had been secured with a digital lock.

In the end it was conceded by Sheltered Housing Management that an obligation to maintain must include, by implication, a right to take access for repairs – a concession which the sheriff (Sheriff L A Drummond QC) considered to have been properly made (para 37). But this did not extend to the type of use actually made by the proprietors and their new manager, which, the sheriff said, went 'far beyond' a use for the purposes of maintenance (para 39). Self-evidently, using the toilet was not the same as – indeed came close to being the opposite of – maintaining it.

What was the juridical nature of this, rather limited, implied right of use? Relying on a passage in D J Cusine and R R M Paisley, *Servitudes and Rights of Way* (1998) para 7.01, the sheriff classified it as a right of servitude. A 'servitude right of access', said the sheriff, 'is necessarily inherent in order to make the obligation to maintain effectual' (para 37). An alternative attribution would be real burden; indeed s 2(3) and 2(4) of the Title Conditions (Scotland) Act 2003 make express provision for real burdens, such as a right to enter, which are 'ancillary' to other real burdens (such as maintenance burdens).

For the sheriff, the right to take access was an inevitable concomitant of the obligation to maintain. A different reading of the maintenance burden might have been to say that, in relation to those parts of the building not owned by the proprietors of the flats, the 'burden of upholding' meant no more than an obligation to pay for the cost of the maintenance carried out by the person who did own the parts. On such a reading, the question of access rights would not arise.

We understand that this decision is being appealed. Another aspect of the case is digested as Case (44) below.

(16) King's Park Heritable Co Ltd v Royal Bank of Scotland
23 January 1963, Court of Session Inner House

This decision of the First Division from 1963 has only recently come to our attention. In terms of the titles of a tenement in central Glasgow, no sign could be erected on a tenement building without the prior consent of a majority of owners. When the defender put up a sign advertising Long John whisky, the pursuer, who owned offices in the building, sought an order requiring the sign to be removed. Meanwhile a majority of owners had agreed that the sign could stay. Nonetheless, the court ordered that it be removed. See **Commentary** p 193.

(17) Inchcolm Land Ltd
2018 GWD 17-221, Lands Tribunal

Section 90(1)(a)(ii) of the Title Conditions (Scotland) Act 2003 empowers the Lands Tribunal, in respect of a title condition or purported title condition which is a real burden, to 'determine any question as to its validity, applicability or enforceability or as to how it is to be construed'. This handy jurisdiction was one of the innovations of the 2003 Act. The facts of the present case are a good example of the kind of circumstances for which it was intended.

Title to a development site in Fife was registered in the Land Register. Among the burdens listed in the D (burdens) section of the title sheet were those contained in a feu disposition granted by Kirkcaldy District Council in 1984. These restricted the use of the site to a car park and hence blocked potential development. The owner/developer made an application to the Lands Tribunal under s 90(1)(a)(ii) seeking a ruling on the validity of the burdens.

On the evidence before it the Tribunal was satisfied that the burdens in the feu disposition were no longer live. The burdens had not been the subject of a preservation notice under s 18 of the Abolition of Feudal Tenure etc (Scotland) Act 2000. Nor did there seem to be any question of third-party rights under ss 52–56 of the Title Conditions (Scotland) Act 2003. That being so the burdens had been extinguished, with the abolition of the feudal system, on 28 November 2004.

In those circumstances one might have expected the Tribunal to pronounce an order to the effect that the burdens were invalid; for, after all, a power to 'determine any question as to its validity' must, it might be thought, include a power to determine that the burdens were invalid. Admittedly, being invalid, they did not qualify as real burdens; but, being listed in the Land Register was surely sufficient for them to qualify as 'purported' real burdens and hence to fall within the Tribunal's jurisdiction under s 90(1)(a)(ii). The topic of 'purported' title conditions is discussed at paras 6.19–6.23 of the Scottish Law Commission's *Report No 181 on Real Burdens* (2000).

That, however, was not the approach taken by the Lands Tribunal. In the Tribunal's view, the invalidity of the burdens was fatal to the application. 'The Tribunal has decided to dismiss this application as incompetent on the basis that there can be no valid title condition or purported title condition.' This result may have been good enough for the applicant – we do not know. But it does not seem entirely satisfactory. As the Tribunal noted in *McCarthy & Stone (Developments) Ltd v Smith* 1995 SLT (Lands Tr) 19 at 26B:

> Dismissal may not be regarded by the parties as a satisfactory or helpful outcome to this application, particularly as our disposal of the matter is not in the form of a declarator that there is no subsisting burden.

That case was decided under the previous legislation, where there was no power to deal with 'purported' real burdens, with the result that dismissal was sometimes an outcome that could not be avoided. One of the ideas behind the revised legislation of 2003 was that dismissal could and should be avoided.

RIGHTS OF PRE-EMPTION

(18) West Lothian Council v Clark
23 August 2018, Livingston Sheriff Court

Today, pre-emptions which were created in a grant in feu can usually be disregarded, and indeed should no longer appear on title sheets. This is because such pre-emptions were normally extinguished, with the feudal system itself, on the 'appointed day' (28 November 2004): see Abolition of Feudal Tenure etc (Scotland) Act 2000 s 17. But there can be exceptions. One is where the superior acted to preserve the pre-emption by registering a notice before the appointed day under s 18 or s 18A of the 2000 Act. That, however, rarely happened. A second exception is where the pre-emption continues to bind the original grantee of the deed as a matter of contract. The present case was concerned with this second exception.

In feuing Westmuir Farm, West Calder, to George Clark in 1986, Lothian Regional Council included a right of pre-emption in the feu disposition. The question to be determined was whether the pre-emption continued to be enforceable, even after the abolition of the feudal system.

If the original parties had remained in place, then there could have been little doubt that the answer was yes. The reasoning here is as follows. (i) Like all conveyances, a feu disposition operates as a contract between the parties to the deed, coming into life when the deed is delivered. (ii) The pre-emption was a term of the contract between Lothian Regional Council and Mr Clark. (iii) For deeds registered before the appointed day, like this one, the contract remains in force notwithstanding registration of the deed. (For deeds registered on or after the appointed day, real burdens cease to be contractual on registration: see Title Conditions (Scotland) Act 2003 s 61.) (iv) Probably, the contract comes to an end if and when the grantee disposes of the land to a singular successor: see Scottish Law Commission, *Report No 181 on Real Burdens* (2000) paras 3.40 and 3.41. (v) The contractual effect of grants in feu is expressly preserved, after the appointed day, by s 75(1) of the 2000 Act; this provides that:

> As respects any land granted in feu before the appointed day, nothing in this Act shall affect any right (other than a right to feuduty) included in the grant in so far as that right is contractual as between the parties to the grant (or, as the case may be, as between one of them and a person to whom any such right is assigned).

In the event, neither of the original parties remained in place. Their successors, however, were in the nature of universal rather than singular successors. Thus, (i) Lothian Regional Council, the original granter, was wound up as a result of the reorganisation of local government by the Local Government etc (Scotland) Act 1994; by virtue of that Act and of the Local Authorities (Property Transfer) (Scotland) Order 1995, SI 1995/2499, West Lothian Council succeeded to the Regional Council's assets and liabilities. (ii) In 2011 the original grantee, George Clark, died. The present litigation was triggered by the wish of his executors to sell part of the property.

The contractual enforceability of the pre-emption would not, of course, have survived a transfer to *singular* successors. So if Mr Clark had sold the property while still alive, the pre-emption could not have affected a subsequent sale by the person who purchased from Mr Clark. A singular successor is unaffected by contractual obligations undertaken by his author. A universal successor, by contrast, takes on his author's rights and liabilities. In principle, therefore, West Lothian Council would have acquired the contractual right conferred originally on Lothian Regional Council by the pre-emption, and Mr Clark's executors would have been subject to the correlative obligation. Although the sheriff (Sheriff Martin G R Edington) did not put matters quite like that, that was the conclusion to which he came.

SERVITUDES

(19) Macgregor v Keig Properties Ltd
12 March 2018, Aberdeen Sheriff Court

The pursuers were the owners of various houses in Montgarrie, Alford, Aberdeenshire, which were bounded on the north by Keig Road, a public road, and on the south by a private road belonging to the defender. The defender owned a house on the other side of the private road. The private road led from another public road, Montgarrie Road, but was a dead-end. Its surface was grass, but sufficiently firm to bear the weight of a vehicle. It was also wide enough for a vehicle, although there was a recurring problem with branches of trees and other foliage.

The defender acquired its property in 2012. Until that time, the pursuers had made occasional use of the private road on foot and by vehicle. The defender, however, had objected to that use and proceeded to block it, first by parking cars across the entrance and then by placing various obstacles. The action was one for declarator of a servitude of pedestrian and vehicular access coupled with interdict of the defender 'from obstructing, blocking or preventing the exercise of the servitude right'.

The pursuers' main case was based on implied servitude. The split-off writs for each of the pursuers' properties were a grant in feu by the Rev William Forbes Leith dating from the period between 1885 and 1896. These provided that the property in question was bounded 'on the south by a proposed new road to be made out by me for the accommodation of my said disponees and my other feuars'.

Following a proof the sheriff (Sheriff Andrew Miller) held that the pursuers' case had been made out. The reference to 'the accommodation of my said disponees' might in itself be seen as decisive – indeed, we might add, came close to being an express servitude. But, in the sheriff's view, this was supported by the facts that (i) all the houses (the plans for which had to be approved by the Rev William Forbes Leith) faced the private road rather than Keig Road; (ii) the private road was the only means of access to the houses from the south; and (iii) the presence of ashpits at the southern end of the gardens; as these were traditionally used for the storage of ash from domestic fires, of the contents of 'dry' toilets, and of other domestic waste, they would have needed to be emptied on a regular basis by horse-drawn cart. All in all, the sheriff concluded (para 242):

> It seems to me that all of these factors considered together give rise to the clear inference that the grantor of the founding titles of the pursuers' properties intended that the owners of those properties would have a servitude right of access over the 'proposed new road' immediately to the south of the properties. Without a right of access over the proposed road it is difficult to understand how it could have served for the 'accommodation' of the adjoining properties.

Furthermore, said the sheriff, such an implied servitude must be held to extend to vehicular as well as to pedestrian traffic. The road was capable of taking vehicles; vehicles were presumably used to empty the ashpits; a number of properties had south-facing garages; and there was clear evidence of vehicular use of the road in modern times.

In reaching this conclusion, no weight was given to the fact that the pursuers' properties could be, and indeed were normally, accessed by means of the public road lying to the north. Yet in a number of previous cases the existence of another means of access has tended to undermine the argument that an access servitude could be implied: see in particular *Gow's Trs v Mealls* (1875) 2 R 729; *McLaren v City of Glasgow Union* (1878) 5 R 1042; *Shearer v Peddie* (1899) 1 F 1201; and *ASA*

International Ltd v Kashmiri Properties (Ireland) Ltd [2016] CSIH 70, 2017 SC 107. The distinguishing feature in the present case, however, is presumably the quasi-express grant of a servitude which could be derived from the reference to the road being for the 'accommodation' of the properties.

The pursuers having succeeded on their main argument, it was not necessary for the sheriff to consider their ancillary argument, which was that a servitude had been constituted by prescription. But here too the sheriff indicated that the pursuers would have succeeded. The use or possession of the road, though meagre, was sufficient bearing in mind the 'terrain and … the fact that the properties are served by the main Kreig Road to the north' (para 216). Nor could that use be attributed merely to tolerance on the part of the defender's predecessor in title, Miss McDonald. This was partly because of her character, as established by evidence at the proof, but mainly because of the quantity of possession (para 264):

> I am satisfied that the evidence establishes that the vehicular use made of the road by the pursuers and their predecessors in title, having regard to the nature and characteristics of the road, had the necessary quality of continuity and indicates that such use was exercised as of right rather than by tolerance or good neighbourliness on the part of Miss McDonald.

(20) North East Promotions Ltd v Emslie
10 October 2018, Banff Sheriff Court

This is another case in which the boundary between express and implied servitudes looks distinctly porous.

When Nigel Wilson sold land in Turriff to the pursuer in 1999, the land was described in the disposition as being bounded on the north by the public road from Turriff to Mill of Colp. The disposition plan, however, showed a small gap between the land and the carriageway of the road, and this gap was reproduced in the title plan in the Land Register. In 2015 Mr Wilson sold the rest of his land to the defender. Subsequently, a disagreement arose as to the right of the pursuer to take access over the gap area in order to reach the public road. In this action the pursuer sought declarator as to the existence of a servitude of pedestrian and vehicular access, and an interdict against the defender from interfering with the pursuer's access.

The pursuer based its case on two separate grounds. The first was that, when the pursuer's land was split off from the area now belonging to the defender in 1999, the disposition must be regarded as including an implied servitude right of way over the gap area.

The second ground was more unusual. In disponing the property in 1999, Mr Wilson had done so

> together with the whole buildings and erections on the subjects hereby disponed, the fittings and fixtures therein and thereon; the parts privileges and pertinents effeiring thereto; and my whole right, title, and interest, present and future in and to the same.

This, of course, was no more than a standard clause. Normally it would carry any existing rights held by the disponer but not create new ones. But this, said the pursuer, was not a normal case. On the contrary, it was a case in which access over the gap area had been taken before the split-off of 1999 and where it continued to be taken thereafter. In those circumstances, by making a grant of 'pertinents' Mr Wilson must be taken to have granted a servitude in order that the access could continue. As authority for this view, the pursuer lodged as a production an Opinion obtained from Professor Roderick Paisley of the University of Aberdeen; and Professor Paisley in turn relied on an unreported decision of Sheriff David B Smith in Kilmarnock Sheriff Court on 16 December 1985: *McFadzean v Currie*.

In the event, neither of the pursuer's arguments was considered in this stage of the litigation. The pursuer was seeking summary decree but the sheriff (Sheriff Robert McDonald) refused to grant it due to the difficulty of the points raised (para 37):

> The question of whether an express servitude of access can be created by a conveyance of 'pertinents' does not have a clear answer and raises a difficult question of law which will require to be gone into in some depth ... I consider that the question ... can only be answered by hearing detailed legal argument presented by both sides either at a diet of debate or on hearing full legal submissions following a proof before answer.

(21) Fraser v McDonald
[2018] SAC (Civ) 8, 2018 SLT (Sh Ct) 157

In selling a plot of land ('plot A') at Stanley in Perthshire to the pursuers, the defenders granted two separate deeds. One, in 2008, was a deed of servitude in respect of an access road. The second, in 2011, was a disposition of plot A itself. Although the servitude was constituted by the deed of servitude, it could not come into effect immediately because the defenders still owned both the benefited and the burdened properties. It was thus only on registration of the disposition in 2011 that the servitude became live: see s 75(2) of the Title Conditions (Scotland) Act 2003.

The deed of servitude conferred a right of access over a private road which led from a public road through land retained by the defenders ('plot B'). The road then continued through land at the foot of plot A ('the disputed strip'). The deed of servitude did not extend to this continuation along the disputed strip, presumably because the original plan was for the disputed strip to be disponed to the pursuers along with the rest of plot A. In the event, however, the 2011 disposition of plot A did not include the disputed strip.

The question then became whether the access servitude could be interpreted as extending to the disputed strip. At first instance the sheriff held that it could: see decision of 18 July 2017 in Perth Sheriff Court (*Conveyancing 2017* Case (13)). The Sheriff Appeal Court has now reversed that decision.

Two main arguments were in play. One was whether the title sheet of plot A could be read as conferring a right of servitude over the disputed strip –

whatever the state of the underlying deeds. The sheriff held that it could. The Sheriff Appeal Court took a different view. We have not seen the title sheet but the reasoning of the Sheriff Appeal Court seems convincing.

The second ground was of more general applicability. At first instance the sheriff accepted that, on a literal reading of the deed of servitude, the servitude did not extend to the disputed strip. That, however, was not necessarily the end of the matter because, in interpreting a conveyancing deed, it was necessary to have regard to the 'general equitable principle in our law that the court will not allow the clear intention of the parties disclosed in a deed to be defeated by a mere inaccuracy or mistake in expression': see *Chalmers Property Investment Co Ltd v Robson* 2008 SLT 1069 at 1073 per Lord Guthrie. The clear intention of the parties in the present case, the sheriff said, was to allow the pursuers to use all of the access road, including the part of the road which was on the disputed strip. Hence the deed of servitude fell to be interpreted so as to extend to the disputed strip.

In commenting on the sheriff's decision (*Conveyancing 2017* pp 11–12) we thought that this second ground of decision stretched the principle of error in expression further than seemed either possible or desirable. The Sheriff Appeal Court has now reached the same view, holding that the *dictum* of Lord Guthrie in *Chalmers Property Investment Co Ltd* was limited to expository matters; and that, the court explained (para 14), 'is not the same as defining a right':

> In *Chalmers*, the dispute was whether a 'spring or well' was the same thing as a streamlet or a burn. By contrast, in the present case the physical limits and descriptions of the servitude granted are plainly set out and are not ambiguous. There is no inaccuracy to be corrected, or overt error in the title deeds. We agree that *Chalmers* does not provide a means of finding a servitude right where none has been granted. It follows that in our view the learned sheriff erred in sustaining that subsidiary submission.

It is understood that the pursuers' pleadings are now to be amended so as to attempt a case on implied servitude. But in the light of decisions such as *ASA International Ltd v Kashmiri Properties (Ireland) Ltd* [2016] CSIH 70, 2017 SC 107 (discussed in *Conveyancing 2006* pp 133–38), the omens for such a case do not look especially good.

(22) Craig v J D Peace and Company (Aberdeen) Ltd
9 February 2015, Aberdeen Sheriff Court

A disposition of land near Echt, Aberdeenshire, granted in 1993, reserved to the retained property of the granter a servitude over a road which, in terms of the deed, was to be constructed by the disponee on his newly-acquired land. The disposition further provided that the road was to be enclosed by post-and-wire fences and to have a maximum width of 6 metres. Later a question arose as to whether the servitude was limited to the surface of the road or whether it included the verges. In what was seen as a matter of interpretation it was held that the verges must be regarded as included within the servitude. Unless that were so, there would be a gap between the dominant tenement and the road, meaning that the servitude could not be exercised. As the sheriff (Sheriff G Garden) explained (paras 4 and 5):

> It is difficult to see ... that whatever was built between the two fences could be categorised as anything other than a road, however that might have been constructed. ... In my view, it is entirely clear from the terms of this disposition that access over the road includes access over the entire width of the road which is effectively defined in the document as the area between the two fences and includes access over any verges which may form part of that construction.
>
> This is not a situation where a third party owns a strip of ground, often referred to as a 'ransom strip', between a point of access and the dominant tenement. It is not a case where access has been granted from an existing road without sufficient care bring taken to ensure that the road borders the subjects. Here the burden is created by reservation on behalf of a proprietor who owns the whole subjects. I agree with the submission made by Mr Guild [for the dominant proprietor] that it would be utterly absurd for such a proprietor to have retained a right of access which he could not exercise.

[Another aspect of this case is digested as Case (50) below.]

(23) McDonald v Young
2 April 1937, Perth Sheriff Court

This decision from 1937 has only recently come to our attention. The pursuer was the proprietor of the farm and lands of Haughend in the Parish of Dunning and County of Perth. The defender was the proprietor of the adjacent farm of Nether Garvock. At one point the boundary between the farms was a service road which ran from north to south and was framed by hedges on either side. The pursuer's farm lay to the west of the road and the defender's to the east. The road was the pursuer's property, but was subject to a servitude of way in favour of the defender which had been established by positive prescription.

The defender improved the road by metalling the surface and extending its width into what had formerly been grass verge. His right to do so was challenged by the pursuer. The sheriff found (i) that the servitude extended to the entire width between the hedges, and (ii) that the defender was entitled to metal the surface as being reasonably necessary for enjoyment of the servitude having regard, in particular, to the fact that use by cars and lorries had replaced use by horses and carts. See **Commentary** p 164.

(24) Don v Gordon
20 January 1986, Stonehaven Sheriff Court

This decision from 1986 has only recently come to our attention. It arose, ultimately, out of the breaking up of the Donnottar (or Kapemi) Estate in Stonehaven in 1962 when various farms were sold to their tenants. The pursuer owned two of those farms: Lindsayfield and Garbertstripes (otherwise

Garbertstryps). The defenders owned a third: Clochnahill. All three names give pleasure. The split-off disposition for the defenders' farm was granted and recorded prior to that of the pursuer's two farms. In the parts and pertinents clause it conferred 'the right to use for all usual purposes all existing roads and ways at present used for the purpose of access to the subjects hereby disponed'. Among the 'existing roads and ways' was a road or track which formed part of Lindsayfield and Garbertstripes.

The litigation concerned two different issues. The first was whether the servitude of way over the road or track, which was admittedly constituted by the 1962 disposition of Clochnahill, had been extinguished by non-use for 20 years. This had become important because of the pursuer's desire to incorporate the road into his fields.

A great deal of evidence was heard by the sheriff (Sheriff R J D Scott) but it did not much impress him:

> It was difficult to accept quite a lot of what was said. This is partly because of the nature of the subject matter, which concerned events and activities over a considerable tract of time. Moreover, this dispute between neighbours has clearly given rise to a great deal of thought and a great deal of discussion. Strong feelings have been aroused … In the result, much of the evidence was, I thought, intended more to persuade than to inform. A degree of disingenuousness seemed to be present in the evidence, on both sides.

Fighting his way through this evidence as best he could, the sheriff rejected as 'incredible' the pursuer's contention that the road had not been used for 20 years. The case for extinction by negative prescription was not, therefore, made out.

The immediate cause of the second issue was certain activities carried out by the pursuer in early 1984. A gate and fence were put across the road; and an adjoining ditch was partially filled in, due to work on the adjacent field, causing the road at that point to become boggy and difficult to use. The defenders responded on 4 July 1984 by removing the gate and fence, and by excavating the ditch, throwing the spoil on to the pursuer's adjacent field. To assist their efforts they used a plough and a tractor. In giving evidence they claimed that they had been taking the plough to the smithy at Fetteresso and that any damage caused was accidental. The sheriff firmly rejected this version of events:

> The inference that I draw is that the parties' intentions were to clear the road, which they saw themselves as entitled to do. In this, as a matter of law, they were wrong. They cast down fencing and a gate which did not belong to them and deposited earth and spoil on the pursuer's endrig. To cause damage in this way is in my judgment a civil wrong.

Accordingly, damages were awarded against them to the tune of £150. None of this is to say that the pursuer was entitled to obstruct the road, if that is indeed what he did. But in the face of such an obstruction it was not for the defenders to take the law into their own hands and to damage the pursuer's property.

(25) Regency Villas Title Ltd v Diamond Resorts (Europe) Ltd
[2018] UKSC 57, [2018] 3 WLR 1603

This decision of the Supreme Court in an English appeal is of importance for the law of servitudes in Scotland. It affirms the decision of the Court of Appeal reported at [2017] EWCA Civ 238, [2017] 3 WLR 644 (*Conveyancing 2017* Case (15)), which in turn affirmed the decision at first instance, [2015] EWHC 3564 (Ch), discussed in *Conveyancing 2016* pp 138–40.

The case concerned land, near Canterbury, Kent, used for the purposes of a timeshare development. Originally the land was owned together with an immediately adjacent property which contained sporting and leisure facilities such as tennis courts, a swimming pool, and a golf course. In 1981 the timeshare land was split off. The conveyance conferred on the grantee and its successors and lessees the right:

> to use the swimming pool, golf course, squash courts, tennis courts, the ground and basement floor of Broome Park Mansion House, gardens and any other sporting or recreational facilities … on the Transferor's adjoining estate.

Later a dispute arose as to whether the right so conferred was merely personal or whether it was an easement (in Scottish terms, a servitude) binding on successors. It has now been held by the Supreme Court that the right was an easement. See **Commentary** p 169.

WAYLEAVES

(26) SSE Telecommunications Ltd v Millar
[2018] SCA (Civ) 14, 2018 SC (SAC) 73

This case concerns the Telecommunications Code set out in sch 2 of the Telecommunications Act 1984. (This has since been replaced, with effect from 28 December 2017, by a new Electronic Communications Code which is inserted as sch 3A into the Communications Act 2003 by s 4 and sch 1 of the Digital Economy Act 2017. For details, see *Conveyancing 2017* pp 71–73.)

The pursuer, having failed to reach agreement with the defender, the owner of land through which the pursuer ran a fibre optic cable, applied to the court for an order under paras 2 and 5 of the Telecommunications Code to impose an agreement on the defender. Two issues were debated in this appeal.

One was whether the pursuer was entitled to rent out some of the fibre optic strands to third parties. The Sheriff Appeal Court held that it was so entitled. All that the Code required was that the network be *provided* by an operator such as the pursuer, not that it be *used* by the operator.

The other issue was the basis of the compensation to be paid to the defender. Paragraph 7(1) of the Code provided, rather unhelpfully, that the amount to be paid should be such 'as it appears to the court would have been fair and reasonable if the agreement had been given willingly'. According to the pursuer, the scheme provided for in the Code was one for the compulsory acquisition of rights. This, if correct, brought into play the *Pointe Gourde* rule, ie the rule, laid down in *Pointe Gourde Quarrying & Transport Co Ltd v Sub-intendant of Crown Lands* [1947] AC 565, that compensation is not to include an increase in the value of the land which is entirely due to the scheme underlying the acquisition. The defender argued that the correct basis of compensation was the value to the operator of obtaining the right and not the value of the land to the owner. On this point the Sheriff Appeal Court agreed with the pursuer. This, however, is of limited importance for the future, because para 24 of the new Electronic Communications Code has detailed provisions on the calculation of compensation.

PLANNING AGREEMENTS

(27) European Development Company (Hotels) Ltd v Aberdeen City Council 12 August 2013 and 14 March 2014, Aberdeen Sheriff Court

This is a rare, and therefore helpful, case on the interpretation of planning agreements. Frequently, such agreements are entered into under s 75 of the Town and Country Planning (Scotland) Act 1997. The agreement in the present case, however, derived from the very general powers found in s 69 of the Local Government (Scotland) Act 1973.

European Development Company (Scotland) Ltd ('EDC 1') applied for planning permission to build a 148-room hotel in the centre of Aberdeen. As a condition of planning permission being granted, EDC 1 entered into an agreement with Aberdeen City Council to make a one-off payment of £40,000. The agreement made provision as to how the money was to be spent. Clause (Second) explained that it was to be used by the Council as a contribution 'towards the cost of improving security at the multi-storey car park at Chapel Street, Aberdeen'. Clause (Third) further provided that:

> The said contribution in Clause (Second) will be used by the Council only for the purpose ascribed to it herein and if the said measures for improving security detailed in Clause (Second) hereof to which the contribution relates are not provided (whether in isolation or as part of a larger scheme) within ten years of the commencement of the use of the Development or any part thereof by members of the public following implementation of the Decision, any payment made by the Developer in respect thereof shall be refunded to the Developer by the Council ...

Payment under the agreement should have been made before the hotel opened for business, on 21 November 2001. In fact it was paid more than two years late. £184,000 was spent by the Council in 2007 on works at the car park, including £12,026 upgrading the CCTV system. Meanwhile ECD 1 had assigned its rights under the agreement to European Development Company (Hotels) Ltd ('EDC 2'), presumably a company within the same group. EDC 2 accepted that the expenditure on CCTV was to improve security, but challenged the other heads of expenditure. In this action EDC 2 sought repayment of £27,974 (being the original £40,000 less the £12,026 spent on CCTV).

At debate, the issue was the proper interpretation of the agreement. As a planning agreement was a commercial contract, it should therefore, said the sheriff (Sheriff Marysia Lewis), be interpreted by reference to the ordinary rules of contract law. That meant that (para 5.5):

> I am required to apply an objective construction to the terms of the disputed phrase by reference to the meaning which a reasonable third party, who is aware of the commercial context in which the contract occurs, would give to the words which the parties have used, and adopt a commercially sensible construction.

Applying such a construction, the sheriff rejected as too narrow EDC 2's view that security was solely concerned with the safety of cars and their drivers. Other relevant matters might include, for example, protecting users of the car park from dangers of all kinds, or certain categories of repair and replacement.

At the proof which followed, the sheriff found much of the evidence of a quality that 'was far from satisfactory' (para 5.4). In the end, she was persuaded only in respect of one additional head of charge: the cost of replacing lights (£10,850) and also emergency lights (£4,200) both of which, on a balance of probabilities, were 'concerned with improving or making better the safe custody of cars, assisting in guarding against theft or damage to cars, attacks on staff and all who enter the car park'. These sums too could be deducted from the original £40,000 paid by EDC 1. Otherwise EDC 2 was entitled to its decree.

VARIATION ETC OF TITLE CONDITIONS BY LANDS TRIBUNAL

(28) Rubislaw Quarry Aberdeen Ltd v Hill of Rubislaw (Q Seven) Ltd
5 January 2018 (merits), 26 June 2018 (expenses), Lands Tribunal

This application concerned a proposal to build a 'granite heritage centre' at Rubislaw Quarry in Aberdeen. The quarry has a distinguished history: see www.rubislawquarry.co.uk/and https://en.wikipedia.org/wiki/Rubislaw_quarry. It was worked from 1740 until 1971, and the City of Aberdeen was built from its granite. In all some 6 million tonnes of granite were extracted for use in Aberdeen and elsewhere in the UK and beyond. At over 140 metres deep, the quarry is said to be the largest man-made hole in Europe. Since its closure, the quarry has begun to fill up with water, and the water levels have continued to rise.

The applicant was the owner of the quarry site, the so-called 'central quarry subjects' ('CQS'). These subjects, together with the land immediately to the north and the south, were subject to a deed of conditions entered into in 2003 and mutually enforceable. In terms of condition 8.3(e):

> the central quarry proprietors shall not develop or seek to develop any part of the central quarry subjects, and in order to preserve the amenity of the quarry subjects generally shall not permit or allow any other occupation or use of the central quarry

subjects for any purpose other than as a designated quarry site, green belt or amenity ground in its existing and/or natural condition, including without prejudice to the foregoing generality any use of the central quarry subjects for tipping or for depositing or storing of any other commercial or industrial substance or material which shall be strictly prohibited.

The application was for the variation of this condition so as to allow the building of the heritage centre.

In the period since 2003, when the deed of conditions was entered into, the land to the south had been developed for six blocks of flats, as indeed was anticipated at the time. The land to the north is also likely to be developed for flats. The application for variation was opposed by the owner of the land to the north as well as the owners of some of the flats to the south.

The applicant's proposal was for a building, faced with granite, on the southern edge of the quarry and accessed from Queens Road. The building would extend over the edge of the quarry, with large overlooking windows as well as windows set into the floor. The project had attracted a significant amount of public interest and support, and planning permission had been granted.

The Tribunal, having considered the various factors set out in s 100 of the Title Conditions (Scotland) Act 2003, refused the application. In the Tribunal's view, the original purpose in imposing condition 8.3(e) (factor (f)) – the preservation of amenity – remained as relevant now as it was in 2003; there had been no significant change of circumstances (factor (a)). The granting of planning permission (factor (g)), often disregarded by the Tribunal, was given weight as supporting the application due to the anticipated public benefit from the heritage centre. But in the end, as so often with Tribunal cases, the result hinged on the relative strengths of factor (b) (the extent to which the condition confers benefit on the benefited property) and factor (c) (the extent to which the condition impedes enjoyment of the burdened property).

In relation to factor (b), the main threat to the owners to the north and south was said to be, not the proposed building itself nor even the destruction of 86 trees, but the fact that the water levels would be lowered by 40 to 50 metres thus exposing potentially unattractive cliff faces. In other words, the value of the site lay, not in the quarry, but in the flooding which had produced what was described as a 'lakeside view'. Many of the flats on the south side of the quarry had been designed so as to enjoy that view. If the heritage centre went ahead, the value of these flats, the Tribunal found, would fall by around 5%. The proposed flats on the north side would also suffer a loss of view. It was true that the deed of conditions said nothing expressly about water levels. But the Tribunal decided, perhaps a little too easily, that 'in preventing development on the CQS, with the practical consequence of there being no incentive to drain the water … the deed of conditions does confer benefit on the amenity of the benefited property' (para 87).

As for factor (c), '[w]e consider that the proposal for a granite heritage centre is a bold and imaginative use for a unique site. If the proposal were to succeed, we accept there would be wider public benefits for Aberdeen and the north east' (para 96). That proposal was prevented by condition 8.3(e) of the deed of conditions. On the other hand, the funding needed for the project to go ahead – perhaps as much as £9.4 million – had yet to be raised, with the result that 'the burden of the condition prevents a development whose prospects are uncertain' (para 98).

There was, the Tribunal concluded, 'a strong case for maintaining the *status quo* and for not rearranging parties' rights under the deed' (para 105). The Tribunal continued:

> The extent to which the condition prevents the bold and imaginative heritage centre project under factor (c), and the public benefits which this might bring in terms of factors (c), (g) and partly (j) are significant and we duly give them weight. However, as we have discussed, we require to take account of the fact that the recent sale of the CQS was a freely entered into transaction involving the existence of a previously negotiated deed of conditions. Also, the prospects for the project are uncertain, and this necessarily reduces the weight we can give to those factors. On balance we do not think these factors outweigh the factors in favour of retaining the *status quo*. We do not therefore think it would be reasonable to vary the condition.

The respondents having prevailed, expenses, taxed on the Court of Session scale, were awarded against the applicant. Although the Tribunal expressed sympathy for the applicant, having regard to the disparity between the parties' resources and also the public spirit of its proposed venture, it was 'unable to find any recognised basis for not applying the general rule' as to expenses (para 26).

Planning permission for the granite heritage centre has since lapsed. That may not, however, be the end of the matter. The *Press & Journal* for 24 December 2018 quotes Hugh Black, the main shareholder in the applicant company, as saying that 'we have a Plan B for 2019 that we are looking at which will give the thousands of supporters of this project the opportunity to be part of our journey and help deliver a unique opportunity for the Granite City'.

(29) Chan v Sanderson-Tolsma
29 November 2018, Lands Tribunal

The applicants owned a house in Dreghorn Link in Edinburgh, part of a small development completed in the early 2000s. In addition to the house and garden they also owned an adjacent area which had not been built on at the time because it contained an underground storm sewer and attenuation tank. Planning permission had now been obtained for building a house on this area in a way which still allowed access to the sewer and tank. But building an additional house, and in this location, was contrary to various provisions in the deed of conditions. The applicants sought to vary or discharge these conditions. The application was opposed by the owners of a number of other houses in the same cul-de-sac.

While finding the various factors set out in s 100 of the Title Conditions (Scotland) Act 2003 to be 'fairly evenly balanced', the Lands Tribunal agreed to vary (but not discharge) the conditions, subject to evidence as to an appropriate wayleave agreement with Scottish Water. The strongest factor in favour of the application was factor (c) (the extent to which the condition impedes enjoyment of the burdened property). In their present form, 'the conditions prevented a development opportunity being realised' (para 51). That opportunity made good use of a difficult site. By contrast, the benefit conferred by the conditions was relatively slight (factor (b)). Quite a bit was made of the modernist style of the proposed new house, as opposed to the arts-and-crafts look of the existing houses. This, thought the Tribunal, was of only limited significance (para 47):

> The extent to which this design contrast can be described as an adverse impact, prevented by the conditions, is however debateable. There are many examples in south Edinburgh of modern architecture sitting next to traditional buildings without damaging, and indeed enhancing, the character of the neighbourhood. The proposed house is not, as it were, in the middle of a row within the residential estate so as to break up a uniform design. Rather, it is at the entrance where a design solution is required for the interface with the commercial service area. While we ourselves might not find the modern design of the house to be particularly attractive in context, we have to recognise that appreciation of architectural design can often be subjective. So although we give some weight to the benefit of the conditions which can be used, in effect, to veto the construction of building of a different style to the existing buildings, the weight we can give is limited in the above circumstances.

Finally, while the overall purpose of the conditions (factor (f)) was the preservation of amenity, inasmuch as the conditions made provision for the particular site they were more concerned with the protection of services rather than the preservation of amenity.

(30) O'Donnell v Craig
2 May 2018, Lands Tribunal

The most important feature of this case is its forthright rejection of the view that a person seeking to object to an application for variation must be able to show interest to enforce by reference to s 8 of the Title Conditions (Scotland) Act 2003 (para 22):

> Section 8 of the 2003 Act has to do with the enforcement of real burdens. It comes into play where someone is positively wanting to enforce such a burden at his or her own insistence in the way, for example, of an action in the Sheriff Court, of which *Barker v Lewis* 2008 SLT (Sh Ct) 48 is an example. Although they can be seen as doing the same thing (enforcing a burden) in different ways, we do not consider that it has any application to s 90. That is because Part 9 of the Act, which has to do with the powers of this Tribunal in relation to title conditions, contains, at s 95, its own provisions as to who can object.

On s 95, the Tribunal continued, 'there is no test of interest to enforce ... only title' (para 23). We have no doubt that this is the correct approach.

The case itself was straightforward. Mr O'Donnell, the applicant, was the owner of a house at the entrance to 'a pleasant development' (para 4) in Beith, Ayrshire, known as the Morrishill Manor Estate. The development dated from the mid-1980s and comprised 88 houses. Mr O'Donnell had obtained planning permission for the erection of three detached houses in his extensive garden. The application was for variation of a real burden in the deed of conditions which prohibited the erection of additional buildings. The application was opposed by the owners of five of the houses, none of whom was an immediate neighbour and only one of whom lived in the same street.

The Tribunal took a properly broad view of factor (c) in s 100 of the Title Conditions (Scotland) Act 2003 (the extent to which the condition impedes enjoyment of the burdened property) (para 34):

> 'Enjoyment of the burdened property' and its predecessor 'a reasonable use of land' have always been interpreted widely (see footnote in Rennie *Land Tenure and Tenements Legislation* 3rd ed page 211 and the cases cited there). Thus, in *Franklin v Lawson* 2013 SLT (Lands Tr) 81 at para 25 the Tribunal (Lord McGhie and Mr Darling FRICS) said 'We have no doubt that the restriction significantly impedes enjoyment of the burdened property. We are satisfied that the term "enjoyment" is used in a wide sense encompassing all the uses an unburdened owner might seek to make of his or her property.'

'But for this condition', the Tribunal continued (para 35), 'the applicant would be free to realise the value of his land by selling it for housing. The condition is, therefore, a very significant impediment to the enjoyment of the property, given the (presumably) substantial sum involved.'

Set against this, benefit conferred by the condition on the five objectors (factor (b)) was 'minimal' (para 27), not least due to their distance from the applicant's house. But even if the broader interests of the whole development were taken into account, under factor (f), there was no real disturbance to the overall amenity. The application was therefore granted.

(31) Martin v Turnbull
26 June 2018, Lands Tribunal

This case concerned the Fairways residential development in Milngavie, Dunbartonshire, which was built in the late 1970s and early 1980s. This was, and is, a 'high-amenity' development (para 24). In the words of the original sales brochure:

> To describe Fairways simply as a development of luxury homes would be to do this scheme a grave injustice. Nowhere in Scotland is there anything to approach its sheer magnificence.... People ... can appreciate the tradition of craftsmanship and concern for ever higher standards that are making Fairways the finest residential development in Scotland.

The applicants, who owned a house in this setting of 'sheer magnificence' wished to build a second house in their back garden. Planning permission was obtained, but the proposed new house would be contrary to several real burdens in two different deeds. The applicants sought to vary these burdens to the extent of permitting the proposed development.

The application, which was opposed by two neighbours, was refused. In what was said to be 'a narrow case' (para 33), the Tribunal concluded that the factors favourable to the applicant – the effect of the burdens in impeding development (factor (c)) and the fact that planning permission had been granted (factor (g)) – were outweighed by the benefit which the burdens conferred on the neighbours in respect of not being overlooked and the preservation of the view of an attractive area of wild amenity ground (factor (b)), especially in the light of the purpose of the burdens, which was evidently to preserve the overall amenity of the development (factor (f)).

Two aspects of this decision stand out. In the first place, the Tribunal placed unusually little weight on factor (c). No doubt the burdens impeded development. But the *status quo* was attractive and many would prefer it to the proposed development. As for that development (para 28):

> [T]he proposed house is fairly large and would be close – we understood some 6m – to the existing house. The construction of the new house is bound to reduce the desirability and value of No 5 with the loss of much of its garden and south aspect.

Although the Tribunal has sometimes taken account of the need, or lack of need, for a proposed development, there is no previous case, we think, where it has sought to pass judgment in quite this way on its overall desirability. There is a marked contrast between the approach adopted in this case and that adopted by a differently constituted Lands Tribunal in the previous case.

In the second place, the Tribunal gave some weight to the loss of view of the amenity area not just in respect of the two houses whose owners had opposed the application but in respect of other houses in the development as well (para 32):

> We have commented under (b) above that the condition is likely to benefit individual proprietors of the estate in that it protects views within the communal open space area. Although only two respondents have entered the process, who are immediate neighbours, we think we can take account of wider interests of the integrity of the estate generally. Experience suggests it is very possible that other benefited proprietors may have not objected because they were not 'immediately' affected and because of the risks of litigation. If not strictly falling under either limb of head (b), we take account of the wider interest under factor (j) ['any other factor which the Lands Tribunal consider to be material'].

(32) Crolla v Reid
18 April 2018, Lands Tribunal

This case adopts the same rather sceptical view of factor (c) as the previous case. The application concerned a seventeenth-century house in Helensburgh, Camis Eskan House, which was set in substantial grounds. In the 1970s it was divided into eight flats and three houses. The applicant, Mr Crolla, was the owner of a substantial four-bedroom flat on the ground floor which could be accessed both from the front, by the original entrance to the house, and from the back. Living on his own and wishing to downsize without leaving a property in which he had lived for 16 years, Mr Crolla proposed to divide his property into a two-bedroom flat accessed from the front and a one-bedroom flat accessed from the rear. His plan was to live in the smaller flat and to sell or let out the larger flat. Subdivision was contrary to the deed of conditions; hence the application. The application was opposed by the owner of the flat immediately above.

The Tribunal was doubtful as to the merits of the proposed conversion and hence as to whether the prohibition on division condition could be said to impede enjoyment of Mr Crolla's flat (para 24):

> Under factor (c) the case being made suggests that the enjoyment of the burdened property is impeded since it cannot be subdivided into more marketable smaller flats. As we have indicated, we are not convinced that two individual flats would necessarily be more marketable than a single large flat. It is by no means clear that a conversion resulting in a net loss of one bedroom, will add value. Moreover the only bedroom pertaining to the smaller flat is a markedly narrow room as it extends towards a front window. The room feels little more than an extension of the corridor leading to it. We think that the marketability of such a flat could thus be challenged.

But slight though the impediment to the applicant's enjoyment might be, it was at any rate greater than the extent to which the condition conferred benefit on the flat belonging to the objector (factor (b)). Given the generous scale of the building and its environs, any impact on the objector would be minimal. Hence the application would be allowed.

(33) Cadman v Cook
2018 Hous LR 64, Lands Tribunal

A grant in feu of land in Cults, Aberdeen, in 1876 restricted the number of houses to be built on the site to three. In due course three substantial houses – Glendarroch, Silverdale and Dunmail – were built and sold separately. So matters remained until 2013 when the owner of Dunmail concluded conditional missives to sell Dunmail to Cala Homes. An indicative plan showed that Dunmail itself was to be demolished and replaced by four houses, although an application for planning permission had yet to be made. As the burden in the 1876 feu was more than 100 years old, the owner of Dunmail served a notice of termination under s 20 of the Title Conditions (Scotland) Act 2003 (the so-called 'sunset' rule). In response, the owners of Glendarroch and Silverdale applied to the Lands Tribunal for the burden's preservation under s 90(1)(b). The application was opposed by the owners of Dunmail.

At first the parties' positions were uncompromising, with the applicants seeking retention of the burden in its entirety and the respondent seeking its removal. But in the course of the proceedings the applicants indicated a willingness to accept two houses on the site, while the respondent argued for six. The Tribunal compromised with four (the number on the indicative plan), but with a restriction to a single storey within 10 metres of Glendarroch and

5 metres of Silverdale. That was round 1 of the saga: see *Cook v Cadman* 2014 SLT
(Lands Tr) 13 (*Conveyancing 2013* Case (18)).

What happened next was that Cala's application for planning permission, for
four houses, was refused, whereupon Cala abandoned the project. McCarthy
& Stone took Cala's place as a potential purchaser and developer, concluding
conditional missives with the owners of Dunmail and drawing up plans for a
sheltered housing development of 21 units in a three-storey building. Planning
permission was initially refused but was granted on appeal. There then remained
the question of the real burden in the 1876 feu charter. Here the variation of 2014
did not help because it only allowed four houses. If the development was to go
ahead it was necessary to return to the Lands Tribunal to seek a further variation.
This, the present application by the owners of Dunmail, was round two. It was
opposed by the owners of Glendarroch and Silverdale.

The application failed. Taking as the baseline, not the burden in its original
form, but the burden as varied in 2014, the Tribunal decided that, insofar as this
impeded the enjoyment of Dunmail at all (factor (c)), it did so only to a limited
degree. It was true that Cala's planning application in respect of four houses had
been refused, but the main ground of refusal was the destruction of trees rather
than the massing of buildings. A different application would probably succeed.
The comparison thus was between (i) a development of four houses and (ii) a
development of a 21-unit sheltered housing development. The Tribunal, however,
had 'no evidence to help us measure the extent to which an ability to develop
retirement flats would be a greater development opportunity than the existing
opportunity for limited housing' (para 79).

By contrast, the burden in its amended form conferred a benefit on the
owners of Glendarroch and Silverdale (factor (b)) which was both 'palpable and
significant' (para 78). This included protection against (i) the greater massing
which would be produced by the McCarthy & Stone development as compared
with a development of four houses; (ii) increased activity and vehicular traffic;
and (iii) in the case of Glendarroch, being overlooked to a greater degree, and
also the significant risk of a diminution in value. To this should be added the
loss of certainty for the future which it had been the purpose of the original
Tribunal decision to procure (factor (f)).

The Tribunal summarised its thoughts in this way (para 83):

> Drawing the threads together we consider that the Tribunal, in varying the condition
> in 2014, did so in a way which purposively excluded the possibility of a future large
> flatted development. This was intended to draw a line in terms of future development
> for anything more than four houses. In this context factor (f) markedly supports
> the respondents. Each respondents' position is further supported by factor (b) and
> we find nothing in the other factors which outweigh these matters in favour of the
> applicants. We are therefore of the clear view that it would not be reasonable to vary
> the title condition.

One imagines that the application would have failed even if this had been
the first time that the parties had troubled the Lands Tribunal rather than the
second. All the same, its prospects do not seem to have been helped by the earlier

application. It was natural for the Tribunal to see its earlier decision as the final resolution of the competing interests at play. Reopening the matter was never going to be easy.

What will happen now? The first projected development had the necessary variation of a real burden but no planning permission. With the second projected development, it was the other way around. Perhaps the owners of Dunmail will reactivate the first development in the hope of producing a version which will find favour with the planning authorities.

One other matter might be mentioned. The applicants sought to argue that the respondents did not have interest to enforce the burden against them. This issue is close to, but distinct from, the question of the degree of benefit conferred by the burden (ie factor (b)). It is, however, the latter which is a matter for the Tribunal and not the former. In rejecting the applicants' submission, the Tribunal explained that (para 50):

> In this case we would therefore propose to follow our normal practice and consider the issue of potential detriment to the benefited property as subsumed within the context of factor (b), and not as a standalone test as the applicants would seek. As will be seen in any event, we are satisfied that the respondents' interest can be seen as more than fanciful or insignificant [being the test for interest to enforce].

The same view, though for a different reason, had been reached by a differently constituted Lands Tribunal in *O'Donnell v Craig* (Case 30 above), a month earlier.

(34) Bennett v Skene
11 May 2018, Lands Tribunal

When domestic rates were abolished in 1989, the legislation (the Abolition of Domestic Rates etc (Scotland) Act 1987 s 5(1)) provided that all existing maintenance obligations apportioned by rateable value (or assessed rental or annual value) should continue to stand; but as there would be no new valuations, the valuation would be frozen as at 1 April 1989. The relevant provision is now s 111 of the Local Government Finance Act 1992. Today, nearly 30 years later, some of these valuations might be seen as unfair, because there may have been changes to the relative values of the properties. And the unfairest case of all is where property that was in commercial use in 1989, and so had a high rateable value, has subsequently changed to domestic use and so should have a lower value.

That was exactly the position in *Bennett v Skene*. The corner tenement at Menzies Road and Grampian Place, Aberdeen, comprised two shops on the ground floor and a flat above. Until 1950 the tenement was owned by a single person. When the shops were sold off, liability for common repairs was imposed on the basis of assessed rental. In the course of time the shops were combined and, after the last valuation in 1989, converted to residential use. In this application to the Lands Tribunal under s 91 of the Title Conditions (Scotland) Act 2003, the applicant, Mr Bennett, was the owner of what is now a ground-floor flat and the respondent, Mr Skene, was his upstairs neighbour.

Section 91 empowers the Tribunal to vary community burdens for the entire community – which, in the present case, meant for both flats in the tenement. Mr Bennett's case was a simple one. Although the lower flat (ie the former two shops) was smaller and worth less than the upper flat, it carried responsibility for 68% of the common repairs on the basis of the frozen valuations. That, said Mr Bennett, should be changed to something more equitable, such as a fixed share of one-third or apportionment by floor area. For this there was a strong precedent. In strikingly similar circumstances, the Lands Tribunal in *Patterson v Drouet* 2013 GWD 3-99 had altered the allocation of common repairs in a tenement from annual value to floor area, resulting in a dramatic reduction in the share attributable to the former shops on the ground floor. See *Conveyancing 2012* pp 137–42.

The Tribunal had no hesitation in following its earlier decision in *Patterson v Drouet*, and for the same reasons. The evident purpose of the burden was to apportion common maintenance by current value (factor (f)). That purpose had been largely defeated by changes in circumstances, namely the combination of frozen valuations and the change from commercial to residential use (factor (a)). Although the proposed variation would be disadvantageous for the upper flat (factor (b)), this was to some extent offset by the likelihood that an equitable apportionment of liability would make repairs easier to manage. The Tribunal concluded that an apportionment of liability on the basis of floor area would be best, but with a small adjustment to acknowledge the storage space available in the attic of the upper flat. This resulted in a split of 55% for the upper flat and 45% for the lower. As in *Patterson* there were no grounds for awarding compensation: there was no evidence that the variation would change the value of the upper flat.

ROADS, PUBLIC RIGHTS OF WAY, AND ACCESS RIGHTS

(35) Renyana-Stahl Anstalt v Loch Lomond and Trossachs National Park Authority
[2018] CSIH 22, 2018 SC 406, 2018 SLT 331, 2018 SCLR 617

Renyana-Stahl Anstalt, a Liechtenstein legal entity, owned an estate of 1,500 hectares, called Drumlean, in the Trossachs, near Ben Venue and Loch Ard. The estate was within the Loch Lomond and Trossachs National Park. The park authority served a notice on Renyana-Stahl, under s 14 of the Land Reform (Scotland) Act 2003, saying that it was unlawfully obstructing access rights, and requiring remedial action. Renyana-Stahl raised the present action to challenge the s 14 notice.

In what is likely to become a leading case on access rights under the 2003 Act, the Inner House had to decide two issues that, hitherto, had been uncertain. The first was whether a s 14 notice can require removal of obstructions that were already on the ground *before* the 2003 Act came into force. (Answer: yes.) The second was whether the 'purpose or main purpose' provision in s 14 is to be interpreted in an objective or a subjective manner. (Answer: objective.) The decision affirms that of the Sheriff Appeal Court: [2017] SAC (Civ) 11, 2017 SLT (Sh Ct) 138, *Conveyancing 2017* Case (18).

[Note: the SC and SLT reports both erroneously give the pursuer's name as 'Anstalt'. This is like reporting an action pursued by Pamela MacGlumphry Limited against Euphemia Turveydrop as *Limited v Turveydrop*.]

(36) Manson v Midlothian Council
[2018] SC EDIN 50, 2018 GWD 33-422

The local authority served an order on the co-owners of a property at Penicuik, Midlothian, requiring them to remove a fence that they had erected which prevented walkers from going along a path on the northern bank of the North Esk. The order was made under s 14 of the Land Reform (Scotland) Act 2003. The owners appealed. After a lengthy hearing the order was upheld. See **Commentary** p 187.

(37) B v C
[2018] SC FORF 27, 2018 GWD 16-213

This was an action for declarator of a right of way. The report omits the names of the parties, of the witnesses, and even the identity of the location, other than that it was (see para 1) 'a picturesque community in the Angus hills'. The reason for these redactions is unknown.

Mr and Mrs B owned a house next to a public path running east–west. Immediately to the north was woodland, owned partly by the defenders, Mr and Mrs C, and partly by Mrs C's father. On the far side of the woodland, at its northern edge, was a village: thus the house of the Bs was at the opposite side of the woodland to the village. Through the woodland, running very roughly in a north–south direction, there was a path that had been, in 2010, designated as a 'core path' by the local authority in terms of the Land Reform (Scotland) Act 2003. The defenders, the Cs, obtained planning permission to build a house in the woodland, close to the core path, the house being completed in about 2015. The Cs asked the local authority to vary the route of the core path through the woodland, so that it would not run so near to their new house, and the local authority did so, this happening in 2016. The Bs then raised the present action for declarator that, notwithstanding the variation of the route of the core path, there was in any case a public right of way which the core path, on its original alignment, had simply followed, the result being that the public (including of course the Bs) could continue to pass by the Cs' new house. (This was not necessary for the Bs to continue to get to the village and back through the woodland. There was always the core path that they could take.) The basis of their claim was prescriptive use.

The prescriptive period for establishing a public right of way is 20 years (Prescription and Limitation (Scotland) Act 1973 s 3). During that time there has to be, among other things, (i) a reasonably definite route and (ii) reasonably frequent usage, that usage being (iii) by the public and not merely by those connected with one particular local property. The pursuers' case had to pass all three tests. As it was, it failed on all three. After hearing the evidence of local people who knew the area, as well as the evidence of the parties themselves, the sheriff (Sheriff Gregor Murray) concluded (i) that whilst there may have been a north–south route through the woodland at certain times in the past, it had had at best an intermittent existence, having frequently been blocked by fencing, overgrowth and so forth, so that what had been designated the core path had come into physical existence relatively recently, (ii) that the pursuers' use of the woodland over the years had been slight, and (iii) that there was little evidence of usage by the public at large, in the sense of crossing the woodland from end to end, as opposed to walking within the woodland. The pursuers, noted the sheriff at para 80, 'led no evidence of use by anyone other than themselves, a visitor … or their servant … While they mentioned seeing others occasionally on the path, there was no evidence those persons used the path end to end …' Here the sheriff cited D J Cusine and R R M Paisley, *Servitudes and Rights of Way* (1998) para 20.25.

Of Mr B as a witness the sheriff observed: 'At no stage did he give the impression that he was willing and/or able to tell things as they truly were. His evidence was … anything but objective. I did not gain the impression he sought to achieve anything other than the furtherance of his own interests' (para 67). The sheriff also noted that, while all this was going on, Mr B had physically blocked the east–west right of way that ran near his own house. 'The irony' observed the sheriff at para 68, 'was apparently lost on him'.

As we have already noted, the failure of this action did not mean that there is now no public path through the woodland. There is, but one that does not run immediately past the defenders' house.

Two final comments. The first is that the pursuers could (as well as using the core path) still exercise their right to roam through the woodland in general. We take it, however, from the fact that they raised this action, that this would not satisfy them, presumably because of the rules in s 6(1)(b)(iv) of the Land Reform (Scotland) Act 2003, whereby the right to roam is restricted in the vicinity of a house. The other comment is to note that the declarator sought by the pursuers was that there was a *public* right of way. They did not seek declarator of a *private* right of way, ie a servitude of way, even though such a declarator would (we surmise) have suited their purposes equally well. Yet the latter would have needed evidence only of their *own* usage, over 20 years, not public usage. Their case would have, therefore, been somewhat more stateable. Nevertheless, the sheriff's evaluation of the evidence would seemingly mean that a claim for a prescriptive servitude would also have failed.

(38) Kolhe v Robertson
[2018] SC ABE 43, 2018 GWD 25-324

Cove is a small harbour near, or in the southern outskirts of, Aberdeen, which has been used by fishing vessels, especially for creel fishing, since beyond living memory. A dispute between the fishermen on the one hand, and the owner of part of the land, Pralhad Kolhe, on the other hand, as to access, has been a fairly significant news story. See for instance the BBC story of 12 July 2018, available at www.bbc.co.uk/news/uk-scotland-north-east-orkney-shetland-44807189.

Mr Kolhe sought to stop the fishermen using the harbour, and did so both by physical means, by placing boulders, and also by legal means, in the form of the present action of declarator and interdict. The defenders responded by counterclaiming. The result of the case was divided, with some points won by the pursuer and others by the defenders. The case is of interest on the facts but also has a point of legal interest: it was held that the public right of way leading to and along the pier (the pier being owned by Mr Kolhe) included an ancillary public right to park vehicles on the pier. See **Commentary** p 191.

COMPETITION OF TITLE

(39) Anderson v Wilson
[2018] CSOH 5, 2018 GWD 4-62

Thomas Paterson owned land at Cobairdy, Aberdeenshire, where he had a dairy farm. In 2011 he sold some of his land to his son-in-law, George Wilson. Mr Paterson died in 2016. Two of his daughters then raised the present action for reduction of the disposition in favour of their brother-in-law. They claimed that the sale had been at 'gross undervalue'. The action failed, primarily because it was held that the pursuers had no title to sue. If the disposition was voidable, then the person with title to sue would be Mr Paterson or, since his death, his executor. See **Commentary** p 198.

(40) Brooke v Kelly
[2018] CSOH 53, 2018 Hous LR 56

In this strange case, allegations of criminality abounded: social security fraud, embezzlement, false affidavits, forgery, theft, witness bribery, witness intimidation ... But the focus of the case was civil law, not criminal law.

Elizabeth Brooke owned a house. She disponed it to a friend, ostensibly gratuitously. In fact the transaction was a sale, the price being paid in cash. She later claimed that she had been induced to sell the house for less than its real value, and raised an action of reduction, based on facility and circumvention. The action failed. See **Commentary** p 205.

(41) Cox v Cox
[2018] CSOH 49, 2018 GWD 17-219

Catherine Cox exercised her right to buy. The price was paid by her son and daughter-in-law. Later she sold the property and agreed that a new property would be bought with the proceeds, the new one being more convenient for an elderly person and, moreover, nearer to her son and daughter-in-law. She agreed that title would be taken in their name rather than hers. She later fell out with them, badly. Her daughter-in-law was prosecuted for assaulting her (but was eventually acquitted). Her son and daughter-in-law raised an action for removal against her. She raised the present action against them, claiming that the title should have been taken in her name, not theirs. Her action was unsuccessful. See **Commentary** p 196.

(42) Barr v Cassels
[2018] CSOH 79, 2018 GWD 27-345

Agnes Barr's father, a farmer, disponed to her, gratuitously, 1.42 hectares of his farm at Bonnyton Moor Farm, Eaglesham, Renfrewshire. The disposition was recorded in the Register of Sasines on 9 June 2006. By a further gratuitous disposition recorded on the same day, Agnes Barr disponed a one-half *pro indiviso* share of the land to James Cassels, with a survivorship destination. Mr Cassels was the family solicitor. Ms Barr and Mr Cassels were in a relationship with each other, and they were planning to build a house on the land and live there together. The house was built. It was large and expensive.

Things then went pear-shaped. Ms Barr fell out with her family, including her father, who considered challenging the validity of the disposition in her favour. She also fell out with Mr Cassels. He raised against her an action of division and sale, and obtained decree. Before this decree could be enforced, Ms Barr raised the present action to have the disposition in his favour reduced. For both actions she received legal aid, a fact that raised the eyebrows of the Lord Ordinary: see para 166.

The action failed. The pursuer's evidence was inconsistent with her written case and also contrary to the more reliable evidence of other witnesses. The defender had not profited at the expense of the pursuer and, applying the test in *Aitken v Campbell's Trs* 1909 SC 1217, the case based on breach of fiduciary duty failed. See **Commentary** p 199.

(43) Khan v Saddique
[2018] CSOH 41, 2018 GWD 16-212

In 1998 Muhammed Khan bought a house in Glasgow. He never lived there, but rented it to Mohammed Saddique. In 2002 a disposition by Mr Khan in favour of Mr Saddique was registered. Eleven years later Mr Khan raised an action to reduce the disposition on the ground that it was a forgery. The Lord Ordinary found that (i) Mr Khan's signature was not by Mr Khan but (ii) whoever was the forger it was not Mr Saddique. Who had in fact signed Mr Khan's name was never determined, and, indeed, much else about this bizarre case was unclear. The action failed on the basis of personal bar. See **Commentary** p 206.

(44) Sheltered Housing Management Ltd v Bield Housing & Care
30 August 2018, Dundee Sheriff Court

In a sheltered housing development the title sheet of each of the flats included, in the A (property) section, a right of common property to a number of parts of the building including the common room, common entrances and hallways, lift, and so on. This list of individual parts concluded with a reference to 'all other services and items not specifically mentioned herein which are of common service to the Development but excluding the access roadway areas and parking areas'. A question arose as to whether these words could be read as including the warden's office, a plant room for the lift, and a toilet adjacent to the common room, or whether these particular parts had been retained by the developer and later passed on to Sheltered Housing Management Ltd, which was the first manager of the development.

It was held, surely correctly, that the parts in question were not encompassed within a general reference to 'services' and 'items ... of common service'.

In reaching that conclusion the sheriff derived some help from the terms of the rest of the title sheet and in particular from a deed of conditions which was set out in the burdens section. This is, perhaps, an indirect and not wholly reliable way of going about things. If words in a deed are unclear, then the place to look for elucidation, in the first place at least, is the deed itself. (See *Craig v J D Peace and Company (Aberdeen) Ltd*, Case (50) below.) The description in the property section would have come from the split-off writ for the flat in question. That would have been the place to start. The deed of conditions would also have been potentially relevant, not only because it was mentioned in the split-off writ, but also because it was more or less contemporaneous with that writ and was granted by the same party. None of this affects the outcome of the case, and either route leads to the deed of conditions. But in matters of interpretation it is the deed which has primacy rather than the information which the Keeper happens to have assembled on the title sheet.

Another consideration in this case which pointed towards the same result was the decision in *PMP Plus Ltd v Keeper of the Registers of Scotland* 2009 SLT (Lands Tr) 2 to the effect that, for land to be conveyed, it must be sufficiently described. That argument too was accepted by the sheriff.

We understand that this decision is being appealed. Another aspect of the case is digested as Case (15) above.

TRUSTS OF HERITABLE PROPERTY

(45) Chemcem Scotland Ltd v Beaton
[2018] SC FAL 32, 2018 SLT (Sh Ct) 371

The pursuer was a company whose shares were wholly owned by a husband and wife, the latter being the defender in this action. It appears that the couple were also the directors of the company. The pursuer sought declarator that certain properties in Linlithgow that the defender had acquired were held by her in trust for the company. The facts of the case were in dispute, but there was also a preliminary plea by the defender that the action should be dismissed as irrelevant, because a trust of heritable property has to be constituted in writing, and here there was nothing in writing. It was held that a trust of heritable property does not have to be constituted in writing. See **Commentary** p 210.

LAND REGISTRATION

(46) Aslam v Keeper of the Registers of Scotland
13 February 2018, Lands Tribunal

This is the first decision on the Keeper's warranty under the Land Registration etc (Scotland) Act 2012 (roughly equivalent to the Keeper's indemnity under the Land Registration (Scotland) Act 1979). It concerns the important transitional provisions, set out in sch 4 of the 2012 Act, which apply to compensation in respect of a rectification of the Register occurring on or after the designated day (8 December 2014) in relation to a title which was itself registered before that day and hence under the 1979 Act. The rather intricate rules which apply in this situation are set out in paras 13.22 and 13.23 of K G C Reid and G L Gretton, *Land Registration* (2017). In brief, they are as follows. (i) Any inaccuracy in a 1979 Act title which would have been capable of being rectified by the Keeper immediately before the designated day (usually because the registered proprietor was not in possession) was automatically corrected on that day in the sense that the relevant rights were redistributed. (ii) But the entry on the Register remained unchanged and hence inaccurate. (iii) That inaccuracy can then be rectified under the normal rules in s 80 of the 2012 Act, which requires that the inaccuracy be manifest. (iv) If rectification occurs, the proprietor whose title is rectified has a claim for compensation under the Keeper's warranty (s 73 of the 2012 Act). (v) Some adjustments, however, are made by sch 4 para 19 to the Keeper's defences to such a claim. On the one hand, the Keeper has available to her any defences which would have been available to her under s 12 of the 1979 Act; on the other hand, she is deprived of the conduct-based defences in s 78(b) and (c) of the 2012 Act. As we will see, these adjustments were of importance in the present case.

Mehmoona Aslam was the owner of a flat, number 257/2 St John's Road, in Corstorphine in Edinburgh. Her title was registered in November 2013, and hence under the 1979 Act. The description of the property in the B (property) section of her title sheet began as follows:

> Subjects within the land edged red on the title plan being the westmost house on the upper storey at 257 St John's Road, Edinburgh EH12 7XD. Together with the garden ground pertaining thereto …

There was indeed garden ground at the rear of the tenement, accessed by a narrow pend, and part of that ground had at one time belonged to the owner of flat 257/2. But by the time of first registration of the title to the flat in 2010, ownership of the garden had been conveyed to the owners of the adjoining tenement. Hence the inclusion of the garden in the title sheet was a mistake.

On 24 November 2016 the Keeper undid the mistake by removing the reference to the garden from the title sheet. Although the issue is not discussed in the Lands Tribunal's Opinion, it is assumed that the Keeper's power to rectify arose because, immediately before the designated day, Mrs Aslam was not in possession of the garden (see (i)–(iii) above). Rectification having taken place, Mrs Aslam claimed compensation under the Keeper's warranty. The present appeal arose because Mrs Aslam was unable to agree quantum with the Keeper. The garden area had long since been dug up and was now used as a car park by the owners of the neighbouring building.

An important preliminary point concerned the relevance, or otherwise, of Mrs Aslam's state of knowledge at the time of her purchase in 2013. She must, it was suggested, have been aware of the frailty of her title to the garden/car park. Read as a whole, the description in the title sheet should have indicated potential problems. The prior Sasine titles gave no support to ownership of the garden. Nor did the state of possession. Finally, the purchase price paid did not suggest that a garden/car park was included in the title.

Quite correctly, the Lands Tribunal dismissed arguments of this kind. It was true that, to a 'regular' claim under the Keeper's warranty, there were certain conduct-based defences, most notably that the existence of the inaccuracy on the Register was known, or ought to have been known, to the claimant or the claimant's legal adviser (2012 Act s 78(b)). But, as already mentioned, such defences were not available for 1979 Act titles. Instead, the 1979 Act defences applied, and under that Act conduct (fraud or carelessness) was relevant only where the conduct had *caused* the inaccuracy (ss 12(3)(n) and 13(4)). As the inaccuracy had come about in 2010, at the time of first registration, it could not be said to be caused by Mrs Aslam's state of knowledge (whatever that was) at the time of her purchase in 2013.

A related issue was whether, as the Keeper urged, quantum should be based on Mrs Aslam's 'real' loss as opposed to the notional loss from being deprived of the garden. For all kinds of reasons, the former might be less than the latter. Again quite correctly, the Tribunal rejected this view (paras 37 and 39):

> Looking at the District Valuer's approach another way, he is suggesting there is no real 'loss' because the appellant had never paid for a property with a value commensurate to a two bedroom flat and five car parking spaces. If the appellant knew she was probably not acquiring or paying for that number of spaces in the transaction, she cannot be said to have 'lost' them by rectification. This argument, which as we have said the Keeper appears to endorse, seems to confuse a common law claim for damages with a claim for breach of warranty. The Keeper's deemed warranty in section 73(1) warrants that the title sheet is accurate insofar as it shows an acquisition by the appellant. The Keeper must pay compensation for loss incurred as a breach of the warranty. . . .
>
> In this case, the warranty is that the description of the subjects as including the garden ground is accurate. The appellant's loss is therefore the extent to which the appellant would have been better off had the information been right and the title not been rectified. Had the description been accurate the appellant would have had a real right in the garden ground: cf s 3(1) of the 1979 Act. On the face of it, therefore, the loss is simply the value of the land removed from the title sheet by the rectification. We do not think it is correct to get into a common law damages approach by seeking

to ascertain an 'overall' loss by reference to what the appellant might have paid for the property in the first place.

As to the value of the garden, there was the usual disagreement between expert witnesses – the District Valuer for the Keeper and Graham & Sibbald for Mrs Aslam. The Keeper argued that, as the boundaries of the garden were not shown on the title sheet, it should be treated as confined to the smaller area which had at one time belonged to the flat in terms of the Sasine titles, but this view was rejected by the Tribunal (para 40):

> The idea that the property section of the land register should be interpreted by reference to a long superseded sasine deed, if that was what was being suggested, seems to undermine the basic purpose of land registration, namely for there to be a mapped system readily showing the extent of land ownership. In terms of section 4(2)(a) of the 1979 Act the Keeper should not have accepted an application for registration if the land was not 'sufficiently described' so as to be identified by reference to the Ordnance Map. So it comes somewhat ill from the Keeper to argue that no claim can be made because the 'lost' area is undefined, where the Keeper appears to have accepted a registration without mapping the details of the land such as the garden area in the first place. By not mapping the details in 1979 Act registrations and by resting upon a potentially ambiguous verbal description it is hard to avoid the conclusion that the Keeper was accepting an increased risk of future problems with the registration in question. But we accept of course that the Keeper made a clerical error, so it is perhaps not surprising there are issues with precisely what the title sheet meant.

The garden ground, the Tribunal concluded, was capable of providing four car-parking spaces. Graham & Sibbald valued each space at £10,000, the District Valuer at £5,000. Having reviewed the evidence, the Tribunal fixed on a figure of £5,600 per space.

(47) Combined Corporation (BVI) Ltd v Souter
15 February 2018, Lands Tribunal affd [2018] CSIH 81, 2019 SLT 127

The same area of land in Peterculter, near Aberdeen ('the disputed area'), extending to around half a hectare, appeared in two different Sasine titles. In due course, the title to one of the properties ('property B') migrated to the Land Register. The other property ('property A') remained in the Sasine Register. This was an application by the owner of property A under s 82 of the Land Registration etc (Scotland) Act 2012 to have it determined that the inclusion of the disputed area in the title sheet of property B was an inaccuracy which fell to be rectified.

It was common ground that the inclusion of the disputed area in the title sheet of property B was originally an inaccuracy, for at that time it was property A that had had the valid Sasine title. But all inaccuracies in titles registered under the Land Registration (Scotland) Act 1979 were cured on the designated day (8 December 2014) unless the Keeper would have been able to rectify the inaccuracy immediately before that day: see Land Registration etc (Scotland) Act 2012 sch 4 para 17. In the absence of fraud or carelessness on the part of the registered proprietor, the main reason why the Keeper might have been unable to rectify the inaccuracy would have been that the registered proprietor was in possession: see 1979 Act s 9(3)(a). The dispute therefore resolved into the question of whether the registered proprietor of property B had been in possession of the disputed area on 7 December 2014. It was held by the Tribunal that the person registered as proprietor of property B had not been in possession, and this finding was upheld on appeal by the First Division. The inaccuracy on the title sheet remained, therefore, and now fell to be rectified. See **Commentary** p 152.

(48) McAdam's Exr v Keeper of the Registers of Scotland
16 May 2018, Lands Tribunal

By s 80 of the Land Registration etc (Scotland) Act 2012 the Keeper must rectify an inaccuracy in the Register but only where the inaccuracy is 'manifest'. The purpose of this limitation is to absolve the Keeper from having to make what may amount to judicial decisions about the title. To count as 'manifest', an alleged inaccuracy must either be obvious or (what really comes to the same thing) the position must be agreed between the interested parties. Otherwise, a person who seeks rectification will first have to have the inaccuracy judicially declared, either by the Lands Tribunal under s 82 of the Act or by the ordinary courts. (A less-than-manifest inaccuracy becomes manifest once the court or tribunal has confirmed it.) But how obvious must an inaccuracy be for it to qualify as 'manifest' without judicial intervention? *McAdam's Exr* is the first case to consider that question.

The facts were unusual. When the title for the terraced house at 3 Morris Avenue, Lochgelly, Fife, was registered for the first time in the Land Register, it was shown as including a small area of ground ('the disputed area') which lay immediately to the front of the adjoining house, number 2 Morris Avenue. This, however, was not a mistake on the part of the Keeper. On the contrary, it reflected the underlying Sasine title. Meanwhile, the title to number 2 continued to be held on the Register of Sasines.

Both properties were former council houses, and the feu dispositions of both properties, when they were sold by the council, included the disputed area. As, however, number 3 was feued before number 2, the disputed area was carried by the feu disposition of number 3.

All of this was done in the early 1980s. Since then, the disputed area had been enclosed and possessed by the owner of number 2. Indeed, from 1992 onwards most of it had been given over to an extension to the house at number 2. In the light of such clear possession it was held by the Lands Tribunal that the disputed area had been acquired by the owner of number 2 by positive prescription. Hence its inclusion in the title sheet of number 3, while originally perfectly accurate, had now come to be inaccurate.

The main interest of this case is the Tribunal's view that such a clear case of prescription created an inaccuracy which was manifest and hence which could have been corrected by the Keeper without recourse to the Tribunal or a court: see **Commentary** pp 147 and 150.

One other aspect of the case may be mentioned. The prescriptive period would have been completed, at latest, in 2002, ten years after the extension was first built. This created an inaccuracy on the title sheet of number 3. As these events occurred before the designated day, the Tribunal sought to apply the transitional arrangements in sch 4 of the 2012 Act (para 9):

> The prescriptive period will have expired by about 2002, and very probably earlier, being a date prior to the designated day for the 2012 Act (8 December 2014). The register will have become inaccurate prior to the designated day by failing to note that the overlap area did not belong to No 3. The transitional provisions of the 2012 Act accordingly apply. In terms of paragraph 17 of Schedule 4 to the 2012 Act, the Keeper would have had the power to rectify the register immediately before the designated day under section 9 of the Land Registration (Scotland) Act 1979. This is because the interested party was not a proprietor in possession in terms of ss (3). It follows from sub-paragraphs (a) and (b) of paragraph 17 that the deceased were proprietors of the overlap area and that the register is presently inaccurate.

The conclusion is, of course, correct: the Register was indeed inaccurate in showing the disputed area as part of number 3. But it is possible to take issue with the Tribunal's reasoning. Immediately before the designated day the Keeper would have been able to rectify, says the Tribunal, because the owner of number 3 was not in possession of the disputed area. That is perfectly true as far as it goes. But it is hard to see why the state of possession mattered. A proprietor in possession was only protected, under s 9(3)(a) of the Land Registration (Scotland) Act 1979, where rectification would be to the proprietor's prejudice. But no prejudice would be suffered by the owner of number 3 in the event of rectification. This is because, despite what the Register said, the title to number 3 no longer included the disputed area and indeed had not done so since 2002. Rectification would simply bring the title into line with the legal position. It would not deprive the owner of number 3 of rights: that had already been done, back in 2002, by operation of prescription.

To put it another way, the inaccuracy in *McAdam's Exr* was an 'actual' inaccuracy and not a 'bijural' one. It was created, not by the Midas touch in the 1979 Act but by the rules of prescription. And, as the heading to paras 17–24 of sch 4 to the 2012 Act makes clear, the transitional provisions are intended only to apply to bijural inaccuracies: see Scottish Law Commission, *Report No 222 on Land Registration* (2010) paras 17.10, 17.11, 17.35 and 36.9. The inaccuracy which arose in 2002 was quite unaffected by the change from 1979 Act to 2012 Act. And by contrast to the redistributive effect of para 17 of sch 4 to the 2012 Act, rectification of the inaccuracy would not alter the legal position of anyone.

[Another aspect of this case is digested as Case (79) below.]

(49) Higgs v Keeper of the Registers of Scotland
29 March 2018, Lands Tribunal

In the year 2000, Auchengool Farm in Kirkcudbrightshire was divided into four separate units. One of the units ('unit 1'), comprising the farmhouse and some

24 hectares of land, was bought by Mr and Mrs Higgs. Access to unit 1 from the public road from Kirkcudbright to Dundrennan lying to the south was by means, firstly, of a shared access road, and then by a steading road which branched off from the shared road in a westerly direction towards unit 1. As the steading road served only unit 1, the intention appears to have been for it to be included as part of that unit.

In the split-off disposition of unit 1 the subjects were described in three different ways: (i) by verbal description in the disposition itself; (ii) by verbal description in an accompanying deed of conditions the terms of which were incorporated by reference into the disposition; and (iii) by plan. None of these was declared to be taxative; but the verbal descriptions were either so vague, or relied on lettering included on the plan, as hardly to qualify as independent descriptions. The plan itself was criticised by Mr and Mrs Higgs as 'fairly crude, unmeasured as it is and with the boundary shown by a thick line' (para 10). But it was at any rate serviceable. It showed the boundary between unit 1 and unit 2 (Auchengool Cottages) as lying to the east of the steading road, so that the whole of the steading road lay within unit 1. Unfortunately, however, the steading road was, for some of its length, depicted in the plan as lying further to the west than it actually did. This mistake appears to have arisen because, at the time of the sale, the steading road, being new, was not shown on the OS map.

The disposition was registered in the Land Register on 7 February 2001. This, of course, was a first registration. In plotting the boundaries of unit 1, the Keeper relied on the deed plan rather than on the two verbal descriptions. This was later to be criticised by Mr and Mrs Higgs but, having regard to the vagueness of the verbal descriptions, it is difficult to see how it could have been otherwise, as the Lands Tribunal noted (para 30). The effect of following the boundary line as shown on the deed plan was to exclude part of the steading road from the title sheet of unit 1 and to include it instead in the title sheet of unit 2. This, however, only became obvious later on when the OS map – and hence the cadastral map – was updated to include the steading road.

The central question to be determined in this application by Mr and Mrs Higgs was whether the Register was inaccurate in showing part of the steading road as lying within unit 2. In arguing that the Register was inaccurate, the applicants placed some reliance on the definition of inaccuracy in s 65 of the Land Registration etc (Scotland) Act 2012, and in particular in the statement in that provision that a title sheet was inaccurate where it 'misstates what the position is in law and fact'. Surely, reasoned the appellants, the title sheet misstated the position in fact where it showed a road which, on the ground, was plainly intended to lie within unit 1 as lying in part in unit 2? This, however, was the wrong test. As the applicants' title was registered under the Land Registration (Scotland) Act 1979, the question as to whether there was an inaccuracy fell to be determined by the transitional provisions in sch 4 paras 17–22 of the 2012 Act; and since the test applied by those provisions is whether the Keeper could, or could not, have rectified the inaccuracy immediately before the designated day, the meaning of inaccuracy is necessarily to be taken to be its meaning under the 1979 Act.

No definition of 'inaccuracy' was given by the 1979 Act but it was generally accepted as meaning an entry on the Register which was not justified by the underlying deed. In the present case, unfortunately for the appellants, the entry was entirely justified by the disposition of unit 1. The title plan showed the relevant boundary line in exactly the same place as was shown in the plan attached to the disposition. No doubt the deed plan was probably wrong. In that case, the appropriate remedy was to seek judicial rectification of the deed, as the Lands Tribunal pointed out (para 51). But where the Register reproduces the terms and legal effect of a deed presented for registration, then the Register is accurate and so cannot be rectified.

It might be added that the result would have been the same if registration had taken place under the 2012 Act, so that the meaning of 'inaccuracy' was to be determined, as the applicants thought, by s 65 of that Act. An entry in the Register does not misstate 'what the position is in law and fact' if it gives effect to a valid deed which is presented for registration. The disposition of unit 1 was a valid deed. In excluding part of the steading road, the title sheet of unit 1 was simply giving effect to its terms.

One other matter was raised by the case. Section 11(7) of the 2012 Act provides that: 'On the base map being updated, the Keeper must make any changes to the register which are necessary in consequence of the updating.' In the present case the base map (ie the OS map) did indeed come to be updated, so as to show the steading road, and hence the fact that the road now wandered from one of the units to the other. Surely, urged the applicants, the Keeper must now alter the Register in the light of this change so as to place the whole of the road within unit 1. The Tribunal disagreed. As the Tribunal pointed out, the purpose of s 11(7) was not to change legal boundaries but simply to enter on the cadastral map such new information (eg the location of a new road) as the revision to the OS map now disclosed. 'If the provision does not operate to enlarge title boundaries and if its application is restricted to the better recording of what is already there, this provision appears to be of no assistance to the applicants' (para 36).

(50) Craig v J D Peace and Company (Aberdeen) Ltd
9 February 2015 and 16 November 2017, Aberdeen Sheriff Court

At one time part of a single property, near Echt, Aberdeenshire, the respective properties of the pursuers and of the defender were divided by a disposition in favour of the defender granted by Trustees for the Firm of John C Harper & Co, the then owners of the whole, recorded GRS Aberdeen on 8 December 1993. The disposition contained a reservation of a servitude in the following terms:

> there will be reserved to us and our successors as proprietors of the whole subjects of which the subjects hereby disponed form part all necessary rights of pedestrian and vehicular access for all purposes over the access road shown coloured yellow on the plan annexed and signed as relative hereto.

Much later, on 7 December 2009, the pursuers acquired part of the property which had been reserved in 1993. This was a first registration, and the pursuers' title was registered under title number ABN103464. The A (property) section mentioned the servitude, but only in a note at the end of the description:

Notes.
1. The Disposition in Entry 2 of the Burdens Section contains a reservation of a servitude in favour of the subjects in this Title and other subjects.

The Disposition in Entry 2 was, of course, the 1993 disposition. It gave the terms of the reserved servitude, but by reference to the title plan rather than the deed plan ('... over the access road tinted green on the Title Plan ...'). Unfortunately, the title plan was incorrect in respect that it showed a gap – representing, presumably, the verge of the road – between the pursuers' property and the green tinting. In effect, therefore, the title sheet disclosed a servitude which, because of the gap, could not actually be exercised.

The parties were in dispute as to the pursuers' right to take access over the road. The present action was one of declarator and interdict.

The sheriff (Sheriff G Garden) accepted, under reference to *Willemse v French* 2011 SC 576, that a prior deed could be used to assist in the interpretation of an entry on a title sheet. (For a brief discussion and a list of further authorities, see K G C Reid and G L Gretton, *Land Registration* (2017) para 5.18; and see also *Sheltered Housing Management Ltd v Bield Housing & Care* (Case (44) above).) But in the present case the terms of the entry were too clear to require interpretation. If the pursuers wished to have the entry altered so as to correspond with the prior deed, this would have to be done by rectification by the Keeper.

On appeal to the sheriff principal the pursuers argued that the servitude was not 'registered' in the Land Register but merely 'noted'. It had been created, not by registration in the Land Register, but by the recording of the 1993 disposition in the Register of Sasines. Thus far, the argument is undoubtedly correct. It was a feature of the Land Registration (Scotland) Act 1979 (as indeed it remains a feature of the replacement legislation of 2012) that registration was only one of the ways by which an entry could be made in a title sheet: see eg Scottish Law Commission, *Discussion Paper No 125 on Land Registration: Void and Voidable Titles* (2004) para 2.21. Other possible methods were: (i) noting of overriding interests (s 6(4)); (ii) making up and maintenance of a title sheet (s 6(1)); and (iii) rectification (s 9). The effect of each was different. As it happens, the entry of the servitude in the present case was more correctly characterised as an example of (ii) rather than (i), for a servitude was an overriding interest only in respect of the title sheet of the *servient* tenement (see s 28(1)). But at any rate the entry did not amount to registration.

Did that make a difference? According to the pursuers it did. As the 1993 disposition had not been registered in the Land Register, there could be no objection to consulting the deed to see whether the account given on the Land Register of that disposition was correct. This was an enterprising argument, and one not without merit. It was accepted by the sheriff principal, although no opinion appears to have been issued. The pursuers were therefore granted decree.

[Another aspect of this case is digested as Case (22) above.]

(51) Taylor v Purves
18 January 2018, Lands Tribunal

In 2014 the respondent bought an upper flat, number 28 Polton Cottages, Lasswade, Midlothian. First registration in respect of this property had taken place some years previously, in 2003. In the title sheet the property was described as including 'the coal cellar being number 28 of the block of coal cellars erected on the back green'. This, however, was a mistake. The coal cellar in fact belonged not to the respondent but to the applicant, on a Sasine title. Indeed the cellar no longer existed as a separate unit because the applicant had knocked down the mutual wall to the adjacent coal cellar, which he also owned. He used the combined cellar to keep classic motor cycles and spare parts. When the respondent acquired the upper flat and hence, she thought, cellar number 28, the result was (para 5):

> a most unfortunate dispute. The applicant apparently discovered his motorcycles being advertised on ebay as a 'barn find' in March 2016. The matter duly escalated to legal proceedings.

The current application, made under s 82 of the Land Registration etc (Scotland) Act 2012, sought a finding that the respondent's registered title was inaccurate in respect of the coal cellar. In the event, the case settled on the first morning of a three-day hearing when the respondent conceded to the applicant. Both parties now sought to recover expenses from the Keeper (who had taken no part in the proceedings) on the ground that the only reason for the application, and for the expense it involved, was the initial registration error by the Keeper in 2003.

The Tribunal refused to make an award of expenses. Following earlier decisions of the Tribunal such as *Gray v Keeper of the Registers of Scotland*, 19 April 2016, the proper focus was the cause of the expense of the *process of litigation*, not the cause of the *dispute* itself. No doubt the dispute was caused by the Keeper's error. But the Keeper had no particular responsibility for the course of the litigation (paras 20 and 21):

> In this case we have sympathy for both the applicant and respondent for the position in which they found themselves. The underlying dispute was not of their making. The inaccuracy in the register had caused a dispute which had to be resolved by one method or another. The applicant appears to have had no choice but to proceed to the Tribunal in order to preserve his property which physically extended beyond cellar 28. The respondent had a title sheet, with indemnity, stating that she was proprietor of cellar 28. Both parties were put in a position of requiring to expend time and money to investigate the respective titles and the

history and degree of possession by each of them and the respondent's predecessors. Only once this was done could a fully informed view be taken on the merits of parties' positions.... Nevertheless, we think the Keeper is well founded in drawing a distinction between the cause of the expense of the process of litigation, as opposed to the cause of the dispute. While the Keeper's action of accepting an application for registration may bring about the latter, it is generally going too far to say that it is the cause of the former, for the reasons discussed in *Gray*. In the present case it would appear that the Keeper's position was known before the start of the Tribunal proceedings. She had accepted the register was inaccurate and adopted a neutral position with regard to the issue of possession. So in general terms we do not think there is a good basis in principle for a finding of expenses against the Keeper.

In the litigation, possession was seen as the crucial issue. This was because, under the transitional provisions in sch 4 paras 17–22 of the Land Registration etc (Scotland) Act 2012, the inaccuracy would be cured, and the respondent would be able to keep the cellar, if she had been in possession of it immediately prior to the designated day (8 December 2014). The issue was not one in which the Keeper could have assisted because it depended on a disputed question of fact. But there was one other matter where the Keeper's conduct was of possible relevance. Shortly before the start of the hearing the Tribunal had emailed all the parties querying whether, in the light of *PMP Plus Ltd v Keeper of the Registers of Scotland* 2009 SLT (Lands Tr) 2, the description in the title sheet was sufficiently clear to carry a right to the coal cellar. 'Had the Keeper ... conceded that the description was invalid, the case might have been short circuited at an earlier stage without reference to the whole tortuous history of possession.' But no such concession was made. The Tribunal doubted the wisdom of that approach but was not prepared to press the matter so far as to make an award of expenses against the Keeper (para 23):

Having read the Keeper's submissions we admit to remaining somewhat puzzled as to how the coal cellar can be said to have been 'sufficiently described by reference to the ordnance map', ie by reference to the second principle identified in *PMP Plus Ltd v The Keeper* at para [57]. The line of coal cellars is not described as such within the red edged area, and coal cellar 28 is not distinguished on the map at all. Indeed the title mapping may have been out of date all along since it does not show the extended and wider storage building developed by the applicant comprising cellars 28, 29 and the other area. There is nothing in the description, verbal or mapped, to show where coal cellar 28 had been or to distinguish it from the remaining cellars. However, we do not think that in present context, ie written motions for expenses – it is appropriate for us to take a view upon the Keeper's practice of a 'steading extent method of mapping' under the 1979 Act and prior to the introduction of section 16 of the 2012 Act. The issue is likely to have wider implications. Parties did not raise the validity issue themselves until the morning of the hearing and, due to the good sense of their agreeing settlement, the matter did not have to be determined. In these circumstances we are not disposed to find the Keeper liable for expenses.

We would simply add that there is a distinction between (i) a description in a deed presented for registration being sufficient to enable identification of the subjects on the OS map, and (ii) what the Keeper actually does with such a description at the point of registration. Under the 1979 Act the first of these was a statutory requirement, so that a deed with an insufficient description fell to be rejected: see s 4(2)(a). As for the second, the position was less clear: see *Conveyancing 2008* pp 140 and 145. On one view, the Keeper was bound the show the subjects on the OS map: after all, s 6(1)(a) provided for 'a description of the land which shall consist of or include a description of it based on the Ordnance Map'; on another view, a merely verbal description might be sufficient if there was some reference to the OS map (eg to the delineation of the tenement steading of which the subjects formed part) even if the subjects themselves were not delineated on the map. The Tribunal in *Taylor v Purves* appeared to favour the first of these views but without settling the question. This uncertainty, however, affects only registration practice in the past. For registrations taking place today, the 2012 Act s 6(1)(a)(i) adopts a rule of 'no registration without mapping.'

(52) Szymanski v Keeper of the Registers of Scotland
8 January 2018, Lands Tribunal

The applicants owned the terraced house, 29 Willow Road, Mayfield, Dalkeith, Midlothian. The front garden of the neighbouring property, number 31, was irregular in shape and included a small section, of less than a metre, which was directly in front on number 29. The title to number 29 was on the Land Register; that of number 31 remained for the moment on the Register of Sasines.

In this application the Lands Tribunal was asked to declare that the title sheet of number 29 was inaccurate to the extent that it did not include a right of access over number 31 for the purposes of repairing the small section of front wall which abutted the garden of number 31. No ground for this alleged inaccuracy was produced by the applicants; nor, on inspection, was the title sheet found to be inconsistent with the split-off writ for number 29. Accordingly, the application was dismissed.

By way of a postscript, the Tribunal said this (para 6):

> it may be the case that the law recognises implied rights of access for the purpose of carrying out repairs in certain cases. No case was made to this effect and we pass no comment upon whether such an implied right may apply here. Such rights, since they are implied, are by definition unlikely to be found on a title sheet. It is therefore questionable whether the Tribunal has jurisdiction to deal with them in referrals concerning the accuracy of the land register, although we would reserve our view on the point.

It does indeed seem likely that there was an implied right to carry out repairs in the present case. For discussion, see *Conveyancing 2017* pp 162–65.

SEARCHES

(53) Commodity Solution Services Ltd v First Scottish Searching Services Ltd
[2018] SC DUNF 14, 2018 SLT (Sh Ct) 117

This is, as far as we know, the first case in which a firm of searchers has been sued by a third party for loss caused by negligence.

Mr and Mrs Gardner owned a property at 6 Arbirlot Place, Arbroath, Angus. In December 2011 Commodity Solution Services Ltd obtained decree against Mr Gardner in the sum of £50,000. In February 2012 it registered an inhibition against him. Soon thereafter Mr and Mrs Gardner sold the property to Paul Gardner and Louise Jones. Paul Gardner was the son of the sellers. A legal report was obtained from First Scottish Searching Services Ltd. The report did not disclose the inhibition. In August 2012 the disposition to the buyers was registered in the Land Register. Like the legal report, the updated title sheet did not mention the inhibition.

Why the search firm failed to disclose the inhibition in the legal report is not known. But the inhibitor averred negligence and the search firm does not seem to have denied it. The case was not about whether there had been negligence, but about whether the inhibitor could found on that negligence to claim damages from the search firm.

The inhibitor said that the decree for £50,000 remained unsatisfied. It said that the search firm owed a duty of care to the inhibitor, a duty that had been breached by the non-disclosure of the inhibition. It said that if the search firm had disclosed the inhibition, the sale would not have happened or, alternatively, that it would have happened on the basis of the inhibition being discharged by payment. As a result the opportunity of recovering the debt from the property had, said the inhibitor, been lost. (What happened to the price is unclear, and nothing is said in the case about the prospects of recovery against Mr Gardner. But in the Register of Insolvencies we see that 'Ian D Gardner' of 1 Gayfield, Dundee Road, Arbroath, was sequestrated, and this would seem to be the same person.)

As mentioned, the case turned on whether there was a duty of care. The sheriff (Sheriff John McSherry) held that there was.

One distinction between the facts of the present case and the facts of the well-known cases cited to the court is that in the latter the claim was made by someone who had relied on a negligent statement – such a person sometimes being known in this area of law as the representee. But in this case the pursuer was not a representee: the pursuer had not relied on the erroneous legal report. (The buyers had relied on it, but they suffered no loss thereby: see the next paragraph.) So the decision does seem to go somewhat beyond the established authorities in this area of the law of delict.

Might the inhibitor have simply raised an action of reduction, notwithstanding the clear legal report and the fact that the inhibition did not show up on the title sheet? The answer was negative – which explains the damages action against the search firm. Section 159 of the Bankruptcy and Diligence etc (Scotland) Act 2007 says that a person who acquires property in good faith takes free from an inhibition against the seller. (Counsel for the defender suggested (see para 20) that, given the relationship between the parties, the buyers might not have been in good faith. But in the pleadings there was no averment to that effect and the sheriff, inevitably, accepted that the buyers must be taken to have acted in good faith: see para 76.)

Why the Keeper did not note the inhibition in the title sheet was not an issue that was explored in the case. But, said the sheriff (para 77), even if the Keeper had noted it, it would have made no difference, standing the terms of s 159 of the 2007 Act. That seems a correct statement of the law.

Postscript: the decision has been appealed without success: [2019] SAC (Civ) 4. The appeal will be covered in next year's volume.

RESIDENTIAL RIGHT TO BUY

(54) Caven v Irvine Housing Association
[2018] CSIH 23, 2018 SLT 401, 2018 SCLR 686

The applicant was originally the tenant of a property at 69 Stakeford Street, Dumfries. In 2003 she exchanged this for the tenancy of another property, at 28 Goldie Crescent, Nithsdale, Dumfries. She was informed:

> Your tenancy will be a Scottish Secure Tenancy and a copy of our tenancy agreement is available on request. You will have the modernised Right to Buy your new home, however, in accordance with legislation, you will not be able to exercise your Right to Buy until 30th September 2012 at the earliest, and this date could be extended.

The suspension was in fact extended by a further ten years, ie to 2022.

In 2015 the applicant applied to buy the property arguing that her right to buy her original property, conferred by the original right-to-buy legislation, carried over to the new property. But the legislation was clear: the exchange in 2003 meant that she was subject to the 'modernised' regime, as the letter to her had correctly stated, and hence was subject to the suspension. Her application to the housing association was accordingly rejected, and she applied to the Lands Tribunal, which held against her: see 2016 GWD 23-433, *Conveyancing 2016* Case (35). She appealed to the Inner House, which has upheld the view of the law taken by the Tribunal.

(55) McGloine v Glasgow Housing Association Ltd
2018 Hous LR 28, Lands Tribunal

James McGloine applied to buy the flat he rented at 3/1, 145 Gatehouse Street, Sandyhills, Glasgow. This was on 26 July 2016. The right to buy was abolished by the Housing (Scotland) Act 2014, but applications could still be made up to 31 July 2016, so that this application was timeous. During the weeks leading up to 31 July 2016 public-sector landlords experienced an avalanche of applications, and did not always meet the two-month deadline for responding. Mr McGloine died on 21 March 2017, by which time no response had been received. During the period after 26 September (when the two-month deadline expired) Mr McGloine could have raised an enforcement action in the Lands Tribunal under s 71 of the Housing (Scotland) Act 1987, but he did not do so. In the present case the family of the late Mr McGloine argued that his rights under s 71 transmitted and could still be enforced. The Tribunal held that the s 71 rights died with Mr McGloine, and accordingly the application was dismissed.

Even if the s 71 rights had been capable of transmission, it is not clear that the applicant, a brother of Mr McGloine, was in a position to assert that he was the beneficiary of such transmission. But this issue did not have to be decided by the Tribunal.

(56) Nimmo v City of Edinburgh Council
19 April 2018, Lands Tribunal

On 28 July 2016 Mr Nimmo applied to buy the flat he rented at 87 Morrison Street, Edinburgh. Eventually, in May 2017, he received an offer to sell. The valuation was £135,000, and, after applying the discount, the council offered to sell the property for £39,000. Mr Nimmo was unhappy and applied to the Tribunal, under s 65(2) of the Housing (Scotland) Act 1987, for the offer to be amended in three respects: (i) that the true value of the property was £125,000 and that the price, after discount, should be reduced accordingly; (ii) that the landlord was liable to carry out repairs, which it had not done, and that a condition about these repairs should be added to the offer to sell; (iii) that the purchase should include a storage cupboard within the building.

The application to the Tribunal was unsuccessful. As to (i) the valuation was by the District Valuer, and the way the legislation was drafted showed that the figure so produced was to be final and binding on both parties. As to (ii) the question of whether the landlord was liable for outstanding repairs was a matter for the law of landlord and tenant and, if in dispute (which it was), would have to be determined in the ordinary courts. As to (iii) it was held that it was too late to seek an order under s 65(2).

(57) Neri v City of Edinburgh Council
31 January 2018, Lands Tribunal

Mr and Mrs Neri applied to buy the property that they rented at 26 Kingston Avenue, Edinburgh. The council agreed that the right to buy existed, but there was a dispute as to whether the price should be determined on the 'modernised' basis or the 'preserved' basis, the latter being more favourable to the tenant. It was held that the 'modernised' basis was applicable, since the current tenancy had come into existence after the 'modernised' regime had come into force, and because, whilst the applicants had been public-sector tenants before, none of the rules preserving the older discount regime was applicable.

(58) Duguid v Sanctuary Scotland Housing Association Ltd
1 June 2018, Lands Tribunal

Mrs Duguid applied to buy the property she rented at 1 Gaitside Road, Aberdeen. The application was refused on the ground that she did not have the right to buy. She then applied to the Lands Tribunal under s 68(4) of the Housing (Scotland) Act 1987. The case is curious: it seems to have been accepted that Mrs Duguid did not have the right to buy in terms of the legislation, but her case was that the landlord had sold properties to other tenants in a comparable position, and that accordingly she was being treated unfairly. This argument did not persuade the Tribunal. It said (paras 5–6), with specific reference to a successful purchase made by the applicant's son:

> The respondents' agents have not given an explanation of how that purchase came about. They are not obliged to do so in this process, since it has no direct bearing on the present applicant's entitlement to buy her home but it would no doubt be helpful, in assuaging the applicant's sense of unfairness, were they, or their clients, to do so now. For our part, all we would say is that the history of legislative changes in this area of housing law since 1980, when the right to buy was first introduced, has been far from straightforward and it is entirely possible that, depending on, among other things, the history of tenancies held, one tenant may be entitled to purchase whereas another is not … Be that as it may, what the respondents and their predecessors may have done in respect of other tenants does not affect the law as it applies to the facts of the present applicant's case and we are unable to find for her on the basis of perceived unfair treatment.

(59) Thomas v Dumfries and Galloway Housing Partnership Ltd
13 December 2017, Lands Tribunal

Some time before the 31 July 2016 deadline, Mrs Thomas posted an application to buy the property that she rented at 18 Broomlands Drive, Dumfries. She sent the application letter by the 'signed for' service (formerly called 'recorded delivery'). The landlord denied having received it, and by the time that the problem came to light the deadline had passed, meaning that it was too late for a new application. Mrs Thomas applied to the Tribunal to enforce her right to buy. The question for the Tribunal was, therefore, whether the application had been received by the landlord.

Section 7 of the Interpretation Act 1978 says that where the fact of posting can be established, there is a rebuttable presumption that the item was delivered 'at the time at which the letter would be delivered in the ordinary course of post'. After hearing extensive evidence, the Tribunal was satisfied that the letter had been posted, but also that it had never arrived, ie it must have been lost in the post. Accordingly, the s 7 presumption was rebutted, and the application failed – through no fault of the applicant herself.

For another case involving s 7 of the 1978 Act, see *EK v City of Edinburgh Council*, 27 September 2017, Lands Tribunal, *Conveyancing 2017* Case (28). And for two other cases of this year about whether a letter had been received, see

Boyce v City of Edinburgh Council (Case (60) below) and *Gateway Assets Ltd v CV Panels Ltd* (Case (61) below).

(60) Boyce v City of Edinburgh Council
18 October 2018, Lands Tribunal

On 29 July 2016, three days before the right to buy was due to be abolished, Angela Boyce applied to buy her council house at 21 Burdiehouse Avenue, Edinburgh. The reason that she left things so late was that she was behind with her rent, and she knew that those with rent arrears could not apply. But she had just been told that social security benefits due to her had been underpaid. The unpaid balance would be enough to clear off the rent arrears and thus open the way to exercise the right to buy. When she applied, however, the council took the view that in fact she did not have the right to buy, and it issued a notice of refusal, which it sent via the 'signed for' service (previously called 'recorded delivery'). But Ms Boyce denied ever receiving this notice and accordingly argued that her right to buy, not having been validly refused, was enforceable.

As mentioned in connection with the previous case, s 7 of the Interpretation Act 1978 says that where the fact of posting can be established, there is a rebuttable presumption that the item was delivered 'at the time at which the letter would be delivered in the ordinary course of post'. After hearing evidence the Tribunal held that the s 7 presumption had not been rebutted, and that accordingly Ms Boyce must be taken as having received the notice of refusal. Accordingly her application failed.

LEASES

(61) Gateway Assets Ltd v CV Panels Ltd
[2018] CSOH 48, 2018 SCLR 736, 2018 Hous LR 34

This was a dispute as to whether a break option had been validly exercised. The lease was for ten years from 3 December 2012. Clause 3.2 said:

> The Tenants shall be entitled to terminate the lease on the 5th anniversary of the Date of Entry by serving upon the Landlords at least 6 months prior written notice thereof (time being of the essence).

On 19 June 2017 a letter was sent by the tenant:

> As per our lease agreement with yourselves, please accept this letter as written confirmation of our desire to terminate our lease on the property located at Unit 2C, Clyde Gateway Trade Park, Dalmarnock Road, Rutherglen G73 1AN. This decision has been previously communicated verbally and in person.

The landlord replied that this letter did not comply with the six-months condition, that accordingly the option had not been validly exercised, and that as a result the lease would run for the full ten years.

The tenant responded by producing a copy of a letter it had, it said, sent in April 2017, exercising the break option. The landlord said it had received no such letter, and thereafter raised the present action for declarator that the break option had not been validly exercised. After hearing evidence, the Lord Ordinary, Lord Clark, concluded that the alleged letter of April 2017 had not been sent. He also concluded that even if, contrary to his finding, it had been sent, it was clear that it had never been received.

That concluded matters in favour of the landlord. Two other arguments advanced by the landlord were rejected, though this made no difference to the result. The first was (para 32) that:

> The April letter gave notice only of an 'intention to terminate the lease on the 5th anniversary of our date of entry in accordance with point 3.2 of our lease'. But clause 3.2 of the lease required intimation that the lease would terminate on the fifth anniversary. That was different from intimating an intention to terminate the lease. For instance, a tenant might indicate to the landlord that it was intending to trigger a break in the hope of extracting improved lease terms.

The Lord Ordinary had no hesitation in rejecting this argument. The meaning of the letter was clear.

The landlord also argued that the letter was invalid because it was sent to the landlord's agent rather than to the landlord itself. This too did not impress the Lord Ordinary. In 2015 the landlord had written to the tenant thus:

> We have appointed David Samuel Asset Management Ltd/David Samuel Management Limited … to act as asset manager and they are authorised to deal with all aspects of management including the collection of rent and service charges … Please therefore remit all rent and other charges etc to the respective company, but deal with all communications and correspondence through the offices of David Samuel Management or David Samuel Asset Management Ltd.

This is not a model of clarity (not least because two distinct companies, David Samuel Asset Management Ltd and David Samuel Management Ltd, are seemingly treated as if they were one and the same), but the Lord Ordinary took the view that the agency extended to such matters as receiving, on behalf of the landlord, a notice exercising a break option.

(62) Ashtead Plant Hire Co Ltd v Granton Central Developments Ltd
[2018] CSOH 107, 2018 GWD 39-477

A lease was entered into for commercial property at West Harbour Road, Granton, Edinburgh. The term of the lease was from 1988 to 2096. There was a provision for rent review every five years, and a provision that in the event of a dispute the rent was to be determined by a qualified surveyor.

The parties were unable to reach agreement on the 2017 rent review, part of the dispute being as to the way that the clause fell to be interpreted. The tenant raised the present action for declarator that the rent review clause was to be interpreted in a certain manner. The landlord argued that the court had no jurisdiction because the matter fell to be determined by the surveyor. The tenant's position was that the surveyor would be an expert on rental values but not on law.

After an extensive review of the authorities, both Scottish and English, the Lord Ordinary (Doherty) held in favour of the tenant, commenting at para 21:

> The critical issue is whether on a proper construction of the lease the contracting parties expressly or impliedly agreed that the legal interpretation of 'the leased subjects' and of the assumptions and disregards were remitted exclusively to the expert. I am not persuaded that they agreed that those issues of construction were removed from the court's jurisdiction. Even on the basis that the expert could obtain legal advice, it would be very surprising if the parties had agreed that a surveyor should have exclusive jurisdiction to decide the correct legal construction of such important provisions. A surveyor would not have the necessary skill and competence to make the required adjudication. He could only obtain and rely upon legal advice. In those circumstances I think that the lease would have to have made it very clear indeed (whether expressly or by implication) that exclusive jurisdiction was being conferred.

(63) FJM v United Kingdom
[2019] HLR 8, (2019) 68 EHRR SE5

If a public-sector landlord of residential property seeks to remove a tenant, the tenant can invoke the protections of the Human Rights Act 1998, and in particular article 8 (right to respect for private and family life): see in particular *Manchester City Council v Pinnock* [2010] UKSC 45, [2011] 2 AC 104. What has been less clear is whether the same is true for private-sector residential tenancies.

Mr and Mrs McDonald had a daughter with serious psychiatric problems. She was unable to work. They bought a property and let it to her. The purchase was financed by a mortgage. The parents got into financial difficulties, and the secured lender decided to enforce the mortgage. The first step was to remove the daughter so that the property could be marketed with vacant possession. An action against her was raised by the lender, in the name of her parents. (This, strange to Scottish eyes, can be done in England under s 109 of the Law of Property Act 1925.) Her defence was that eviction would violate her article 8 rights.

The daughter was unsuccessful in the county court. She appealed to the Court of Appeal, where again she was unsuccessful. She then appealed to the Supreme Court, where yet again she was unsuccessful: *McDonald v McDonald* [2016] UKSC 28, [2017] AC 273 (*Conveyancing 2016* Case (42)). We quote from the Supreme Court judgment (paras 40–41):

> Although it may well be that article 8 is engaged when a judge makes an order for possession of a tenant's home at the suit of a private sector landlord, it is not open to the tenant to contend that article 8 could justify a different order from that which

is mandated by the contractual relationship between the parties, at least where, as here, there are legislative provisions which the democratically elected legislature has decided properly balance the competing interests of private sector landlords and residential tenants. In effect the provisions of the Protection from Eviction Act 1977, s 89 of the Housing Act 1980 and Chapters I and IV of the 1988 Act [ie the Housing Act 1988], as amended from time to time, reflect the state's assessment of where to strike the balance between the article 8 rights of residential tenants and the A1P1 rights of private sector landlords when their tenancy contract has ended. To hold otherwise would involve the Convention effectively being directly enforceable as between private citizens so as to alter their contractual rights and obligations, whereas the purpose of the Convention is, as we have mentioned, to protect citizens from having their rights infringed by the state.

We quote this *in extenso* because though we believe the ratio of the decision probably lies within this passage, we would hesitate to attempt to state precisely what it is.

Having lost in the Supreme Court the daughter then raised the present action in the European Court of Human Rights. Once more she has been unsuccessful. The approach of the court was the same as that of the Supreme Court.

Whilst there may be difficulties in identifying the ratio, either that of the Supreme Court decision or that of the European Court of Human Rights, the practical result is that the chances of article 8 being used in future as a defence against a private-sector landlord are remote.

STANDARD SECURITIES

(64) UK Acorn Finance Ltd v Holt
29 September 2014, Aberdeen Sheriff Court

In this 2014 case, which has only recently come to our attention, the pursuer sought to enforce a standard security. The secured loan was for a term of six months, at a rate of 21%. The defender's position was that the pursuer had assured the defender that long-term financing at a lower rate of interest would be available when the loan matured, and that accordingly enforcement would not be reasonable. It was held that no such assurance had been given, and accordingly decree was granted as craved. See **Commentary** p 142.

(65) Stewart v UK Acorn Finance Ltd
[2018] CSOH 31, 2018 GWD 13-174

This case was in some ways similar to the previous case – not least the fact that the same lender was involved in both. Mr Stewart owned a farm at Thrumster, Caithness. He borrowed money from UK Acorn Finance Ltd, secured by standard security. The term of the loan was nine months. He did not repay, and UK Acorn Finance Ltd raised an action in the sheriff court for the enforcement of the security, and was successful. See **Commentary** p 143.

(66) Peart v Promontoria (Henrico) Ltd
[2018] CSIH 35, 2018 SC 581, 2018 SCLR 757

This case is primarily about the law of sequestration, but has some conveyancing interest. Barry and Susan Peart owned a property, and borrowed several hundred thousand pounds secured on that property, the purpose of the loan being to buy and develop another property, with the idea of eventually selling the first property. The loan contract provided that the loan was an on-demand one. When the creditor sought to enforce, the Pearts pled that, side by side with the loan contract, there had been an oral agreement that the loan would not be called up until the first property had been sold. This argument was admitted to proof. See **Commentary** p 145.

(67) Unicorn Tower Ltd v HSBC plc
[2018] CSOH 30, 2018 GWD 13-179

The pursuer wished to carry out a mixed commercial/residential development in central Glasgow. There were to be two phases, the cost of the first being estimated at £14 million. In 2007 the pursuer obtained a loan facility from the defender in the sum of £7,965,000. The idea was that the loan would be repaid in stages as the first-phase properties were sold. But that was not what the loan contract said. The loan contract said that all moneys advanced were repayable on an on-demand basis. A standard security was granted.

Problems developed, and in 2009 the defender, deciding to bail out, demanded repayment of all outstanding sums. The pursuer responded by raising the present action for declarator that the defender had not been entitled to demand repayment. It argued that the loan 'was a fixed term facility and (absent a breach by the First Pursuer of its terms) would not be terminated until the completion of the development' (para 6). This was on the basis of an alleged unwritten collateral agreement. The pursuer's case was dismissed on grounds of relevancy. See **Commentary** p 144.

(68) Joint Administrators of Granite City Assets Ltd, Ptrs
[2018] CSOH 55, 2018 GWD 23-290

Granite City Assets Ltd bought a property at 96–126 John Street, Aberdeen, with a view to demolishing it and replacing it with a hotel and retail units. A complex funding arrangement was entered into between (i) Granite City Assets Ltd, (ii) BridgePoint Ventures LLC, (iii) SES Equity Partners Ltd, (iv) FirstPoint Agent Ltd, (v) Red Friar Private Equity Ltd, (vi) Northern & Western Insurance Co Ltd, and (vii) FirstPoint Security Trustee Ltd. One element of the arrangement was that Granite City Assets Ltd would grant a standard security to FirstPoint Security Trustee Ltd, the latter holding the security in trust for a variety of parties including 'the BridgePoint Purchasers', who were the intended tenants, and who might suffer financial loss in the event of the insolvency of Granite City Assets Ltd.

These 'purchasers' (ie tenants) paid deposits, amounting in all to £4.5 million, to Granite City Assets Ltd. That company then became insolvent. The joint administrators of the company, having sold the property for £4 million, raised the present action to have it determined whether the repayment of the deposits was covered by the terms of the standard security. It was held by the Lord Ordinary (Doherty) that it was. At para 36 he said:

> The BridgePoint Purchasers were not parties to the Master Agreement but, on the hypothesis that the Agreement was followed by delivery to them or an equivalent, third party rights were constituted by the contracting parties in terms of, and by means of, that Agreement and subsequent action. As a result the BridgePoint Purchasers were added to the persons who had the right to enforce the relevant clause 15 and clause 21 obligations. On that scenario the sensible view would be that Granite's counterpart obligations are 'liabilities or obligations … owed or expressed to be owed to … the BridgePoint Purchasers … under the Master Agreement' in terms of clause 1.20 of the Standard Security.

Hence, whilst 'the BridgePoint Purchasers' were not directly secured, in that they were not creditors in the standard security itself, they were indirectly secured, in that the sums they were owed were payable, from the proceeds of the sale, to the trustee for their behoof.

(69) Green v Southern Pacific Mortgage Ltd
[2018] EWCA Civ 854, [2018] 2 P & CR 12

In this English case, Jacqueline Green bought a property at 164 Claverham Road, Bristol, in 1994. In 2006 she remortgaged it, the new loan being for £96,000 and for a term of 20 years. The new mortgage was of the 'repayment' type. She soon fell into arrears and in 2009 the lender began enforcement proceedings. Despite contributions towards the mortgage payments by the Department of Work and Pensions, the debt snowballed. 'By the date of the hearing before the Recorder [the first-instance judge] in September 2015 the total figure for principal, arrears and costs was £181,703.37. It is now put at the staggering sum of about £300,000, divided broadly into one-third mortgage arrears, two-thirds costs and expenses' (para 30).

The borrower's defence to the action was that she was depressed; because she was depressed she was disabled; because she was disabled she was protected by the Disability Discrimination Act 1995 and its replacement the Equality Act 2010. Her position was that, because she was disabled, and as a result unemployed, the lender should be offering her an interest-only loan to replace the existing repayment loan.

It seems that this is the first time that such an argument has been presented in court. The Court of Appeal, affirming the decision at first instance, held that the refusal to allow a change from the repayment loan to an interest-only loan had not been discriminatory and accordingly found in favour of the lender.

There is another aspect of this case to be mentioned. The loan contract provided that enforcement costs were to be met by the borrower. Lord Justice Jackson commented at paras 96–97:

> While Miss Green's own misfortunes and the decisions taken by her and on her behalf are the root cause of her unintended predicament, there must be concern about a situation where a borrower ends up paying for every bad argument that a lender chooses to run. The unreasoned approach of Southern Pacific must have added considerably to the legal costs and may have led Miss Green and her advisers to believe that their position was stronger than it was. Southern Pacific's practices, policies and procedures, insofar as they existed, were opaque from start to finish. It gave wholly inadequate answers to a routine customer request, presented a disingenuous defence to the proceedings and pursued a disorganised case at trial. The Recorder was left to interpret the disabilities legislation in relation to an organisation for whom the legislation might as well not have existed.
>
>   I find this state of affairs disturbing. Despite the dismissal of Miss Green's appeal, if any good purpose might now be served by this court directing an account of whether the contractual costs that have been claimed were all reasonably incurred (as they must be to be recoverable under clause 23 of the mortgage deed), I would favour that course.

'There must be concern about a situation where a borrower ends up paying for every bad argument that a lender chooses to run.' Indeed. The same issue can arise in Scots law: thus sch 3 para 12 of the Conveyancing and Feudal Reform (Scotland) Act 1970 provides that:

> The debtor shall be personally liable to the creditor for … all expenses reasonably incurred by the creditor in calling-up the security and realising or attempting to realise the security subjects, or any part thereof, and exercising any other powers conferred upon him by the security.

In most cases, excessive expenses on the part of the lender are likely to make little difference to the borrower, for a borrower who cannot afford to repay the loan is unlikely to be able to pay the expenses, so that a lender that incurs unnecessary expenses in enforcement is likely to bear the loss itself. But this will not always be true: in some cases the property can be sold for more than the amount of the loan, and in such cases the level of expenses may be crucial to the (ex-)borrower. It is true that the expenses have to be 'reasonable'. But that this proviso is always enforced in practice is far from clear.

(70) J H & W Lamont of Heathfield Farm v Chatisham Ltd
[2018] CSIH 33, 2018 SC 440, 2018 SLT 511

The owners of land with development potential entered into a contract with a development company whereby the latter, in exchange for making an advance payment, acquired an option to buy the land. The owners granted to the developer a standard security, securing their obligations under the option agreement.

Planning permission for development was never obtained, and the option period eventually came to an end. The owners asked for the standard security to be discharged. The developer refused, claiming that the owners had been in material breach of their obligations under the contract and claiming, moreover, substantial damages for that alleged breach. The developer argued that the standard security must be understood as being a valid security in respect of the money due in terms of the damages claim.

It was held in the Outer House that, whatever the position might be as to alleged breach by the owners, the standard security fell to be discharged: [2017] CSOH 229, 2017 GWD 30-470, *Conveyancing 2017* Case (60). The defender reclaimed, but the Inner House has affirmed the decision.

The case was argued on the basis of the law of contractual retention. Each of the three judges in the Inner House case, namely Lord Carloway, Lord Drummond Young and Lord Malcolm, gave opinions, which, whilst agreeing as to the disposal of the case, took differing views about the law of retention. For discussion, see Lorna Richardson, 'What do we know about retention now?' (2018) 22 *Edinburgh Law Review* 387.

In our view, the Conveyancing and Feudal Reform (Scotland) Act 1970, on a proper construction, says that a standard security expressed to be for a non-monetary obligation is a security for damages for breach of that obligation: see *Conveyancing 2017* pp 136–41. It is to be regretted that that basic issue was not put to the court, either in the Outer House or in the Inner House.

(71) Kennedy v Royal Bank of Scotland plc
[2018] CSIH 70, 2018 SLT 1261

David Kennedy was a car dealer and was also the landlord of nine residential properties. He had loan finance from the RBS, secured by standard securities over all nine properties. The finance consisted of term loans. In February 2010 the bank demanded immediate repayment of the sum of £532,077.88. Mr Kennedy did not have the funds available to repay, and also had difficulty in finding new sources of finance. In April 2010 he sold all nine properties to his wife at a discount to their market value, the discount being £159,078. The price paid by his wife was sufficient to pay off the bank.

After some years Mr Kennedy sued RBS for £159,078 plus interest. He argued that the bank had acted in breach of contract in demanding early repayment, and that this breach had forced him to sell the properties at a loss. Accordingly the bank was liable in damages.

In the sheriff court it was held that the bank had indeed been in breach of contract. But the bank also pled that any liability was now barred by the running of negative prescription, and this was also the issue in the present phase of the case, which had been remitted for decision to the Court of Session. The Inner House held that Mr Kennedy's claim had indeed prescribed.

We offer two incidental thoughts on the case. The first is that if the bank's demand for repayment was indeed in breach of contract, Mr Kennedy could, presumably, have refused to pay, and any enforcement action by the bank would have failed, for the simple reason that a debt not yet due cannot successfully be claimed in court. But of course one can well understand how, faced with the threat of immediate enforcement, Mr Kennedy may have felt that there was no realistic alternative to what he chose to do.

The second thought is that, whilst Mr Kennedy may have sold at undervalue, the sale was to his wife, so that there was, it would seem, no loss to the family considered as a unit. So if he had been successful in his claim for damages from the bank, the odd result would seemingly be that the family would have profited very considerably.

(72) Bridging Loans Ltd v Hutton
[2018] CSIH 63, 2018 Hous LR 83

The defender, Sandra Hutton, bought Cotterton Lodge, Padanaram, near Forfar, Angus, in about 2013. For the purchase she obtained funding from two lenders, one a company in the Halifax group and the other the pursuer, Bridging Loans Ltd. Both loans were secured by standard securities. The Bridging Loans Ltd security, which was second-ranked, secured a 12-month loan. When the defender failed to repay the loan, the pursuer raised the present action to enforce the security. Matters proceeded slowly. Over time, more than one law firm withdrew from acting for the defender. Several diets of proof were discharged at her request. She averred ill health. She averred that she was seeking alternative finance. She averred that she was attempting to sell the property. When, during one hearing, she walked out of the sheriff court, decree against her was granted by default.

She appealed to the Sheriff Appeal Court, without success. She then appealed to the Inner House, which has now rejected her appeal. The Inner House commented (para 10):

> This was ... a summary application which had proceeded, for such an application, at a glacial pace by reason of repeated discharges of diets of proof at the defender's instance. There is no defence to the action. The defender owes the pursuers ever-increasing sums, now in the region of £150,000. The defender has had ample opportunity, in what will shortly become three years since the application was lodged, to take whatever steps could be taken in relation to the sale of the Lodge. In these circumstances the court has no hesitation in refusing this appeal. No error on the part of the sheriff has been discovered which would justify interfering with his decision.

SOLICITORS

(73) NRAM Ltd v Steel
[2018] UKSC 13, 2018 SC (UKSC) 141, 2018 SLT 835

A bank held standard securities over three properties owned by a company. When the company sold one of the properties, the bank discharged that security, being paid the bulk of the proceeds of sale. At the same time it also discharged the securities over the other two properties. Some years later, when the company went into insolvent liquidation, the bank claimed that the discharges of the latter two securities had been a mistake, caused by the negligence of the debtor company's law firm (the bank had not used its own solicitors) and it sued for damages, suing both the law firm and the relevant partner.

In the Outer House the action failed: [2014] CSOH 172, 2015 GWD 10-191 (*Conveyancing 2014* Case (63)). The pursuer reclaimed, and the Inner House, by a two-to-one majority, reversed the decision, ie found in favour of the bank, awarding damages of £369,811.18, plus interest and expenses: [2016] CSIH 11, 2016 SC 474 (*Conveyancing 2016* Case (62)). There has been a further appeal, to the Supreme Court, which, reversing the decision of the Inner House, has reinstated that of the Lord Ordinary. See **Commentary** p 155.

(74) Khosrowpour v Taylor
[2018] CSOH 64, 2018 GWD 22-276

The facts of this dispute are in many respects unclear, because neither of the two actions that the pursuer brought (the present action, and *Khosrowpour v Mackay's Exr* [2016] CSIH 50, 2016 GWD 21-366, *Conveyancing 2016* Case (17)) went to proof.

In or about 1989 Ann Mackay bought the property that she tenanted at 7 Partick Bridge Street, Glasgow. In 2012 she passed away. Her will seems to have said that £7,200 was to be paid to a daughter, declaring 'that this sum is to represent her contribution to the purchase of my former council house', and that the residue of the estate was to be divided equally three ways, between that daughter and her two siblings.

In the first action Hamid Khosrowpour, the former husband of the daughter in question, sued the estate on the alleged basis that it was he, not his former wife, who had provided the money and that Mrs Mackay had, in return, promised to leave the house to him exclusively. He claimed that Mrs Mackay had indeed done so. But he could not produce a copy of this alleged will, which, if it had in fact been made, would in any event have been superseded by the will that took effect when Mrs Mackay passed away in 2012. No documentation existed to support his averment about an agreement between himself and Mrs Mackay. Since it was held that an agreement to make a legacy of heritable property (even if there was one, which was never established) requires to be in writing, his first action, against the estate, failed.

He then raised the present action for damages against the solicitor who had, it was said, acted for him in 1989, claiming that it was negligent not to have advised that the alleged agreement should have been put into formal writing. The defender pled negative prescription, and this plea was upheld.

There are several puzzles about the case, one or two of which we will mention. One is that the pursuer averred that the money had been advanced by him, whereas Mrs Mackay's will said that it had been advanced by her daughter.

Another is that the pursuer averred in the second action that, following the failure of the first action, Mrs Mackay's executor had agreed to pay him £22,000, this being the original sum plus interest. If that is true, the implication seems to be that the original sum had been by way of loan. But then that would not be very easy to reconcile with the pursuer's stance, in both the first and the second actions, in both of which the pursuer's case was that the payment had not been a loan, but a payment to secure title to the property when Mrs Mackay died.

Another puzzle: the pursuer also averred that Mrs Mackay had in 1991 (well after the purchase of the house had taken place) granted him a standard security for all sums due or to become due. This was, by its terms, a security for a money debt, and so seemingly did not secure the obligation (if any such obligation had ever been entered into) to bequeath. So what *did* the standard security secure? No answer to this rather obvious question emerges from the two actions.

What really happened as between Mr Khosrowpour and Mrs Mackay? After two no doubt expensive Court of Session actions, the first of which went up to the Inner House, the answer is: entirely unclear.

(75) P & P Property Ltd v Owen White & Catlin LLP
Dreamvar (UK) Ltd v Mishcon de Reya
[2018] EWCA Civ 1082, [2018] 3 WLR 1244, [2018] 4 All ER 277

These two cases, which had similar facts, were heard together in the Court of Appeal, and there is a single report covering both cases. Collectively they are being referred to in England as the *Dreamvar* case.

First, the facts of *P & P Property Ltd v Owen White & Catlin LLP*. Clifford Harper was the owner of 52 Brackenbury Road, Hammersmith, London. The property was let out, the most recent tenant being Mark Armstrong, or at any rate someone calling himself by that name. The property was mortgage-free. On 20 November 2013 someone who identified himself as Clifford Harper telephoned a law firm, Messrs Owen White & Catlin LLP, to say that he wished to borrow £800,000 on the security of the property, because he wished to buy another property using the borrowed money. The other property was said to be in Dubai, where he said he lived. He needed the loan to be in place in no longer than ten days. Shortly after this he said that, instead of borrowing, he wished to raise the money by selling.

All of the fake Mr Harper's communications with Messrs Owen White & Catlin LLP were by telephone or email. He never set foot in the office. The identity checks carried out by the law firm were inadequate.

The property was sold to P & P Property Ltd for £1,130,000. As soon as the transaction completed, the money was paid to the fake Mr Harper. Neither the money nor the fake Mr Harper was ever seen again. When the deed of transfer was presented for registration, the Land Registry rejected it because it appeared not to be genuine. Accordingly the real owner suffered no loss. The loss was suffered by the buyer, who had paid out £1,130,000 in exchange for nothing.

We pause at this point to note that these facts are absolutely typical for identity-theft cases. Lights flash; klaxons sound. (i) There is a property that is well above average house values. (ii) It is mortgage-free, a fact which of course can be found out from the register. (If there is a mortgage, the thief will not usually know how much is outstanding, and so will not know the value of the equity. From the thief's standpoint, high equity is essential.) (iii) The real owner is not in occupation. (iv) The 'owner' does not have an existing relationship with the law firm that he approaches. (v) The 'owner' never sets foot in the law firm. Everything is done by telephone and email. (vi) The 'owner' wishes the transaction to be carried out at high speed. There is strong pressure to achieve this, the pressure being on the fraudster's law firm, on the seller's estate agent (which in England will be separate from the law firm), on the buyer and on the buyer's law firm. (vii) The 'owner' says that he lives abroad or at any rate that he spends much time abroad for business reasons. A country furth of Europe is usually mentioned.

Next, the facts of *Dreamvar (UK) Ltd v Mishcon de Reya*. This involved an unoccupied property, 8 Old Manor Yard, Earl's Court, London, owned by David Haeems. The report does not say whether or not there was a mortgage over it, but we presume that there was no mortgage: see above. A person claiming to be Mr Haeems approached Mary Monson Solicitors Ltd saying he wished to sell. The identity checks carried out by the law firm were inadequate. The property was sold to Dreamvar (UK) Ltd for £1,100,000. 'Mr Haeems' disappeared with the money. When the deed of transfer was presented for registration, the Land Registry rejected it because it appeared not to be genuine. Accordingly the real owner suffered no loss. The loss was suffered by the buyer, who had paid out £1,100,000 in exchange for nothing.

In both cases, the Land Registry detected the fraud, with the result that no registration took place. How? The English Registry has something called the 'property alert service' (see *Conveyancing 2016* p 202) whereby an owner can request to be contacted in the event of a proposed entry in the register (eg sale). Whilst the report does not say if that is what happened, it is no doubt the explanation. In both cases the owner must have signed up to this service, and when the application was received by the Registry it was notified to the owner, who promptly contacted the Registry saying 'this is a scam'. In Scotland the Keeper does not offer this service.

The Court of Appeal held that the fraudster's solicitors were not liable in tort, but that they were liable for breach of trust, for when they received the price they did so in trust for the true owner, and so acted in breach of trust in paying out to a non-owner. Likewise the solicitors for the buyers were in breach of trust in paying over the price when there was no genuine transaction. Thus both law firms were liable to the defrauded buyer. The Court of Appeal did not apportion liability between them.

The underlying legal position in England, with its extensive use of trust law, is different from the position in Scotland, so even if a similar result were to be arrived at here, it would not be on the same legal basis. What the law of Scotland is in this area we are not sure. But we will pick up two particular issues.

The first is this: when X acts as agent for Y, X is in principle liable in the event that the agency does not in fact exist, for an agent is deemed to 'warrant his authority'. Might the law firm acting for a fraudster be liable on this basis, the argument being that it purported to act for the owner of the property when in fact it did not? This argument was indeed advanced in one Scottish case, *Frank Houlgate Investment Company Ltd v Biggart Baillie LLP* [2009] CSOH 165, 2010 SLT

527 (*Conveyancing 2009* Case (80) but was rejected. (For a full account of this complex litigation see *Conveyancing 2014* pp 189 ff). In *Dreamvar* the argument was, by contrast, accepted in principle, though in the event it was rejected because it was held that the buyer had in fact not relied on the warranty.

The other issue worth noting is that the Court of Appeal took the view that a failure to comply with the requirements of the Money Laundering Regulations is not, as such, tortious.

An article by Gail Cook at 63 (2018) *Journal of the Law Society of Scotland*/July/44 has some sensible suggestions for safe conveyancing in the light of these cases.

JUDICIAL RECTIFICATION

(76) Britannia Invest A/S v The Scottish Ministers
[2018] SC EDIN 12, 2018 SLT (Sh Ct) 133, 2018 Hous LR 8

New premises were built at the West Port, Edinburgh. The owner was West Port SARL, seemingly a French company. It entered into a ten-year lease, from 2012 to 2022, with the Scottish Ministers, for occupation of the premises by NHS Education Scotland, the leased property being two and a half floors of the building. In 2015, following the insolvency of West Port SARL, ownership passed to a Danish company, Britannia Invest A/S ('A/S' = *Aktieselskab* = public limited company). The new landlord and the tenant disagreed as to how the amount of the service charge should be calculated. An action for payment was raised. When the court held that the relevant clause in the lease fell to be interpreted according to the position adopted by the tenants (the defenders), the pursuer amended its pleadings so as to add a crave for rectification of the lease, under s 8(1)(a) of the Law Reform (Miscellaneous Provisions) (Scotland) Act 1985, arguing that the wording of the clause (as interpreted by the sheriff) was disconform to the actual intentions of the parties when the terms of the lease were being negotiated.

The lease as signed had a lengthy provision, clause 5.13, about the service charge, which read in part:

> The Tenant's liability for that element of the Service Charge that does not include the cost of utility supplies shall be capped so that it shall be a maximum of:
> 5.13.1 The rate of £5 per square foot (exclusive of VAT) for the first period running from the Date of Entry to 31 December 2013;
> 5.13.2 For each subsequent period of 12 months commencing on 1 January 2014, the rate payable in the period to the foregoing 31 December (exclusive of VAT), subject to annual RPI increases.

The pursuer asked the court to rectify 5.13.2 so as to read:

> For each subsequent period of 12 months commencing on 1 January 2014, the rate of £5 per square foot (exclusive of VAT) subject to annual RPI increases.

The sheriff (Sheriff William Holligan), after hearing evidence of the negotiations that had taken place prior to the signing of the lease, agreed that the crave for rectification should be granted. In doing so, he endorsed and quoted extensively from the views of Lord Hodge in *Patersons of Greenoakhill Ltd v Biffa Waste Services Ltd* [2013] CSOH 18, 2013 SLT 729 at 734–35, views which emphasised the need to take an objective approach in ascertaining the intention of the parties; the subjective intention of a party was not relevant unless it had been communicated to the other side. For a case based on s 8(1)(a) to succeed, it was necessary to show that the words in the document were disconform to some antecedent agreement between the parties (which need not in itself be legally binding). That (non-binding) agreement in the present case was provided by heads of terms which had been accepted by both parties.

Even where s 8(1)(a) is satisfied, the court has a discretion to refuse the remedy, but in practice this seems never to be done. The sheriff reviewed such authority as exists on the exercise of the discretion before concluding as follows (para 62):

> Section 8 gives no guidance as to in what circumstances the court may grant or not grant the remedy. Given that the rectification provisions are designed to deal with a defectively expressed document, if it is proved that the agreement fails to express accurately the common intention of the parties to the agreement, then it is difficult to envisage in what circumstances the remedy should be withheld. However, it is also difficult to envisage all the circumstances which might arise in a rectification case. In my opinion, characterising the power as discretionary permits the court to withhold the remedy where it would be inequitable to grant it. Whether it would be inequitable to grant it depends upon all the circumstances of the case.

There were no circumstances in the present case to justify withholding the remedy of rectification.

(77) Bumpers Ltd v Broxburn Motorzone Ltd
[2018] CSOH 43, 2018 Hous LR 45

This case adopts the same objective approach as in the previous case but with the result, this time, that rectification was refused.

The pursuer owned commercial premises at 67 Inglis Green Road, Edinburgh. The premises were let out. In 2015 the pursuer granted what was, in effect, an interposed lease to the defender, the ish being in 2035. The lease was expressed as being for the whole premises. The pursuer brought the present action to have the lease rectified, so as to cover only part of the premises, namely the showroom and forecourt.

There was a proof as to the events leading up to the signing of the lease. The Lord Ordinary (Lord Doherty) concluded that the pursuer's director who had negotiated the lease may well have intended that it should extend to just part of the premises. But 'Mr Adam's subjective intention is not relevant unless he communicated it to Mr Barnes [who negotiated for the defender] by statement or conduct. The court requires to assess objectively whether the suggested antecedent agreement and common intention exist' (para 48). 'In my opinion Mr Adam's evidence that he made it clear to Mr Barnes that only the showroom and the forecourt were being let was unconvincing' (para 49). 'It follows that the pursuer's case for rectification of the Minute fails. It has not established that the parties' common intention at the time of the antecedent agreement was that only the showroom and forecourt be let' (para 56).

It was said above that the lease was 'in effect' an interposed lease. In fact, it was rather more complicated than that. The property had first been leased, and, after the creation of a sublease, the head lease had been assigned to the owner. The question of whether the head lease might have been extinguished by *confusio* (or perhaps by *consolidatio*) was not discussed in the case, the understanding of both parties having been that the lease had continued in existence, so that Bumpers Ltd was taken to be, at one and the same time, landlord to itself and tenant to itself. (For the question of whether *confusio*, or *consolidatio*, will operate in such cases see Scottish Law Commission, *Discussion Paper No 165 on Termination of Leases* (2018) ch 8, discussed at p 106 below.) Then later there was a 'minute of extension and variation' whereby Broxburn Motorzone Ltd was 'substituted' as the new holder of the head lease. It was this 'minute of extension and variation' that was at issue in the present action.

BOUNDARIES AND POSITIVE PRESCRIPTION

(78) MacDonald v Keeper of the Registers of Scotland
2019 GWD 5-63, Lands Tribunal

In 1992 Mr and Mrs Kay acquired Gateyard Cottage, Balcurvie, Leven, Fife. On the south-east, between what was indisputably part of Gateyard Cottage and a public road known as Durie Place, lay a small triangular area of land ('the triangular area'). This comprised (i) a footpath, (ii) an area of hardstanding, and (iii) a grassy area. The ownership of the triangular area was obscure. The council cut the grass and seemed to regard the triangular area as a (rather broad) verge of the road. But Mr and Mrs Kay, too, considered that they had a claim to the triangular area. Sometimes Mr Kay cut the grass, and in 2011, when neighbouring property to the south, known as Old School House, was on the market and questions arose as to the right to take access from that property to Durie Road, Mr and Mrs Kay granted a servitude over the triangular area to the owners of Old School House. This was expressed as: 'A servitude right of access and egress at all times and for all purposes for pedestrians and private motor cars over and across the servitude area.'

The restriction of the servitude to 'private' motor cars was to cause friction with the new owners of Old School House, Mr and Mrs MacDonald, because it prevented delivery vans and other commercial vehicles from reaching Old School House. Meanwhile, Mr and Mrs Kay were making their claim to the triangular area more overt by erecting wooden posts and by planting a hedge to cordon off the area from the carriageway of the public road.

In due course, each party resorted to conveyancing. Mr and Mrs Kay were first off the mark, applying to the Keeper for voluntary registration of their Sasine title. In this they were successful, and the cadastral unit for the property included all of the triangular area. Meanwhile, Mr and Mrs MacDonald had obtained a disposition of the triangular unit from the person who owned the residue of the Durie Estate. But the application for registration was refused on the ground that the triangular area was already in the Kays' title and could not also be in a different cadastral unit. For under the 2012 Act overlapping titles are not allowed: see s 12(2) and, for discussion, para 5.11 of K G C Reid and G L Gretton, *Land Registration* (2017). If Mr and Mrs MacDonald were to succeed with their application for registration, they would first have to procure the rectification of the Kays' title by having the triangular area removed. To that end, Mr and Mrs MacDonald made the present application to the Lands Tribunal to have it determined that the presence of the triangular area in the Kays' title was an inaccuracy.

The application was opposed by Mr and Mrs Kay, who asserted ownership of the triangular area on the basis of positive prescription. Prescription, of course, requires a registered/recorded title followed by ten years' possession. Mr and Mrs Kay were to fail on both requirements.

As the title on which prescription had run, Mr and Mrs Kay put forward the disposition of 1992 by which they had acquired Gateyard Cottage. This incorporated the description from an earlier disposition of 1919. The relevant boundary was given as being 'bounded by the high road', the 'high road' in question being Durie Road. Mr and Mrs Kay would succeed if it could be shown that their boundary to the east, at least for the purposes of a prescriptive title, was either (i) the mid-point of Durie Road or (ii) the near (western) edge of its carriageway.

The normal rule is that, when property is stated to be 'bounded' by a physical feature, such as a wall, the physical feature is regarded as excluded from the property. But some authority exists to suggest that this rule does not apply, or at least always apply, in the case of public roads (such as Durie Road). In particular, in *Magistrates of Ayr v Dobbie* (1898) 25 R 1184 it was held that, where a proprietor dispones two pieces of ground, one on each side of a public road, there is a presumption that the boundary between them is the *medium filum* of the road. What has always been less clear is whether the same presumption applies even in the case of a single disposition of ground on one side of the road only. The Lands Tribunal decided that the presumption did not apply in the present case and that, in any event, other terms of the 1992 disposition (including the grant of a servitude of access over the triangular area) were inconsistent with a boundary at the *medium filum* of the road (paras 69–76).

It followed, therefore, that the eastern boundary of Gateyard Cottage was the western edge of the road, and indeed the western edge of the road as it had been in 1919 when the description was first drawn up (although it was not thought that the road had significantly changed since 1922). A considerable quantity of extrinsic evidence was considered in order to determine whether the triangular area was part of the road, as its verge (as Mr and Mrs MacDonald maintained), or whether the triangular area was excluded from the road (as was argued for Mr and Mrs Kay). The evidence comprised: (i) maps, (ii) a Council plan, (iii) evidence of use of the area by members of the public, and (iv) the presence of electricity cables under the area.

The use of extrinsic evidence in prescription cases is often a tricky matter. On the one hand, s 1(1) of the Prescription and Limitation (Scotland) Act 1973 requires only that the deed founded on is 'sufficient *in respect of its terms* to constitute' a right of ownership (or other real right). On the other hand the 'terms' of a deed may be impossible to understand without recourse to extrinsic evidence. The danger is that the extrinsic evidence used goes beyond explaining a particular term and colours the interpretation given to the deed. There is then a risk of focusing on what the description in the deed *actually* means instead of, as the 1973 Act requires, focusing on whether it is *possible* to read the description as including the targeted property. There are perhaps some signs of this tendency in the present case. For the purposes of prescription the question to be asked of a description is not 'what does it mean?' but 'what *could* it mean?'

In the event, the Tribunal concluded that the triangular area was part of Durie Road. Hence, when the 1919 description said that Gateyard Cottage was 'bounded by the high road' it necessarily excluded all of Durie Road, including the triangular area. Hence the title was not *habile* for the purposes of positive prescription.

Even if the title had been sufficient, there was not, said the Tribunal, sufficient evidence of possession. Any grass-cutting by Mr Kay was sporadic in nature, and while the Kays often parked their car on the triangular area, this was not 'unequivocally referable to the assertion of a right of ownership in the land' (para 90), as the law requires, because 'there is an undoubted practice in general terms of the motoring public to park upon the verge of a public road' (paras 90 and 91). This last point is perhaps hard to follow. A consideration of possession was only relevant on the assumption that the title was good for the purposes of prescription, and the title was only good for that purpose if the triangular area did *not* form the verge of Durie Road.

The Kays having failed on both points, the Tribunal found that the inclusion of the triangular area within their title was an inaccuracy.

(79) McAdam's Exr v Keeper of the Registers of Scotland
16 May 2018, Lands Tribunal

When the title for the terraced house at 3 Morris Avenue, Lochgelly, Fife, was registered for the first time in the Land Register, it included a small area of ground ('the disputed area') which lay immediately to the front of the adjoining house, number 2 Morris Avenue. This, however, was not a mistake on the part of the Keeper. On the contrary, it reflected the underlying Sasine title. The title to number 2 continued to be held on the Register of Sasines.

Both properties were former council houses and the feu dispositions of both properties, when they were sold off by the council, included the disputed area. As, however, number 3 was feued before number 2, the disputed area was carried by the feu disposition of number 3.

All of this was done in the early 1980s. Since then, the disputed area had been enclosed and possessed by the owner of number 2. Indeed, from 1992 onwards most of it had been given over to an extension to the house at number 2. In the light of such clear possession it was held by the Lands Tribunal that the disputed area had been acquired by the owner of number 2 by positive prescription. Hence the title sheet of number 3 fell to be rectified to exclude the disputed area.

The case is a useful illustration of the way in which prescription – even on the basis of a Sasine title – can undermine a title held on the Land Register. Registration in the Land Register confers ownership, but it does not guarantee that ownership will be retained.

[Another aspect of this case is digested as Case (48) above.]

NEIGHBOUR LAW

(80) National Rail Infrastructure Ltd v Williams
[2018] EWCA Civ 1514, [2018] 3 WLR 1105

Japanese knotweed (*fallopia japonica*) is, as the name indicates, an alien species. In the words of the Master of the Rolls, Sir Terence Etherton (para 3), referring to a report by the Royal Institution of Chartered Surveyors, 'it can affect drains, patios, paths, drives, boundary walls, retaining walls, outbuildings, conservatories and gardens. It can block drains; disrupt drain runs; grow between slabs of concrete drives; disrupt brick paving; undermine garden walls; and overwhelm poorly built outbuildings and conservatories.' Its presence may materially prejudice saleability and mortgageability.

In this case the claimants owned residential properties adjacent to land owned by National Rail Infrastructure Ltd. The latter was infested with Japanese knotweed, which to some extent had begun to spread to the adjacent properties. The claimants argued that the infestation constituted a nuisance, and they sued for damages, and also sought an order requiring the defendants to take steps to control the infestation. They were successful at first instance, and the judgment in their favour has now been upheld by the Court of Appeal.

CRIMINAL PROPERTY LAW

(81) HM Advocate v Younas
[2018] CSOH 9, 2018 SLT 227 affd [2018] CSIH 7, 2018 SLT 1303

This is a sequel to *HM Advocate v Younas* [2014] HCJ 123, 2015 SCL 162 (*Conveyancing 2014* Case (75)). An enforcement administrator, acting under the Proceeds of Crime Act 2002, wished to sell the property of a career criminal, Mr Younas. The latter's sister applied for the flat that he owned to be exempted from the sale. See **Commentary** p 224.

(82) HM Advocate v Housley
2017 JC 294

Richard Housley was a partner of Paul Gebal & Co, solicitors, Bathgate. He acted for a fraudster, Michael Voudouri. (For Mr Voudouri see *Conveyancing 2015* p 69.) Mr Housley was convicted of fraud and money laundering. He was sentenced to prison and was also struck off. In the present proceedings the Crown sought a confiscation order against him.

Mr Housley had acted for Mr Voudouri in various conveyancing transactions, and, in so acting, £1,399,329 had passed through the firm's hands. It was held by Lord Bannatyne that the whole of this sum was, for the purposes of the Proceeds of Crime (Scotland) Act 1995, to be regarded as the property of Mr Housley: 'The money in the account gave rise to a thing in action in favour of the respondent' [Mr Housley]' (para 61). (We make no comment on the introduction to Scotland of English property law terminology.)

Mr Housley was also held liable for certain other, smaller, sums. He was, however, successful on another matter. The matrimonial home was owned solely by his wife, yet the Crown argued that, because of the marriage, one half of it fell to be regarded as 'realisable property' for the purposes of the confiscation order. The Crown's argument on this point was rejected, surely rightly. Unlike some countries, in Scotland the property of spouses is not automatically co-owned.

The sum awarded is not stated in the case as reported, but according to *Scottish Legal News*, 30 January 2017, it was £97,378.

INSOLVENCY

(83) O'Boyle's Tr v Brennan
[2018] CSOH 90, 2018 GWD 29-369

In September 2014 the defender, Karen Brennan, bought 16 Attlee Road, East Kilbride, taking title in her sole name. Her partner, John O'Boyle, provided her with the price, £190,960. So she acquired the property with his money. It seems that there was no documentation (eg a loan contract) about this funding. Shortly thereafter, in February 2015, Mr O'Boyle was sequestrated. His trustee at first seems to have done nothing to query the transaction. In January 2017 the defender sold the house for £200,000, and immediately paid £197,462.20 to Mr O'Boyle, who by this time had been discharged from his sequestration. For this payment too there seems to have been no documentation. 16 Attlee Road, East Kilbride, seems to have been a low-documentation zone.

The trustee in sequestration then raised the present action, seeking (i) declarator that the original payment (£190,960) by Mr O'Boyle to Ms Brennan had been a gratuitous alienation, and (ii) decree ordaining her to pay that sum to the pursuer.

The first defence was that the money had been repaid. But of course it had been paid not to the trustee but to the debtor, and this defence was repelled.

The second defence was that the mere fact of repayment meant that 'adequate consideration' had been given for the original payment. The defence, which seems to us unstateable, also failed.

The third defence was that the trustee should have made the claim before the debtor's discharge. This too failed: a sequestration is not ended by the debtor's discharge. The defender does not seem to have framed this defence as a plea of mora and taciturnity, which might have been an argument worth considering.

It was also said for the defender that it would be 'inequitable' if she had to pay the trustee, for in that case she would have paid back the same money twice. This argument does not seem to have been developed and is not addressed in the judgment of the Lord Ordinary (Lord Doherty). Possibly the money she must pay to the trustee would now be recoverable by her from Mr O'Boyle on the basis of unjustified enrichment.

The reason for the original payment seems to have been accepted by both sides as having been donation. Yet it seems more likely that it was (i) deposit or (ii) loan or (iii) trust: why else would Ms Brennan have returned it? (The reason for the return of the money seems not to have been discussed in the case.) But this would have made no difference, for if there existed any right on Mr O'Boyle's part to require repayment, that right would have vested in his trustee anyway.

(84) Joint Liquidators of Grampian Maclennan's Distribution Services Ltd v Carnbroe Estates Ltd
[2018] CSIH 7, 2018 SC 314, 2018 SLT 205, 2018 SCLR 532

Grampian Maclennan's Distribution Services Ltd fell into acute financial difficulties. It decided to sell its chief asset, a property at 9 Stroud Road, East Kilbride. That type of property would typically need a long period of marketing – probably at least a year. Instead, the company decided on an immediate off-market sale at a figure, £550,000, that was below full market value. The company soon went into insolvent liquidation, and its liquidators raised the present action to reduce the sale as a gratuitous alienation. The action was unsuccessful at first instance, but was successful after a reclaiming motion to the Inner House. An appeal to the Supreme Court is pending. The case is chiefly of interest from the standpoint of insolvency law, but there are implications for conveyancers too. See **Commentary** p 211.

PART II

STATUTORY DEVELOPMENTS

STATUTORY DEVELOPMENTS

Forestry and Land Management (Scotland) Act 2018 (asp 8)

This Act transfers the powers and duties of the Forestry Commissioners in Scotland to Scottish Ministers and repeals, for Scotland, the Forestry Act 1967. Under Part 2 of the Act Scottish Ministers have a duty to promote sustainable forest management and to publish a forestry strategy. Part 3 deals with management and the provision of information. Part 4 updates the regulatory regime for felling trees, and provides for the registration of a number of notices in the Land or Sasine Register (s 42), including notices to comply (s 38) and notices of variation (s 40). At the time of writing the Act was, for the most part, not yet in force.

Land and Buildings Transaction Tax (Relief from Additional Amount) (Scotland) Act 2018 (asp 11)

This short Act gives retrospective effect to the Land and Buildings Transaction Tax (Additional Amount–Second Homes Main Residence Relief) (Scotland) Order 2017, SSI 2017/233. The 2017 Order prevents additional dwelling supplement ('ADS') from being charged where an existing main residence of spouses, civil partners or cohabitants is replaced by another main residence, notwithstanding that the old house was in the name of only one party and the new house is in the name of both. For details, see *Conveyancing 2017* pp 190–91 and p 233 below. The effect of the Act is to backdate the relief to 1 April 2016.

Prescription (Scotland) Act 2018 (asp 15)

This legislation is based on the Scottish Law Commission's *Report No 247 on Prescription* (2017). The Act makes a large number of amendments to the provisions on negative prescription in the Prescription and Limitation (Scotland) Act 1973. As, however, it says nothing about positive prescription, the legislation is of limited interest for conveyancers.

The main impetus behind the legislation was the decision of the Supreme Court in *David T Morrison & Co Ltd v ICL Plastics Ltd* [2014] UKSC 48, 2014 SC (UKSC) 222 as to the correct construction of the 'discoverability' test in s 11(3) of the Prescription and Limitation (Scotland) Act 1973 which triggers the start of the five-year negative prescription in relation to claims for reparation arising out of an act, neglect or default. The Supreme Court held, contrary to prior decisions in the lower courts, that the five-year period began to run as soon as the claimant knew that he or she had sustained loss, injury or damage, even if the claimant did not (yet) know that the loss was cause by fault or negligence (and hence likely to give rise to a claim). The decision is reversed by s 5 of the 2018 Act. This amends s 11(3) to provide that the claimant, before the five-year prescriptive period can begin, must know each of (a) that loss, injury or damage has occurred; (b) that this was caused by a person's act or omission; and (c) the identity of that person.

Three other changes introduced by the Act may be mentioned. First, the list in sch 1 para 1 of the 1973 Act of the obligations which are subject to the five-year negative prescription is expanded to include, as a new sub-para (h), 'any obligation to make a payment arising under an enactment (whenever passed or made), not being an obligation falling within any other provision of this paragraph': see s 3 of the 2018 Act. This broad provision allows some weeding out of particular statutes mentioned in para 1, but also requires the addition of some new exceptions to para 1 in para 2. Obligations by the Keeper to make payments which derive from the Land Registration etc (Scotland) Act 2012 will be caught by para 1(h) and hence subject to the five-year prescription; but a new para 2(ea) specifically exempts from the five-year prescription (and hence, by default, applies the 20-year prescription to) obligations of the Keeper to pay compensation under the Keeper's warranty or in respect of realignment (ie under ss 77 and 94 of the 2012 Act).

The second change is that the 20-year negative prescription will no longer be capable of being interrupted judicially or by acknowledgement by the debtor; but court proceedings begun before the end of the prescriptive period will lengthen that period until such time as the claim has been finally disposed of. This affects both s 7 and s 8 of the 1973 Act (see ss 6 and 7 of the 2018 Act). 'Final disposal' of a claim is defined in a new s 9A of the 1973 Act, inserted by s 12 of the 2018 Act.

Finally, provision is made as to burden of proof. A new s 13A is added to the 1973 Act by s 14 of the 2018 Act: 'If a question arises as to whether the obligation or right has been extinguished by the expiry of the applicable prescriptive period, it is to be presumed that the obligation or right has been so extinguished unless the contrary is proved by the creditor.'

At the time of writing the Act was, for the most part, not yet in force.

Scottish Crown Estate Act 2019 (asp 1)

Although this Act did not receive Royal Assent until 15 January 2019, it completed its passage through the Scottish Parliament on 21 November 2018 and can thus be regarded as legislation which was, in substance, a product of 2018.

The background to the Act is as follows. The Crown Estate is owned by the Crown but, until recently, was administered on a UK basis by the Crown Estate Commissioners, all profits being paid to the Treasury. That changed on 1 April 2017. While ownership remains with the Crown, the power of administration of the Crown Estate in Scotland was transferred to the Scottish Ministers by virtue of s 90B of the Scotland Act 1998, a provision which was added by s 36 of the Scotland Act 2016. Today all profits from the Crown Estate in Scotland are paid into the Scottish Consolidated Fund, although this has been fiscally neutral as there is a baseline deduction from the Scottish Government's block grant from Westminster equal to the net profit generated by Crown Estate assets in the year before the transfer.

An interim body, Crown Estate Scotland (Interim Management) (in Gaelic, Oighreachd a' Chrùin Alba (Stiùireadh Eadar-amail)), was set up by the Crown Estate Scotland (Interim Management) Order 2017, SSI 2017/36, to manage the Crown Estate on behalf of the Scottish Ministers. Following consultation (see *Conveyancing 2016* pp 105–06), the Scottish Crown Estate Act 2019 now provides for long-term management of the Crown Estate.

Once it is in force, the Act will make the current interim body permanent but under a different name: Crown Estate Scotland (in Gaelic, Oighreachd a' Chrùin Alba). SSI 2017/36 is renamed as the Crown Estate Order 2017 (see sch 1 para 11). But while Crown Estate Scotland (www.crownestatescotland.com/) is the default manager, the management of particular assets can, and in some cases will, be further devolved to local authorities, harbour authorities, other public authorities, community organisations, or even to the Scottish Ministers. 'Community organisation' is defined in s 6 and is broader in scope than its counterpart which, under the Land Reform (Scotland) Act 2003 and other legislation, has a statutory right to buy. Community organisations can be designated as such by Scottish Ministers by regulations; otherwise they are any body corporate which 'relates to a community' and has a written constitution which covers certain specified matters. The devolution of management in respect of particular assets can be long-term (a 'transfer' under s 3) or more short-term and limited in scope ('delegation' under s 4).

For as long as the Crown Estate in Scotland was administered by the Crown Estate Commissioners, there was a statutory duty, under s 1(3) of the Crown Estate Act 1961, 'to maintain and enhance its value and the return obtained from it'. The equivalent provision in the Scottish Crown Estate Act, s 7, qualifies that duty by requiring the 'manager' – whether Crown Estate Scotland or some devolved body – to (a) 'act in the way best calculated to further the achievement of sustainable development in Scotland', and also to (b) 'seek to manage the assets in a way that is likely to contribute to the promotion or the improvement in Scotland of (i) economic development, (ii) regeneration, (iii) social wellbeing, and (iv) environmental wellbeing'.

Spaceflight servitudes

The relevance to Scottish conveyancing law of the **Space Industry Act 2018 (c 5)** is perhaps not immediately obvious. The purpose of the legislation is to facilitate commercial space launches from UK soil, including the launching of small satellites and scientific experiments. By s 39, the Secretary of State may make an order granting rights over land if satisfied that it is appropriate to do so:

(a) to secure the safe and efficient use for the carrying out of spaceflight activities of any land which is vested in a qualifying person or which a qualifying person proposes to acquire,

(b) to secure the provision of any services required in relation to any such land, or

(c) to secure that spacecraft and carrier aircraft may be navigated safely.

A 'qualifying person' is (a) the Secretary of State; (b) the holder of a range control licence; or (c) the holder of a spaceport licence (s 39(3)). Among the rights which the Secretary of State may grant is a servitude (s 39(4)(a)). The servitude does not take effect against third parties without registration of the order in the Land or Sasine Register (s 45(2)). There is no mention of dual registration, ie the registration against both dominant and servient tenement that is required for normal servitudes by s 75(1) of the Title Conditions (Scotland) Act 2003. Whether a requirement for dual registration can be read into s 45 of the 2018 Act is unclear.

Registers of beneficial ownership of companies

Since 6 April 2016 UK companies have been required to maintain a public register of those who have significant control over the company (the 'PSC register'), 'significant control' being defined to include direct or indirect ownership of more than 25% of the shares or direct or indirect control of more than 25% of the voting rights. The relevant provisions can be found in part 21A (ss 790A–790ZG) and sch 1A of the Companies Act 2006, both of which were added by the Small Business, Enterprise and Employment Act 2015. The aim is to increase transparency, especially in the cause of detecting money laundering, tax evasion, and other forms of crime. One result of the PSC register is that, where land is owned by a UK company, it is possible, at least in theory, to find out from Companies House the 'true' owner or owners of the company.

More recently, the UK Government has indicated an intention to establish a comparable regime for overseas companies and other legal entities but only where they own or are purchasing UK land and buildings. See **Commentary** p 175. A draft Bill – the Registration of Overseas Entities Bill – has been published for comment and, in a small way, there has been legislation. Section 50 of the **Sanctions and Anti-Money Laundering Act 2018 (c 13)** requires the Secretary of State to publish and lay before Parliament three reports on the progress that has been made to put in place a register of beneficial owners of overseas entities. Each report will be due after the expiry of a 12-month reporting period. The first and second reports must set out the steps that will be taken in the next reporting period towards putting the register in place and an assessment as to when the register will be put in place. The third and final report must include a statement setting out what further steps, if any, are to be taken towards putting the register in place. Section 50 came into force on the day on which the Act was passed, ie 23 May 2018 (s 64(1)).

Meanwhile, s 51 of the same Act seeks to extend a scheme of registration of beneficial ownership to the British Overseas Territories, that is to say, to Anguilla, Bermuda, British Antarctic Territory, British Indian Ocean Territory, the Cayman Islands, the Falkland Islands, Gibraltar, Montserrat, Pitcairn, Henderson, Ducie and Oeno Islands, St Helena, Ascension and Tristan da Cunha, South Georgia and the South Sandwich Islands, the Sovereign Base Areas of Akrotiri and Dhekelia, the Turks and Caicos Islands, and the British Virgin Islands. As quite a number of these are tax havens, the initiative by the Mother Parliament to legislate on this topic has generally been controversial. Section 51 offers a mixture of help and compulsion. Subsection (1) provides the promise of help:

> For the purposes of the detection, investigation or prevention of money laundering, the Secretary of State must provide all reasonable assistance to the governments of the British Overseas Territories to enable each of those governments to establish a publicly accessible register of the beneficial ownership of companies registered in each government's jurisdiction.

Where, however, no such register has been set up by 31 December 2020, subsection (2) requires the Secretary of State to prepare an Order in Council requiring the government of the territory in question to do so. At the time of writing, s 51 had yet to be brought into force.

Money Laundering Regulations

The money-laundering event of 2017 was the passing of new regulations, the Money Laundering, Terrorist Financing and Transfer of Funds (Information on the Payer) Regulations 2017, SI 2017/692: see *Conveyancing 2017* pp 73–74. Minor amendments are now made to the 2017 Regulations by the **Money Laundering and Terrorist Financing (Miscellaneous Amendments) Regulations 2018, SI 2018/1337**. More significant from a Scottish point of view are the changes made by reg 6 of the 2018 Regulations to s 34(1D) of the Solicitors (Scotland) Act 1980. Prior to the change, this provision empowered the Council of the Law Society of Scotland to make rules 'as to the way in which solicitors and incorporated practices are to comply with the Money Laundering, Terrorist Financing and Transfer of Funds (Information on the Payer) Regulations 2017'. Since 10 January 2019 this has been replaced with a new version of s 34(1D) which allows for Law Society enforcement. The new version reads:

> Rules made under this section may make provision as to—
>
> (a) the way in which solicitors and incorporated practices are to comply with the Money Laundering, Terrorist Financing and Transfer of Funds (Information on the Payer) Regulations 2017;
>
> (b) the action which the Council may take to enable them to ascertain whether or not such rules are being complied with; and
>
> (c) the recovery from solicitors of fees and other costs incurred by the Council in ascertaining whether or not a solicitor who has failed to comply with such rules has remedied that failure and is complying with the rules.

Community right to buy abandoned, neglected or detrimental land

A new community right to buy abandoned, neglected or detrimental land was inserted into the Land Reform (Scotland) Act 2003, as part 3A (comprising ss 97A–97Z), by s 74 of the Community Empowerment (Scotland) Act 2015. The provisions came into force on 27 June 2018: see **Community Empowerment (Scotland) Act 2015 (Commencement No 11) Order 2018, SSI 2018/139**. Also coming into force on 27 June 2018 were ss 52 and 53 of the Land Reform (Scotland) Act 2016 which provide for the setting up by the Keeper of the Registers of Scotland of a new register, the Register of Applications by Community Bodies to Buy Land ('RoACBL'): see **Land Reform (Scotland) Act 2016 (Commencement No 8 and Saving Provision) Regulations 2018, SSI 2018/138**. A helpful overview was published by Ann Stewart in the online edition of the *Journal of the Law Society*: see bit.ly/2MQTA3g.

Detailed guidance has been issued by the Scottish Government to assist communities in exercising the right to buy: see www.gov.scot/publications/land-reform-scotland-act-2003-part-3a-community-right-buy-abandoned-neglected-detrimental-land-full-guidance/. There are also shorter guides: see (i) www.gov.scot/publications/easy-read-version-community-groups/; (ii) www.gov.scot/publications/information-leaflet-community-bodies-landowners-interested-parties-regarding-applications/; and (iii) www.gov.scot/publications/information-communities/. Finally, guidance has also been prepared for landowners and creditors: see www.gov.scot/publications/information-landowners-creditors/.

The right to buy applies to land which, in the opinion of the Scottish Ministers, is wholly or mainly abandoned or neglected or 'the use or management of the land is such that it results in or causes harm, directly or indirectly, to the environmental wellbeing of a relevant community' (Land Reform (Scotland) Act 2003 s 97C). Much will depend on how these criteria are interpreted. Various matters to which Ministers are to have regard in determining the eligibility of land are set out in regs 2–6 of the **Community Right to Buy (Abandoned, Neglected or Detrimental Land) (Eligible Land, Regulators and Restrictions on Transfers and Dealing) (Scotland) Regulations 2018, SSI 2018/201**. Section 97C(5) of the 2003 Act makes certain exclusions from the right to buy, including private homes, and these are augmented by regs 8 and 9 of SSI 2018/201 to include, for example, land that is held by a Minister of the Crown or government department.

The right-to-buy procedure involves a community ballot followed by an application to Scottish Ministers, the application being registered in the new Register of Applications by Community Bodies to Buy Land (https://roacbl.ros.gov.uk/) (ss 97F, 97G and 97J). Details and forms are set out in the **Community Right to Buy (Abandoned, Neglected or Detrimental Land) (Applications, Ballots and Miscellaneous Provisions) (Scotland) Regulations 2018, SSI 2018/140**. Ministers cannot approve an application unless satisfied that the acquisition is in the public interest and compatible with furthering the achievement of sustainable development, and that the achievement of sustainable development would be unlikely to be furthered by the existing owner (s 97H(1)). There is a right of appeal to the sheriff (s 97V). Market value is payable, calculated by a valuer in accordance with s 97S and subject to a right of appeal to the Lands Tribunal (s 97W). Further details are in the **Community Right to Buy (Abandoned, Neglected or Detrimental Land) (Compensation) (Scotland) Order 2018, SSI 2018/137.**

As soon as a pending application is registered in the Register of Applications by Community Bodies to Buy Land, a restriction period comes into operation during which period the land cannot be transferred except in furtherance of the community right to buy: see 2003 Act s 97N(1) and SSI 2018/201 regs 12–14. Other transactions are not permitted unless they fall within one of a number of listed exceptions. These include gifts of land, and also transfers in implement of missives or option agreements entered into prior to the registration of the application. A disposition granted in reliance on an exception must contain a declaration which identifies the exception in question. The Property Standardisation Group (www.psglegal.co.uk/) has provided a clause for inclusion in missives to deal with the possibility of land being abandoned, neglected or detrimental: see cl 7.6 of the Offer to Sell with vacant possession.

What would be the status of a disposition granted and registered in breach of these provisions? This question is not easy to answer. There is no equivalent of s 40(2) of the 2003 Act which, in relation to a community interest registered in the Register of Community Interests in Land, declares unauthorised transfers to be of no effect.

It is already good practice, in buying land, to search in the Register of Community Interests in Land, and this practice should now be extended to the Register of Applications by Community Bodies to Buy Land. Like the first of these registers (http://rcil.ros.gov.uk/RCIL/default.asp?category=rcil&service =home), the second is also maintained by the Keeper and held online (https:// roacbl.ros.gov.uk/), and can be searched without charge.

The Scottish Government produces an annual survey of vacant and derelict land: see p 121 below for the most recent survey.

Installation of service pipes in tenement buildings

Section 19 of the Tenements (Scotland) Act 2004 empowers the Scottish Ministers to make regulations allowing owners within a tenement to lead pipes, cables and other equipment through the common parts of the building. The background is explained in paras 10.6–10.8 of the Scottish Law Commission's *Report No 162 on the Law of the Tenement* (1998). Until now, no regulations had been made under s 19, and the provision had lain unused. That has now changed. The **Tenements (Scotland) Act 2004 (Heating Services) Regulations 2018, SSI 2018/163**, applies s 19 to communal heating within a tenement building as well as to heating provided by a wider ('district') network. More significantly, the **Tenements (Scotland) Act 2004 (Gas Services) Order 2018, SI 2018/658**, fills a gap noticed by the Scottish Law Commission by extending s 19 to the provision of gas supplies; for reasons of legislative competency this is a statutory instrument of the UK Government. The first of these had previously been the subject of public consultation: see www.gov.scot/Publications/2016/01/3668.

An identical procedure is provided in each case. An owner who wishes to lead service pipes of the permitted kind must notify the other owners of the common parts. A form of notice is prescribed. If a recipient of the notice objects within 28 days, the initiating owner must try to reach agreement (which might involve the service of a revised notice) or, failing agreement, must seek authority from the sheriff court under s 6 of the 2004 Act. Further provision is made for the costs of installation (the initiating owner must pay unless the titles or other legislation says otherwise), and for the repair of any damage caused.

Registration of letting agents

Part 4 (ss 29–62) of the Housing (Scotland) Act 2014 introduced a registration system for those who act as letting agents for private-sector residential tenancies. The primary legislation was supplemented by the Letting Agent Registration (Scotland) Regulations 2016, SSI 2016/432, which came into force on 31 January 2018. This prescribed additional information to be included in the application for registration and on the register itself (regs 3 and 4). It also provided that applicants require to have a qualification at level 6 or above of the Scottish Credit and Qualifications Framework which includes training on matters such as the legal obligations relating to letting agency work, the rights and responsibilities of landlords and tenants, managing repairs, and handling money (regs 5–7). A minor amendment is made to the 2016 Regulations by the **Letting Agent Registration (Scotland) Amendment Regulations 2018, SSI 2018/196**, removing the requirement for applicants to have a dedicated client bank account.

Since 31 January 2018, letting agents have been subject to a Code of Practice provided for by s 46 of the Housing (Scotland) Act 2014 and set out in the Letting Agent Code of Practice (Scotland) Regulations 2016, SSI 2016/133. Minor amendments have since been made by the Private Housing (Tenancies) (Scotland) Act 2016 (Consequential Provisions) Regulations 2017, SSI 2017/405, and by the Letting Agent (Registration and Code of Practice) (Scotland) (Miscellaneous Amendments) Regulations 2017, SSI 2017/428. A consolidated print of the Code of Practice was issued by the Scottish Government on 31 January 2018, the day on which the Code came into force: see www.gov.scot/publications/letting-agent-code-practice/.

Tenements: repayment charges for registered social landlords

Where a repair is authorised by scheme decision, any owner in the tenement can arrange and pay for the repair and then look to the other owners for a contribution to the cost: see Tenement Management Scheme (set out in sch 1 to the Tenements (Scotland) Act 2004) and especially rr 3.1, 4 and 8.3. In tenements with a mix of privately-owned flats and flats let as social tenancies, the social landlord might find itself in that position. If the social landlord is a local authority, s 172 of the Housing (Scotland) Act 2006 allows the local authority to secure the amount due by means of a repayment charge. A similar power is now created for registered social landlords ('RSLs', ie landlords other than local authorities) by the **Registered Social Landlords (Repayment Charges) (Scotland) Regulations 2018, SSI 2018/301**.

A style of the new repayment charge is given in the 2018 Regulations. The charge is registered in the Land Register and ranks before standard securities, even those of an earlier date (reg 10). It is for the RSL to divide the sum due into annual or monthly instalments, but the flat-owner can pay the whole amount due at any time (regs 5 and 6). On repayment, a discharge is granted and registered (reg 9(2)).

Standard securities: restrictions on the right to redeem after 20 years

Section 11 of the Land Tenure Reform (Scotland) Act 1974 gives borrowers the right to redeem a standard security over a private dwelling house after it has been in force for 20 years. Its purpose – rather oddly, to modern eyes – was to prevent the use of sales, in which the 'price' was repayable over a very long period and secured by a standard security, as a substitute for the leases of more than 20 years which, for dwellinghouses, were banned by s 8 of the Act. (See J M Halliday, *Conveyancing Law and Practice* vol 2 (2nd edn, 1997) para 55–65.) In practice, if that particular device was ever known it is unknown now. On the other hand, the 20-year rule has caused difficulty, especially in respect of the stipulation in subsection (4) of s 11 that the amount due on redemption cannot be larger than, in essence, the amount originally advanced plus interest. This does not fit in well with certain types of financing arrangements that now exist such as shared equity loan and equity release schemes. With this in mind, an exemption was added to s 11 by s 93 of the Housing (Scotland) Act 2014 in respect of 'a heritable security which is in security of a debt of a description specified in an order made by the Scottish Ministers'. Following consultation, an order has now been made exempting heritable securities granted under a number of listed schemes to the Scottish Ministers, Places for People Scotland, and to social landlords: see the **Redemption of Heritable Securities (Excluded Securities) (Scotland) Order 2018, SSI 2018/376**.

PART III
OTHER MATERIAL

OTHER MATERIAL

Land registration

Completion of the Land Register

According to the Registers of Scotland *Annual Report 2017–18* (p 15), 65% of property titles (around 1.8 million), amounting to 31.7% of Scotland's land mass, are now on the Land Register.

Keeper-induced registration

One of the main vehicles for completion of the Register is Keeper-induced registration (KIR). In the year 2017–18, some 26,000 titles (comprising 63,000 addresses) entered the Land Register by KIR.

Hitherto the Keeper has declined to give individual notification to the owners of property affected by KIR. This has been much criticised – see eg a letter by Keith Robertson published at (2018) 86 *Scottish Law Gazette* 33. We understand that this practice has been reviewed and that some form of notification may be introduced.

Another criticism, though perhaps not (yet) one grounded on much evidence, has been concern about the quality of KIR titles. A detailed study carried out by Keith Robertson on two small residential developments in Kingussie uncovered some troubling errors: see (2018) 63 *Journal of the Law Society of Scotland* Sept/32. There is a special form on the RoS website for querying errors in a KIR registration: see www.ros.gov.uk/services/keeper-induced-registration/how-kir-works.

Since a KIR title is created without input from an applicant, and could suffer in quality as a result, something more than the ordinary reports may be appropriate, and accordingly some search firms have introduced special reports for KIR titles, which include checks against the Sasine search sheet and the underlying descriptive deed.

Delays in registration

According to the RoS *Annual Report 2017–18* (p 6), there were 541,622 applications for registration in the Land Register, and 45,422 for recording in the Register of Sasines. So far as the Land Register is concerned, ordinary transactions are registered expeditiously. Increasing concerns, however, were expressed in 2018 about lengthy delays in some first registrations and in transfers of part. For example, a letter to the *Scottish Law Gazette* (p 32) complained that:

> The delays we are now experiencing with the Land Registers are getting to such a stage that, on some files, correspondence from lenders chasing up titles and correspondence to the Registers enquiring about the position is forming a substantial portion of the file and a portion for which there is no provision for a fee. I have had cases where we are approaching two years since the application was lodged and I have in those circumstances been recommending to clients to raise the issue with their MSP to see if there is a political solution that can resolve matters and put pressure on the Keeper. The problems with registration reflect badly on the profession as a whole as clients will see the delay as one caused by solicitors and not by the Registers despite our trying to explain this to clients.

None of this augers well for completion of the Land Register by the target date of 2024.

The statutory position is that applications must be dealt with 'without unreasonable delay': Land Registration etc (Scotland) Act 2012 s 35(3). For standard first registrations, the target figure of Registers of Scotland is 20 working days. Last year this was achieved in around 80% of cases: see Registers of Scotland, *Annual Report 2017–18* (p 13). The main problem, as might be expected, has been with more complex cases. It was announced by RoS in the July issue of the *Journal of the Law Society* (p 9) that almost 40,000 such cases are in significant arrears, including 3,000 cases in which the delay amounts to almost two years. 'The Keeper has made a firm commitment to addressing the backlog', according to the article, 'and our teams have worked to develop a plan of action to make real, demonstrable progress in clearing it'. Since then, monthly reports have been published in the *Journal*, the most recent of which (on p 9 of the issue for December 2018) says that 40% of cases that were older than two years have now been dealt with.

Meanwhile, RoS have accepted that in exceptional circumstances applicants need to be able to jump the queue. To that end there is now a formal process to request that an application is expedited. A form is available at www.ros.gov. uk/support/contact-us/expedite-requests. RoS assess applications against three criteria concerning the effect of the delay: (i) financial loss or hardship, (ii) the loss of future transactions, and (iii) personal loss or hardship. The request must be accompanied by an explanation of how the criteria are met, supported (except in the case of (iii)) with appropriate evidence.

Delayed rejections

Delays in processing applications lead to delays in rejections. Fortunately, most rejections happen quickly, as a result of the initial sift of applications. But in more complex cases, especially in first registrations, an error may only come to light much later in the registration process. For practitioners and clients alike, the combination of late-stage rejections and delayed processing can be toxic, especially where something untoward has occurred during the intervening period, such as the insolvency of the granter. One correspondent to the *Scottish Law Gazette* (p 29 of the volume for 2018) suggested that, for applications not processed within the target time-frame, the Keeper should be liable for any loss which results. The Scottish Law Agents Society is arguing for applications to be conclusively deemed to have been accepted if they have not been rejected after, say, one or three months.

In this connection it may be noted that s 35(3) of the Land Registration etc (Scotland) Act 2012 says that 'the Keeper must deal with an application without unreasonable delay'. More specifically, s 35(1) says that 'the Keeper's decision as to whether to accept or reject an application for registration must be made within such period as may be prescribed' and s 35(2) adds that 'different periods may be ... prescribed for different kinds of application'. This power remains unused. Perhaps it should be used.

Rather puzzlingly, RoS have promised ((2018) 63 *Journal of the Law Society of Scotland* Sept/9) 'that no case that has been with us for longer than three months will be rejected unless it absolutely legally has to be' – puzzling because s 21 of the 2012 Act largely removes the Keeper's discretion in matters of acceptance and rejection.

In fact, the number of rejections continues to decline. The figures for the year ending 31 March 2018 are given in an article by Frances Rooney published on p 32 of the *Journal of the Law Society* for July 2018. For ordinary dealings with a registered title, the rejection rate over the year was 6.05%; for first registrations it was 11.53%. The most common reasons for rejection, in order, were:

(1) witness has not signed or been named/designed (9.1% of total rejections);
(2) application form not signed (5.7%);
(3) application created in error (5.4%);
(4) signatory/attorney not named/capacity not designed (5.3%);
(5) information in form different from that in deed (4.8%);
(6) LBTT requirements not met: 4.7% of rejections;
(7) links in title question answered inappropriately – granter not recorded owner etc (4.6%).

Some of these grounds have been eliminated or made less likely by the new application form for registration (for which see below).

Rejections: letter of undertaking by borrower's solicitor to lender

The perception that rejections have become more common has resulted in some lenders seeking letters of undertaking from borrower's solicitors in relation to funding arrangements. The Property Standardisation Group (www.psglegal. co.uk) has now produced a style letter. Among other things, the borrower's solicitor undertakes: (i) within two business days of completion to apply for registration of the disposition (or lease or assignation, as the case may be), discharge, and standard security; (ii) not to withdraw the application; (iii) to notify the lender of any rejection within one business day; (iv) to use reasonable endeavours to correct any errors in the application and to re-submit; (v) if the advance notice has expired, to apply for a new one; and (vi) to submit the LBTT return to Revenue Scotland by electronic submission within one business day of completion.

A *non domino* dispositions

The suggestion mentioned above on the part of the Scottish Law Agents Society in relation to late rejections comes from material which accompanied the launch of the Society's new Consumer Property Group: see (2018) 86 *Scottish Law Gazette* 35. Its purpose is 'to look at particular issues where the interest of consumers and solicitors are aligned and action required to improve the situation of both in relation to Property in Scotland'. Apart from late rejections, the other issue which is pressed in the launch material is the virtual impossibility of using the procedure under the 2012 Act for *a non domino* dispositions, with the result that many small areas of land are and will remain unaccounted for:

> [The 2012 Act procedures] are not an effective way of filling in gaps in the Land Register. Most legal practitioners are simply not using them now and rely on Title (or more accurately Dispossession) Indemnity Insurance Policies which once taken out will mean the Title will never be cured for the future as any attempt will invalidate cover under the Policy. Thus the Land Register Cadastral Map will have 'black holes or slivers of land' whose ownership cannot be effectively backed up with indemnity insurance for large numbers of Titles.

This is a view with which we have considerable sympathy. Yet we doubt whether a reform of the rules affecting *a non domino* dispositions is practical politics, at least for the time being, given the suspicion with which positive prescription is regarded by many members of the Scottish Parliament. It is, we fear, a suspicion that is based on a lack of understanding.

For a recent radical proposal to make it easier to obtain a good title on the basis of prescriptive possession, see G L Gretton, 'Reforming the law of prescriptive title to land', in D Bain, R Paisley, A Simpson and N Tait (eds), *Northern Lights: Essays in Private Law in Memory of Professor David Carey Miller* (2018) 66.

The cadastral map and the registration of unmapped areas

In taking up this new initiative, the Scottish Law Agents Society appears largely to have abandoned its previous campaign against the 2012 Act which was directed, in particular, at the Keeper's refusal to register unmapped areas. In last year's volume we suggested a number of reasons why this campaign was ill-founded: see *Conveyancing 2017* pp 150–54. Linked to the campaign was a questionnaire, first issued with the *Scottish Law Gazette* for August 2017 and later reissued, which asked: 'Have you had any problems with the Land Register since December 2014?' It is reported in the January 2018 issue of the *Scottish Law Gazette* (on p 27) that 'virtually no response' had been received – although an absence of responses should not, of course, be equated with satisfaction with the registration procedures under the 2012 Act.

Updates to OS map

Underlying the cadastral map is the OS map. This is in a constant state of change and improvement. Where a section of the OS map is updated, s 11(7) of the 2012 Act requires the Keeper to 'make any changes to the register which are necessary in consequence of the updating'. Two articles in the *Journal of the Law Society* in 2018 question the accuracy of the OS updates, and hence their knock-on effect on the cadastral map and individual titles: see Andrew Upton (Dec/34) and Tony Rosser (bit.ly/2Q3QajF).

New application form for registration

A new application form for registration was introduced on 21 March 2018: for background, see *Conveyancing 2017* p 145. Following a transitional period, the old form has now been phased out. Some of the differences between the two forms are discussed in an article by Frances Rooney on p 32 of the *Journal of the Law Society* for July 2018.

Document return

Since 20 November 2018, Registers of Scotland have scanned applications in respect of registered plots immediately upon receipt and posted the documents back to the submitting solicitor within 24 hours. RoS emphasise, however, that returning the documents does not mean that the deed has been registered. The documents should not be destroyed at least until notification by email that registration has taken place. This new procedure does not apply to dual registrations.

Registers Direct: the end

The Registers Direct service was withdrawn on St Andrew's Day 2018. Its replacement, ScotLIS (= Scotland's Land Information Service: scotlis.ros.gov. uk) was launched on 24 October 2017 and now includes access to the Register of Inhibitions as well as to the Land and Sasine Registers. The cost of a RoI search done through ScotLis is £1 (as compared to the normal fee of £3).

Digital Discharge Service

In the issue of the *Journal of the Law Society* for September 2018 (p 9), RoS report as follows in relation to the Digital Discharge Service ('DDS'):

> DDS was launched in May of last year, and has been an overwhelming success. Digital discharges deliver the highest level of security, offering peace of mind to both solicitors and their clients. One of the challenges of operating in a modern business environment is that people want, and expect, everything to be done more quickly – DDS delivers that, while also managing to cost the customer less rather than more. We have completed 27,802 digital discharges to date, and in July this year 36% of all securities were discharged via DDS.

By the December issue of the *Journal* (p 9), the number of discharges completed had risen to 'nearly 40,000', and a plea was also made to use the DDS (rather than the eForms service) even for paper applications.

It is not clear at what point the DDS will become compulsory. Nor is it clear when the next stage in the digital journey, the digital registration of standard securities, will begin. The pace of travel seems to have slowed.

Shared plots

Normally, RoS treat areas of common ground as shared plots (except for areas within tenement steadings). A shared plot is given its own title sheet which is separate from the title sheets of the individual plots (the primary or 'sharing' plots) which hold the rights in common. Since 21 January 2019, however, RoS treat areas which are essential to the use of the primary plot (such as bin stores, paths and driveways) as pertinents and so include these in the primary-plot title sheet. This is to reduce work at RoS and hence to speed up first registrations. Other areas of land owned in common (such as amenity areas) continue to be treated as shared plots.

Register of Persons Holding a Controlled Interest in Land

Part 3 of the Land Reform (Scotland) Act 2016 requires the Scottish Ministers to make provision by regulations for the collection and publication in a public register of information as to the persons who have controlling interests in owners and tenants of land. As s 41 requires, a public consultation was launched in September 2016 and closed in December 2016: see Scottish Government, *Improving transparency in land ownership in Scotland: a consultation on controlling interests in land* (www.gov.scot/Publications/2016/09/6681). Draft regulations were published on 20 June 2018 (www.gov.scot/publications/delivering-improved-transparency-land-ownership-scotland-consultation-draft-regulations/), and comments invited by 8 November 2018. This important subject is discussed elsewhere in this volume: see p 174 below.

Property Market Report 2007–08 to 2017–18

According to figures released by Registers of Scotland on 6 March 2018, the 2017 calendar year saw increases in the average price of a residential property as well as in the volume and market value of Scottish property sales. The *2017 Calendar Year Market Review* shows a 4% increase in the average price for a residential property in Scotland in 2017, compared to 2016, to £172,779. This continues the generally upward trend seen since 2012. East Renfrewshire and the City of Edinburgh showed the highest average prices in 2017 at £252,870 and £249,651 respectively. The largest annual changes were seen in South Lanarkshire and Glasgow City, with increases of 8.6% and 7.8% respectively.

There was a 4.2% year-on-year rise in the volume of sales of residential property, with 103,617 total sales. This growth was experienced across most of the country, with Na h-Eileanan Siar and East Lothian showing the largest increases between 2016 and 2017, at 16.8% and 16.6% respectively. Only three local authorities reported decreases: Clackmannanshire (–7.6%), Midlothian (–2%), and Dundee City (–1%). The value of the Scottish market for residential property increased by 8.5% in 2017, compared to 2016, to £17.9 billion, continuing the upward trend since 2011.

These figures are put in perspective by another Registers of Scotland publication, *Property Market Report 2007–08 to 2017–18*. For residential property, the total number of sales in 2017–18 is still 31.3% less than before the recession, in 2007–08. For non-residential property the decline since 2007–08 is 15.4%, although there was a 71.4% increase in sales between 2012–13 and 2017–18. The total market value of non-residential sales in 2017–18 was £4.3 billion (which is around a quarter of the value of residential sales). Some 725 commercial leases were registered in 2017–18 (1,178 in 2007–08). Cash sales have become much more common in the residential sector, accounting for 31.7% of all sales in 2017–18 as compared with only 15.5% of sales in 2007–08.

New edition of the Scottish Standard Clauses

The third edition of the Scottish Standard Clauses 'came into force' on 1 November 2018 – although there is nothing to stop parties from using earlier editions, whether deliberately or by inadvertence. The text of the third edition can be found at www.lawscot.org.uk/members/rules-and-guidance/rules-and-guidance/section-f/division-c/advice-and-information/scottish-standard-clauses/.

The November 2018 issue of the *Journal of the Law Society* (p 34) carries a helpful article by Ross Mackay, the chair of the Standard Clauses Review Group, setting out the main changes from the second edition. Only a few need be mentioned here. There is now a warranty that the seller is not a corporate body registered in any jurisdiction outwith the UK (cl 19.5). Clause 28.2 asks that the seller should have been in possession for a year, which is the period stipulated in s 86(3)(a) of the Land Registration etc (Scotland) Act 2012 in relation to realignment. There is now, for the first time, a clause (cl 31) on home reports. This includes a warranty by the seller that the information in the property questionnaire is true and correct, and is unchanged since the questionnaire was first issued. Finally, a new clause 31 acknowledges the coming into force on 26 February 2018 of the Contract (Third Party Rights) (Scotland) Act 2017 by excluding any third-party rights under that Act.

No doubt ideas for further amendments will continue to circulate. For example, one solicitor (Ed Wright), troubled by the difficulty of extracting discharges of standard securities from certain lenders, would like a new clause assigning to the seller's solicitor, and also to the buyer and buyer's solicitor, the seller's right to require the lender to discharge the security: see (2018) 63 *Journal of the Law Society of Scotland* July/6.

Another solicitor (Willie MacRae) argues for a clause allowing buyers to withdraw from the contract up until 14 days before the date of entry on payment of a penalty of, say, 3% of the price: see bit.ly/2u7oKve. This ready means of exiting is conceived of as an encouragement to buyers to conclude missives more swiftly, the point being that it would make it safer for them to conclude even though their finance is not yet fully in place.

Law reform

Three publications of the Scottish Law Commission in 2018 (all available on the Commission's website: www.scotlawcom.gov.uk) deal with or touch on conveyancing law and practice.

Termination of commercial leases

A discussion paper published for consultation in May 2018 – *Discussion Paper No 165 on Aspects of Leases: Termination* – examines various aspects of termination of commercial leases. The consultation closed on 14 September 2018.

There is much in the paper about notices to quit (chs 3 and 4). A number of open questions are posed. Should such notices by governed by the Sheriff Courts (Scotland) Act 1907? Should there be a prescribed form of notice or only a list of essential content (and, if the latter, what should that content comprise)? Is 40 days an appropriate period of notice, and should it be possible for parties to make provision in the lease for a longer, or even a shorter, period? Should the rules as to the content and period be the same for all commercial leases or should there be different rules depending on, for example, duration or extent or type of lease subjects? Should it be possible to serve a notice by electronic means?

The importance of notices to quit, however, will diminish if the doctrine of tacit relocation is either abolished or made capable of being excluded in the lease. Both possibilities are canvassed in the Law Commission's paper (ch 2). Under current law, it is not possible to have a lease which comes to an end automatically at the contractual ish. In the absence of a notice to quit, the lease will always continue by tacit relocation. By contrast to the position in other countries, it appears that tacit relocation cannot be contracted out of.

The other topics covered in the paper are (i) apportionment of rent (ch 5), (ii) the Tenancy of Shops (Scotland) Act 1949 (ch 6), (iii) irritancy (ch 7), and (iv) *confusio* and *consolidatio* (ch 8).

In relation to (i), the paper asks whether, in the light of the decision of the Supreme Court in the English case of *Marks and Spencer plc v BNP Paribas Securities Services Trust Co (Jersey) Ltd* [2015] UKSC 72, [2016] AC 742, it should be possible to recover rent paid in advance, *pro rata*, in the event of the early termination of lease.

In relation to (ii), the Scottish Law Commission is attracted to the idea of repealing the 1949 Act on the ground that its provision for security of tenure (a series of one-year extensions by application to the court) has become outdated in the modern market where many 'shop-keepers' are multi-national companies.

On irritancy, the paper draws attention the Scottish Law Commission's earlier but unimplemented recommendations, contained in *Report No 191 on Irritancy in Leases of Land* (2003), and asks whether the law is still in need of reform.

Finally, the paper analyses the law of confusion/consolidation as it applies to leases and, finding it to be unclear, asks whether it should be reformed so that consolidation operates only on the performance of some positive act such as the registration of a minute. Alone among the chapters in the discussion paper, this chapter applies to all leases and not merely to commercial leases.

Section 53 of the Title Conditions (Scotland) Act 2003

Section 53 of the Title Conditions (Scotland) Act 2003 was added by the Scottish Government to the then Title Conditions Bill at a late stage in its Parliamentary progress. The addition was opposed by the Scottish Law Commission, which had been responsible for preparing the Bill. Unfortunately, s 53 has caused a great deal of trouble. The policy behind it – to confer mutual enforcement rights in relation to real burdens within housing estates and other 'communities', if the burdens were created as a common scheme before the appointed day (28 November 2004) – is unexceptionable. But the chosen means, with its reliance on the idea of 'related properties', are fatally unclear, meaning that it is often difficult to know when s 53 does or does not apply – and hence, often, whether real burdens were extinguished on the appointed day (28 November 2004) or, on the contrary, continue on in vigorous good health.

Public attention was drawn to these difficulties by a report issued by the Justice Committee of the Scottish Parliament on 5 June 2013: *Inquiry into the effectiveness of the Title Conditions (Scotland) Act 2013* (www.scottish.parliament.uk/parliamentarybusiness/CurrentCommittees/64203.aspx): see *Conveyancing 2013* p 93. This recommended that s 53 be referred to the Scottish Law Commission, and a formal reference to the Commission was made by the Scottish Government on 31 August 2013. The Commission's preliminary proposals were issued for consultation in May 2018: see *Discussion Paper No 164 on Section 53 of the Title Conditions (Scotland) Act 2003*. The consultation closed on 31 August 2018. A final report is expected in the course of 2019.

Rather than the open questions of the discussion paper on termination of leases (discussed above), the discussion paper on s 53 offers a set of fully-worked proposals. A single provision would replace both s 53 and also s 52, a provision which covers similar territory to s 53 but which does so by restating the former common law. In place of the indicative but non-exhaustive examples of 'related' properties found in s 53 there would be a clear set of rules as to when mutual enforcement rights arise in respect of burdens imposed on a number of properties under a common scheme. Three main rules are proposed. Owners of properties affected by common scheme burdens should have mutual rights of enforcement where: (i) the properties are tenement flats; (ii) the burdens provide for common management in respect of the community; or (iii) the properties are close together – leaving open for the moment the question of what 'close' might mean for this purpose.

Law of contract

The Scottish Law Commission's longstanding project on contract law has already resulted in two Acts of Parliament: the Legal Writings (Counterparts and Delivery) (Scotland) Act 2015 (see *Conveyancing 2015* pp 125–33 and 167–69) and the Contract (Third Party Rights) (Scotland) Act 2017 (see *Conveyancing 2017* p 71). Now, a final report on contract law, *Report No 252 on Review of Contract Law: Formation, Interpretation, Remedies for Breach, and Penalty Clauses*, published in March 2018, brings the project to a close.

Assuming that the recommendations in the report are accepted by the Scottish Government, the main legislative outcome will be a restatement of the rules of formation of contract, as set out in part 1 of the draft Bill which forms an appendix to the report. The main substantive change is the abolition of the postal rule (ie the rule that a contract is formed when an acceptance of an offer is put in the post). Instead, an acceptance, like an offer – or indeed a withdrawal, revocation, or rejection – will be subject to the normal rule, which is that it takes effect only upon notification to the intended addressee. Notification is the subject of s 13 of the draft Bill. Notification occurs on the offer etc reaching the person in question, that is to say, 'when it is made available to the person in such circumstances as make it reasonable to expect the person to be able to obtain access to it without undue delay'. This formulation is intended to be sufficiently general to cover electronic communications. In addition, the opportunity of a restatement is taken to fill one or two gaps in the existing law. For example, s 6 provides that an offer lapses 'on a fundamental change of circumstances', which is defined to include the death or incapacity of either of the parties.

At one time, the ambitious plan was to have a restatement of the rules of breach of contract, as well as detailed provisions on interpretation. Abolition of penalty clauses was also under consideration. For various reasons, including the response of consultees to earlier papers, none of this was in the end proceeded with. Instead, the draft Bill makes three specific changes (only) to the rules in relation to breach, of which perhaps the most important is a new general rule which limits the damages due where the claimant has contributed by his or her conduct to the loss (s 22). Under the current law, the equivalent law is tied to a requirement of showing concurrent contributory negligence in delict.

Working group on tenement maintenance

A working group was formed in March 2018 to consider new initiatives and mechanisms for facilitating communal repairs by owners within tenements. Initially convened by Ben Macpherson MSP, the working group is now convened by Graham Simpson MSP. Details of the group's membership as well as minutes of its meetings – there had been four at the time of writing – can be found at www.befs.org.uk/policy-topics/buildings-maintenance-2/.

One possible mechanism which has attracted attention is the Development Management Scheme ('DMS'), which was introduced in 2009 and provides a straightforward but fairly comprehensive scheme of management, including provision for annual budgeting: for a summary, see K G C Reid and G L Gretton, *Conveyancing* (5th edn, 2018) paras 16–08 ff. As matters currently stand, however, the DMS is optional, and take-up, while increasing, has been fairly poor. Registers of Scotland report that a total of 59 deeds have been registered applying the DMS. This breaks down by year as follows: 2011 – 1; 2012 – 6; 2015 – 8; 2016 – 13; 2017 – 12; and 2018 – 19. In interim recommendations for reform, published on its website on 16 January 2019, the working group suggests that the DMS might be made compulsory for new tenements (but with an exception for tenements with a small number of units), and that a version of the DMS might replace the Tenement Management Scheme even for existing tenements. Other proposals are that there should be a compulsory sinking fund, and a compulsory five-year inspection of the common parts by a qualified building professional. Monitoring and enforcing compliance would be an obvious difficulty here. The closing date for responses to these proposals was 27 February 2019.

Mention may also be made of another publication on the working group's website: Douglas Robertson's *Common Repair Provisions for Multi-Owned Property: A Cause for Concern* (10 January 2019).

Maintenance of Glasgow tenements

The need for a stronger culture of repairs is borne out by research on the physical condition of tenements in Glasgow. Back in 2012 Glasgow City Council set up a Commission to look at problems concerned with the factoring of residential properties and especially of flatted property, which comprises 70% or more of the housing stock in Glasgow. In its final report, published on 21 February 2014, the Glasgow Factoring Commission presented a gloomy, if familiar, picture of unpopular factors, recalcitrant owners and undone repairs. Although little in the way of evidence was presented, the Commission concluded that the condition of tenements in Glasgow was deteriorating. Possible reasons were said to include the decline in owner-occupation and the consequent rise of absentee landlord-owners concerned only with financial returns, and an influx of new owners who were unfamiliar with the traditional culture of joining together to carry out repairs. In what was often a thoughtful analysis, the Commission had a whole range of suggestions for making things better. The rights and responsibilities of tenement owners should be set out in a simple and accessible guide and publicised on a website. Factors should be more open and transparent with their clients and seek feedback on their services. Owners should be encouraged, or even required, to have regular 'MOT' surveys of the building, establish reserve funds, and take out policies of common insurance.

Building on this earlier work, Glasgow City Council is currently engaged on a research project on the city's pre-1919 tenement stock – some 70,000 flats in all. An interim report issued in November 2018 noted that around £5–6 million of Council money was being spent each year to assist with repairs to tenements. Nonetheless, tenements were at increased risk of catastrophic failure (para 3.2):

In the past 2/3 years a growing number of tenement properties have either had to be evacuated or had emergency stabilisation works carried out, having been classed as dangerous buildings. Many require extensive repair works which could cost in excess of £500,000 to return them to a good state of repair.

Three case studies are given.

A working group is to be formed with commercial property factors and property owners to determine and quantify the extent of disrepair within the pre-1919 tenement stock and to report back by the end of 2019. This will be supplemented by a stock-condition survey of around 500 tenements across a minimum of ten different areas of the city.

Amendments to Code of Practice for Factors

Around 400 property factors are registered under the Property Factors (Scotland) Act 2011, with approximately 620,000 property addresses and 2,500 land records searchable on the register. In addition to registration, the 2011 Act provided for a Code of Conduct to be prepared by the Scottish Ministers (s 13). This was implemented by the Property Factors (Code of Conduct) (Scotland) Order 2012, SSI 2012/217; the Code itself can be found at www.scotland.gov.uk/Publications/2012/07/6791/0. In 2017 the Scottish Government consulted on whether amendments were required to the Code, and for that purpose a draft revised Code was prepared: see www.gov.scot/Publications/2017/10/5817. The main proposed changes were summarised in *Conveyancing 2017* pp 91–92.

The consultation closed on 15 January 2018, and an analysis of the rather mixed responses from some 102 individuals and organisations was published on 29 June 2018 (www.gov.scot/publications/consultation-draft-revised-code-conduct-registered-property-factors-analysis-responses/). Further developments are awaited.

Review of tenancy deposit schemes

Tenancy deposit schemes were introduced for the residential private-rented sector by the Tenancy Deposit Schemes (Scotland) Regulations 2011, SSI 2011/176, made under ss 120–122 of the Housing (Scotland) Act 2006. The purpose was to deal with what was seen as the abuse of the deposit typically exacted of tenants at the beginning of a lease and sometimes retained without good reason at the end. One of the findings of the Scottish Government's *Review of the Private Rented Sector* in 2009 (see *Conveyancing 2009* pp 75–76) was that between 8,000 and 11,000 tenants per year may have part or all of their tenancy deposits unfairly withheld.

The 2011 Regulations allow private providers to set up nationwide schemes for the safeguarding of tenancy deposits. Three such schemes have been set up: Letting Protection Service Scotland; MyDeposits Scotland; and Safe Deposits Scotland. The last of these is used by more than half of all landlords, while the second is used by around a third.

Under the Regulations, landlords must pay deposits into one of the schemes within 30 working days of receipt (see reg 3(1) and, for the sanctions for breach, reg 10). There are some exemptions, corresponding to the leases exempt from landlord registration under the Antisocial Behaviour etc (Scotland) Act 2004 s 83(6) (eg holiday lets). The deposit is held until the end of the lease. It is normally released following a request by the landlord, which must state how much is to be paid to the landlord and how much to the tenant, and requires to be approved by the tenant, who is contacted directly by the scheme administrator (regs 24 and 25). If landlord and tenant are unable to agree, the tenant can refer matters to the dispute resolution service which every scheme must provide free of charge. Some disputes have reached the courts, mainly in relation to a landlord's initial failure to pay a deposit into a scheme: see eg *Fraser v Meehan* 2013 SLT (Sh Ct) 119 and *Tenzin v Russell* 2014 Hous LR 17. Jurisdiction has now moved from the sheriff court to the Housing and Property Chamber of the First-tier Tribunal: decisions can be found here: www.housingandpropertychamber.scot/previous-tribunal-decisions.

The Scottish Government commissioned a review of the operation of tenancy deposit schemes, based on questionnaires and online surveys involving users, and this was published on 21 December 2018: see https://www2.gov.scot/Publications/2018/12/2976. The response to the schemes was generally favourable, and in most cases the schemes were working well. For example, almost eight out of ten tenants received their deposit back on time and the majority received it in full. The most common reason for deductions was damage to the property, followed by rent arrears. Some tenants – mainly students, especially those from overseas – failed to claim their deposits. Low interest rates were a source of concern for the schemes, which rely on interest for income (as they are not allowed to charge fees to landlords or tenants).

Consultation on a review of landlord registration applications and fees

On 15 March 2018 the Scottish Government launched a consultation, *Landlord Registration in Scotland: Consultation on a review of landlord registration applications and fees* (www.gov.scot/publications/landlord-registration-scotland-consultation-review-landlord-registration-applications-fees/), seeking views on a possible requirement for landlords to provide additional information about compliance with legal duties, and on a range of options for increasing application fees.

In total, there were 239 responses to the consultation, of which 80 were from organisations, 95 from individuals and 64 from those who identified themselves as landlords. The analysis of responses (www2.gov.scot/Publications/2018/11/6101/0), published on 23 November 2018, showed general support for the proposals in respect of additional information, subject to some concerns as to increased workloads for landlords, but general opposition to the proposals as to fees. In addition, a number of general themes emerged:

- A need for changes to the online registration system which is currently perceived not to be user-friendly or fit for purpose.

- Concerns over how the proposals will fit with current data protection and GDPR requirements.
- The need for enforcement to be applied in order to deal with rogue landlords, with a perception from some that landlords who do register are currently subsidising rogue landlords who do not register.
- A need for consistent administration across Scotland, with some suggestions for a national registration system to be operated across Scotland rather than having 32 different systems which lead to duplication of effort and inconsistency across Scotland.
- Requests for transparency in how local authorities make up their charges.
- The suggested proposals (or some of them) will duplicate information provided which is already required through other legislation.

Registration of small landholdings

Small landholdings and their close cousins, statutory small tenancies, are one of the mysteries of the law of landlord and tenant. They are largely absent from standard general works on landlord and tenant such as Angus McAllister's *Scottish Law of Leases* (4th edn, 2013) (but see paras 16.3 and 16.4) and *Leases* (2015) by Robert Rennie et al (but see para 30-10), although books on crofting tend to provide some coverage. A little is said about their history by Ewen Cameron, in *No Ordinary Court: 100 Years of the Scottish Land Court* (2012) pp 25 ff.

It comes as something of a surprise, therefore, to find that the whole topic has recently been investigated with a view to the possible creation of a scheme of registration. The investigation was funded by the Scottish Government and led by Dr Annie Tindley, a historian at Newcastle University, with legal input from Malcolm Combe of Aberdeen University. The result was published on 16 November 2018 as *Small Landholdings Landownership & Registration: Project Report* (www2.gov.scot/Publications/2018/11/3809). It is a fascinating account of the history of this type of tenancy based on selective archival work especially in the archives of the Board of Agriculture in Scotland and the Scottish Land Court. Both of these bodies were set up by the Small Landholders (Scotland) Act 1911, the legislation which also established small landholdings. The 1911 Act remains the principal legislation today.

Small landholdings were conceived of as a sort of crofting-like tenure for the non-crofting counties. The Board of Agriculture was charged with matching demand for this type of tenure to supply by negotiating with landowners to provide suitable land. Once a farm was identified, and innumerable legal and administrative hurdles surmounted, the farm would be divided into, say, half a dozen small landholdings. As with crofting, there was security of tenure and controlled rent. Landowners were paid compensation although, oddly, only where they objected to the scheme. In time this came to be fixed at 25 years' worth of rental value, ie of the difference between the previous rent and the new 'fair' rent set by the Scottish Land Court. Once a small landholding was established, the maintenance of the scheme became the responsibility of the landowner who had, for example, to find a replacement tenant if the original tenant died or gave up the tenancy.

After a slow start, the number of small landholdings grew in the 1920s, partly to provide a livelihood for men returning from the war. At its peak in the 1930s there were around 476 such holdings. Today there are thought to be only 68. Factors contributing to this decline were rural depopulation and also the capital cost of mechanisation which could often hardly be justified for a small agricultural holding.

The archives are rich for the early period, when many schemes were being set up, but sparse thereafter, so that it is often difficult to trace current tenants of smallholdings or the history of their title. The creation of a register would therefore be of value. As to whether it could be done, Dr Tindley and her team acknowledge the difficulties but think that a register could be compiled by a team which included a PhD student at a cost of around £130,000. It is to be hoped that the Scottish Government will be willing to support this initiative.

As part, presumably, of the same exercise, the Scottish Government has also published a useful booklet by Sir Crispin Agnew of Lochnaw QC on *Small Landholdings Legislation: A guide to the law in Scotland* (available at www.gov.scot/publications/small-landholdings-legislation-guide-law-scotland/).

Common good property

In provisions which came into force on 27 June 2018, the Community Empowerment (Scotland) Act 2015 requires every local authority to compile a 'common good register', ie a register of all property which is held as part of the common good. This must be made available for public inspection free of charge, including on a website (s 102). In addition, before taking any decision to dispose of or change the use of common good property, a local authority must publish details of its proposal, notify community councils and any community body with an interest in the property, and consider representations (s 104).

During the course of 2017 the Scottish Government undertook a public consultation on statutory guidance for local authorities as to how to fulfil these requirements: see www.gov.scot/Publications/2017/06/7704. An analysis of the responses to the consultation was published on 24 November 2017 (www.gov.scot/Publications/2017/11/9276). For details, see *Conveyancing 2017* p 101.

The statutory guidance itself was published on 23 July 2018: see www.gov.scot/publications/community-empowerment-common-good-property-guidance-local-authorities/. In relation to the common good register, for example, the guidance says that (para 1.7):

> The list of common good property should include enough detail about each item to enable members of the public to identify and locate individual assets. The minimum information which should be included is given in Table 1. An example of what entries in the common good register might look like is given at Annex A.

Table 1: Minimum Information for Entries in a Common Good Register

Information	Detail
Former Burgh	The name of the burgh to which the property originally belonged.
Name of property	The name by which the asset or cash fund is generally known.
Description of	A brief description of what the asset is, or was, if now held as property cash.
Location of property	Information about the location of the asset, including a map or postcode/Unique Property Reference Number (UPRN)/OS reference if available. A member of the public should be able to use this information to accurately identify where the asset is. Where the property is a common good income fund or an item is in secure storage, it is not necessary to include a precise location. For income funds, the location details should include a statement that the annual accounts of the common good will provide more information on any use of income funds.

The guidance adds (para 1.9):

> When setting out the list of property, it is recommended that the list is split into sections for each of the former burghs, and then further subdivided by the type of property e.g. land, buildings, funds etc. to make it easy to navigate. Where the list contains a lot of information, the local authority should ensure that it has a search facility so that readers can easily find the information they are looking for.

Foreign ownership of land

For reasons which are unclear but may be the subject of speculation, Registers of Scotland have begun to issue data as to foreign ownership of land and buildings in Scotland. An initial report, issued in February 2018, was updated in August to show the position as at 30 June: see www.ros.gov.uk/data-and-statistics/land-and-property-titles-by-country-of-origin. Further reports can presumably be expected. The figures refer mainly to owners but also include those holding under a long lease.

Of the 1.54 million titles registered on the Land Register as at 30 June 2018, whether residential or non-residential, 7% (108,621 titles) related to titles for which one or more of the registered owners (buyers or tenants) had an identifiable address outside Scotland. For the most part (6%), this comprises owners based in other parts of the UK, so that only 1% of all registered titles are registered in the name of one or more owners from overseas. Of that 1% (15,730 titles in all), 83.5% cent of the proprietors were individuals and 11.5% were overseas companies. More than half (53.6%) of titles owned or leased by overseas companies were accounted for by four countries: Jersey, Isle of Man, British Virgin Islands and Guernsey (in that order). The USA was the most common country for individuals.

With regard to the absolute number of titles, Renfrewshire was the most popular area of Scotland for purchasers/tenants from abroad to buy or lease (18%). RoS, however, speculates that some of these holdings may relate to very small parcels of land such as parking spaces and storage facilities near to Glasgow airport; a large proportion (83.1%) relate to commercial leases. The next most popular areas are Fife (7.8%), Edinburgh (6.9%), Highland (6.4%), and Glasgow (5.5%).

Interesting as these figures are, however, they deal with title numbers and not extent, and so give no indication of the percentage of Scotland's land mass which is currently in foreign ownership. Furthermore, the significance of the figures may be questioned. For example, if Mr Smith in Leeds gets a job in Glasgow and buys a house there, he will be noted as being an 'English' owner even although his address and domicile from that point on will be 'Scottish'.

Land value tax

In a short briefing paper published on 10 December 2018, the Scottish Land Commission (https://landcommission.gov.scot/) became the latest body to examine the viability of some form of land value tax. Land, says the Commission, comprises just over half the net worth of the UK. Land values have increased more than 450% since 1995. Even allowing for inflation, some of that increase is created by society, or public bodies acting on behalf of society, rather than by the efforts of the landowner. In particular, it is created by (i) improvements in infrastructure; (ii) the grant of planning permission; and (iii) wider societal changes which make a particular area more valuable to live in. Currently, planning obligations are one of the main tools for capturing land value. That is the subject of a separate briefing note by the Scottish Land Commission (*Land Value Capture*) as well as a separate paper in the Commission's 'Land Lines' series written by Tony Crook (for which see below). But whereas planning obligations are one-off charges on developers, land value tax is typically a recurrent annual levy on all or a significant number of owners of land.

Land value tax is based on the unimproved value of land (ignoring buildings or infrastructure) but for the land's optimum use. Such a tax would be an innovation in the UK, although it has been tried in a number of other countries such as Denmark, Australia, Estonia, New Zealand, South Africa and Namibia. Apart from raising money, one of the claimed benefits of land value tax is that, since land is taxed on the basis of optimum use, it encourages the more productive use of land. It might have a useful role, for example, in respect of vacant or derelict land, although only where such land has development value.

A warning note is sounded by research commissioned by the Scottish Land Commission from the University of Reading which suggests that, 'although the theoretical case for the introduction of a land value tax is strong, there is a lack of empirical evidence that land value taxes have actually delivered the theoretical benefits attributed to them' (p 2): see *Investigation of Potential Land*

Value Tax Policy Options for Scotland: Final Report, published on the Commission's website on 23 July 2018. Any steps towards the introduction of such a task must therefore, the Land Commission says, 'be taken with caution' (p 2). Nonetheless, the Land Commission's stance is generally supportive, and work on the topic is continuing.

Scottish Land Commission: 'Land Lines' discussion papers

The Scottish Land Commission (https://landcommission.gov.scot/) has published a number of papers in its 'Land Lines' series. These are commissioned but independent studies, often on controversial topics, and are intended to stimulate debate to inform the Land Commission's longer-term research priorities. The first paper, on the housing land market, was published at the end of 2017: see *Conveyancing 2017* pp 96–97. Five further papers were published in 2018 and are described briefly below.

Limitations on the scale of landownership

In *Land: For the many, not the few? Limitations on the Scale of Land Ownership*, Peter Peacock argues that there should be limitations on the amount of land which can be owned by any one person, and also, perhaps, limitations on the concentration of ownership. As justifications, Mr Peacock mentions in particular: (i) fairness and social justice in sharing out a resource which, in Scotland, is concentrated in an unusually small number of hands; (ii) increased levels of economic activity following the breaking-up of large landholdings; (iii) addressing market failure: if estates are large, they can only be bought by the rich; and (iv) reducing local land monopolies and their consequent concentration of power.

Possible solutions are only lightly sketched. For new acquisitions, there could be an absolute limit to the extent of permitted ownership (though no actual figure is suggested), or alternatively certain types of acquisition might trigger a public-interest inquiry. The breaking-up of existing landholdings is not ruled out although the ECHR problems are acknowledged. A residency requirement could be introduced. There could also be nudge mechanisms to discourage large landholdings, such as higher or different taxation or the withdrawal of public grants and subsidies.

Mention should also be made of a research paper on this general topic. *Research on interventions to manage land markets and limit the concentration of land ownership elsewhere in the world* was written at the invitation of the Scottish Land Commission and can be found on the Commission's website. The authors are Jayne Glass, Rosalind Bryce, Martin Price, Leonie Schulz, Diana Valero (Centre for Mountain Studies, Perth College, University of the Highlands and Islands), Malcolm Combe (School of Law, University of Aberdeen), and Norman Hutchison (Centre for Real Estate Research, University of Aberdeen). Approval requirements for the ownership of land were found to exist in 18 of the 22 countries surveyed, either in respect of foreign ownership (12 countries) or of ownership by anyone of agricultural land (six countries). Outright bans on foreign ownership were uncommon, as were upper limits to the amount of land that any one individual or entity can own. Where upper limits did exist, they tended 'to be targeted at foreign land acquisitions and/or used as planning control mechanisms, rather than being used to restrict ownership rights or as mechanisms for redistribution'. Indeed, it was notable that the motivations for restrictions of various kinds were often rather different from likely motivations in Scotland.

Public-interest-led development

Steven Tolson and Archie Rintoul, both chartered surveyors, argue in *The Delivery of Public Interest Led Development in Scotland* that in the last 30 years the state has done too little in the way of organising development and instead relied too heavily on private developers. This, they argue, can be seen particularly in housing, where private developers concentrate on family homes at the expense of the smaller units which are in short supply. The state, perhaps acting through a new development agency, should take the lead in providing sites, infrastructure, capital, and so on. It is only in this way that significant new areas can be released for development, as was once done for the new towns. The authors hold up as models certain developments in countries such as Germany and the Netherlands, where public bodies have shown a more active, and more long-term, view of development.

Capturing development value

The question of how public bodies might capture development value, which was touched on in the previous paper, is one of the main subjects covered in *Local authority land acquisition in Germany and the Netherlands: are there lessons for Scotland?* The author is Tony Crook, Emeritus Professor of Town & Regional Planning at the University of Sheffield. The background is that a certain amount of development value is captured by way of taxation (CGT and LBTT) and by contributions to infrastructure and other planning obligations imposed as a condition of the grant of planning permission. The question is whether more development value could be captured. A related question is whether public bodies should be able to acquire land at existing-use value rather than, as at present, at market value. On the second question, Professor Crook warns of the risk of creating 'two market values, one for land CPO'd and another for land subject to private transactions' (p 26). There are ways of mitigating this but they are not straightforward. Drawing on the experience of Germany and the Netherlands, Professor Crook suggests a number of other possible approaches. For example, the clear and consistent use of planning obligations would allow developers to take this cost into account on deciding how much to pay for land, with the result that market values would decrease (if not down to existing-use value).

Human rights

Insofar as human rights have been discussed in the context of land reform, the discussion has tended to focus on the potential obstacle to reform created by the property protection clause in article 1 of the First Protocol ('A1P1') to the European Convention on Human Rights. In *Human Rights and the Work of the Scottish Land Commission*, Kirsteen Shields, a lecturer in international law at Edinburgh University, argues that it is wrong to focus exclusively on the ECHR, and indeed that the demands of the property protection clause can to some extent be balanced by recourse to other human rights instruments. Of particular importance, she says, are the economic, social and cultural rights embodied in the United Nations International Covenant on Economic, Social and Cultural Rights (ICESCR). Indeed, the ICESCR is expressly mentioned as an example of a relevant human rights instrument in s 1(6)(b) of the Land Reform (Scotland) Act 2016.

As well as including a range of economic, social and cultural rights, such as the rights to housing, work, education, cultural life, and health and food, the ICESCR also includes, in article 2, a positive obligation on ratifying states (such as the UK) to use their resources to their maximum availability to progress such rights. As a public body, and as one subject to the 2016 Act, the Scottish Land Commission is bound by the ICESCR.

In a concluding section, Dr Shields considers how the ICESCR might be relevant to different aspects of the Scottish Land Commission's current programme of work. For example, the Land Commission's interest in redeveloping vacant and derelict land for housing potentially promotes a number of ICESCR rights (p 11):

> For example, by using vacant land to create space for affordable homes, redevelopment could progress the right to housing. Also, by using the land to create community greenspaces or other public goods, redevelopment could progress the right to health (Art 12) and the right to take part in cultural activities (Art 15).

Encouraging lettings of agricultural land

In *Encouraging agricultural land lettings in Scotland for the 21st century*, Jeremy Moody, the Secretary and Advisor to the Central Association of Agricultural Valuers, charts the decline in the number of farm tenancies over the last century and makes proposals for their revitalisation. Today most farms are owner-occupied and are passed down families. Not only does this mean that farms rarely come on the market, it also carries the risk that land is being farmed by those with only limited aptitude for farming: after all, 'the next Olympics team would not be drawn solely from the children of past Olympians' (p 7). Mr Moody attributes the decline in the tenanted sector partly to the complexity of the agricultural holdings legislation and partly to a growing perception among landowners that tenancies are 'high risk and low return'. In respect of the latter, Mr Moody writes (p 6) that:

> Whether or not substantial land reform is under way, the rhetoric accompanying the topic is deterring those anxious to avoid anything that makes their position less flexible, especially as the market for farmland is relatively illiquid when compared to many financial assets. As owners, whether estates or farmers, typically have long term perspectives, they can reduce their exposure to such risks by using other

arrangements or adopting other land uses, in turn reducing the supply of land to the formal let market.

Among the possible methods of encouraging more letting of agricultural land, the paper proposes in particular (i) simpler and shorter legislation which focuses on essentials, and (ii) a significant measure of income tax relief for rental income from agricultural land.

Review of community ownership mechanisms

In 2017 the Scottish Land Commission was asked by the Scottish Government to review the existing mechanisms for the community right-to-buy. The first step was the commissioning of a research report from a team comprising Rob McMorran (Scotland's Rural College), Anna Lawrence (Random Forest Ltd), Jayne Glass (Perth College UHI), Jon Hollingdale (Community Woodland Association), Annie McKee (James Hutton Institute), Diane Campbell (Independent Consultant), and Malcolm Combe (School of Law, University of Aberdeen). Their report, *Review of the effectiveness of current community ownership mechanisms and of options for supporting the expansion of community ownership in Scotland*, is available on the Land Commission website (https://landcommission.gov.scot/). Their overall conclusions (p vi) were as follows:

> The mechanisms and support frameworks through which communities can achieve ownership have evolved considerably and further opportunities for increasing community ownership clearly exist. Nevertheless, in relation to the existing mechanisms communities often report challenging, frustrating and exhausting experiences: relationships with public and private asset owners are at times undermined and attempts to acquire assets via legislative routes can take many years to accomplish, or are unsuccessful. Negotiated sales and transfers are widely considered the preferred route to ownership; however, often communities are channelled towards legislative processes and more could be done to facilitate and support negotiated routes to ownership. The processes of community acquisition are widely perceived as unduly complex, onerous and time-consuming. Considerable scope exists for further simplification and alignment of legislative processes, and for enhancing guidance and support.
>
> The provision of sufficient post-acquisition development funding is critical to ensuring long-term sustainable development of assets and communities, particularly in the most disadvantaged communities. Currently asset acquisitions often occur in a reactive way and considerable scope exists for developing a more strategic approach to community asset transfer as part of local community planning processes. Furthermore, the current fiscal and policy framework contributes to increasing land values. This reinforces existing patterns of ownership and inhibits community ownership and, by extension, sustainable development.

On the basis of these conclusions, and of the research paper as a whole, the Scottish Land Commission on 15 November 2018 published a brief paper, *Community Ownership and Community Right to Buy: Recommendations to Scottish Ministers*. Its 'key recommendation' was that 'a clear vision is now needed for the way in which community ownership matures over the coming decades to be a mainstream route to delivering sustainable development for communities across rural and urban Scotland' (p 2). The vision should address:

- a clear articulation of the outcomes that community ownership delivers – recognising that it is not an end in itself but a means to delivering wider development and regeneration outcomes;
- a shift from community acquisition being driven either by specific problems or being reactive to land coming to the market, towards being a normal, designed part of community planning, development, and regeneration;
- a presumption for negotiated transactions between a willing seller and willing buyer being the norm, with statutory rights to buy or asset transfer being used only where this is not possible; and
- a recognition that community ownership is entirely normal, and a pathway that is open to all communities.

'In order to build this vision and delivery', the paper continued (p 3), 'the Commission propose to work with the Scottish Government to bring relevant stakeholders together in a Community Ownership Delivery Group (CODG). To support this work, the paper sets out seven 'strategic delivery recommendations'. These are:

1. Proactive consideration of community land and asset ownership is embedded as an integral part of local place planning processes.
2. Development of a new suite of indicators to replace the 'million acres' target with targets and indicators that reflect the outcomes sought from community ownership and are relevant to both rural and urban contexts.
3. Support for enabling community ownership should be further developed to:
   - provide consistent support equivalent to that provided by Highlands & Islands Enterprise (HIE) across the whole of Scotland (including within the remit of the South of Scotland Enterprise Agency);
   - provide support to landowners as well as communities in order to encourage and enable negotiated transfers; and
   - include a proactive communications strategy and programme of education and awareness raising for communities across Scotland.
4. Adopt a more proactive and strategic approach to the potential transfer of publicly owned land.
5. Consider long term financial support beyond the immediate commitments to the Scottish Land Fund including capital and development funding.
6. The Scottish Land Commission consider the impact of tax and fiscal policy on the expansion of community land ownership as part of its wider Programme of Work.
7. Consider opportunities for simplification and consolidation of statutory right to buy provisions.

Land reform: NGOs and community groups

A report carried out by Amelia Kuch on behalf of the Scottish Government examines the relationship between environmental NGOs and local communities: see *Environment and Land Reform: Examining relations between Non-Governmental*

Organisations and Community Groups (www.gov.scot/publications/environment-land-reform-examining-relations-between-non-governmental-organisations-community-groups/). Eight environmental organisations – National Trust for Scotland, RSPB, John Muir Trust, Scottish Wildlife Trust, Woodland Trust Scotland, Borders Forest Trust, Plantlife and Trees for Life – own between them around 2.6% of Scotland's land mass. On the basis of interviews with representatives from some of these bodies and also from other organisations, the report suggests a slightly troubled relationship between NGOs and their local communities, with difficulties of reconciling NGO objectives with local needs, and a pattern of communication which is often sporadic in nature. Incompatible working paces and capacity – a professional organisation set alongside a group of part-time volunteers – have tended to limit the amount of long-term co-operation.

The most interesting part of the report is the view of NGOs on the shortcomings of the various community rights to buy (para 4.4):

> Overall, NGOs interviewed highlighted that Land Reform Act 2016 prioritises ownership over the type and style of management and that communities that come into land ownership struggle to access resources for improving land management. As one participant explained:

>> 'We are concerned that the Land Reform was very focused on land ownership and not on how land was used and managed. We want a better link between these two things. Changing who owns the land doesn't necessarily influence how it's managed unless you have a clear idea of what you want that difference to be.'

> The discussion about ownership vs. management of land was a prominent trope in many interviews with landowning NGOs. When asked about community land ownership on or around NGOs' estates, research participants expressed sceptical views, highlighting challenges community groups were likely to encounter, such as: lack of access to financial resources following the buyout, shortages of time, lack of land management knowledge, lack of coherence and sustainability within the community groups themselves, lack of clear vision for the newly acquired assets. The majority of the respondents identified the main problem in the disproportionate amount of funding available for the purchase of land as compared to the resources available for developing and managing the land.

Scottish Vacant and Derelict Land Survey 2017

The Scottish Government conducts an annual survey of vacant and derelict land based on returns from local authorities. 'Vacant' land is land which is unused for the purposes for which it is held and is viewed as an appropriate site for development; the land must either have had prior development on it or preparatory work must have taken place in anticipation of future development. 'Derelict' land (and buildings) is land which has been so damaged by development that it is incapable of development for beneficial use without rehabilitation. The annual surveys may be watched with greater attention following the introduction of a community right to buy abandoned, neglected or detrimental land by s 74 of the Community Empowerment (Scotland) Act 2015, which came into force on 27 June 2018: see p 92 above.

Key findings from the 2017 survey (published on 26 June 2018: www.gov. scot/publications/scottish-vacant-derelict-land-survey-2017/) include (pp 7–9):

- The total amount of derelict and urban vacant land in Scotland has decreased by 844 hectares (7%) in the latest year, from 12,493 hectares in 2016 to 11,649 hectares in 2017.
- The net decrease of 844 hectares (7%) between 2016 and 2017 is the result of 857 hectares being brought back into use (includes 514 hectares of former Royal Ordnance sites in Renfrewshire), 109 hectares recorded as naturalised, the addition of 229 hectares in new sites and a net decrease of 107 hectares as a result of changes to existing sites.
- Of the 11,649 hectares of derelict and urban vacant land recorded in the 2017 survey, 2,075 hectares (18%) were classified as urban vacant and 9,574 hectares (82%) were classified as derelict.
- For those sites where the previous use is known, 38% of derelict land recorded in 2017 had been previously used for mineral activity (3,559 hectares), 21% for manufacturing (1,922 hectares), and a further 14% for defence (1,260 hectares). For urban vacant land, where previous use is known, the largest area was previously in residential use (17%, 302 hectares) and the second largest area had a previous use for agriculture (16%, 279 hectares).
- Of the 229 hectares of new derelict and urban vacant land reported by local authorities, the largest area had previous land uses related to mineral activity, 61 hectares, 27% of new land reported.
- East Ayrshire has the largest amount of recorded derelict and urban vacant land, with 2,401 hectares (21% of the Scotland total). Highland has the second largest amount with 1,342 hectares (12%), North Ayrshire is third with 1,335 hectares (11%), followed by North Lanarkshire with 1,282 hectares (11%) then Glasgow City with 1,069 hectares (9%).
- 29.8% of Scotland's population are estimated to live within 500 metres of a derelict site in 2017. This varies by local authority area from 0.9% in Shetland and 1.0% in Orkney to 61.7% in Glasgow and 75.8% in North Lanarkshire.
- 59% of people living in the most deprived decile in Scotland are estimated to live within 500 metres of derelict land, compared to 12% of people in the least deprived decile.
- 2,685 hectares (25%) of derelict and urban vacant land in 2017 was reported to be developable in the short term, with an expectation of development within five years. A total of 2,784 hectares (26%) of derelict and urban vacant land is seen by local authorities as being uneconomic to develop and/or is viewed as suitable to reclaim for a 'soft' end use (i.e. non-built use).
- The most common use for derelict and urban vacant land brought back into use since the previous survey was residential, with 152 of the 317 listed reused sites (48%) reclaimed for this purpose – covering 194 hectares. The largest area of land was brought back into use as passive open space, 527 hectares (61%) – 506 hectares of this was a single former Royal Ordnance site in Renfrewshire.
- Of the 857 hectares of derelict or urban vacant land reused in 2017, a total of 62 hectares (7%) involved some form of public funding, either a full or partial contribution.
- Since its inception in 2005/06, the Scottish Government's Vacant and Derelict Land Fund has contributed (either fully or partially) to the reuse of 386 hectares

(in total) of previously derelict and urban vacant land across Dundee City, Glasgow City, Highland, North Lanarkshire, South Lanarkshire and more recently Fife.

- The total amount of derelict and urban vacant land has decreased each year between 2011 and 2017 (annual decreases ranging from 1.2% to 6.8%), except for 2014 when there was an increase of 2,090 hectares (18.8%) compared to 2013, largely due to over 2,200 hectares of former surface coal mine sites in East Ayrshire that had become derelict following the liquidation of Scottish Coal and ATH Resources in 2013.

- There has been a cumulative increase of 258 hectares (2 per cent) in the total amount of derelict and urban vacant land recorded since 2011 – from 11,391 hectares in 2011 to 11,649 hectares in 2017. However when excluding derelict mineral sites there has been a cumulative decrease of 1,393 hectares (15%) in the total amount of derelict and urban vacant land since 2011.

Compulsory sales orders

Mention was made above of the community right to buy abandoned, neglected or detrimental land, which was introduced by s 74 of the Community Empowerment (Scotland) Act 2015. In theory, another way of dealing with derelict land and buildings is for the relevant local authority to use compulsory powers to acquire it. The difficulty here, however, is that the local authority might well have no wish to make the acquisition, or have no use for the property once acquired. Against this background it has been suggested that a useful additional power for planning authorities would be a power to require that derelict land be put on the market and sold by auction. The suggested mechanism is a compulsory sales order ('CSO'). This idea apparently has the support of the Scottish Government, so that there is likely to be legislation in due course. Meanwhile, the Scottish Land Commission (https://landcommission. gov.scot) has published a paper, *Compulsory Sales Orders*, as a way of testing how such a scheme might work.

Under the Land Commission's proposals, the power to use a CSO would be restricted to, for example, sites that (i) are relatively small, (ii) are not used for any productive purpose, (iii) are causing demonstrable harm to the surrounding community, (iv) are located within or on the immediate periphery of existing settlements, and (v) have previously been developed (ie brownfield rather than greenfield sites) (para 3.1.1). The owner of the site would, of course, have a right to object to the CSO, and there would be a mechanism for adjudication of the different interests at stake. The Commission sees CSOs as a stimulus to regeneration even in cases where, in the end, they do not have to be used (para 2.4).

Scottish Housing Condition Survey 2017

Key findings from this informative annual study (published on 4 December 2018: www2.gov.scot/Publications/2018/12/8868) include the following:

- In 2017, 42% of Scottish homes were rated as EPC band C or better and half had an energy efficiency rating of 67 or higher (SAP 2012). This is a significant increase from 39% in 2016 and continues the improving trend from 35% in 2014, the first year in which data based on SAP 2012 is available.
- The level of disrepair was unchanged from last year, with 68% of all dwellings having some degree of disrepair, however minor. Disrepair to critical elements stood at 50%, while 28% of dwellings had some instance of urgent disrepair, and 5% had some extensive disrepair. While these figures are not statistically different from 2016, there is still a longer-term trend of improvement.
- Levels of damp and condensation improved slightly compared to 2016. 91% of properties were free from any damp or condensation, up from 89%
- Levels of compliance with the tolerable standard in 2017 remained similar to 2016: 1% (or 24,000) of all dwellings fell below the tolerable standard. Longer term this represents an improvement of 3 percentage points since 2012.
- Across the stock as a whole, Scottish Housing Quality Standard (SHQS) compliance improved on 2016 levels. In 2017, 40% of Scottish homes failed to meet the SHQS, down from 45% in 2016.
- The SHQS failure rate in the social sector was 37%, not allowing for abeyances and exemptions. This has fallen from 60% in 2010. 26% of properties did not meet the Energy Efficient criterion.
- Overcrowding levels in Scotland remain unchanged: 3% of all households (66,000) were living in overcrowded accommodation in 2017.

Housing Statistics 2017–18

The annual survey of housing discloses the fifth consecutive increase in completion of new-build homes, this now being at the highest level since before the recession in 2009–10. Full details of the housing statistics can be found in *Housing Statistics for Scotland 2018: Key Trends Summary* (www.gov. scot/publications/housing-statistics-scotland-2018-key-trends-summary/). In summary:

Housing Supply (Private and Public Sector)
- *New housing supply:* New housing supply (new build, refurbishment and conversions) increased by 745 homes (4%) between 2016–17 and 2017–18, from 18,683 to 19,428 units. Housing association new builds increased by 382 homes (14%) and local authority new builds increased by 381 homes (34%), whilst private-led new builds decreased by 325 homes (2%). Refurbishments (rehabilitations) increased by 359 homes (60%) and net conversions decreased by 52 homes (7%).
- *New house building:* In 2017–18, 17,731 new build homes were completed in Scotland, an increase of 438 homes (3%) on the 17,293 completions in the previous year, the fifth consecutive annual increase and the highest annual number of completions since 2008–09. During the same time-period the number of homes started decreased by 129 homes (1%) from 19,724 to 19,595.
- *Affordable housing:* In 2017–18, there were 8,534 units completed through all Affordable Housing Supply Programme (AHSP) activity, an increase of 1,198 units (16%) on the previous year. Approvals increased by 1,401 units (14%) in the latest year to reach 11,677 in 2017–18, and starts increased by 1,261 units (14%) to reach 10,569. This activity represents the first two years in the target period to build

50,000 affordable homes, including 35,000 for social rent, over the five year period from 2016–17 to 2020–21.

Local Authority Housing

- *Local authority housing stock:* At 31 March 2018, there were 314,482 local authority dwellings in Scotland, a slight decrease of 334 units (0.1%) from the previous year.
- *Sales of local authority dwellings (Right to Buy):* Sales of public authority dwellings (including local authorities with total stock transfers) fell by 40% in 2017–18, to 2,101. This decrease follows the Right to Buy scheme closing to all new applicants in July 2016. It is expected that sales will continue to fall further in the next year as the number of applications remaining in the system falls closer to zero.
- *Vacant stock:* Local authorities reported 7,140 units of vacant stock at 31 March 2018, 976 units (16%) more than the 6,164 vacant units in the previous year, driven by increases in units awaiting demolition (an increase of 503 units), units part of a modernisation programme (an increase of 310 units), and vacant normal letting stock (an increase of 319 units). Vacant units used as temporary accommodation for the homeless fell by seven, and vacant units in low demand areas fell by 149 units.
- *Lettings:* During 2017–18 there were 25,666 permanent lettings made, a slight decrease of 122 units (0.5%) compared to 25,788 lettings in the previous year. There were 10,805 lets to homeless households in 2017–18, which equates to 42% of all permanent lets by local authorities.
- *Evictions:* Eviction actions against local authority tenants resulted in 1,460 evictions or abandoned dwellings in 2017–18 (1,023 evictions, 437 abandoned dwellings). This is up by 3%, or 39 actions of evictions or abandonments, on the 1,421 in the previous year.
- *Housing lists:* Household applications held on local authority or common housing register lists decreased by 3% or 4,346 households to 157,806 at March 2018, the tenth consecutive annual decrease.

Local Authority Housing Assistance and Licensing

- *Scheme of assistance:* There were 9,049 scheme of assistance grants paid to householders in 2017–18, 1,434 grants (14%) fewer than in 2016–17. Spend on scheme of assistance grants totalled £29.8 million, around £2 million less than in 2016–17. The majority of grants in 2017–18 were for disabled adaptations; 5,599 grants totalling £21.9 million.
- *Houses in multiple occupation:* In 2017–18, 9,025 applications were received in respect of the mandatory licensing scheme for houses in multiple occupation (including new applications and applications for renewal). At 31 March 2018 there were 15,671 licences in force, representing an increase of 2% over the previous year.

Books

Douglas Bain, Roderick R M Paisley, Andrew R C Simpson and Nikola J M Tait (eds), *Northern Lights: Essays in Private Law in Memory of Professor David Carey Miller* (Aberdeen University Press 2018; ISBN 9781857520712)

Malcolm M Combe, *The ScotWays Guide to the Law of Access to Land in Scotland* (Birlinn Ltd 2018; ISBN 9781910900284)

George L Gretton and Kenneth G C Reid, *Conveyancing*, 5th edn (W Green 2018; ISBN 9780414032545)

John MacAskill, *Scotland's Foreshore: Public Rights, Private Rights and the Crown, 1840–2017* (Edinburgh University Press 2018; ISBN 9781474436915)

Kenneth G C Reid and George L Gretton, *Conveyancing 2017* (Avizandum Publishing Ltd 2018; ISBN 9781904968900)

Articles

James Aitken, 'Purchasing property with cryptocurrency' (2018) 156 *Greens Property Law Bulletin* 5 and 157 *Greens Property Law Bulletin* 5

Mike Blair, 'Confusion about *confusio*' (2018) 156 *Greens Property Law Bulletin* 1 (considering *confusio* in the context of leases)

Stewart Brymer, 'Artificial intelligence in conveyancing' (2018) 157 *Greens Property Law Bulletin* 3

Stewart Brymer, 'Delays in registration of title' (2018) 155 *Greens Property Law Bulletin* 1

Stewart Brymer, 'More information or better information?' (2018) 154 *Greens Property Law Bulletin* 1 (considering the case for a property logbook)

Stewart Brymer, 'Old habits die hard' (2018) 156 *Greens Property Law Bulletin* 4 (advocating the use of digital signatures)

Stewart Brymer, 'Risk management in commercial property transactions' (2018) 153 *Greens Property Law Bulletin* 3

Iain Buchan, 'The perils of parking' (2018) 63 *Journal of the Law Society of Scotland* July/24

George Clark, 'The First-tier Tribunal Housing and Property Chamber' (2018) 157 *Greens Property Law Bulletin* 1

Malcolm Combe, 'Better access to the law' (2018) 63 *Journal of the Law Society of Scotland* Oct/34 (considering *Renyana Stahl Anstalt v Loch Lomond and Trossachs National Park Authority* [2018] CSIH 22, 2018 SLT 331 and *Manson v Midlothian Council* [2018] SC EDIN 50, 2018 GWD 33-422)

Malcolm Combe, 'Revisiting access to land under the Land Reform (Scotland) Act 2003' 2018 SLT (News) 51 (considering *Renyana Stahl Anstalt v Loch Lomond and Trossachs National Park Authority* [2018] CSIH 22, 2018 SLT 331)

Malcolm M Combe, '*Manson v Midlothian Council*, 2018 GWD 33-422' 2018 SLT (News) 149

Malcolm M Combe and Malcolm I Rudd, 'Abandonment of land and the *Scottish Coal* case: was it unprecedented?' (2018) 22 *Edinburgh Law Review* 301

Gail Cook, 'Conveyancers beware!' (2018) 63 *Journal of the Law Society of Scotland* July/44 (considering *Dreamvar (UK) Ltd v Mishcon de Reya* [2018] EWCA Civ 1082, [2018] 3 WLR 1244)

Iain Doran, 'Breaking up is hard to do: problems operating lease break clauses' (2018) 154 *Greens Property Law Bulletin* 1 and (2018) 155 *Greens Property Law Bulletin* 3

Caroline Drummond, 'How we deal with leases at termination' (2018) 63 *Journal of the Law Society of Scotland* June/34 (introducing the Scottish Law Commission's *Discussion Paper No 165 on Aspects of Leases: Termination*)

George Duthie, 'Fire damage to property' (2018) 154 *Greens Property Law Bulletin* 5 (considering fire damage in the context of leases)

Laura Hay, 'The Lands Tribunal's discretion to vary title conditions: *Rubislaw Quarry Aberdeen Ltd v Hill of Rubislaw (Q Seven) Ltd*' (2018) 153 *Greens Property Law Bulletin* 3

Caragh Jenkins, 'Compulsory sale orders: a practical proposal?' (2018) 156 *Greens Property Law Bulletin* 7 (considering the recent proposal by the Scottish Land Commission that local authorities should be able to force owners to sell vacant or derelict land or buildings)

Austin Lafferty, 'GSPC: eulogy for a friend' (2018) 63 *Journal of the Law Society of Scotland* Sept/22

Hannah Leslie, 'Draft revised Code of Conduct for Registered Property Factors – a summary' (2018) 152 *Greens Property Law Bulletin* 7

Ross Mackay, 'Missives: third way' (2018) 63 *Journal of the Law Society of Scotland* Nov/34 (reviewing the changes made in the third edition of the Scottish Standard Clauses)

Roddy MacLeod, 'The remedy of reduction in executry cases' 2018 SLT (News) 17 and 21 (considering *O'Neil v O'Neil* [2017] SC GLA 40, 2017 GWD 22-361)

Francis McManus, '*Steel v NRAM Ltd* – a search for clarity?' 2018 *Juridical Review* 191

Alisdair D J MacPherson, 'Floating charges and trust property in Scots law: a tale of two patrimonies?' (2018) 22 *Edinburgh Law Review* 1

Alisdair D J MacPherson, 'The circle squared? Floating charges and diligence after *MacMillan v T Leith Developments Ltd*' 2018 *Juridical Review* 230

Willie MacRae, 'Missives: time to add a penalty' (2018) 63 *Journal of the Law Society of Scotland*, online edition: bit.ly/2u7oKve (advocating a fixed penalty for withdrawing from a concluded contract, so as to encourage early conclusion)

Douglas S K Maxwell, 'Broadening the human rights discourse, realising socio-economic rights, and balancing rights to property: moving beyond the rhetoric of socio-economic rights and Scottish land reform' 2019 *Public Law* 121

Douglas S K Maxwell, 'Enforceable rights or progressive policy goals?' (2018) 63 *Journal of the Law Society of Scotland* March/18 (considering socio-economic rights, as set out in the 1976 International Covenant, in the context of land reform in Scotland)

Megan Rea, 'The Digital Economy Act 2017 – what do landowners need to know?' (2018) 152 *Greens Property Law Bulletin* 2 (considering the new Electronic Communications Code)

Lorna Richardson, 'The scope and limits of the right to retain contractual performance' 2018 *Juridical Review* 209

Lorna Richardson, 'What do we know about retention now?' (2018) 22 *Edinburgh Law Review* 387 (considering *J H & W Lamont of Heathfield Farm v Chattisham Ltd* [2018] CSIH 33, 2018 SLT 511)

J Keith Robertson, 'KIR: the time bomb explodes' (2018) 63 *Journal of the Law Society of Scotland* Sept/32

Peter Robson, 'Reviving tenants' rights? The Private Housing (Tenancies) (Scotland) Act 2016' 2018 *Juridical Review* 108

Jill Robbie, 'Death, divorce and defective drafting' (2018) 22 *Edinburgh Law Review* 301 (considering the effect of divorce on survivorship destinations)

Frances Rooney, 'Putting the squeeze on rejections' (2018) 63 *Journal of the Law Society of Scotland* July/32

Tony Rosser, 'Land registration errors: an owner's view' (2018) 63 *Journal of the Law Society of Scotland*, online edition: bit.ly/2Q3QajF (considering a reduction in mapped extent caused by an OS update)

Michael Skilling, '*St Andrew's Forest Lodges Ltd v Grieve*: the lease's fifth element in action' 2018 *Juridical Review* 122

Anneli Spence, 'See-through titles: setting the scene' (2018) 63 *Journal of the Law Society of Scotland* Aug/36 (considering draft regulations for the establishment of a Register of Persons Holding a Controlled Interest in Land)

Addi Spiers and Lynsey Walker, 'Tide runs for lenders' (2018) 63 *Journal of the Law Society of Scotland* April/32 (considering *OneSaving Bank plc v Burns* [2017] SC BAN 20, 2017 SLT (Sh Ct) 129)

Andrew Steven, 'Clarifying real burden enforcement rights' (2018) 63 *Journal of the Law Society of Scotland* June/33 (introducing the Scottish Law Commission's *Discussion Paper No 164 on Section 53 of the Title Conditions (Scotland) Act 2003*)

Ann Stewart, 'Community right to buy: the new scope' (2018) 63 *Journal of the Law Society of Scotland*, online edition: bit.ly/2MQTA3g (considering the right to buy abandoned, neglected or detrimental land)

Calum Stewart, '*Confusio*' (2018) 153 *Greens Property Law Bulletin* 4 (considering *confusio* in the context of leases)

Calum Stewart, 'Tenancy of shops' (2018) 152 *Greens Property Law Bulletin* 6

Ken Swinton, 'Agents' liability to third parties in identity fraud cases' (2018) 86 *Scottish Law Gazette* 21 (considering *P & P Property Ltd v Owen White & Catlin LLP* [2018] EWCA Civ 1082, [2018] 3 WLR 1244)

Ken Swinton, 'Liability for misrepresentations as to flooding' (2018) 86 *Scottish Law Gazette* 25 (considering *Anwar v Britton* [2018] SC FAL 31, 2018 GWD 20-251)

Ken Swinton, 'The right to roam – definitely not a boar' (2018) 86 *Scottish Law Gazette* 9 (considering *Renyana Stahl Anstalt v Loch Lomond and Trossachs National Park Authority* [2018] CSIH 22, 2018 SLT 331)

Andrew Todd, 'Follow England? Latest developments in law and policy for new homes' (2018) 155 *Greens Property Law Bulletin* 4

Andrew Todd and Hannah Leslie, 'Short-term lets and title conditions: a house builder's perspective' 2018 *Juridical Review* 197

Viktoria Wahle, 'Private residential tenancies – a new form of lease?' (2018) 152 *Greens Property Law Bulletin* 4

Lucy Weaver, 'The art of rectification' (2018) 63 *Journal of the Law Society of Scotland*, online edition: bit.ly/2Q50xPT (advocating challenging the Keeper's initial refusal to rectify)

PART IV
COMMENTARY

COMMENTARY

INTERPRETING THE SCOTTISH STANDARD CLAUSES

The Scottish Standard Clauses have been one of the success stories of recent years. Growing out of a number of separate initiatives to produce regional missives for residential conveyancing, the Scottish Standard Clauses were launched in 2015 as an all-Scotland style and are already in their third edition.[1] Being relatively new, the Clauses have yet to attract much in the way of litigation. But two cases from 2018 shed helpful light on their interpretation.

Representations and contractual terms

Textualism v contextualism

Anwar v Britton[2] concerned the purchase for development of property at Strathblane in Stirlingshire. After settling the transaction and taking entry, the buyers discovered that a burn which crossed the property had flooded within the last year. They sought recovery from the sellers on the basis of clause 2 of the Scottish Standard Clauses, which had been incorporated into the missives.

In the then current (second) edition of the Clauses used by the parties in *Anwar*, clause 2 read:

> **2 AWARENESS OF CIRCUMSTANCES AFFECTING THE PROPERTY**
>
> 2.1 So far as the Seller is aware (but declaring that the Seller has made no enquiry or investigation into such matters) the Property (including in respect of Clauses 2.1.3 and 2.1.4 the Building, if appropriate) is not affected by:
>
> 2.1.1 any Notice of Potential Liability for Costs registered in terms of the Tenements (Scotland) Act 2004 or the Title Conditions (Scotland) Act 2003;
>
> 2.1.2 any Notices of Payment of Improvement/Repairs Grants;
>
> 2.1.3 flooding from any river or watercourse which has taken place within the last 5 years;
>
> 2.1.4 other than as disclosed in the Home Report for the Property any structural defects; wet rot; dry rot; rising damp; woodworm; or other infestation.

---

1 The third edition came on-stream on 1 November 2018: for details, see p 105 above.
2 2018 GWD 20-251 affd [2018] SAC (Civ) 27, 2019 SLT (Sh Ct) 23. The Sheriff Appeal Court comprised Sheriff Principal M M Stephen QC, Sheriff Principal M W Lewis, and Appeal Sheriff P Braid. The Opinion was a joint one. All subsequent references are to the decision of the Sheriff Appeal Court. The decision at first instance was discussed in Ken Swinton, 'Liability for misrepresentations as to flooding' (2018) 86 *Scottish Law Gazette* 25.

The buyers' argument was that there had been a breach of the warranty in clause 2.1.3.

The sellers disputed that view. As they pointed out, the controlling verb ('is not affected') was in the present tense. Read literally, therefore, the warranty was merely that the property was not affected *now*, at the date of missives, by any flooding within the last five years.[1] So if flooding had come and gone, and the property had dried out, the warranty would not, on this approach, be breached.

But a literal interpretation is not the only type of interpretation on offer. Under reference to a number of leading cases, including the decisions of the Supreme Court in *Rainy Sky SA v Kookmin Bank*,[2] *Arnold v Britton*,[3] and *Wood v Capita Insurance Services Ltd*,[4] the parties were agreed that it was also of relevance to look at the background circumstances[5] and, in cases of ambiguity, to have regard to business common sense.[6] Thus the court's task, as the Sheriff Appeal Court put it:[7]

> is to ascertain the objective meaning of the words used, having regard to the language used – textualism – and the consequences of the rival constructions – contextualism. It is an iterative process, by which the court arrives at the correct meaning.

In the court's view, the literalist meaning proposed by the sellers (and defenders) made 'little sense'. The court continued:[8]

> It is unlikely that a purchaser would wish to have a warranty that the property is not presently affected by flooding when such a circumstance might be expected to be obvious to the purchaser or his surveyor in any event. It is also unlikely that he would not wish to know about the propensity to flood. The defenders' construction also gives rise to uncertainty, since it introduced an element of subjective assessment into what must be disclosed. How is a seller to judge whether the property is or is not [still] affected by flooding? ... Conversely, the pursuers' interpretation not only makes sense but is easy for a seller to comply with. All they need to do is disclose any flooding which, to their knowledge, has occurred within the last five years. Whether it was big or small makes no difference. The risk will then be a matter for the purchaser to take an informed decision on.

There seems little doubt that this is the meaning intended for the clause even if it is not, precisely, what the clause says. So in this case the court's helping hand is a welcome one.

---

1 Even that view can be challenged, and indeed was to some extent challenged by the Sheriff Appeal Court: see paras 28–30.
2 [2011] UKSC 50, [2011] 1 WLR 2900.
3 [2015] UKSC 36, [2015] AC 1619.
4 [2017] UKSC 24, [2017] AC 1173.
5 Though, as senior counsel for the buyers conceded (para 25), this was unlikely to be of much assistance in interpreting a standard-form contract.
6 For a brief discussion in the context of missives, see G L Gretton and K G C Reid, *Conveyancing* (5th edn, 2018) para 3–24.
7 Paragraph 27.
8 Paragraphs 30 and 31.

Misrepresentation v breach of contract

The sellers being in breach of a provision of the missives, it might be thought that the buyers' action was one for breach of contract. But instead of pursuing a case for breach the buyers sought reduction of both missives and disposition,[1] repetition of the purchase price, and damages on the ground of misrepresentation.[2]

The background is that the buyers, who were buying the property for development, had been worried all along about the possibility of flooding. The flood-risk report on which they had insisted said that the risk of flooding was low but recommended that the sellers be asked whether the property or surrounding area had flooded before. By email the sellers' solicitors confirmed that their clients had had no experience of flooding at the subjects. Perhaps surprisingly, that was not the representation founded on by the buyers.

The buyers' argument was both different and also more interesting. It went like this. We, the buyers, made an offer to buy the property on the basis of the Scottish Standard Clauses. You, the sellers, issued a qualified acceptance of the offer without qualifying the warranty as to flooding contained in clause 2.1.3. In issuing such an acceptance you must therefore be taken to have represented that no flooding had taken place in the last five years. The representation pre-dated any contract. On the basis of the representation we entered into a contract to buy the property. The representation turned out to be false. Hence the contract, and the disposition which followed, were both induced by the misrepresentation of you, the sellers.

We do not know why the buyers risked an argument based on misrepresentation when they could have had an easy victory on the basis of breach of contract, but the answer may lie in the remedies sought. An action based on breach of contract would have resulted in an award of damages but not, probably, in the termination of the contract because the sellers' breach is unlikely to have been sufficiently material to allow for rescission. If, therefore, the buyers wanted out of the bargain, and their money back, it was only misrepresentation which provided the necessary remedy.

Only misrepresentation too would allow reduction of the disposition. One of the oddities of the *Anwar* case is that reduction was sought not by the granter of the deed but by the person in whose favour the deed was granted. In seeking to reduce the disposition the buyers were seeking to destroy their own title to the property. It seems doubtful that this was necessary or even, perhaps, wise. A reduction of the missives (alone) would have entitled the buyers to repetition of the price against a reconveyance of the property, on the

---

1 As Scotland has an 'abstract' system of transfer, the validity of the disposition is viewed independently from the validity of the missives, and a failure of the latter does not necessarily lead to the failure of the former. In the present case the buyers' argument was presumably that the misrepresentation had induced the disposition as well as the missives.

2 [2018] SAC (Civ) 27 at para 37.

principle of unjustified enrichment.[1] It might have been better to wait for an assurance of repayment before surrendering title to the property.[2]

Two defences

To the buyers' action of reduction the sellers offered two defences. The first was that a claim based on misrepresentation was excluded by the entire agreement clause in the contract, clause 27 of the Scottish Standard Clauses. This read:

> The Missives will constitute the entire agreement and understanding between the Purchaser and the Seller with respect to all matters to which they refer and supersede and invalidate all other undertakings, representations, and warranties relating to the subject matter thereof which may have been made by the Seller or the Purchaser either orally or in writing prior to the date of conclusion of the Missives.

As the sellers pointed out, this clause is very widely expressed. It supersedes prior agreements and collateral warranties, of course. But with its references to 'agreement *and understanding*', and to 'representations', it might seem also to exclude the buyers' remedy in respect of any representation – or, rather, misrepresentation – made by the sellers.[3]

The Sheriff Appeal Court disagreed. Even as a matter of language, said the court, it was wrong to read the clause in the way suggested by the sellers. 'Agreement and understanding' was a stock phrase of no particular significance. The force of the word 'representations' was largely taken away 'when the position of the word in the sentence is noted, namely, between undertakings and warranties both of which do signify matters of contractual significance'.[4] Furthermore, while the words 'supersede' and 'invalidate' were apposite in the case of collateral warranties, they made little sense in the context of misrepresentations:[5]

> As counsel for the pursuers submitted, those words convey the meaning that the parties agree that something which otherwise would have had legal effect should not have that effect, rather than an intention to surrender a potential legal remedy which would otherwise be available in respect of a wrong which may have been committed. Those are two entirely different concepts.

Contextual considerations gave further support to this view:[6]

---

1 This is because, with the reduction of the contract, the legal basis for the parties to hold on, respectively, to the property and the price would have ceased to exist. There would therefore be the *restitutio in integrum* which is essential in cases of reduction. See H L MacQueen and J Thomson, *Contract Law in Scotland* (4th edn, 2016) para 4.5.
2 Although admittedly the reduction would not have real effect until presented for registration in the Land Register by the buyers/pursuers: see Conveyancing (Scotland) Act 1924 s 46A.
3 It is competent for an entire agreement clause to exclude reliance on representations, other than fraudulent misrepresentations: see W W McBryde, *The Law of Contract in Scotland* (3rd edn, 2007) para 5–56.
4 Paragraph 19.
5 Paragraph 19.
6 Paragraph 19.

We note that this is a standard form contract designed to be used for many years in a variety of situations in contracts for the purchase and sale of residential property in Scotland. It is unlikely that the drafters intended that a purchaser of heritable property should, in ordinary course, not be entitled to pursue a legal remedy which he would otherwise have had. Had that been the intention, one would have anticipated that it would have been made crystal clear. It is one thing to provide for certainty as to what the contract comprises; quite another to agree not to rely on a pre-contractual misrepresentation.

In summary, the entire agreement clause had no bearing on whether the buyers had a remedy in respect of pre-contractual misrepresentations.

The second defence went to the very heart of the remedy sought. This was that clause 2.1.3 could not be both a term of the contract and, at the same time, a pre-contractual misrepresentation; and since it was indisputably the former, it could not also, said the sellers, be the latter. On this topic there was, it seemed, no clear prior authority in Scotland,[1] and both parties sought to argue from first principles. Looking at matters in that way the Sheriff Appeal Court saw no reason why the same statement should not be both a pre-contractual representation and thereafter a term of the contract itself.[2] In such a case the buyers would have a choice of remedies. There was, thought the court, nothing wrong with that. Proof was accordingly allowed of the sellers' averments and especially, it may be supposed, on the question of the buyers' alleged reliance on the sellers' misrepresentation.

This is an important decision. In relation to contractual warranties, at least,[3] it means that a buyer may sometimes be able to circumvent the rules on rescission for breach of contract by seeking to reduce the contract for pre-contractual misrepresentation. Whether this approach is sound in law or in policy is, however, likely to be controversial.[4]

Implications for practice

By unlucky timing, the declaration incorporating the third edition of the Scottish Standard Clauses was registered in the Books of Council and Session

---

1 The issue had, however, arisen before, in *Fortune v Fraser* 1993 SLT (Sh Ct) 68 but a decision in principle was avoided due to the fact that (unlike in *Anwar*) the seller's acceptance of the buyers' offer had been unqualified, so that the very time of the supposed misrepresentation (based on a clause in the original offer, now accepted) was also the moment at which the contract was concluded. This fact pattern removed any possibility of a pre-contractual misrepresentation: see pp 74–75. The decision of the sheriff principal went on appeal to the Inner House where, following amendment of the pleadings, the buyers relied on earlier and different statements by the seller as the basis of misrepresentation and a proof was allowed: see 1995 SC 186 and especially at 200–01 per Lord Morison. *Fortune* is not referred to in the opinion of the Sheriff Appeal Court in *Anwar*.

2 Paragraph 37.

3 But not, as the Sheriff Appeal Court pointed out in *Anwar* (at para 37), to obligations to do something.

4 The law in England and Wales appears to be different: see *Idemitsu Kosan Co Ltd v Sumitomo Corp* [2016] EWHC 1909 (Comm), [2016] 2 CLC 297, especially at paras 14–23. This decision is not cited in the opinion in *Anwar*. See also eg *Spencer Bower and Handley: Actionable Misrepresentation* (5th edn, by K R Handley, 2010) paras 2.11–2.13.

on 3 October 2018, a mere five days before the Sheriff Appeal Court handed down its judgment in *Anwar v Britton*. There was thus no opportunity for the drafting committee to take account of the decision and to consider whether either of the clauses under scrutiny should be amended.

In fact an amendment *was* made to clause 2.1.3 in the light, presumably, of the decision in *Anwar* at first instance. The revised clause reads as follows (with the added words given in italics):

> So far as the Seller is aware (but declaring that the Seller has made no enquiry or investigation into such matters) the Property (including in respect of Clauses 2.1.3 and 2.1.4 the Building, if appropriate) is not affected by ... *(nor has been affected by)* flooding from any river or watercourse[1] which has taken place within the last 5 years.

This achieves the necessary fix, in the sense at least of making clear that the warranty covers flooding which took place at any time in the previous five years regardless of whether the flooding still affects the property today. It does, however, leave in place the words 'is not affected by' which are not only now unnecessary but which were also criticised by the Sheriff Appeal Court.[2] It may be that the words should be removed when the Scottish Standard Clauses next come to be revised.

The other clause – the entire agreement provision in clause 27 – remains unamended. Presumably this was because the drafting committee was content both with the policy (ie that pre-contractual misrepresentations should found reduction of the contract) and with the drafting (at least in the light of the decision at first instance in *Anwar*). The policy does indeed seem satisfactory, but in the light of certain comments made by the Sheriff Appeal Court the drafting may need some attention on the next occasion that the Standard Clauses are revised. In particular, the court commented that the use of the word 'understanding' in the expression 'entire agreement and understanding' was, 'we suspect, more due to the innate prolixity of conveyancers and a tendency to use two words where one might do, rather than a tightly worded but oblique attempt to state that both parties agree not to rely on misrepresentation in support of any remedy which they might seek'.[3]

None of this should cause much concern to practitioners. An obvious advantage of using the Scottish Standard Clauses is that responsibility for imperfections does not, in the normal case at least, lie with the solicitor-user. Fixing the Standard Clauses is someone else's problem. But in any event the message from *Anwar v Britton* is reassuring enough. True, the clauses under scrutiny were found to be not beyond reproach, but in the end they still managed to do the job that they were supposed to do.

---

1 As a river is a type of watercourse, this might be better expressed as 'river or other watercourse'.
2 At para 30: 'The defenders' construction also gives rise to uncertainty, since it introduced an element of subjective assessment into what must be disclosed. How is a seller to judge whether the property is or is not [still] affected by flooding?'
3 Paragraph 19. To a critical reader, this sentence will seem an example of the very vice which it seeks to condemn.

Twelve weeks since substantial completion

Another provision of the Scottish Standard Clauses which might benefit from revision in the light of judicial deliberation is clause 8.3. Clause 8 is about consents to alterations, but half-hidden amidst provisions about planning permission, building warrants and the like, there is the following warranty:

> 8.3 The Seller warrants (i) that any building work carried out to the Property has been in a state of substantial completion for a period of not less than 12 weeks prior to the date of conclusion of the Missives; and (ii) that no valid objection to the work was made at any time by a person with title and interest to do so under a valid real burden.

On an initial read-through, the first part of this warranty is surprising and unexpected. A clue as to its purpose, however, can be found in the second part. As well as the consent of planning authorities and other public bodies, alterations may also need the consent of neighbours if they turn out to be contrary to real burdens which the neighbours have title and interest to enforce. Preferably there should then be a formal minute of waiver. But even if no consent or waiver is obtained, the effect of s 16 of the Title Conditions (Scotland) Act 2003 is for neighbours to lose their right to enforce – and for the real burden to be extinguished to the extent of accommodating the alterations – if the neighbours fail to object within 12 weeks of substantial completion of the works.[1] Hence the warranty in clause 8.3: if 12 weeks pass, without complaint, following substantial completion, then there is nothing to fear from real burdens.

The focus of the first part of the warranty is on the period of 12 weeks. But another layer of meaning exists because, as well as warranting that 12 weeks have passed since the works were substantially completed, clause 8.3 also necessarily warrants that the works were completed in the first place. That seems to take clause 8.3 into uncharted and, we assume, unintended regions. Suppose, for example, that works have been started by the sellers but not finished. They intended, say, to put up a new garden fence but became discouraged after completing only one section. They then sell the property. Are they in breach of clause 8.3? Are the buyers entitled to the cost of completing the fence by way of damages?

Cooper v Skene[2] suggests that the answer might often be yes. In that case, the defender built a house and sold it to the pursuers. The house, or so the pursuers averred,[3] turned out to be without running water. The pursuers sought damages for breach of the missives. One of their grounds for doing so was clause 7(b) of the Aberdeen and Aberdeenshire Standard Clauses (2013 Edition), which was in identical terms to clause 8.3 of the Scottish Standard Clauses.[4] The argument

---

1 See K G C Reid and G L Gretton, *Conveyancing* (5th edn, 2018) para 14–25.
2 2 March 2016, Aberdeen Sheriff Court.
3 The judgment was in relation to a debate on the relevancy, and no proof had taken place.
4 The Scottish Standard Clauses, of course, give other grounds for a claim in respect of a defective water supply, notably in clauses 4.1 and 11.3. But the interest of *Cooper v Skene* lies, not in the issue of water supply as such, but in the more general issue of unfinished repairs.

was simple. The defender had built the house but, in respect at least of the water supply, he had failed to attain the status of substantial completion at least 12 weeks before the date of missives – or, indeed, at all. The sheriff[1] thought the argument potentially a good one:[2]

> If it be the case that the pursuers' averment is correct and that the property had no water supply to it, then it does not seem to me that the building work carried out at the property can be said to have been in a state of substantial completion at the date of entry let alone for a period of 12 weeks prior to the date of conclusion of Missives. If it is correct that the property had no water supply that may well entitle the pursuers to argue that the defender is in breach of Clause 7(b). The pursuers may or may not be able to demonstrate that the property had no water supply but that it seems to me is a matter for proof. It seems to me that the pursuers are entitled to proof of those averments.

In the light of this decision, clause 8.3 seems likely to be looked at again when the Scottish Standard Clauses are next revised. In the meantime, it may sometimes be prudent for sellers to qualify or exclude clause 8.3, especially if the house being sold has been subject to a programme of half-hearted improvements.

SECURED LOANS AND COLLATERAL UNDERSTANDINGS

'Yes, that's the paperwork, but what the lender actually said was ...'

What business representatives say in their sales pitch and what the written contract says do not always tally. This is a general issue of contract law. In recent years it is an issue that has become more prominent in loans. The lender's representative allegedly said one thing, but the paperwork does not reflect what was allegedly said. Of course, to seek to modify, supplement or contradict the terms of a written contract is difficult, but not necessarily impossible. One route is to argue that, side-by-side with the written contract, there was a collateral oral agreement. Another is to argue that the contract was induced by misrepresentation.

A case that sparked the current interest in this area of law, in relation to loans, was *Royal Bank of Scotland plc v Carlyle*, decided by the Supreme Court back in 2015.[3] In that case Mr Carlyle obtained a loan to purchase land for development. There was, naturally, a written loan contract. But to construct the proposed buildings he would need a further loan, and this was, he said, agreed with the bank – orally. The bank then refused to make further funding available. When the bank sued Mr Carlyle for repayment of the loan, he counterclaimed for damages for the bank's failure to honour its undertaking to make the additional loan. Mr Carlyle was victorious.

---

1 Sheriff W H Summers.
2 Paragraph 105.
3 [2015] UKHL 13, 2015 SC (UKSC) 93, 2015 SLT 206. See *Conveyancing 2010* p 42; *Conveyancing 2013* p 53; *Conveyancing 2015* pp 151–54.

This year we bring news of a number of such cases (though their facts were different from *Carlyle*), including one from 2014 that has only recently come to our attention. In all four the borrower failed to persuade the court of the existence of a binding collateral agreement. Such arguments are very difficult to run successfully. Some fail at the threshold of relevancy and specification;[1] others fail at proof.

We are here dealing with collateral understandings. There are also cases where lenders breach the written contract itself, typically by demanding repayment before it is due. The best-known such case is an English one, *Alexander v West Bromwich Mortgage Co Ltd*.[2] 2018 saw another example, *Kennedy v Royal Bank of Scotland plc*,[3] but details are sparse, the case as reported having been fought out on a different issue, namely prescription.

The *Acorn Finance* cases

UK Acorn Finance Ltd was a sub-prime lender, specialising in short-term loans to farmers at high rates of interest, secured against the farms. It attracted national publicity of a negative type. For example, there was a BBC programme entitled 'The Country Rogue', the reference being to the founder of UK Acorn Finance.[4] Other references include the London *Evening Standard* report on 15 May 2017,[5] and that major international news outlet, familiar to all our readers, the *Chew Valley & Wrington Vale Gazette*, which ran an interesting story on 23 December 2016, 'Local agricultural solicitor struck off for dishonesty'.[6] A common feature of the allegations is that the company inveigled farmers into signing up to high-interest loans on the understanding (not in writing) that further finance, on a longer-term basis, and at more reasonable rates of interest, would become available when the short-term loan ran out. We do not know whether these allegations were true. We would, however, offer the thought that a business model of this type was likely to be highly profitable provided that customers could be found to sign up. The interest rate was high, and in practice recovery rates would be high because the loans were well secured. If the customer failed to repay at the contractual date (typically about six months after the making of the loan) that would in a sense be good, not bad, news for the lender, since the high interest would run for longer.

In this volume there are two cases involving UK Acorn Finance Ltd. They are somewhat similar to each other and to the cases discussed in the news media.

---

1 As in *Promontoria (Chestnut) Ltd v Ballantyne Property Services* 2016 GWD 35-633 (*Conveyancing 2016* pp 52–53), and in *Unicorn Tower Ltd v HSBC plc* [2018] CSOH 30, 2018 GWD 13-179 (below).
2 [2016] EWCA Civ 496; [2017] 1 All ER 942 (*Conveyancing 2016* pp 149–52).
3 [2018] CSIH 70, 2018 SLT 1261.
4 Broadcast on 16 April 2014 (available at www.bbc.co.uk/programmes/b040hzz5).
5 'Farmers' loans firm to stop trading amid scandal claims' (available at www.standard.co.uk/business/farmers-loans-firm-to-stop-trading-amid-scandal-claims-a3539526.html).
6 Available at www.chewvalleygazette.co.uk/article.cfm?id=101523&headline=Local%20agricultural%20solicitor%20struck%20off%20for%20dishonesty&sectionIs=news&searchyear=2016.

In the first *Acorn Finance* case,[1] Angela Holt was the owner of a farm at Auchenachie, Ruthven, Aberdeenshire. There were two title sheets, one covering two cottages, and the other about 57 hectares of land. In July 2011 she was offered and accepted a loan of £420,000 from UK Acorn Finance Ltd, to be drawn down in September, repayable in March 2012, the interest rate being an eyebrow-raising 21%. Her solicitors, Peterkins, told her that they were 'not happy'[2] but she went ahead anyway. To secure the loan a standard security was granted over both properties.

What was the purpose of the loan? Partly it was by way of refinancing, because Ms Holt 'had been under some pressure from her existing lender'[3] though details are unclear. But the main purpose was the construction of a hydroelectric scheme on the land. By the time of the hearing in September 2014 much work had been done but more remained to be done and the scheme was still not producing electricity. Hydroelectricity seems to be the fashion. A hydroelectric scheme was also involved in *Peart v Promontoria (Henrico) Ltd* (below).[4]

A document signed in 2011 by Ms Holt said that:[5]

The borrower intends to repay Acorn from a combination of asset sales, sale and contract farming and refinancing. The applicant understands that it will be necessary to demonstrate to any new lender that the financial projections contained in these proposals have been met and that the business complies with a new lender's requirements and that there is no guarantee that a new lender will be found. In the event that it is not possible for the applicant to obtain replacement finance, the applicant understands that the Acorn loan will be repaid by the sale of the security property.

This is on the whole clear and coherent, though there are one or two oddities. What, for example, does 'asset sales, sale ...' mean? And why does the last sentence mention only refinancing as the means of repayment, when the first sentence mentions other possibilities?

Ms Holt's position was that when she and her husband met Acorn Finance's representatives, the latter assured them that new finance would be available, longer-term, and at a much lower rate of interest. It was, she said, in reliance on those assurances that she had agreed to the loan.

When the loan matured, in March 2012, Ms Holt did not have replacement finance, either from Acorn Finance or from any other lender. In October 2013 Acorn Finance served a calling-up notice and thereafter raised the present action. It proceeded on the basis that the property fell within the 'residential' rules in the enforcement provisions of the Conveyancing and Feudal Reform (Scotland) Act 1970. That was evidently the case for the plot that had two cottages on it

---

1   *UK Acorn Finance Ltd v Holt*, Aberdeen Sheriff Court, 29 September 2014, unreported.
2   Paragraph 26. Seemingly the advice not to sign was repeated: see para 64.
3   Paragraph 32.
4   According to the Scottish Government, 'Scotland is a world leader on tackling climate change': see www.gov.scot/Topics/Environment/climatechange. We hope that the Holts, the Pearts and others are now contributing to Scotland's world leadership.
5   Paragraph 7. This is similar, though not identical, to the wording in *Stewart v UK Acorn Finance Ltd* (below).

but it does not seem that the other property of 57 hectares was residential. This point is not discussed in the case. It may be that the view was taken that, since there was a single standard security, the 'residential' rules were applicable, even though one of the two plots of land was non-residential. We merely speculate.

Under the 'residential' rules in the 1970 Act, decree is to be granted only if it is 'reasonable'.[1] The defender's case was that, standing the assurances of replacement finance, enforcement of the security would not be reasonable. The defence failed, and decree in favour of the pursuer was granted. By this time the running of the high interest rate meant that the £420,000 debt had ballooned to £753,845. A reason for the decision was that the recollections of Ms Holt and her husband as to what had been said at the meeting differed:[2]

> The defender thought that the interest rate [on the future financing] would be quite low in the region of 1.5%, and that no term had been agreed. Mr Holt thought that the interest rate was to be between 5% and 8% over a period of 15 to 20 years. Thus there can have been no agreement reached.

As a result, the conclusion was that since there had been no definite collateral agreement, enforcement of the standard security was reasonable.

In the second Acorn case,[3] Peter Stewart was the owner of a farm at Thrumster, Caithness. He borrowed money from UK Acorn Finance Ltd, secured by standard security. The term of the loan was nine months. A document signed by Mr Stewart said:

> The applicant intends to repay the Acorn loan on the due date (or sooner) by obtaining refinance from another lender. The applicant understands that it will be necessary to demonstrate to any new lender that the financial projections contained in these proposals have been met and that the business complies with a new lender's requirements and that there is no guarantee that a new lender will be prepared to refinance his business … In the event that it is not possible for the applicant to obtain replacement lending, the Acorn loan will be repaid by the sale of the security property.

Mr Stewart did not repay the loan when it matured after nine months, and UK Acorn Finance Ltd raised an action in the sheriff court for the enforcement of the security. It was successful.

Mr Stewart then raised the present action, seeking reduction of the sheriff court decree. His main arguments were as follows. (i) The property included a structure that was residential, and therefore the lender ought to have adopted the special enforcement procedure appropriate to residential properties, because s 24(1A) of the Conveyancing and Feudal Reform (Scotland) Act 1970 applies the special procedure to 'land used *to any extent* for residential purposes'. (ii) When the loan was being negotiated, it had been agreed, orally, between Mr Stewart and the representative of Acorn Finance that, when the loan term ran out, Acorn

---

1 Conveyancing and Feudal Reform (Scotland) Act 1970 s 24(1B), (5)(b).
2 Paragraph 63.
3 *Stewart v UK Acorn Finance Ltd* [2018] CSOH 31, 2018 GWD 13-174.

Finance would offer to Mr Stewart a replacement loan for a term of 'around 8–12 years'.[1] No such replacement loan had been offered.

The action was unsuccessful. The structure on the farm could not be regarded as residential. It had, indeed, electricity, but it had no water supply and was essentially unfurnished apart from a 'couch'. It was used merely as an occasional shelter, and also for storage of farming materials. As to the oral agreement, the Lord Ordinary[2] held that no such oral agreement had ever existed. He accepted that there had been some discussion of the possibility of replacement finance but nothing definite had been agreed. Mr Stewart's case thus foundered on an evidential rock: no collateral agreement could be proved. Of course, seeking to reduce a decree already granted is in itself extremely difficult.

The *Unicorn* case

In the two *Acorn Finance* cases, the debtor sought to use the alleged collateral agreement as a shield. In the next case, *Unicorn Tower Ltd v HSBC plc*,[3] the debtor deployed the alleged agreement not only as a shield but also as a sword, counterclaiming against the lender for £8 million damages for breach of contract. This seems the preferable tactic: if there was in fact a collateral agreement, its breach should in principle be the basis of a damages claim. Using an alleged agreement solely as a shield is perhaps somewhat half-hearted. Apart from the pure question of law, a damages counterclaim is more likely to bring the lender to consider settling the case on terms acceptable to the debtor.

In *Unicorn Tower Ltd* the pursuer wished to carry out a mixed commercial/residential development in central Glasgow. There were to be two phases, the cost of the first being estimated at £14 million. In 2007 the pursuer obtained a facility from the defender in the sum of £7,965,000. The idea was that the loan would be repaid in stages as the first-phase properties were sold. But that was not what the loan contract said. The loan contract said that all moneys advanced were repayable on an on-demand basis. A standard security was granted. Problems developed, and in 2009 the defender decided to bail out, and demanded repayment of all outstanding sums.

The pursuer responded by raising the present action for declarator that the defender had not been entitled to demand repayment. It argued that the loan 'was a fixed term facility and (absent a breach by the First Pursuer of its terms) would not be terminated until the completion of the development'.[4] This was on the basis of an alleged unwritten collateral agreement. In addition, the pursuer sought damages of £8 million for breach of contract.[5] The defender counterclaimed for repayment of the loan. It is curious that the bank did not itself raise an action for repayment: in the action as raised, the bank was the defender. It is also curious

---

1 See para 11.
2 Lord Tyre.
3 [2018] CSOH 30, 2018 GWD 13-179.
4 Paragraph 6.
5 The pursuer also had pleas based on personal bar and on the defender's alleged failure to act in good faith.

that a 2009 demand for repayment of a commercial loan has been heard and determined only after nine years.

The Lord Ordinary (Lady Wolffe) held that the pursuer's case fell to be dismissed as irrelevant and lacking in specification. The requirements for invoking an unwritten collateral agreement that allegedly varies a term of the written agreement are stringent, in which connection she cited the comments of Lord Tyre in *Scanmudring SA v James Fisher MFE Ltd*.[1] There may be some tension between this case and the next.

The *Peart* case

The *Peart* case[2] is primarily about the law of sequestration, but has some conveyancing interest. Barry and Susan Peart owned the Old Golf House, Newbattle, Midlothian, a property dating from the late seventeenth century.[3] The Pearts were in partnership with each other. Presumably they held title to the property in trust for the firm, though this point is not wholly clear. In 2007 they decided that they would buy another property and on it would develop a hydroelectric scheme. To finance the purchase and the development they borrowed money (how much is unclear) from Clydesdale Bank plc, the loan being secured by standard security over the Old Golf House, which at that time was valued at £1.25 million. What happened to the hydroelectric scheme does not appear from the judgment. As for the loan, the general idea seems to have been that it would be paid off from the sale of the Old Golf House. But, be that as it may, the documentation said that it was an on-demand loan. The Old Golf House was put on the market by the Pearts but failed to find a buyer.[4] The bank, claimed the Pearts, entered into an oral collateral agreement with them that repayment of the loan would not be demanded until the Old Golf House had been sold.[5]

The bank thereafter assigned the loan to an Irish company, Promontoria (Henrico) Ltd.[6] That company demanded repayment, and served charges, which expired without payment.[7] Since the days of charge had expired, the

---

1 [2017] CSOH 91, 2017 GWD 21-334.
2 *Peart v Promontoria (Henrico) Ltd* [2018] CSIH 35, 2018 SC 581, 2018 SCLR 757.
3 The Old Golf House, or at least the woodland adjacent to it, has featured in the law reports before. See *Peart v Legge* [2007] CSIH 70, 2008 SC 93 in which the same parties, Barry and Susan Peart, had a notable victory in arguing that a servitude of way held by neighbour was not *res merae facultatis* and hence could be extinguished by negative prescription: see *Conveyancing 2007* pp 117–21.
4 That failure seems to be ongoing: we note that the property continued to be advertised for sale in December 2018, the upset price being £850,000.
5 The terms of this alleged agreement, for instance as to term and as to interest, are unclear.
6 Clydesdale Bank plc seems to have assigned many loans to companies in the Promontoria group. For an example from last year see *Burnside v Promontoria (Chestnut) Ltd* [2017] CSOH 157, 2018 GWD 2-35 (*Conveyancing 2017* pp 52–53).
7 The judgment does not indicate the basis for these charges. A charge usually follows a court action completed by decree, but no such action is mentioned, and had there been such an action the Pearts would presumably have defended it. We would guess that either the loan contract or the standard security, or both, contained a consent to summary diligence, and that what happened was that Promontoria (Henrico) Ltd registered the loan contract, or the standard security, or both, for execution in the Books of Council and Session and then charged on the basis of an extract.

Pearts were now 'apparently insolvent'[1] and the company applied for them to be sequestrated.[2] At this stage the Pearts raised the present action, seeking to interdict the company from seeking their sequestration. In the Outer House, interim interdict was granted; Promontoria (Henrico) Ltd then reclaimed. Much of the case was concerned with whether the Pearts could competently seek interdict in this type of situation. It was held that they could. That being the case, the Inner House took the view that the Pearts had pled a relevant case and that the decision in the Outer House to grant interim interdict had been sound. The case now proceeds to a full hearing. The case shows that a plea based on a collateral oral understanding, though a long shot, is not necessarily doomed.

Some reflections

An argument based on 'what the lender said' can take many forms. One is as a 'reasonableness' defence to an action to enforce a standard security: this was the line taken in *UK Acorn Finance Ltd v Holt*.[3] Another would be to assert that there had been an agreement with contractual force, collateral to the written contract. A third would be a similar approach but based on promise rather than contract: that was the line taken in *Royal Bank of Scotland plc v Carlyle*.[4] A fourth would be to seek rectification of the written agreement under s 8 of the Law Reform (Miscellaneous Provisions) (Scotland) Act 1985. Contract, promise and rectification all need evidence of a definite agreement which, as has been seen, can be difficult. In some situations a misrepresentation argument would be better. In the recent crop of cases neither the rectification line nor the misrepresentation line has been adopted. So there is plenty of scope for creative litigation.

One final thought. It sometimes happens that the written agreement fails to track what was in fact agreed not because of any questionable statements made by the representatives of the lender but simply because whoever drew up the documentation used the wrong style, by adopting an 'on demand' style whereas what was asked for was a style for a term loan. This can happen in more than one way, but a simple example is where a form A standard security has been used: form A means (unless expressly qualified) that the creditor can demand repayment at any time.[5]

POSITIVE PRESCRIPTION AND THE LAND REGISTER

Of the many changes made by the Land Registration etc (Scotland) Act 2012 not the least important was the reintroduction of positive prescription for Land

---

1   Notour bankrupt in oldspeak.
2   We surmise that the application was for the sequestration of all three, ie (i) Mr Peart, (ii) Mrs Peart, and (iii) the partnership. But this is not wholly clear from the judgment.
3   See above.
4   See above.
5   Conveyancing and Feudal Reform (Scotland) Act 1970 s 10.

Register titles.[1] The previous law had been different. Except in respect of titles where indemnity was excluded by the Keeper, positive prescription had been abolished by the Land Registration (Scotland) Act 1979 on an optimistic and, as it turned out, mistaken view as to the impregnability of titles on the Land Register.[2] The 2012 Act performed a notable service in bringing prescription back.[3]

Prescription can operate to fortify a Land Register title. But it can also operate to undermine it. It fortifies a title – if, unusually, the title is void or voidable and so in need of fortification – where the registered proprietor or successive registered proprietors are in possession for the prescriptive period of ten years.[4] But potentially prescription can also undermine a registered title if possession is in the hands of a competing title-holder. A straightforward example of the latter from 2018 is *McAdam's Exr v Keeper of the Registers of Scotland*.[5]

McAdam's Exr concerned two adjacent terraced houses, numbers 2 and 3 Morris Avenue, Lochgelly, Fife. Formerly council houses, they were feued by Dunfermline District Council in the 1980s as part of the right-to-buy programme. Number 3 was the first to be sold. By mistake, the feu disposition included as part of the subjects feued a small area of ground lying immediately to the front of number 2. The same area ('the disputed area') was also included in the subsequent feu disposition of number 2, to Mr and Mrs McAdam; but as the Council no longer had title to the disputed area, the feu disposition was ineffective to that extent. The disputed area thus belonged to the owner of number 3. On the ground, however, nothing had changed, and the area continued to be possessed by Mr and Mrs McAdam as owners of number 2.

Years passed. Number 3 changed hands and entered the Land Register. Number 2 continued to belong to Mr and Mrs McAdam and to be held on a Sasine title. In 1992 the McAdams added an extension to the front of their house which occupied nearly all of the disputed area. Later Mr McAdam died and then Mrs McAdam. All this time the title discrepancy lay unnoticed. It was only when, after Mrs McAdam's death, some conveyancing needed to be done and a plans report was obtained that the title problem came to light.

Was the Land Register inaccurate in showing the disputed area as part of the title of number 3? On an application by Mrs McAdam's executrix, under s 82 of the Land Registration etc (Scotland) Act 2012, the point fell to be determined by the Lands Tribunal. The owner of number 3 did not enter the process.

---

1 Land Registration etc (Scotland) Act 2012 sch 5 para 18(2), amending s 1(1) of the Prescription and Limitation (Scotland) Act 1973.

2 Land Registration (Scotland) Act 1979 s 10, amending s 1(1) of the Prescription and Limitation (Scotland) Act 1973.

3 For discussion, see Scottish Law Commission, *Discussion Paper No 125 on Land Registration: Void and Voidable Titles* (2004) paras 3.4–3.8; Scottish Law Commission, *Report No 222 on Land Registration* (2010) para 35.3.

4 The bulk of this ten-year period can be before the day on which the 2012 Act came into force, on 8 December 2014, provided that some part of the possession, however small, occurred on or after that day: see Land Registration etc (Scotland) Act 2012 s 120(1) and, for discussion, K G C Reid and G L Gretton, *Land Registration* (2017) para 17.11.

5 16 May 2018, Lands Tribunal.

The applicant's case was simple. Originally, the disputed area had belonged to the owner of number 3. That might still have been true at the time of first registration of the title to number 3. But since then the disputed area had been acquired by Mr and Mrs McAdam by positive prescription. The two requirements for prescription, title and possession for ten years, had plainly been met.[1] Title was provided by the original feu disposition from the Council. As for possession, the building and occupation of the extension were conclusive in that respect. The Lands Tribunal agreed, without hesitation, and pronounced the title sheet of number 3 to be inaccurate in respect of the overlap area.

Two observations may be made. First, as the decision illustrates, a title on the Land Register may be lost by positive prescription. Whilst registration of a disposition, if valid, confers ownership at the time of registration, it does not guarantee that ownership will continue forever. Prescription is one of the ways in which ownership may be lost.

Secondly, prescription may proceed on a Sasine title, so that a title on the new register is, as it were, defeated by a title on the old. That was what occurred in *McAdam's Exr* and that indeed is the typical case. Conversely, ownership is unlikely to be lost to a neighbour by prescription on a Land Register title because, overlapping titles not now being allowed on the Land Register, the neighbour is unlikely to have the necessary title to support his possession.[2] The important topic of overlapping titles is considered in the next section.

OVERLAPPING TITLES

Introduction

You are acting for a client in the purchase of a property – let's call it property A. Property A is held on a Sasine title, so that the disposition in favour of your client will trigger first registration. Bad news arrives with the plans report. There is a title overlap between property A and a neighbouring property, property B, which, being already registered, has beaten property A to the Land Register. That victory in timing is, as we will see, of significance. The example just given is of a purchase but the issue can equally arise where property A enters the Register by some other means, such as voluntary registration or Keeper-induced registration.

As more properties come on to the Land Register, so the discovery of potential title overlaps is, unfortunately, becoming more frequent. Title overlaps can have many different causes, including blundered conveyancing, inaccuracies on the OS map, wrongly-sited buildings or boundary fences, or simple error on the part of the Keeper on first registration. But whatever the cause, the issues to be confronted are much the same. Faced with a potential overlap, what should the purchaser of property A do? Tempting though it may be, it is unwise to ignore the

---

1 Prescription and Limitation (Scotland) Act 1973 s 1.
2 It is true that, in a change from the previous law, the title needed for prescription is a registered deed rather than a title sheet itself: see PL(S)A 1973 s 1(1)(b) and Reid and Gretton, *Land Registration* para 17.3. But the Keeper will not in practice register a disposition which carries an area which is included in another title sheet.

problem in the hope that the overlap can be slipped past the Keeper. Whatever the position might have been under the 1979 Act,[1] the Keeper will not, today, register overlapping titles. Indeed the 2012 Act expressly forbids her to do so.[2] So if the disposition of property A includes the overlap area, the application for registration will simply be rejected by the Keeper.[3]

Two options

What, then, are the options available to a purchaser?[4] Assuming that the purchase proceeds at all, which of course it may not,[5] the options are really only two. One is to give up on the overlap area and register a disposition of the rest of property A. The other option is to make a claim to the overlap area. This too may involve the registration of a disposition shorn of the area. But that would only be an interim measure pending resolution of the issue.

A number of factors are likely to influence the choice between these options. One is the importance or unimportance of the area in question. How much does it matter to the purchaser? Is it worth a fight? Another is whether the owner of property B is willing to co-operate to put matters right. A third is the prospects of success in the event of a dispute. That will depend both on the state of the underlying Sasine title and also on the state of possession. In general, the prospects are better if the overlap area is possessed by the owner of property A than if it is possessed by the owner of property B.

The difficulty of making a challenge must also be borne in mind. The owner of property B, having got to the Land Register before the owner of property A, has the advantage of incumbency. For the purchaser of property A to be able to include the overlap area in his disposition, the area must first be dislodged from the title sheet of property B. There must, in other words, be rectification of the title sheet of property B. On the subject of rectification the 2012 Act contains both good news and bad news.[6] The good news is that the Keeper must rectify an inaccuracy on the Register; she has no discretion in the matter. The bad news is that she must, indeed can, only do so where the inaccuracy is 'manifest'. So the task of any challenger is to convince the Keeper that there is a manifest inaccuracy.

Understandably, the Keeper is not easily convinced. Not being a judge (indeed, not necessarily even being legally qualified), she lacks the power or the means to determine disputed questions of law and fact.[7] Her frequent response to a

---

1 Ie the Land Registration (Scotland) Act 1979.
2 Land Registration etc (Scotland) Act 2012 s 12(2).
3 The Keeper's policy is outright rejection. For discussion as to whether the Keeper should, rather, accept the application but exclude the overlap area from the applicants' title, see Reid and Gretton, *Land Registration* para 11.23 n 148.
4 For general discussion, see Reid and Gretton, *Land Registration* paras 11.20–11.26.
5 The purchasers may simply walk away from the transaction. If missives have already been concluded, the purchasers will usually be able to rescind on the basis that the sellers are in breach of their obligation to provide a good and marketable title to the whole subjects: see eg *Campbell v McCutcheon* 1963 SC 505.
6 Land Registration etc (Scotland) Act 2012 s 80.
7 In some countries (eg Germany) the equivalent of the Keeper is a type of judge.

request for rectification, therefore, is to refuse it on the ground that the alleged inaccuracy is not manifest. The challenger must then choose between giving up or seeking to establish the existence of the inaccuracy by judicial process. A court declarator would be sufficient for this purpose, but the normal route is to seek a ruling from the Lands Tribunal under s 82 of the 2012 Act.

A judicial process is not always needed. If both parties – if the owners of property A and property B – are agreed that the Register is inaccurate, that will be enough for the Keeper. There will also be cases where the error really is beyond dispute.[1] *McAdam's Exr v Keeper of the Registers of Scotland*,[2] mentioned earlier,[3] is an example – indeed is the first example of a manifest inaccuracy to have come before the courts. In *McAdam's Exr* the title of the challenger had been fortified by positive prescription. Accordingly, the inaccuracy in the title sheet of property B was not in doubt. As the Lands Tribunal put it:[4]

> In the light of the evidence presented it appears to us that the inaccuracy is manifest. The evidence about possession is clear and uncontradicted. We are therefore doubtful why this case required a determination by the Tribunal, given that the 2012 Act makes separate provision for the rectification of manifest inaccuracies.

These words are an encouragement to those attempting to convince the Keeper that an inaccuracy is manifest. At the same time, however, the particular facts of the case should be borne in mind. The challenge rested on prescriptive possession, and the Keeper is usually unwilling, indeed unable, to determine questions of possession. But in *McAdam's Exr* the building of an extension on the overlap area made the possession incontrovertible. In that respect this is far from being a typical case.

Initial inaccuracies and their cure

If neither the neighbour nor the Keeper is open to persuasion, a challenger must litigate if he is to succeed in obtaining rectification. This may seem unfair on the challenger. But it is the price which the legislation exacts for the neighbour having reached the Land Register first.

At this point it may be helpful to return to a version of the example with which we began. The owner of property A, Anna, seeks to challenge the presence of an overlap area in the registered title of property B, which is owned by Billy. Property A is held on a Sasine title. In order to have the inaccuracy judicially declared, Anna applies to the Lands Tribunal under s 82 of the 2012 Act. Her case is that the overlap area should not have been included within property B on first registration of that property. But establishing that initial inaccuracy, assuming she is able do so, may still not be enough for victory, because an entry on the

---

1 For an account of a case where the Keeper was, in the end, persuaded that this was so, see Lucy Weaver, 'The art of rectification' (2018) 63 *Journal of the Law Society of Scotland*, online edition: bit. ly/2Q50xPT.
2 16 May 2018, Lands Tribunal.
3 See p 147 above.
4 Paragraph 11.

Register which begins as inaccurate can, over time, cease to be so. Inaccuracies, in other words, can be cured and, once cured, can no longer be rectified. So there may be a question as to whether what was an inaccuracy at the time of first registration remains an inaccuracy today.

How might an inaccuracy be cured? The answer depends on whether first registration of property B took place under the Act of 1979 or the Act of 2012. The law here is regrettably, but unavoidably, complicated.

For first registrations under the 2012 Act the risk of cure is relatively low. Suppose that first registration of property B took place in 2016, and that the subjects registered included an area of land which was actually part of property A. Anna, the owner of property A, lost nothing by Billy's registration as owner of property B, for there is no Midas touch under the 2012 Act.[1] The overlap area is still Anna's and not Billy's. So long, therefore, as Anna can satisfy the Tribunal as to the mistake made on first registration, the Register will be rectified to remove the area from Billy's title. Yet there are risks for Anna if the overlap area is possessed by Billy. For if Billy, possessing the area, then dispones property B to someone else, the disponee, if in good faith, will receive a good title to the overlap area by virtue of the doctrine of realignment.[2] Alternatively, if Billy (or Billy and his predecessors) possess the overlap area for ten years, Billy will acquire ownership by positive prescription.[3] In either case ownership will have been lost by Anna, curing the initial accuracy in Billy's title, and rectification by Anna will cease to be possible.

The position is different and more difficult where first registration of property B occurred before the designated day (8 December 2014) and hence under the Act of 1979. The strange and unsettling logic of that Act would have applied at the time of first registration and continues to govern the position even today. Thus Billy would have become owner of the overlap area immediately on registration, due to the Midas touch,[4] and Anna would have ceased to be owner. The Register would be (bijurally) inaccurate[5] and so capable, in principle, of rectification;[6] but if Billy was in possession of the overlap area, rectification would not normally have been possible because of the protection given by the 1979 Act to proprietors in possession.[7]

Understandably, this protection for proprietors in possession has been carried forward into the current law. This is by virtue of transitional provisions,

---

1 Land Registration etc (Scotland) Act 2012 ss 49(4) and 50(2).
2 LR(S)A 2012 s 86. This provision imposes some other requirements of which the most important is that the overlap area has been possessed by Billy, or by Billy and the acquirer in turn, for a period of a year.
3 Prescription and Limitation (Scotland) Act 1973 s 1(1); for discussion, see pp 146–47 above.
4 Land Registration (Scotland) Act 1979 s 3(1)(a).
5 Bijural inaccuracies only arose under the 1979 Act. They occurred where an entry on the Register was accurate as a matter of registration law, owing to the Midas touch, but inaccurate as a matter of the general law of property. For discussion, see Reid and Gretton, *Land Registration* para 2.8.
6 LR(S)A 1979 s 9(1).
7 LR(S)A 1979 s 9(3)(a). That protection, however, was withdrawn in the four circumstances set out in s 9(3)(a) of which the most important was where the inaccuracy had been caused by the fraud or carelessness of the proprietor in possession. So there could sometimes be rectification even where the registered proprietor was in possession.

contained in schedule 4 of the 2012 Act,[1] which are perhaps less well known than they ought to be. Under the transitional provisions, if an inaccuracy on the Register was one which, immediately before the designated day, the Keeper was unable to rectify, then the inaccuracy was cured on the designated day and cannot be rectified now.[2] Whether the Keeper could have rectified depends, in turn, on the state of possession on 7 December 2014. So if on that day it was Anna (or at least someone other than Billy) who possessed the overlap area, the Keeper could have rectified the inaccuracy and can still rectify it today; but if it was Billy who was in possession, the Keeper could not normally have rectified, with the result that the inaccuracy was cured forever on the designated day. Anna's only recourse is against the Keeper for compensation.[3]

Hence for Anna to succeed in an application in respect of a title the first registration of which took place under the 1979 Act, the Lands Tribunal must be satisfied that Billy did *not* possess the overlap area on 7 December 2014. Furthermore, Anna's task is made more difficult by a statutory presumption that it was the registered proprietor (Billy) who was in possession on that day.[4] The onus of proving the contrary lies with Anna. Sometimes that onus will be easy to discharge, for example because the overlap area lies clearly within a long-standing wall or fence which marks the boundary of property A. But sometimes the matter can only be determined by the Tribunal after a lengthy consideration of conflicting evidence. That was the position in *Combined Corporation (BVI) Ltd v Souter.*[5]

Combined Corporation (BVI) Ltd v Souter

The facts of *Combined Corporation (BVI) Ltd v Souter* were these. The same area of land in Peterculter, Aberdeenshire ('the disputed area'), extending to around half a hectare, appeared in two different Sasine titles from the same granter. How this came about we do not know, but in each case the disputed area was disponed as part of larger subjects. The respective split-off dispositions dated from 1979 and 1990; and since ownership of the disputed area passed with the recording of the first disposition, the second disposition was ineffective to convey the area.

The disponee in 1979 was a Mr Souter. The subjects conveyed by the 1990 disposition were acquired by a Mr Stamper in 1994 and then passed through the hands of companies controlled by the Stamper family ending up, in 2006, in the ownership of Combined Corporation (BVI) Ltd ('CCL'). By this time, the title was on the Land Register. Mr Souter, however, continued to hold his property on a Sasine title.

1 LR(S)A 2012 sch 4 paras 17–24. For discussion of these complex provisions, see Reid and Gretton, *Land Registration* paras 11.9–11.12. Note that the provisions apply only to bijural inaccuracies: cf *McAdam's Exr v Keeper of the Registers of Scotland*, discussed at p 54 above.
2 LR(S)A 2012 sch 4 para 22.
3 LR(S)A 2012 sch 4 paras 23 and 24.
4 LR(S)A 2012 sch 4 para 18. This presumption has the important practical purpose of providing a rule in cases where, with the passing of the years, there is little or no evidence of the state of possession on 7 December 2014.
5 15 February 2018, Lands Tribunal affd [2018] CSIH 81, 2019 SLT 127.

Changes to the Aberdeen Local Plan resulted in the disputed area becoming a recommended site for residential development. Independently, both Mr Souter and CCL determined to build houses on it. To that end, Mr Souter, in 2015, disponed part of his property, including the disputed area, to a company he owned called Casa Developments SCO Ltd.[6] The application for registration was rejected by the Keeper on the basis that the disputed area was already registered as part of CCL's title, a registration which had taken place under the 1979 Act. Mr Souter applied to the Lands Tribunal to have it established that the Land Register was inaccurate in attributing the disputed area to CCL, and hence that CCL's title sheet should be rectified. One result of rectification would be to allow the registration of the disposition in favour of Casa Developments. The application to the Tribunal was opposed by CCL.

That the inclusion of the overlap in CCL's title had been an inaccuracy was accepted by both parties. So the first hurdle in Mr Souter's way was readily surmounted. But a second hurdle remained. In *Combined Corporation*, as in a growing number of other cases, the dispute resolved into the question of whether the registered proprietor, CCL, had been in possession of the disputed area on 7 December 2014, immediately before the designated day.

After six days of evidence, the Tribunal held that CCL had not been in possession, and hence that the Register could be rectified so as to remove the disputed area from CCL's title.[7] As so often, the evidence as to possession was convoluted and contradictory. In assessing its effect, the Tribunal placed particular reliance on the decision of the Inner House in *Safeway Stores plc v Tesco Stores Ltd*.[8] There Lord Hamilton had said that, for a proprietor to be in possession for the purposes of the 1979 Act, there had to be 'some significant element of physical control'; and for this purpose it was necessary to look at the position, not just on a single day, but over 'an appropriate tract of time preceding it'.[9] The appropriate tract of time in the present case, said the Tribunal, was the period of CCL's ownership, which had begun eight years before the designated day, in April 2006.

What, then, was the evidence of possession on the part of CCL? In the Tribunal's assessment:[10]

> it comprises a number of people visiting the land and walking over the disputed area for the purpose of showing it to intending developers and allowing those developers to work up a planning proposal for the eventual development of the land. There is no element of physical control; they never even marked out the boundaries of their property on the ground. There is no element of use of the land; nothing was done on it, not a spade was put in the ground (we have rejected Mr Stamper's evidence of tree-planting for the reasons given when discussing credibility) and it was not even surveyed, for aught heard in the evidence. Any 'enjoyment' of it by Mr & Mrs Stamper

6 This was presumably in tribute to Mr Souter's own house, which was called 'Nostra Casa'.
7 The decision is dated 15 February 2018. The Tribunal comprised Lord Minginish and A Oswald FRICS.
8 2004 SC 29.
9 2004 SC 29 at paras 77 and 80.
10 Paragraph 48 of the Lands Tribunal's judgment.

was recreational and cannot in our opinion be attributed to the interested party [CCL] which did not, so far as we know, have as one of its purposes recreational use of the land. Similarly negotiations with the planning department do not, on Lord Hamilton's view, constitute acts of possession, albeit those were informed by site visits.

By contrast, there was clear evidence of possession on the part of Mr Souter. His possession of the disputed area could be divided into three distinct periods. (i) From his acquisition of ownership in 1979 until the early 1990s Mr Souter was plainly in possession of the disputed area. (ii) From the early 1990s until 2009 there were no acts of possession apart from some dog-walking. (iii) From 2009 onwards Mr Souter's possession was 'very obviously affirmed again, first by the depositing of spoil from the site of Pauline Souter's house and the re-profiling of land around *Nostra Casa*, and then by the continuing work of clearance of trees as the applicant worked his way northward over his land'.[1]

Two questions required to be considered. The first was whether, having acquired possession during period (i), Mr Souter could be regarded as having retained it in period (ii) when he was making little or no use of the disputed area. The answer, as the Tribunal pointed out under reference to Stair's *Institutions* II.1.20, depended on whether Mr Souter's previous acquisition of possession had been usurped by contrary possession on the part of CCL. The Tribunal's assessment of the evidence was that there had been no usurpation:[2]

> What acts there were [on the part of CCL] were not even such as put the applicant on alert that his possession was being challenged. Had they been he would undoubtedly have challenged them. In those circumstances the applicant's possession is to be taken as having continued until 2009 when it came to be very obviously affirmed again.

The second question was whether the possessory acts in period (iii) could be regarded as merely a 'tennis match', ie acts artificially done in response to the challenge which was now being presented by CCL. The Tribunal did not think that that was the case.

CCL appealed to the Inner House, but without success.[3] The First Division was fully supportive of the judgment of the Lands Tribunal. On only one point did they differ. As previously mentioned, the 2012 Act creates a rebuttable presumption that the property was possessed by the registered proprietor, ie in this case CCL, immediately before the designated day.[4] But how strong is this presumption? In the Tribunal's view it could not be rebutted simply by evidence of non-possession on the part of the registered proprietor. Rebuttal required positive evidence of possession on the part of the challenger (ie Mr Souter). As it happened, such evidence was available. The First Division, surely correctly, disagreed. The absence of possession by CCL 'in itself, demonstrated that "the contrary" to the appellants' [CCL's] possession had been shown, even without

1 Paragraph 53.
2 Paragraph 53.
3 [2018] CSIH 81, 2019 SLT 127. Lord Carloway, the Lord President, was sitting with Lords Brodie and Drummond Young. The Opinion of the Court was delivered by the Lord President.
4 Land Registration etc (Scotland) Act 2012 sch 4 para 18.

any consideration of the respondent's [Mr Souter's] position'.[1] It was 'nevertheless open to the Tribunal to include in the equation the nature and extent of the respondent's possession of the disputed land', and no criticism could be made of the Tribunal's findings in that regard.[2]

SOLICITORS: LIABILITY TO THE OTHER SIDE?

Potential liability to one's client is an inevitable and, alas, familiar aspect of legal practice. Mistaken advice or other errors will occasionally happen, and a damages claim may then be the result. But is there also the possibility that a law firm might become liable to a damages claim by the party on the *other* side of a transaction? The answer is yes, though such claims are not easy to establish. *NRAM Ltd v Steel*, decided in the Supreme Court in 2018, is an important contribution to the law in this area.[3]

The facts

In many reported cases the full story never quite comes out. Sometimes the case as reported seems a complete story, but one discovers from other sources that the contrary is true. And sometimes it is apparent from the report itself that the story is incomplete. The latter is the position here. What the full story was, we do not know.

The sale of the four units

Headway Caledonian Ltd owned four units – numbers 1, 2, 3 and 4 – at Cadzow Business Park in Hamilton, Lanarkshire. Headway had substantial borrowings from NRAM. These borrowings were secured against all four units by means of standard securities and an all-assets floating charge. Headway had bought the properties in 1997/98 and the standard securities had been in place since that time. The floating charge had been granted in 2002. In 2005 Headway sold unit 3. NRAM discharged its standard security over unit 3 at the time of sale. Its standard securities over units 1, 2 and 4 remained in place.

In the course of 2007 the remaining three units were sold. The sale of unit 1 was completed in March 2007. In September/October 2007 the sale of unit 4 was completed, and finally in December 2007 the sale of unit 2 was completed. So by the end of 2007 all four units had been sold. In 2010 Headway went into insolvent liquidation.

---

1 Paragraph 23.
2 Paragraph 24.
3 [2018] UKSC 13, 2018 SC (UKSC) 141, 2018 SLT 835. (In the SLT report the name of the case is given incorrectly as *Steel v NRAM Ltd*.) In the course of the litigation the bank changed its name twice. When the litigation began it was Northern Rock (Asset Management) plc. Then it became NRAM plc. By the time the case reached the Supreme Court it was NRAM Ltd. There had been earlier name changes too: see *Conveyancing 2009* pp 58–59 and *Conveyancing 2012* pp 77–78.

In March 2007, on the eve of the sale of unit 1, the total debt to NRAM was £1,221,850. Unit 1 sold for £560,000. By agreement, £495,000 out of that amount was remitted to NRAM, as a result of which the debt was reduced to £726,850. Units 4 and 2, when they were sold, realised £750,000 and £325,000 respectively. What happened to these two sums is not disclosed in the litigation. Clearly not all the money was used to pay off the debt. We know that by the time that the present action was raised the amount outstanding was £458,723.99, or £440,162.68 if certain debits fell to be taken into account.[1] So between March 2007 and 2010, when Headway went into liquidation, more than £200,000 of capital must have been repaid, though the source of that repayment is not known.[2] As for interest, Headway continued to pay it until shortly before it went into liquidation.

The premature discharges

What happened to the standard securities and the floating charge? In a case of this sort, the lender would typically discharge the securities held, one by one, so as to enable the properties to be sold on the basis of unencumbered titles, and, in return, would be paid all or a large part of the sum realised on sale. At the same time, in relation to the floating charge, certificates of non-crystallisation would be given, one by one for each sale. If that straight-forward process had happened here, by the end of 2007 the amount owing to NRAM would have been paid off, because the total value of the units was larger than the total debt. But that was not what happened. It had, it is true, happened for the sale of unit 3 in 2005. But for the other three units, the story becomes strange.

NRAM, at the time of the sale of unit 1, in March 2007, discharged not only the standard security over unit 1 (as one would expect), but also the standard securities over the other two units, whose sales were not to be completed until some months later. Why? To that we will return, but it was this event – the early discharge of the standard securities over units 2 and 4 – that formed the basis of the present action. NRAM claimed that these discharges were granted in error, an error induced by the negligence of Headway's law firm, and that had the discharges not been granted, it would have made a full recovery of all sums owed to it.

What about the floating charge? When unit 1 was sold, in March 2007, a certificate of non-crystallisation was (as one would expect) granted, and the same happened later in the year for the sales of units 2 and 4. That was all in accordance with normal conveyancing practice – except for the mystery that the non-crystallisation certificates for units 2 and 4 did not bring about payment to the bank of the proceeds of sale, or such part thereof as might be agreed. To this puzzle we return below.

---

1   The difference between these figures does not matter for present purposes. For some discussion of the figures see para 51 of the case when at first instance: [2014] CSOH 172.
2   The question of what happened to the proceeds of the sales of units 4 and 2 is not explored in the case. Nor is the question of the repayment of over £200,000 of capital prior to liquidation.

In the liquidation NRAM was able to make a substantial recovery, but nevertheless overall there was a large shortfall. The shortfall, after deducting the amount recovered already from the liquidator, plus the further, smaller, amount that the bank could be expected to recover from the liquidator by the end of the winding-up process, was £369,811.18.[1] The bank raised the present action in delict to recover this shortfall from the law firm that had acted for Headway in 2007, plus the partner concerned, personally. The law firm did not act for the bank, which was unrepresented in relation to the transactions.

The mystery email

Central to the litigation was an email that the solicitor acting for Headway had sent to the bank during the sale of unit 1, at 5pm on 22 March 2007.

> Subject: headway caledonian limited sale of Pavilion 1 Cadzow Park Hamilton (title nos LAN 6421 and LAN 124573)
>
> Helen/Neil
>
> I need your usual letter of non-crystallisation for the sale of the above subjects to be faxed through here first thing tomorrow am if possible to 0141 221 0123 marked for my attention – I have had a few letters on this one for previous other units that have been sold. I also attach discharges for signing and return as well as the whole loan is being paid off for the estate and I have a settlement figure for that. Can you please arrange to get these signed and returned again asap.
>
> Many thanks
> Jane A Steel
> Jane Steel
> Partner
> For Bell & Scott LLP

The heading of the email referred to unit 1 as being 'title nos LAN 6421 and LAN 124573'. These two title numbers covered the three units that the company still had: 1, 4 and 2. The draft discharges attached were for the standard securities over the whole of both title units, ie not only unit 1 but also the units that were sold later in the year, namely 4 and 2.

When it received the email, the bank opened the attachments, printed them off, executed them, and returned them. The discharges were promptly registered, the result being that all three units were disencumbered of the standard securities.

Just why the email said that the *whole* remaining sums were being repaid, and all the standard securities were, therefore, to be fully discharged, was investigated in the proof. No answers were obtained.

As for the floating charge, the bank granted the following certificate, which, unlike the discharges of the standard securities, was restricted to unit 1:

---

1 See [2014] CSOH 172 at para 83.

PRIVATE AND CONFIDENTIAL[1]

FAO Jane Steel
Bell & Scott LLP ....

Dear Sirs

Commercial Mortgage Account Number: C2/14150T-00260
Headway Caledonian Limited
Pavilion 1 Cadzow Business Park Hamilton

We Northern Rock plc, the holders of a Floating Charge dated 27 June 2002 hereby confirm we have taken no steps to Crystallise the said Floating Charge.

Northern Rock consent to the sale of the subjects and will release the subjects from the floating charge on delivery of the disposition to the purchaser.[2]

Yours faithfully

Martin Clarke
Manager – Loan Reviews

The litigation

NRAM's case

NRAM's case against the defenders was set out in its pleadings:[3]

> Due to the formalities of settling Scottish conveyancing transactions (the purchase price will only generally be released, in exchange for inter alia a discharge of the security over the sale subjects), executed Discharges were as a matter of course provided to the borrower's solicitors in advance of funds being made available to NR.[4] It was therefore necessary for NR to rely exclusively on the borrower's solicitor where direct requests were made, such as here, for discharge documentation. This was the process which NR followed for the partial discharge of unit 3. By way of further example, the same solicitor had in November 2005 requested the execution of a full discharge (drafted by her firm) of a security over other subjects owned by HCL[5] (Macdonald Drive, Lossiemouth). This was provided to her in advance of funds being received for the redemption of the loan. Ms Steel was accordingly well aware that any request by her for discharge documentation from NR would generally be acted upon by them without question. She was also aware that it would be provided to her, and could be passed to the purchaser, in advance of redemption funds being transferred. This was on the implicit understanding that such funds would then be

---

1 Why the letter was headed 'private and confidential' we do not know. The normal purpose of a certificate of non-crystallisation is where a third party is transacting with the debtor company (as of course happened here). Were the certificate to be kept private as between the bank and the debtor company it would fail in its purpose, for the third party will not normally agree to complete the transaction without seeing the certificate.
2 The certificate uses the future tense, as if on delivery of the disposition the bank was to grant a further deed. But clearly that is not the meaning: the meaning is that on delivery of the disposition by Headway to the buyer the charge would cease to apply to unit 1.
3 See [2014] CSOH 172 at para 4.
4 'NR' means Northern Rock, later renamed as NRAM.
5 'HCL' means Headway Caledonian Ltd.

held by her to the strict order of NR and, in the absence of any contrary instruction, should be remitted to them forthwith ...

The members of the pursuers' CMT team who received the email ... the members of the pursuers' Admin Team who were responsible for having the discharges executed and the signing officer who executed both discharges were misled into believing that the first defender would repay or arrange repayment of the whole borrowings on receipt by her of the executed discharges. They were misled into believing that the first defender would not deliver the discharges to the purchaser of unit 1 or would not otherwise cause or permit the discharges to be registered without effecting or arranging repayment of the whole borrowings. If they had not been misled in this way they would not have arranged for the discharges to be executed or returned to the first defender ... NR are content to execute the discharge documents in advance of funds being received by them only because they rely on the requesting solicitor not releasing those documents without receiving in exchange a sum sufficient to redeem the outstanding loan and thereafter to hold those funds to NR's order. The first defender knew that this was a common practice in transactions where a solicitor acts for a party selling heritable property in Scotland which is burdened by security. She knew that the pursuers were relying on her not to release the discharges or otherwise cause or permit their registration unless or until they were repaid in full ...

The Outer House decision[1]

The Lord Ordinary[2] was unpersuaded by NRAM's argument. He said:[3]

The email was vague and ambiguous. There was tension between the subject heading and the body of the email. The email did not state what the settlement figure was, or by whom the first defender had been provided with it. It cried out for clarification ... I have no real difficulty in concluding that it was not reasonable for a bank in the position of the pursuers to rely on the misstatement information without checking its accuracy; and that a solicitor in the position of the first defender would not foresee that such a bank would reasonably rely on that information without carrying out such a check. Any prudent bank taking the most basic precautions would have checked the information provided by seeking clarification from the first defender and/or looking at their file.

The Inner House decision[4]

When the case went to the Inner House the Lord Ordinary's decision was reversed by a two-to-one majority. We quote from Lady Smith, giving the leading opinion for the majority:[5]

The Lord Ordinary required, when applying the law to the facts, to give careful consideration to, and answer, the question of whether or not Ms Steel fell to be treated by the law as having assumed responsibility for the misstatements and their consequences. I readily accept that the particular circumstances weighed heavily in

1 [2014] CSOH 172, [2015] PNLR 16. For discussion, see *Conveyancing 2014* pp 51–52.
2 Lord Doherty.
3 Paragraphs 77 and 78.
4 [2016] CSIH 11, 2016 SC 474, 2016 SLT 285. For discussion, see *Conveyancing 2016* pp 175–84.
5 Paragraphs 45–47.

favour of NRAM's contention that, on the question of assumption of responsibility alone, they were, when the email was written and sent, owed a duty of care by Ms Steel. The representations made in an email which she 'signed' in her capacity as a solicitor, particularly those to the effect that the circumstances were such as to require the attached discharges to be signed, were within her area of professional skill. The information was supplied – looking at matters objectively – for the purpose of being relied on by NRAM. Ms Steel had demonstrated in two previous transactions where NRAM did not have their own solicitor acting for them that she could be trusted. She knew that 'Helen/Neil' were not solicitors and that NRAM did not have a solicitor acting for them in relation to the Unit 1 transaction; indeed, there was, on the Lord Ordinary's findings nothing to afford NRAM justification for thinking she could not be trusted on this occasion. NRAM did in fact rely on her word 'as a solicitor' (see Lord Ordinary's opinion at para 25). The representations made were, on the terms of the email, Ms Steel's representations; they were not, for instance, qualified under reference to what her client had told her. Further, she had no authority for the representations of fact in the email or for the representation that NRAM required to sign and return discharge documents. The email was sent at close of business on 23 March and related to a transaction that was to settle the following day; there was a palpable sense of urgency in its terms.

Further, I consider that there is merit in Mr Clancy's[1] submission that, properly understood, this was not an arms' length transaction. It was in the interests of both NRAM and HCL to ensure that the sale of the unit was completed. Both would benefit financially from the proceeds of sale ... The key aspects of the email were unequivocal: NRAM needed to provide Ms Steel with a letter of non-crystallisation and signed discharges in the form attached, as a matter of some urgency, and they needed to do so in circumstances where the whole loan due (for which she had a settlement figure) was being paid off. That was the purpose of the email; its message was clear and unequivocal. It was also, of course, wrong but there was nothing in the body of the email to cause doubt as to the veracity of that message. For reasons which I explain below, resultant harm to NRAM in the form of economic loss was reasonably foreseeable.

In these circumstances, the Lord Ordinary required to ask whether this was one of those cases where the law attributes assumption of responsibility to the solicitor and, in doing so, provides a complete answer to the duty of care question, obviating the need for further inquiry including inquiry as to whether or not NRAM could or should have checked their file. I cannot read his opinion as indicating that he did so. Had that question been asked, I consider it to be inevitable that the conclusion would have been that this was one of those cases. The factors I have referred to – which are all drawn from the Lord Ordinary's findings in fact and are more extensive than those listed by him in para 73 – weigh heavily in favour of the law attributing assumption of responsibility to Ms Steel and thus, without further inquiry, imposing on her a duty of care. It being conceded that if she did owe the duty then it was breached, that would be an end of matters.

The Supreme Court decides

The defenders sought leave to appeal to the Supreme Court. Perhaps surprisingly, given the importance of the case, and the fact that the Court of Session judges

---

1   Ronald Clancy QC represented the pursuer.

were themselves evenly divided,[1] this request was refused by the Inner House, but the Supreme Court itself authorised an appeal to proceed. The appeal took place and the result was that the Supreme Court unanimously reversed the decision of the Inner House, thereby reinstating the decision of the Lord Ordinary.[2]

Referring to the *fons et origo* of delictual liability in this area, *Hedley Byrne & Co Ltd v Heller & Partners Ltd*,[3] the court noted 'the emphasis given in the decision in the *Hedley Byrne* case to the need for the representee reasonably to have relied on the representation and for the representor reasonably to have foreseen that he would do so'.[4] The court also quoted with approval the remarks of Lord Jauncey in a later case:[5]

> Four factors are relevant to a determination of the question whether in a particular case a solicitor, while acting for a client, also owes a duty of care to a third party: (1) the solicitor must assume responsibility for the advice or information furnished to the third party; (2) the solicitor must let it be known to the third party expressly or impliedly that he claims, by reason of his calling, to have the requisite skill or knowledge to give the advice or furnish the information; (3) the third party must have relied upon that advice or information as matter for which the solicitor has assumed personal responsibility;[6] and (4) the solicitor must have been aware that the third party was likely so to rely.

In a fairly short judgment, the Supreme Court agreed with the Lord Ordinary and with Lord Brodie, who had dissented when *NRAM* was in the Inner House. The nub of the decision can be found in the following passage:[7]

> A commercial lender about to implement an agreement with its borrower referable to its security does not act reasonably if it proceeds upon no more than a description of its terms put forward by or on behalf of the borrower. The lender knows the terms of the agreement and indeed, as in this case, is likely to have evolved and proposed them. In so far as the particular officers in Northern Rock who on 23 March 2007 saw and acted upon the e-mail had never been aware of the terms or had forgotten them, immediate access to the correct terms lay – literally – at their finger-tips. No authority has been cited to the court, nor discovered by me in preparing this judgment, in which it has been held that there was an assumption of responsibility for a careless misrepresentation about a fact wholly within the knowledge of the representee.

---

1 Two judges (one Outer House judge and one Inner House judge) held for the defenders; two judges (both Inner House) held for the pursuer.
2 [2018] UKSC 13, 2018 SC (UKSC) 141, 2018 SLT 835. The justices who sat were Lady Hale, Lord Wilson, Lord Reed, Lord Hodge, and Lady Black. A single judgment was given, by Lord Wilson.
3 [1964] AC 465.
4 Paragraph 19.
5 *Midland Bank plc v Cameron, Thom, Peterkin & Duncans* 1988 SLT 611. This was when Lord Jauncey was still in the Court of Session; in the same year he was elevated to the House of Lords.
6 Without questioning the overall soundness of Lord Jauncey's approach, we would note that the existence or non-existence of a duty of care at the time of giving the advice can hardly depend on a *later* event, ie on whether the representee *actually did* rely on the advice. Actual reliance is a *sine qua non* of the existence of *liability*. Put in other words, whether or not there is actual reliance is a *causation* issue not a *duty* issue.
7 Paragraph 38.

The explanation is, no doubt, that in such circumstances it is not reasonable for the representee to rely on the representation without checking its accuracy and that it is, by contrast, reasonable for the representor not to foresee that he would do so.

Some reflections

Reliance

The pursuer's case was based on reliance. It pled: 'It was ... necessary for NR to rely exclusively on the borrower's solicitor ...'[1] This seems to us a remarkable statement. A lender is under no necessity whatsoever to rely on the borrower's law firm.

Unbillable hours

The pursuer's case was delictual not contractual: there was no suggestion that Messrs Bell & Scott had been retained by *both* sides. But in substance NRAM was asserting that it was entitled to treat Bell & Scott as its law agents, obtaining the benefit of their services free of charge. There can be cases where X reasonably relies on the law firm that acts for the other side, and *Dean v Allin & Watts* (below) may be one of them. But it is difficult to feel sympathy with a bank that was seeking legal services without having to pay for them.

Dean v Allin & Watts

We took the view in our 2016 volume that the Inner House decision was wrong and hence we welcome the decision of the Supreme Court.[2] We will not repeat at length what we said in that volume, but it is perhaps worth commenting on the *Dean* case,[3] given the weight that that case was accorded in the Inner House, and given that the Supreme Court, though mentioning it, says little about it.

Dean was a case in the English Court of Appeal in which Mr Dean had wished to lend money on mortgage. Messrs Allin & Watts were a law firm that acted for the borrower from Mr Dean. Mr Dean was legally unrepresented. He was granted a mortgage of a type that had once been valid, but was no longer valid.[4] The borrower became insolvent, and Mr Dean sued Messrs Allin & Watts in negligence. He succeeded. The decision is significant. But there are two factors which make it very different from the facts in *NRAM*. In the first place, in *NRAM* the lender was a bank; in *Dean* the lender was a car mechanic. In the second place, the negligence in *Dean* concerned a matter of *legal* knowledge: what type of mortgage was or was not valid in English law. In *NRAM* the bank was not relying on the legal knowledge of Messrs Bell & Scott LLP. The question was whether the whole indebtedness was being repaid. That was a banking question, not a conveyancing question. The question of whether all the standard securities

---

1 See above for the full passage.
2 See *Conveyancing 2016* pp 175–84.
3 *Dean v Allin & Watts* [2001] 2 Lloyd's Rep 249.
4 The mortgage was by simple deposit of the title deeds. This type of mortgage had ceased to be valid as a result of s 2 of the Law of Property (Miscellaneous Provisions) Act 1989.

fell to be discharged was a wholly subsidiary one, depending on the answer to the primary, factual question.

Decision in *NRAM* quite narrow

Conveyancers will welcome the Supreme Court's decision in *NRAM*. But the ratio of the case seems to be fairly narrow. The decision does not say 'conveyancers are never liable to the party on the other side of the transaction'. What determined the outcome of the case was the conclusion that it had not been reasonable for NRAM to rely on the email. In coming to that conclusion the court stressed that the representee was a 'commercial lender' and that the true facts of the transaction 'lay – literally – at their finger-tips'.[1] Whether reliance on a representation is reasonable will always depend on the facts and circumstances of the case. So: from a solicitor's point of view, two cheers only.

The floating charge

The case as reported does not fully explore the facts, and so it may not be out of place to offer a few further remarks.

The bank not only had standard securities, but also an all-assets floating charge. And the story about that is as strange, or stranger, but largely unexplored in the litigation. The core of the bank's case was that it had thought, relying on the email, that the whole loan was being paid off. That account is consistent with the fact that discharges of all the standard securities were granted. But is it consistent with what happened to the floating charge? The bank granted a certificate of non-crystallisation *but only for unit 1*. Why? How can this overtly limited certificate be reconciled with the idea that immediate full repayment was expected?

Next, what happened to the floating charge after the events of March 2007? It will be recalled that the debtor company was selling all four units, the last two being sold later in the same year as unit 1: unit 4 in September/October 2007 and unit 2 in December 2007. It will also be recalled that the bank still had security over these properties by way of its all-assets floating charge. It could be reasonably sure of being paid out of the proceeds of these two sales for the simple reason that refusal to grant the necessary certificates of non-crystallisation would prevent the sales from taking place. In other words, notwithstanding the discharge of the standard securities in March, the bank still had the leverage to obtain full repayment. So what happened? It happily granted the certificates for units 2 and 4 *without repayment*. Hence the simple story told by the bank – namely, 'we were misled by the defenders, in March 2007, into thinking that we would be receiving full payment, and acted accordingly, and thereby incurred loss' – is not easy to understand.

One could also put the matter more technically, and suggest that even if an actionable wrong had been committed by the defenders in March 2007, the chain of causation was thereafter broken, not once, but twice – in September/October

---

1 See the passage quoted above.

2007, and again in December. The pursuer had, after all, to establish that, had the discharges of the standard securities not been granted in March 2007, it would have made a full recovery of all sums owed to it. It is difficult to discern, on the facts as disclosed in the case, any solid basis for that view. This large aspect of the matter – what happened to the floating charge after March 2007 – is almost undiscussed in the litigation. It is not mentioned either in the Inner House or in the Supreme Court, and only briefly in the Outer House.[1] We do not know why it was almost entirely left on one side. And as to what actually happened from March to December 2007 we are more or less in the dark.

SERVITUDES

Using and improving roads

Introduction

McDonald v Young is not a new case but an old one which has only recently come to light. It was decided in Perth Sheriff Court on 2 April 1937.[2] The Opinion of the sheriff-substitute[3] deals with some important matters and repays study.

Mr McDonald was the proprietor of the farm and lands of Haughend in the Parish of Dunning and County of Perth. Mr Young owned the neighbouring farm of Nether Garvock. At one point the boundary between the farms was a service road which ran from north to south and was framed by hedges on either side. Mr McDonald's farm lay to the west of the road and Mr Young's to the east. The road was Mr McDonald's property, the boundary being two march stones in the hedge which separated the road from a field forming part of Mr Young's farm.[4] Mr Young had a servitude of pedestrian and vehicular access over the road which had been constituted by positive prescription.

Originally the road was no more than a cart track with grass verges on either side. In 1935, however, Mr Young took steps to widen and improve the road so as to make it suitable for motorised traffic. This involved constructing a new surface of road metal extending over a width of 10 feet 6 inches.

The immediate result was an outbreak of letters between the farmers' respective solicitors. First in the frame was a letter from Messrs Thomas E Young of Auchterarder on behalf of Mr McDonald, sent on 25 June 1935:

> Mr McDonald informs us that your client, Mr Young, is now laying down metal on his (Mr McDonald's) road, which runs along the west side of the march between Haughend and Garvock. Will you kindly let us know why and under what authority this is being done?

---

1 [2014] CSOH 172 at paras 50 and 82.
2 Like quite a number of other cases in this volume, this case was excavated by Professor Roderick Paisley of the University of Aberdeen. We are grateful to him for drawing it to our attention and for providing a copy of the judgment.
3 Sheriff G D Valentine.
4 The precise line of the boundary was itself a matter of contention in the litigation.

To that polite but icy inquiry Messrs Condie Mackenzie & Co of Perth sent the following reply on 2 July, having first met with Mr McDonald's law agent:

> With reference to your letter of 25th ulto, and our meeting with your Mr Peter Young this afternoon, we have since spoken to our client, who informs us that the work he is carrying out on the service road is to make good the damage occasioned by the Harts when they were tenants of Nether Garvock and by timber haulage.
> Mr Young[1] seemed surprised at the attitude your client is taking up as he feels that the repairs he is effecting to the road will be beneficial both to your client and himself. So far Mr Young has not asked your client for a contribution towards the repairs, and he suggests that if your client is prepared to admit Mr Young's right of access to his fields from the road[2] that he will not ask your client for any contribution in respect of the repairs[3] now being carried out. It seems to us that this is a very generous offer on the part of Mr Young, and we trust your client will see his way to agree to it and get this question amicably settled.

Any hopes of an 'amicable' settlement were, however, dashed by the curt response of Messrs Thomas E Young on 12 July:

> We refer further to your letter of 2nd inst, about which we have now heard from our client. The proposals, however, made by your client are not acceptable to Mr McDonald. It would appear therefore that this matter is not to be settled out of Court, and an Action has consequently been instructed.

The action was indeed raised shortly afterwards. Among other craves Mr McDonald sought to interdict Mr Young 'from widening and/or altering and/or improving said service road or interfering with the verges of the same without the approval of the pursuer'. The main issue between the parties was thus the right of a servitude-holder such as Mr Young to improve the road over which the servitude was held. But an important preliminary issue was whether the servitude, constituted as it was by prescription, was limited to the original cart track or whether, on the contrary, it extended to the grass verges.

Verges

There is no fixed rule as to whether a servitude of way extends to the verges of a road. As was said by Lord Macfadyen in *Stansfield v Findlay*,[4] giving the Opinion of the First Division:

> We did not find support in any of the authorities cited to us for the view that, as a matter of law, the track over which access is to be provided must be construed as including its 'verges' ... We accept that there may be cases in which it can be inferred that a right of way which passes between fenced enclosures extends to the full width between the fences and is not limited to a worn or metalled track lying within that

---

1 Ie Condie Mackenzie's client and the defender in the ensuing action.
2 A separate ground of dispute as to which see below.
3 The use of the word 'repairs' was no doubt intended to minimise the extent of the works actually being carried out.
4 1998 SLT 784 at 787–88.

area. That may, for example, be the case with former drove roads. Each case depends on its own facts, however.

Where the servitude in question is constituted by deed, the matter must be resolved by interpretation of the deed coupled, if the deed is unclear, with a consideration of the circumstances at the time of grant.[1] In some cases this has led to the conclusion that the verge was included within the servitude,[2] in others that it was not.[3]

In the present case, however, the servitude was constituted not by deed but by prescription. There the usual rule is that the extent of the servitude is measured by the extent of possession: *tantum praescriptum quantum possessum*. That rule was indeed applied relatively recently in *Garson v McLeish*,[4] a decision of Sheriff Daniel Kelly QC, where there was said to be insufficient possession for the servitude to extend over the verges. But in cases like this, evidence of possession is often both hard to find and also disputed. Accordingly, the sheriff in *McDonald v Young* took a broader – some might say, a more common-sense – view, following a proof:[5]

> With regard to the use made of the road it admittedly is a service road. It is common ground that up till lately there was only a cart track along it. There has been a great deal of discrepant evidence as to the breadth of this track. That is not surprising. An access road to a farm is a familiar object and everyone knows that it would be difficult, if not impossible, to state the breadth of the track. At times and places there may be only a single pair of wheel tracks, at other places, particularly where the ground is soft, the tracks are spread out as the cart sought for firmer ground. Where carts have to meet they will pass each other by leaving the ordinary track and going on to the verge. Even in the same place the track might at one time consist of only two wheel marks, and at another of a number.

Although not referring to the *tantum praescriptum* rule the sheriff accepted the principle 'that the breadth of the road is measured by the breadth of the cart tracks that may be on it at any time'. But in applying that principle, some generous assumptions might appropriately be adopted:

> It is obvious here that the whole strip between the hedges ... has been set aside for passage though it was not usually required. So far as not required at the time for that purpose it was simply overgrown by weeds and brambles. It seems to me that a person having the right to use this road is entitled to use any part of the strip and

---

1 *Wimpey Homes Holding Ltd v Collins* 1999 SLT (Sh Ct) 16 at 19H per Sheriff-Principal G L Cox QC.
2 *Alvis v Harrison* 1991 SLT 64; *Wimpey Homes Holding Ltd v Collins* 1999 SLT (Sh Ct) 16; *Craig v J D Peace and Company (Aberdeen) Ltd*, 9 February 2015, Aberdeen Sheriff Court, unreported (Case (22) above).
3 *Stansfield v Findlay* 1998 SLT 784; *Thomas v Allan* 2004 SC 393.
4 2010 SLT (Sh Ct) 131; see *Conveyancing 2009* pp 13–14.
5 An obvious criticism of this approach is that it comes close to removing the onus of proof from the servitude-holder. A holder of a servitude who is unable to prove possession over the verge must, on the traditional view, fail in the action.

that so long as he does not go out of it he is not increasing the burden of the servitude by using any part of it, or the whole of it.

Mr Young's servitude, it seemed, included a right to take access over the verges.

Improvements

But that decision merely cleared the ground for the main issue: was Mr Young entitled to carry out improvements, thereby transforming a soft cart-track into a metalled road? The general rule here is well-settled. A servitude-holder can carry out such repairs and improvements as are reasonably necessary for the servitude's exercise or enjoyment.[1] Yet if the rule is clear there is relatively little case law on its practical application. A new case – or an old case freshly exhumed – is thus greatly to be welcomed.

In one reported case, improving a road's surface by means of hard core and gravel was allowed although, unlike in *McDonald v Young*, there was no question of increasing the width.[2] In another case, improvements to a path over sand dunes so as to make it suitable for the vehicular traffic for which the servitude had been granted was also permitted.[3] In *McDonald v Young*, however, it was the change in technology from horse and cart to motor vehicles which made it necessary and hence justifiable to metal the surface of the road. As the sheriff explained:

> The introduction of motor cars and motor lorries has made the track which formerly gave sufficient access to Nether Garvock quite insufficient for the purpose. It is not merely a matter of convenience, but of necessity, to improve the road as has been done. Formerly tradesmen's horse vans could go up with supplies over the old road, but now tradesmen do not have horse vans. Tradesmen's motor vans cannot safely do so, and therefore the tenant of Nether Garvock has the choice of making a road that they can go over, or going without supplies. Again motor lorries cannot go up the old road. It has been proved that some of them tried to do so and came to grief. It is true that it is not a matter of absolutely necessity that motor lorries should go up the road as they could discharge manure and so forth at the end of it, and the goods could then be carted up. But the inconvenience in this is so great that I think it must be regarded as an economic impossibility.

This is a valuable decision. Nor is it confined to roads, because changes in technology can require physical changes to be made in relation to other types of servitude as well such as servitudes for pipelines and cables.

That was not quite the end of the matter because even an improvement which is needed for a servitude's exercise or enjoyment must give way to the fundamental principle that the burden on the servient tenement is not to be increased.[4] But here, said the sheriff, no such increase could be anticipated:

---

1 D J Cusine and R R M Paisley, *Servitudes and Rights of Way* (1998) paras 12.124–12.126. These passages were approved and applied in *Garson v McLeish* 2010 SLT (Sh Ct) 131 at paras 68 ff.
2 *Lord Burton v Mackay* 1995 SLT 507 especially at 510.
3 *Pullar v Gauldie*, 25 August 2004, Arbroath Sheriff Court, noted in *Conveyancing 2010* pp 15–16.
4 Cusine and Paisley, *Servitudes and Rights of Way* paras 14.15–14.17; *Lord Burton v Mackay* 1995 SLT 507 at 510D per Lord Coulsfield.

The servient tenant is bound to give passage over any part of the road lying between the hedges. The defender [Mr Young] has confined his operations to the part over which he is entitled to passage and I cannot see that he has increased the burden of the servient tenant to any extent.

One final matter remained to be considered. Who was to bear the cost of making and thereafter maintaining the road? An offer to pay the former, it will be recalled, was one of the carrots dangled by Mr Young before Mr McDonald in the hope of securing the latter's agreement to the improvements. As the making of the road was an initiative of Mr Young's, carried out in the face of opposition from Mr McDonald, there could be no question of requiring a contribution from the latter. But what about ongoing maintenance? On first principles, there is no requirement on a servient owner to maintain the servient property, for servitudes impose obligations which are passive in nature (*in patiendo*) rather than active (*in faciendo*). But nor is there a requirement on the dominant owner to maintain except in a case where this was a condition of the creation of the servitude. In the sheriff's view, however, it was for Mr Young to attend to maintenance:

> I may add, though it is not perhaps strictly relevant, that in my view he [Mr Young] is bound to keep up this new road himself and cannot call upon the pursuer [Mr McDonald] to share the expense. The pursuer also makes use of the road for access to his fields, and to the stockyard, but for these purposes the old road was good enough. Accordingly, I do not think he can be required to bear any portion of the expense of making or upholding the new road.

It is not quite clear what this passage means. If it means that Mr Young could not look to Mr McDonald for a contribution to maintenance, then it is both correct and unexceptional. But if it means that Mr Young is bound, as opposed to entitled, to maintain the road, then it goes beyond the existing authorities. No ground of decision is given, but a possible ground would be that, by making a new road, Mr Young was taken to have assumed responsibility for its maintenance. It need hardly be added that the responsibility would potentially be a heavy one.

Additional access points

One final bone of contention concerned the manner in which the road was accessed. In the recent past, Mr Young had opened up two new access points in the hedge between his field and the road. Mr McDonald challenged his right to do so. If the hedge had belonged to Mr Young, there could presumably have been no objection as to this method of access.[1] But it seems that the hedge belonged in whole or in part to Mr McDonald, with the result that access through it required the existence of a servitude (ie through the thickness of the hedge).

Mr Young sought to argue that such a servitude had been constituted by prescription. The evidence of possession, however, was slight and patchy. One witness claimed to have opened the two gaps for carts in the early years of the Great War. Other witnesses spoke to carts using the gaps when the fields were

---

1 See *Alvis v Harrison* 1991 SLT 64.

in crop in various years going back to 1884. But for much of the time the gaps had been closed up by wire and other barriers. Such meagre acts of possession, the sheriff thought, employing a mode of reasoning which is familiar from cases on prescriptive servitudes,[1] was 'attributable, and naturally attributable, to indifference and neighbourly tolerance on the part of those who saw it'. No right had been established by prescription.

Servitudes of recreation

Regency Villas

From the sheriff court in 1937 to the Supreme Court in 2018. *Regency Villas Title Ltd v Diamond Resorts (Europe) Ltd*,[2] although a decision in an English appeal, is likely to be influential in Scotland where the law of servitudes shares many features with the law of easements in England.[3] In the same way that the decision of the House of Lords in the Scottish case of *Moncrieff v Jamieson*[4] is often treated, south of the border, as an English decision, so *Regency Villas* may in time come to be treated in Scotland as if, virtually, it was a Scottish decision.

The case has been mentioned in these volumes before as it was working its way through the lower courts.[5] It concerned two neighbouring timeshare developments near Canterbury, one large and the other small. Broome Park, the larger development, was centred on a seventeenth-century mansion which had once been the home of Lord Kitchener of Khartoum. The smaller development next door was known as Regency Villas. Both properties were developed and owned by the same company, Gulf Investments Ltd, and both used the same recreational facilities, all of which were located in Broome Park. These were lavish in nature and included an 18-hole golf course, an outdoor heated swimming pool, tennis and squash courts, Italianate gardens, a croquet lawn and a skating rink, riding stables, and, within the mansion house itself, a restaurant, lounge, billiard room and a gym with sauna and solarium.

In 1981, shortly after the development at Regency Villas was completed, Gulf Investments conveyed Regency Villas to another company in the same group. And so Regency Villas came to be, and remained, in separate ownership from Broome Park. Yet those with timeshares in the former continued to use the recreational facilities in the latter. This had been the subject of express provision in the conveyance of Regency Villas, which conferred on the grantee and its successors and lessees the right:

---

1 Another example from this year's crop of cases, but reaching the opposite conclusion on the basis of the substantial amount of possession, is *Macgregor v Keig Properties Ltd*, 12 March 2018, Aberdeen Sheriff Court (Case (19) above).

2 [2018] UKSC 57, [2018] 3 WLR 1603. The principal judgment was given by Lord Briggs, with whom Lady Hale and Lords Kerr of Tonaghmore and Sumption agreed. Lord Carnwath dissented.

3 This is mainly because Roman law has been influential in the English law of easements, albeit often mediated through French law and especially the *Code civil*: see C Seebo, *Servitus und Easement: Die Rezeption des römisches Servitutenrechts in England* (2005).

4 [2007] UKHL 42, 2008 SC (HL) 1.

5 *Conveyancing 2016* pp 138–40 covering the decision at first instance; *Conveyancing 2017* pp 13–15 covering the decision in the Court of Appeal.

to use the swimming pool, golf course, squash courts, tennis courts, the ground and basement floor of Broome Park Mansion House, gardens and any other sporting or recreational facilities ... on the Transferor's adjoining estate.

There was, however, no corresponding obligation to contribute to the cost. Nor was the owner of Broome Park taken bound to maintain the facilities; indeed in English law a positive covenant of that sort would not have been enforceable against successors.

Over time the two developments came to be owned by unconnected companies. The facilities began to deteriorate. Some were closed, others replaced. The owners of Regency Villas started to make voluntary payments in aid of maintenance. Ultimately, timeshare holders from Regency Villas were being charged for any facilities that they used. At this point the owner of Regency Villas protested, and, protests being of no avail, raised the present action for a declaration that the timeshare holders at Regency Villas were entitled, by way of easement, to the free use of all the sporting or recreational facilities from time to time provided within Broome Park. Also sought was an injunction restraining interference by the defendants, who were the current freehold and leasehold owners of Broome Park.

The Supreme Court accepted, as a matter of construction, that the owner and users of Regency Villas had been granted a right to use, free of charge, such recreational facilities as existed from time to time at Broome Park. But unless this was an easement, it would not bind successors as owner of Broome Park such as the defendants. The question to be determined, therefore, was whether a right of recreation of this kind and extent could be and had been constituted as an easement.

The main obstacle was what in Scotland would be called the requirement of praediality. An easement, like a servitude, must benefit property and not merely people. Furthermore, the connection to the property – to the dominant tenement – must be palpable and must support a normal use of that property. As Lord Briggs put matters in *Regency Villas*:[1]

> [I]t is not enough that the right is merely appurtenant or annexed to the dominant tenement, if the enjoyment of it has nothing to do with the normal use of it. Nor is it sufficient that the right in question adds to the value of the dominant tenement. Thus for example, a right granted to the owners and occupiers of a house in Kennington to have free access to the Oval cricket ground on test match days might be annexed to the ownership of that house, and add significantly to its value. But it would have nothing to do with the normal use of the property as a home.

A particular difficulty with a recreational right was that it could 'fairly be described as an end in itself, rather than a means to an end (ie to the more enjoyable or full use of the dominant tenement)'.[2] Could an activity giving pleasure in itself, and which usually existed without reference to any property

---

1 Paragraph 40.
2 Paragraph 44.

at all, nonetheless be created as an easement? The Supreme Court thought that it could:[1]

> In the present case the dominant tenement was to be used for the development, not of homes, still less townhouses, but of timeshare apartments. Although in terms of legal memory timeshare is a relatively recent concept, timeshare units of this kind are typically occupied for holidays, by persons seeking recreation, including sporting activities, and it is to my mind plain beyond a doubt (as it was to the judge) that the grant of rights to use an immediately adjacent leisure development with all its recreational and sporting facilities is of service, utility and benefit to the timeshare apartments as such, just as (although for different reasons) the grant of rights over a communal garden is of service, utility and benefit to a townhouse.

Furthermore, behind this particular example was a larger point of principle. This was 'that the grant of purely recreational (including sporting) rights over land which genuinely accommodate adjacent land may be the subject matter of an easement'.[2]

Some awkward questions

The right recognised in *Regency Villas* is no ordinary easement (or servitude), and it has the potential to create problems which do not arise, or arise to the same extent, with other kinds of servitude. To be usable, sporting facilities need work and attention. Swimming pools must be cleaned and filled. In golf courses the grass must be cut and the greens manicured. All sporting facilities, moreover, will deteriorate with use and with the passage of time, as indeed happened in the Broome Park development, and so will require maintenance or replacement. What, then, is the position of the dominant proprietors in the servitude? Can the servient proprietors be made to maintain the facilities and, if necessary, to replace them? Or alternatively can the dominant proprietors take matters into their own hands and carry out the works of maintenance and replacement by themselves?

There was no question, in *Regency Villas*, of the servient proprietors being under a duty to maintain and replace.[3] That indeed stems from the very nature of a servitude, the burden of which can only be passive in nature.[4] In Scotland, however, though not in England, the difficulty can be solved by combining the servitude with a real burden of maintenance. According to taste, this could provide for maintenance by the servient proprietor alone or by the dominant proprietor alone or by both proprietors acting together. There is even a name for such a real burden in the Title Conditions (Scotland) Act 2003: it is a facility burden.[5]

Suppose, however, that no such real burden has been imposed, and that the facilities begin to deteriorate. Can the dominant proprietors step into the place

---

1 Paragraph 53.
2 Paragraph 81.
3 Paragraphs 68 and 69.
4 This point was emphasised in *Regency Villas*: see paras 66 and 68.
5 Defined in Title Conditions (Scotland) Act 2003 s 122(1).

of the servient proprietors and do the work themselves, at their own expense? Is managing and maintaining a swimming pool a right of the same order as maintaining and improving a road (the subject of the litigation in *McDonald v Young*, discussed above)? Can it really be said to flow from the right of use which the servitude primarily confers?

These issues were discussed but not fully resolved in *Regency Villas*. Lord Briggs ventured the view 'that step-in rights are, by definition, rights to reasonable access for maintenance of the servient tenement, sufficient, but no more than sufficient, to enable the rights granted to be used'.[1] Swimming pools could be filled, but it seemed doubtful that there could be powers of day-to-day management. That in itself would exclude certain types of recreational facilities from easements:[2]

> It is not difficult to imagine recreational facilities which do depend upon the active and continuous management and operation by the servient owner, which no exercise of step-in rights by the dominant owners would make useable, even for a short period. Free rides on a miniature steam railway, a covered ski slope with artificial snow, or adventure rides in a theme park are examples which would probably lie on the wrong side of the line, so as to be incapable of forming the subject matter of an easement. But the precise dividing line in any particular case will be a question of fact.

The position in Scotland

Would *Regency Villas* be followed in Scotland? Are we witnessing the dawn of a new age of recreational servitudes? In Calvinist Scotland, the traditional view was sceptical if not downright hostile. Writing in 1821 about the alleged 'servitude of walking (*spatiandi*) for sport or amusement on another man's land', Baron Hume commented that:[3]

> There is certainly at present no Judgement which acknowledges such a servitude; and indeed the general precepts of our practice seem rather to be against such a privilege. It seems rather to be in the nature of a personal privilege (which our law does not recognise) and for the gratification of an individual – than a matter of substantial benefit to a tenement, so as to bring it under the maxim of *praedium servit praedio*.

When, therefore, the issue of recreational rights was considered in 1867 in the leading case of *Patrick v Napier*,[4] the court refused to recognise as a servitude a right 'of angling or rod-fishing in the river Echaig'.

Yet *Patrick v Napier* is not the end of the story. The decision itself can be explained, at least in part, by the distance between the alleged dominant tenement and the river in which the fishing rights were to be exercised. It might be a different matter if, as in *Regency Villas*, the properties were next-door.

---

1 Paragraph 65. As his primary authority, Lord Briggs gave *Gale on Easements* (20th edn, by Jonathan Gaunt and The Hon Mr Justice Morgan, 2016) para 1–93. The equivalent of 'step-in' rights in Scots law would be ancillary rights.
2 Paragraph 72.
3 *Baron David Hume's Lectures 1786–1822* vol III (ed G C H Paton, Stair Society vol 15, 1952) 269.
4 (1867) 5 M 683.

Two other factors suggest that the law in this area is on the move. One, of which much was made in *Regency Villas*, is the greatly enhanced role of exercise in contemporary living:[1]

[T]he advantages to be gained from recreational and sporting activities are now so universally regarded as being of real utility and benefit to human beings that the pejorative expression 'mere right of recreation and amusement, possessing no quality of utility or benefit' has become a contradiction in terms, viewed separately from the issues as to accommodation of the dominant tenement. Recreation, including sport, and the amusement which comes with it, does confer utility and benefit on those who undertake it. ... Whatever may have been the attitude in the past to 'mere recreation or amusement', recreational and sporting activity of the type exemplified by the facilities at Broome Park is so clearly a beneficial part of modern life that the common law should support structures which promote and encourage it, rather than treat it as devoid of practical utility or benefit.

The other factor, which applies to Scotland alone, is s 76 of the Title Conditions (Scotland) Act 2003. Up until the enactment of that provision, servitudes in Scotland had been restricted to a more or less fixed list of permissible servitudes.[2] Section 76 abandons that list in the case of new servitudes created by writing and registration. Thus the fact that recreational servitudes have not been recognised in the past is no barrier to their recognition in the future.

Will, then, *Regency Park* be followed in Scotland? It may be that a right to swim or play golf lies on the edge of what is likely to be accepted as a servitude or that, if it is accepted, it will be allowed only for the benefit of timeshare developments, hotels and the like, as indeed the late Professor W M Gordon once suggested.[3] But lying behind *Regency Villas* is a case which has considerable promise for Scotland.[4] In *In re Ellenborough Park*,[5] decided in 1955, the Court of Appeal in England held that houses surrounding private gardens could have an easement to use the gardens for walking and for other recreational purposes. More than swimming or golfing, such a right confers a clear benefit on the houses in question, 'for just as the [sole] use of a garden undoubtedly enhances, and is connected with, the normal enjoyment of the house to which it belongs, so also would the right granted, in the case supposed, be closely connected with the use and enjoyment of the part of the premises sold'.[6] In this sort of reasoning may lie a solution to the problem of amenity areas in housing estates in cases where the areas do not belong to the householders. A developer who is minded to retain

---

1 Paragraphs 59 and 81.
2 For a detailed assessment of this list, see ch 3 of Cusine and Paisley, *Servitudes and Rights of Way*. Cusine and Paisley doubt whether recreational rights fall within this list: see paras 2.50 and 3.71.
3 W M Gordon, *Scottish Land Law* (2nd edn, 1999) para 24–19: 'When it is possible to have a servitude right to a water supply to drive a mill, there seems nothing anomalous in, say, a hotel having a servitude right of fishing or golfing, although it may be questionable whether a private house should have it.'
4 *In re Ellenborough Park* has also had a considerable influence throughout the common-law world. See *Regency Villas* para 77 and the cases there cited.
5 [1955] Ch 131.
6 At 174 per Evershed MR.

ownership of recreational areas, perhaps with a view to conveying them to a land management company such as Greenbelt,[1] can still give use rights to the householders by means of an express servitude.[2]

TRANSPARENCY: TWO NEW REGISTERS?

Introduction

The property registration system, which began with the Registration Act 1617, means that it is possible to find out who owns land. If anyone wishes to find out who owns the semi-detached house at 47 New Street, Dunbar, it will not take long to discover that the answer is: Mr and Mrs Gloag. The public registration of title information is vital to the functioning of the conveyancing system, and indeed the 1617 Act was passed primarily as an aid to conveyancing.

But whilst conveyancers may feel that the property registers are 'their' registers, the registers have come to interest others too: central government, local government, the police, a variety of public agencies, including HMRC, investigative journalists, community organisations and activists of varying hues, all consult the property registers. Indeed, it was the 'who owns Scotland?' political agenda that was key to the Scottish Government's decision to enact the Land Registration etc (Scotland) Act 2012, because it is far easier to obtain title data from the Land Register than from the Register of Sasines, and the 2012 Act provided for a much more rapid extension of Land Register coverage.

But for some purposes to be able to find out who owns land, though necessary, is not seen as enough. Mr and Mrs Gloag might be acting as nominees for ABCD Ltd, a company incorporated in the British Virgin Islands whose share ownership is a riddle, and which, even if you could answer that riddle, would merely show that the shares are held by a Malta-based trust whose sole trustee is a Belize company owned by a private-purpose foundation registered in Mordor. The 'who owns this property?' question thus splits into two: (i) the literal question, which can be answered from the Land Register, or, for a diminishing number of properties, the Register of Sasines, and (ii) the 'who pulls the strings?' or 'who has beneficial ownership?' question. For most properties, of course, the two questions have the same answers. Mr and Mrs Gloag own their semi-detached house and they live in it. That is that: there is no more story to be told.

The demand that the 'beneficial ownership' of land should be disclosed is often made but often not thought through. Edinburgh Castle belongs to the Scottish Government.[3] Who pulls the strings? The answer is the 5.14 million people of Scotland, or, more narrowly, the 4.12 million of them who are registered voters. To list their names in relation to Edinburgh Castle would be hardly possible and indeed pointless, and the moment the task was done it would be out of date, because the 'beneficial ownership' of Edinburgh Castle changes by

---

1 See eg *Conveyancing 2015* pp 137–38.
2 See also p 223 below.
3 Registered in the Land Register under title number MID 1.

the hour. Similar remarks could be made about land that is owned by a major company, which may have a vast number of shareholders, who change day by day as the shares are traded on the London stock exchange. Registration of the 'beneficial ownership' of such land would be pointless and virtually impossible. So some more meaningful and workable concept of 'beneficial ownership' had to be developed if a workable disclosure regime was to be launched.

That launch happened at a UK level with the Small Business, Enterprise and Employment Act 2015, which introduced the 'People with Significant Control' (PSC) reporting system.[1] The PSC concept is an attempt to make the idea of 'beneficial ownership' workable in relation to companies, using the threshold of 25% of shareholding, direct or indirect, or 25% of voting rights.

Two policy agendas

The demand to know who pulls the strings has behind it two separate policy agendas. The first agenda is crime control, and this has been the driver for what has been happening in the UK Parliament. It could be called the Westminster agenda. To illustrate the first agenda, we would quote the UK Government's *Overview Document* concerning a new draft Bill, the Registration of Overseas Entities Bill (for which see below).[2] It says:[3]

> The Register has the following primary objective: to prevent and combat the use of land in the UK by overseas entities for the purposes of laundering money or investing illicit funds by increasing transparency in overseas entities engaged in land ownership in the UK.

Much the same was true of the 2015 legislation mentioned earlier.

The other agenda has nothing to do with crime, but is simply an aspect of the 'who owns Scotland?' agenda. It could be called the Holyrood agenda, because provision for it is made by Part 3 of the Land Reform (Scotland) Act 2016 (of which, more below). The matter could be put thus. If all human beings were suddenly to become honest and law-abiding,[4] the Westminster transparency agenda would be needless and could be scrapped. But the transformation of human nature would leave the Holyrood transparency agenda unaffected.

The road to 2021

Two pieces of legislation are in the offing to advance the cause of transparency. Both were published in draft form during 2018, one by the Scottish Government and the other by the UK Government.

---

1 The provisions are to be found in sch 3 to the Small Business, Enterprise and Employment Act 2015, which inserted a new Part 21A into the Companies Act 2006.
2 www.gov.uk/government/consultations/draft-registration-of-overseas-entities-bill.
3 Paragraph 8. Also worth quoting is a passage in para 3: 'Overseas entities are often used as a vehicle by criminal organisations and corrupt individuals to hide and launder the proceeds of bribery, corruption and organised crime.'
4 'Juris praecepta sunt haec: honeste vivere, alterum non laedere, suum cuique tribuere': Ulpian, *Digesta* 1.1.10.

The first is the draft statutory instrument to give effect to Part 3 of the Land Reform (Scotland) Act 2016. It is called the Register of Persons Holding a Controlled Interest in Land (Scotland) Regulations. The other is the Registration of Overseas Entities Bill.[1]

The timetable for these pieces of legislation is not yet fully clear. The Scottish draft regulations actually have '2021' as part of their title, but there are indications that this date may be brought forward to 2020. In any event, actual commencement will (on current information) be on 1 April 2021. The UK Government has said that it expects its Westminster Bill to come into force in 2021, which presumably means that the intention is for it to be passed in 2019 or 2020. Meanwhile, the Government is under a statutory duty to produce annual progress reports.[2]

Although neither legislative measure is yet in its final form, both promise, or threaten, to be significant for conveyancers and accordingly some overview of both measures is called for.

The draft Westminster Bill

The PSC system introduced by the 2015 Act applies to all UK companies, whether they own land or not. It is not, as such, a land-related piece of legislation. But its proposed twin, the Registration of Overseas Entities Bill, is land-related, for it is to apply only to overseas entities that hold land in the UK. If enacted, the Bill will establish a new register, the Register of Overseas Entities, to be kept by the Registrar of Companies.[3] Registration will be necessary in the sense that (i) unregistered overseas entities will not be allowed to acquire ownership of land in the UK (or a registrable lease),[4] and (ii) unregistered overseas entities that are already owners of land (or holders of registered leases) will not be allowed to grant registrable deeds. If that sounds simple, the Bill takes 41 pages to say it, so it is not really so simple.[5]

An 'overseas' entity is any juristic person (typically this will be a company) incorporated outwith the UK.[6] In this context it should be borne in mind that Jersey, Guernsey and the Isle of Man are not part of the UK so that companies registered in those jurisdictions are overseas entities. A trust is not a juristic person and so is not covered.

---

1 Published for consultation in July 2018 as Cm 9635. The consultation period closed on 17 September 2018. The Bill was preceded by a Government response to an earlier call for evidence: see www.gov.uk/government/consultations/property-ownership-and-public-contracting-by-overseas-companies-and-legal-entities-beneficial-ownership-register, published in March 2018. For the earlier stages of the proposals see *Conveyancing 2017* pp 93–94.
2 Sanctions and Anti-Money Laundering Act 2018 s 50.
3 To be precise, the Registrar for England and Wales, in Cardiff. The Scottish Registrar has no role.
4 Short leases are not relevant. Thus if an Italian clothing company opens a shop in Glasgow's Argyle Street, taking the property on a 15-year lease, it will not have to register.
5 The draft Scottish statutory instrument is no sylph either, with a girth of 26 pages.
6 In this connection it is worth noting that s 51 of the Sanctions and Anti-Money Laundering Act 2018 requires each of the British Overseas Territories to establish its own publicly accessible register of the beneficial ownership of those companies that are incorporated in the Territory in question. See also p 91 above.

Registration will involve the disclosure of 'beneficial ownership', that concept being much the same as in the current PSC regime for UK companies.[1] But the registration requirement is not limited to entities that have 'registrable beneficial owners'. *Any* foreign entity (if it owns land in the UK, or has a registrable lease of such land) is covered by the legislation. By contrast, the draft Scottish regulations apply only to owners or tenants that have separate 'beneficial ownership'.

To bring about these rules the Bill makes extensive prospective amendments to the Land Registration etc (Scotland) Act 2012. It amends ss 21 and 27, it adds a new s 112A (an additional type of offence, just to make everyone jump for joy), and it adds a long new schedule, sch 1A. As well as these extensive amendments to the 2012 Act, it also amends s 4A of the Conveyancing (Scotland) Act 1924.

What will be the practical implications for Scottish conveyancers? The overall answer is simple enough. (i) If you are acting for an overseas entity in a property transaction you need to make sure that it is registered. (ii) If in a property transaction the party on the *other* side is an overseas entity you again need to make sure that it is registered. No doubt a standard clause will be added to missives. It will be mainly commercial and rural transactions that are affected, but ordinary residential transactions will sometimes be as well, so from the standpoint of the conveyancer the legislation will be potentially relevant to all properties in Scotland.

If an overseas entity owns (or leases) land already, does it need to do anything when the Bill comes into force, or can it simply wait until it needs to transact (eg sell) and then register at that point? The basic answer (there are exceptions) is that the entity will have to register even if it has no intention of selling (etc) the land it owns. There will be a grace period of 18 months.[2] This requirement is backed by criminal sanctions.

Registered entities will be issued with an 'overseas entity ID' and this number will be needed for Land Register transactions. Registration in the Register of Overseas Entities will not be a once-and-for-all affair. There will be a duty, backed by criminal sanctions, of annual updating. Subject to certain qualifications, the register will be open to the public.[3]

We would repeat that at present this is no more than a draft Bill. Its final form cannot yet be known with certainty, and indeed it cannot be known with certainty that it will ever be enacted. Nevertheless, the probability of enactment is fairly high, and it is doubtful whether the text will be changed substantially.

The draft Scottish regulations

Section 39(1) of the Land Reform (Scotland) Act 2016 says:

---

1 See sch 2 of the draft Bill.
2 The UK Government's original proposal was that the grace period should be 12 months. In the draft Scottish regulations the grace period is only six months. See below.
3 As is required by the fifth Money Laundering Directive: Directive (EU) 2018/843 of the European Parliament and of the Council of 30 May 2018 amending Directive (EU) 2015/849 on the prevention of the use of the financial system for the purposes of money laundering or terrorist financing.

The Scottish Ministers must by regulations make provision (a) requiring information to be provided about persons who have controlling interests in owners and tenants of land, and (b) about the publication of that information in a public register kept by the Keeper of the Registers of Scotland.

The remainder of s 39 says in very general terms what provisions 'may' be included in the regulations and the remainder of Part 3 of the 2016 Act is about such matters as consultation. In other words, Part 3 is skeletal. It enables, and requires, regulations to be made, but it says little about what those regulations are to look like. A consultation document was published later the same year,[1] and in 2018 draft regulations were published, the Register of Persons Holding a Controlled Interest in Land (Scotland) Regulations.[2] The Scottish Parliament's Environment, Climate Change and Land Reform Committee has issued a report that is critical in a number of respects.[3] It is expected that the Scottish Government will in 2019 issue a revised version. Everyone who has looked at the existing draft agrees that it is not easy to understand.

Like the Westminster Bill, the regulations apply to those who own land or hold a registrable lease. Like the Westminster Bill, a new register is created, so that, assuming that both measures go ahead, there will be two new registers detailing the 'beneficial ownership' of land in Scotland,[4] one kept in Cardiff by the Registrar of Companies and the other kept in Edinburgh by the Keeper.

Given the background to Part 3 of the 2016 Act, one might suppose that the legislation will apply to large estates in Argyll or Perthshire or Sutherland, and so on, and so it will. But as with the Westminster Bill, the legislation applies to land and buildings of any kind, including commercial and residential.

An accompanying consultation document says:[5]

> The draft Regulations primarily seek to address two particular scenarios in which there is currently a lack of transparency as to the control or influence of the decision-making of an owner or tenant of land. Firstly, where the legal owner or tenant of the land is an opaque legal entity, such as an overseas company, or secondly, where they hold the title or lease in an arrangement which is not necessarily discernible from the Land Register itself, such as a trust arrangement.

The word 'primarily' should be noted, for the coverage is, strictly speaking, wider than this summary account indicates, but nevertheless these are the main

---

1 Scottish Government, *Improving Transparency in Land Ownership in Scotland: A Consultation on Controlling Interests in Land* (www.gov.scot/Publications/2016/09/6681).

2 At the same time a consultation document was published seeking views on the draft regulations: *Improving the Transparency of Land Ownership: A Consultation on Draft Regulations* (www.gov.scot/publications/delivering-improved-transparency-land-ownership-scotland-consultation-draft-regulations). The consultation period closed on 8 November 2018.

3 SP Paper 416 9th Report (Session 5) published 8 November 2018: see https://digitalpublications.parliament.scot/Committees/Report/ECCLR/2018/11/8/Land-Reform--Scotland--Act-2016--Register-of-Persons-Holding-a-Controlled-Interest-in-Land---Scotland--Regulations-2021--draft-#Membership.

4 Of course, the Westminster Bill applies to land throughout the UK. But here we are concerned with Scotland.

5 *Improving the Transparency of Land Ownership*, para 19.

categories. And there is an immediate issue: one of these two categories will be covered by the Westminster Bill. The policy of the regulations is that any owner or tenant who is subject to some *other* transparency regime will be exempt from the regulations. That means that UK companies will be exempt (because they are already subject to the PSC regime) and, assuming that the Westminster Bill is enacted, overseas entities will also drop out of the regulations. The result would be that only trusts, plus one or two bits and bobs, would be subject to the regulations. The measure would come close to being what might be dubbed the Beneficial Ownership of Trusts Holding Land Regulations. That, at any rate, is what the Scottish Government intends. But the Scottish Parliament's Environment, Climate Change and Land Reform Committee has some concern that different transparency regimes would mean that investigators would have the trouble of looking in different places for their information. It is also concerned that, whereas the intention is that access to the Scottish register will be free of charge, access to the Register of Overseas Entities is expected to involve payment, as of course is generally the position for public registers. The Committee considers that to be unacceptable.[1]

The new Scottish register is to be called the Register of Persons Holding a Controlled Interest in Land ('PCI Register').[2] It is to have entries giving (i) the name of the 'recorded person' (ie the owner[3] or tenant), (ii) the 'associate' (ie the persons pulling the strings), and (iii) the property. As we understand it, if a trust (etc) owns more than one piece of land, there will be separate entries for each separate property. The register is to be public and is to be searchable by property and by name. The duty to register is backed by criminal sanctions. There is an updating obligation. Unlike the Westminster Bill, however, it is not an annual obligation, but an obligation triggered by any significant change.

Where, as at 1 April 2021, land is already held by a 'recorded person' subject to the powers of an 'associate', registration must take place within six months, ie by 1 October 2012. This seems too short a period. By contrast the grace period in the Westminster Bill is 18 months.

The regulations are enforced solely by criminal law. There are no civil law aspects. Here the difference from the Westminster Bill is a marked one. The Scottish Parliament's Environment, Climate Change and Land Reform Committee was critical. It said:[4]

> The Committee cannot see any reason why completion of the PCI registration process for recorded persons and associates should not be introduced into the Regulations as a pre-condition for undertaking other administrative and financial changes and/ or transactions relating to the land, for example: when entering a title into the Land Register; when mortgaging or re-mortgaging the property; and when any other changes are made to the title deeds of the property. The Committee recommends

---

1 See p 13 of the committee's report.
2 The abbreviation is used in the regulations themselves.
3 Regulation 2(3) defines 'owner' as someone with a completed title in the Land Register (or the GRS as the case may be). Thus unregistered holders (uninfeft proprietors as these were called before feudal abolition) would seem not to be covered.
4 Paragraph 230.

completion of the Register is a pre-condition for undertaking other administrative and financial changes and/or transactions relating to the land. This should ensure clarity of responsibility for registration where land transactions occur and at the point of sale.

This is perhaps not very clear, but probably the idea is that there should be rules similar to those in the Westminster Bill, barring unregistered entities from Land Register transactions. If so, we would respectfully suggest that matters may not be so straightforward. Under the Westminster Bill, it will be obvious enough if a party to a Land Register transaction is an overseas entity. But under the Scottish regulations it will often be uncertain whether the rules apply or not. For example, Titania wishes to transact, perhaps as a disponer, or the granter of a standard security, or perhaps as a disponee. The counterparty is Vitruvius. How does Vitruvius know whether Titania might not be acting as a nominee or some other type of trustee? How could the Keeper? If Titania is registered, then no problem. And if she is in fact not a trustee, there is nothing to worry about anyway. But what if she is a trustee but is keeping silent about it? Is Vitruvius to suffer thereby?

Privacy

Both proposed new registers are to be public, but both will have mechanisms for protecting privacy as well. The mechanisms, however, are very different. We will not enter into details here, but merely make the obvious point that there are policy problems in this area that cannot really be solved. Compromises are possible, as in the two proposed measures, but they are necessarily rather messy and less than satisfying. Indeed, forget 'beneficial ownership' for a moment and consider land registration itself. Even here there is a problem, for land transactions must involve publicity (or shall we return to the balmy days of pre-1617 conveyancing?) and yet publicity contradicts privacy.[1] A few countries, most notably Germany, actually say that public access to the land register is allowed only to those with a 'legitimate interest'.[2] Political activism of the 'who owns Bavaria?' type is not regarded as a legitimate interest. It does not trump privacy.

Final comments

We conclude with three points, two of them points already made. First, the two proposed measures – the Westminster Bill and the Scottish regulations – are long and complex, and the foregoing is far from being a comprehensive treatment. The second point is that these measures are still only in draft form, and while eventual enactment is highly probable, there are likely to be at least some changes before the two new registers go live in (probably) 2021. The third and final point is

---

1 In 2018 a book was published on this problem: Anna Berlee, *Access to Personal Data in Public Land Registers: Balancing Publicity of Property Rights with the Rights to Privacy and Data Protection.*
2 'Die Einsicht des Grundbuchs ist jedem gestattet, der ein berechtigtes Interesse darlegt': *Grundbuchordnung* § 12(1).

evaluation. Will these two measures prove workable? Cost-effective? Sufficiently sensitive to privacy issues? Practically enforceable? To such questions we would hesitate to hazard any answers.

TENEMENTS: UNALLOCATED PARTS

A key advantage of the Tenements (Scotland) Act 2004, as compared to the common law which it replaced, is the provision of rules for allocating parts of the building and surrounding ground to particular flats.[1] These are default rules, of course. Where titles provide, titles prevail.[2] But insofar as the titles are silent, the Act fills in the gaps. *Mackay v Dickinson*[3] is a helpful illustration of how this works.

The tenement at issue was a Victorian sandstone building on two floors, part of a terrace of houses in Dalrymple Loan, Musselburgh, East Lothian. Originally a single dwelling, the building came to be divided into two flats. Access to the lower flat (number 41) was by a front door leading directly from the street. Access to the upper flat (number 39) was by a passageway or vennel leading from the street, by way of the side of the building, to a small patio at the rear; an external staircase then led from the patio to the upper flat. The vennel was a covered passageway, its roof being formed by a portion of the upper flat which then joined on to the neighbouring building. There was a locked door at the entrance to the vennel.

The properties were split as to title in 1972 when the lower flat was sold. The conveyancing does not seem to have been well done. In the split-off disposition nothing was said as to the vennel or patio. Indeed nothing was said even as to the extensive rear garden, an omission which was only repaired in 1982 when the respective owners entered into a minute of agreement under s 19 of the Land Registration (Scotland) Act 1979 dividing the garden in two, with each flat allocated one of the halves.

The current disagreement was about the ownership of the vennel and of the patio to which the vennel led. It was prompted by the sale of the lower flat and the resulting title sheet produced on first registration. The title sheet showed the vennel and patio as common property of the two flats. The proprietors of the upper flat, held still on a Sasine title, objected and sought rectification. In their view, they were the sole owners of the vennel and patio.

Under s 80 of the Land Registration etc (Scotland) Act 2012 the Keeper can rectify an inaccuracy only where the inaccuracy is 'manifest'. The alleged inaccuracy in the present case – if indeed it was an inaccuracy at all – fell far short of that exalted standard. If the proprietors of the upper flat were to succeed, therefore, they would have to have the inaccuracy judicially declared. Their preferred route, as is now the standard practice, was to apply to the Lands

---

1 These rules can be found mainly in ss 2 and 3 of the Act.
2 Tenements (Scotland) Act 2004 s 1.
3 28 March 2018, Lands Tribunal. The Tribunal comprised R A Smith QC and C C Marwick FRICS.

Tribunal under s 82 of the Act for a determination as to the accuracy of the Register.[1]

Who, then, owned the vennel and patio? In the absence of anything in the titles, the answer turned on the Tenements (Scotland) Act 2004 and in particular on s 3 of that Act, which determines which parts of the building and ground are the pertinents of which flat or flats. For present purposes the governing provision was s 3(4):

> If a tenement includes any part (such as, for example, a path, outside stair, fire escape, rhone, pipe, flue, conduit, cable, tank or chimney stack) that does not fall within subsection (1) or (3) above[2] and that part –
>
> (a) wholly serves one flat, then it shall attach as a pertinent to that flat;
> (b) serves two or more flats, then there shall attach to each of the flats served, as a pertinent, a right of common property in (and in the whole of) the part.

This provision allocates parts by reference to a service or function test. The question, as applied to the present context, was: which flat was served by the vennel and patio? Was it the upper flat alone, as maintained by the owners of that flat? Or was it *both* flats, as the title sheet of the lower flat seemed to suppose? If the first was correct, the vennel and patio were the sole property of the upper flat; if the second, then they were owned in common, in equal shares,[3] by the proprietors of both flats.

On the evidence, the Lands Tribunal concluded that the vennel and patio served both flats. It was true that the rear garden belonging to the lower flat could already be reached from the back door of that flat. There was thus no necessity for another route. Nonetheless, a number of factors indicated that the vennel and patio were intended as an alternative means of access to the garden. (i) The plan attached to the 1982 minute of agreement indicated, by arrows and words, that the vennel was the 'entrance to No 39 and rear of No 41'. (ii) Day-to-day access was in fact taken by this route to the rear garden belonging to the lower flat; for that purpose the proprietor of the lower flat had a key to the locked door. (iii) A gate led from the patio to the rear garden of the lower flat. Taken together, this evidence suggested that the vennel and patio served the lower flat as well as the upper. Hence it was common property. Hence the title sheet of the lower flat was correct and would not be rectified.

Two remarks seem worth making. First, in determining whether the vennel and patio served the lower (as well as the upper) flat, the Tribunal had regard, not just to the physical layout of the tenement, but to the attitude and beliefs of the affected parties as evidenced by the minute of agreement and the history of access-taking. No indication is given of the relative importance to be given to these factors; but it is thought that physical layout must be the dominant consideration, and often the decisive one.

---

1 See generally K G C Reid and G L Gretton, *Land Registration* (2017) para 11.14.
2 Provisions which deal with the close, any lift, and the garden ground.
3 Tenements (Scotland) Act 2004 s 3(5).

Secondly, in concluding that the vennel and patio served the lower flat because they served its garden, the Tribunal was giving the word 'flat' an extended meaning. At first sight that might seem at odds with the definitional scheme of the Act, which appears to confine 'flat' to a part of a *building* – to the indoors and not to the outdoors. Thus 'flat' is defined as including 'any *premises* whether or not (a) used or intended to be used for residential purposes; or (b) on the one floor'.[1] Elsewhere in the interpretation section 'flat' is given as an example of a 'sector', a sector itself being defined as any 'three dimensional space', with the provision going on to add that 'the tenement building shall be taken to be entirely divided into sectors'. If, however, a flat is distinct from its garden, then it might seem to be stretching s 3(4) of the Act to say that the vennel and patio served the lower flat. Yet the approach of the Tribunal appears to be correct. As a garden is a pertinent of a flat,[2] it seems justifiable, in the context of s 3, to treat the latter as including the former. Indeed, if this were not so, the result would be a gap in the Act, and hence the possibility of unallocated property.

ACCESS RIGHTS

Introduction

2018 brought with it an important Inner House case on public access rights under the Land Reform (Scotland) Act 2003, *Renyana-Stahl Anstalt v Loch Lomond and Trossachs National Park Authority*,[3] and another significant case on the same subject in the sheriff court, *Manson v Midlothian Council*.[4] There was also a significant case on common-law public rights of way, *Kolhe v Robertson*.[5]

We begin with the Land Reform (Scotland) Act 2003 itself. This introduced public 'access rights' or, to use a common term, 'the right to roam'.[6] Under the Act, public access rights exist over any land unless some exception applies.[7] An exception of particular importance is provided by s 6(1)(b)(iv), which says that access rights do not apply to land which 'comprises, in relation to a house ... sufficient adjacent land to enable persons living there to have reasonable measures of privacy in that house ... and to ensure that their enjoyment of that house ... is not unreasonably disturbed'. As will be seen, the application of that exception was one of the issues in the *Manson* litigation.

---

1 T(S)A 2004 s 29(1); our emphasis.
2 T(S)A 2004 s 3(3).
3 [2018] CSIH 22, 2018 SC 406, 2018 SLT 331, 2018 SCLR 617.
4 [2018] SC EDIN 50, 2018 GWD 33-422.
5 [2018] SC ABE 43, 2018 GWD 25-324.
6 For a valuable and up-to-date account, see Malcolm M Combe, *The ScotWays Guide to the Law of Access to Land in Scotland* (2018); and in relation to the cases to be discussed, see the following articles by the same author: 'Better access to the law' (2018) 63 *Journal of the Law Society of Scotland* Oct/34; 'Revisiting access to land under the Land Reform (Scotland) Act 2003' 2018 SLT (News) 51; 'Manson v Midlothian Council, 2018 GWD 33-422' 2018 SLT (News) 149.
7 Land Reform (Scotland) Act 2003 s 1.

The drafters of the legislation realised that the simple existence of access rights is not enough if, on the ground, there are serious obstacles to their exercise. For instance, if the Duke of Omnium builds a Trump-style wall all round his vast estate in Sutherland, access rights would still exist, but those seeking to exercise them would (i) need to come equipped with very high ladders and (ii) need to be physically fit.[1] Access rights over the estate would still exist in theory, but in practice would border on non-existence. The Duke of Omnium would have successfully cocked the snook.[2]

So the legislation has a battery of provisions to ensure that access rights should exist not merely in theory but also in practice. Section 13, for example, imposes a general duty on local authorities[3] 'to assert, protect and keep open and free from obstruction or encroachment any route, waterway or other means by which access rights may reasonably be exercised'. Under sections 12 and 15, local authorities have a range of powers to give substance to access rights, s 12 conferring power to make byelaws and s 15 conferring a range of practical powers, including (for we cannot resist quoting this) power to 'install and maintain ... gates, stiles, moorings, launching sites ... and seats, lavatories and other means of contributing to the comfort and convenience of persons exercising' access rights. We understand that the s 12 and s 15 powers have been little used.

Section 3 imposes various obligations on landowners, its opening provision being:

> It is the duty of every owner of land in respect of which access rights are exercisable –
> (a) to use and manage the land; and
> (b) otherwise to conduct the ownership[4] of it,
> in a way which, as respects those rights, is responsible.

Then there is s 14, a provision that has proved to be of considerable importance in practice, and was involved in two of this year's cases, *Renyana-Stahl Anstalt* and *Manson*. Section 14 has two aspects: a set of specific duties on the landowner, and a set of powers vested in the local authority. Section 14 is so important that we quote here its first three sub-sections:

> (1) The owner of land in respect of which access rights are exercisable shall not, for the purpose or for the main purpose of preventing or deterring any person entitled to exercise these rights from doing so –

---

1   For the fashion-conscious rambler there would also be the option of helicopter hire. Lest we be accused of incomplete discussion, we would also note that s 1(6) says that access rights can exist 'below ... the surface of the land' so that tunnelling should doubtless be considered as a further possibility.

2   But probably so vulgar a gesture is inconceivable for members of the nobility.

3   By s 32 this term includes national park authorities. Hence the involvement of the Loch Lomond and Trossachs National Park Authority in the *Renyana-Stahl Anstalt* case.

4   A strange phrase. One can think of Simon Rattle conducting the London Symphony Orchestra. But conducting *ownership*? But given that the phrase must mean something, the question is: what? How does 'conducting ownership' differ from the 'use and management' of the land required in the previous paragraph? The implication is that a landowner who uses and manages the land in the most perfect manner conceivable can still be in breach of the legislation, but precisely how is obscure.

    (a) put up any sign or notice;

    (b) put up any fence or wall, or plant, grow or permit to grow any hedge, tree or other vegetation;

    (c) position or leave at large any animal;

    (d) carry out any agricultural or other operation on the land; or

    (e) take, or fail to take, any other action.

(2) Where the local authority consider that anything has been done in contravention of subsection (1) above they may, by written notice served on the owner of the land, require that such remedial action as is specified in the notice be taken by the owner of the land within such reasonable time as is so specified.

(3) If the owner fails to comply with such a notice, the local authority may –

    (a) remove the sign or notice; or, as the case may be,

    (b) take the remedial action specified in the notice served under subsection (2) above, and, in either case, may recover from the owner such reasonable costs as they have incurred by acting under this subsection.

The section goes on to provide that 'section 14 notices' (as they have come to be called) can be challenged by the landowner in the sheriff court.[1]

With the provisions of the 2003 Act, especially s 14, in mind, we proceed to the *Renyana-Stahl Anstalt* and *Manson* cases.

Liechtenstein in the Trossachs

The dispute in the first of these cases[2] concerned Drumlean Estate in the Trossachs, between Loch Ard and Ben Venue, owned by a Liechtenstein entity (an 'Anstalt'), Renyana-Stahl Anstalt. Drumlean Estate consists of about 3700 acres of land. Most of the estate was freely open to the public, but public access was denied or hindered in respect of a fenced area of around 300 acres (less than 10% of the estate) at the southern-most point.[3] Within this area were a farm and farmhouse and also a red deer population of between 120 and 150. Access was by three gates, all of which were kept padlocked. There was also a sign saying 'DANGER WILD BOAR', though boar were at the time not present. None of this was new. It had been the situation since before the 2003 Act came into force.

The local authority served a s 14 notice requiring the owner to unlock the gates and to remove the sign.[4] The owner raised the present action to have the notice quashed. The padlocks and the sign, argued the owner, were not 'for the purpose or for the main purpose of preventing or deterring' the exercise of access

---

1 This explains why so in many cases it is the landowner who appears as the pursuer.

2 *Renyana-Stahl Anstalt v Loch Lomond and Trossachs National Park Authority* [2018] CSIH 22, 2018 SC 406, 2018 SLT 331, 2018 SCLR 617.

3 The acreages have been subject to some confusion. We take the figures from para 6 of the Inner House judgment.

4 The main function of the 'signs' bit of s 14 is to deal with signs that say things such as 'PRIVATE PROPERTY – NO ENTRY'. But *any* signage deterring access to legally-accessible land is subject to s 14 (though specific context is relevant, of course).

rights, as was required to bring them within s 14.[1] There were two strands to this argument.

The first was that that the padlocks and sign predated the commencement of the 2003 Act. There were at that time no access rights capable of being obstructed. It might have been otherwise if the padlocks and sign had been placed there more recently. But that was not the position.

Moreover – and this was the second strand to the argument – even if the first strand of the argument was wrong, obstruction of access rights had not been 'for the purpose or for the main purpose' of obstructing access, but for the purpose of legitimate land management, and that 'purpose' was something that had to be tested according to the actual intentions of the landowner – a 'subjective' test. In the words of the court, summarising this second strand of argument, 'when the court is determining the purpose of the action complained of, it ought to be looking into the mind of the landowner in order to ascertain, subjectively, his honesty or "bona fides" in maintaining that the act was not to prevent or deter exercise of the public's 2003 Act rights'.[2]

For both these strands of argument there was substantial authority. As to the first, there was the decision of the sheriff principal in *Aviemore Highland Resort Ltd v Cairngorms National Park Authority*.[3] Here the owner of land, shortly before the 2003 Act came into force, erected a fence which had the effect of obstructing the exercise of access rights, when, later, those rights came into existence. Claiming that the erection of the fence constituted a breach of s 14, the local authority served a notice requiring the fence to be removed. The owner sought an order from the court quashing the notice. The order was granted on the basis that the action complained of had taken place before the Act came into force:[4]

> [W]hen they erected the fence, the pursuers were not the owners of land in respect of which access rights were exercisable, and in any event they could not have erected the fence for the purpose or for the main purpose of preventing or deterring any person entitled to exercise those access rights from doing so since the rights did not then exist. Nor in my view is it correct to characterise the erection of the fence as a continuing state of affairs. It was an act which was completed before Pt 1 of the Act, and with it the access rights in question, came into force, and it is nothing to the point that the continuing presence of the fence has the effect now of preventing or deterring any person entitled to exercise access rights under Pt 1 from doing so.

As to the second strand of argument there was also authority, this time from the Inner House itself, in one of the leading cases on access rights, *Tuley v Highland Council*.[5]

---

1 The owner was thus not claiming that the land was exempt from access rights (though for a minor qualification to this see para 55 of the judgment). The question was the different one, namely whether the padlocks and the sign amounted to unlawful obstruction.
2 Paragraph 62.
3 2009 SLT (Sh Ct) 97 (*Conveyancing 2009* Case (46)). The sheriff principal was Sir Stephen Young QC.
4 Paragraph 14.
5 [2009] CSIH 31A, 2009 SC 456: for discussion, see *Conveyancing 2009* pp 165–68.

So the landowner had a strong case, and at first instance the sheriff held in favour of the landowner and quashed the s 14 notice. The local authority appealed to the Sheriff Appeal Court, which allowed the appeal.[6] The case was appealed again, this time by Renyana-Stahl Anstalt. The First Division has refused the appeal, so victory rests with the local authority.[7] The case is one of the most important so far on access rights.

The court held that a s 14 order can competently deal with locks, signs etc that pre-date the 2003 Act, and that the term 'purpose' in s 14 is to be understood in an objective rather than a subjective sense.

As to the first, we would suggest that s 14 is, in this aspect, not well drafted, and probably the drafters, if they had anticipated this litigation, would perhaps have used somewhat different wording. The practical significance of this part of the decision is obvious. No distinction is to be drawn on the basis of date. Thus as the years roll by – increasingly fast for some of us – it becomes more and more difficult to know just when a particular hedge, dyke, ditch, fence or gate came into being; as a result of the decision of the First Division, that difficulty ceases to matter. The effect of the decision is that the word 'purpose' in s 14(1) means something like 'ongoing purpose'.

As to the second aspect of the decision, namely that 'purpose' is to be assessed objectively, not subjectively, this has the advantage pointed out by the court that it brings about uniformity, rather than depending on who happens to be the owner of a particular property, something that will change from time to time; indeed, a single owner may have different purposes at different times. It also has the advantage, pointed out by the court, that objective purpose is easier to determine than subjective purpose: 'It is to be hoped that, in the future, an appeal to the sheriff on similar grounds will be dealt with far more expeditiously by what ought to be a relatively simple task of ascertaining the purpose objectively. This ought to be capable of determination by doing little more than understanding the physical characteristics of the land in question.'[8]

One final observation before leaving this important case. The First Division remarked that 'the SAC were correct in holding that the percentage area over which access was sought, relative to the total estate owned by the pursuers, was irrelevant'.[9] The fact was that the locked gates prevented access. This is not new law, but is useful as a succinct statement.

Checkpoint Penicuik

Introduction

Through Penicuik, Midlothian, runs the North Esk. It is bridged at a street called, oddly, Bridge Street. A few hundred yards to the west of Bridge Street are the

---

6 2017 SLT (Sh Ct) 138 (*Conveyancing 2017* Case (18)).
7 [2018] CSIH 22, 2018 SC 406, 2018 SLT 331, 2018 SCLR 617. There were two minor exceptions. The First Division held that only two of the three gates had to be opened (the SAC had ordered the opening of all three) and it held that the sign could remain because it accepted the evidence that said it had been erected at the request of the local authority.
8 Paragraph 76.
9 Paragraph 71.

beautiful and extensive policies of Penicuik House, which are open to the public.[1] The policies can be accessed by more than one route, but in some respects the most convenient is from Bridge Street. The hopeful walker begins there, and goes westward, in the direction of the policies, along Cairnbank Road. The road then divides into two branches, both, rather confusingly, called Cairnbank Road. Our walker, aiming for the Penicuik House policies, takes the left (southern) branch, keeping the river on her left-hand (southern) side. The last house belongs to Mr and Mrs Manson, the pursuers in this action.[2] The edge of the road is just a few yards from the house: between the road and the house is a garden, screened from the road by a high fence. Somewhat further – about 20 metres – beyond this point the road ceases to be a road and becomes a footpath, and, if the hopeful walker could continue, she would enter the policies of Penicuik House. And that is what she could have done until June 2016.

It was then that the path was severed by the Mansons, by the construction of a barrier. The *solum* of the path in this section was part of their property. We quote the sheriff:[3]

> The barrier takes the form of an eight foot (2.438 metres) high solid wooden fence with an integrated wooden padlocked gate ... The fence/gate is about three metres in width. ... It is painted with anti-climb non-drying paint. The pursuers have placed yellow warning signs on both sides of the fence/gate to warn members of the public of the existence of CCTV cameras.

The hopeful walker's boyfriend, to whom she said a tender goodbye in Bridge Street, can find another way into the Penicuik House policies and he can then eventually reach the same path, and they can fondly greet each other. But fond greeting is one thing, fond meeting another. Physically meet they cannot. They are on the opposite sides of Checkpoint Penicuik.

There is no way through. Is there a way round? In practical terms the answer is no. To the north of the path, away from the river, are the houses and gardens of a street called St James Gardens. To the south, towards the river, the ground slopes down steeply towards the water, and is fenced off. For walkers, it is the path or nothing.

Midlothian Council served an order on the Mansons requiring them to open the path up again, on the basis that the blockage was an unlawful interference with public access rights. The notice was served under s 14 of the Land Reform (Scotland) Act 2003. The Mansons responded with the present action.

Public right of way?

One preliminary, parenthetical, point. Much evidence was led about the usage of the road and path over the years, and, looking at that evidence, one cannot

---

1   http://www.penicuikhouse.co.uk/.
2   *Manson v Midlothian Council* [2018] SC EDIN 50, 2018 GWD 33-422. The judgment of Sheriff Fiona Lennox Reith QC runs to a remarkable 43,900 words, so of necessity the account given here omits some of the detail.
3   Findings-in-fact 11 and 13.

help wondering whether in fact there existed a prescriptive public right of way. Indeed, the local authority expressly stated in its written pleadings that 'the path has been in use by the public since at least 1980'.[1] If so, access rights under the 2003 Act would not matter, for blocking a public right of way is simply unlawful as a matter of common law. Why the local authority did not add this plea to their defence of the s 14 notice (a plea which, if successful, would have made the s 14 issue more or less irrelevant) we do not know.

Grounds of challenge

The action had two prongs. (i) The pursuers sought declarator, in terms of s 28 of the 2003 Act, that 'the land to which the notice relates is not land in respect of which access rights are exercisable'.[2] If that declarator was successful, the s 14 notice would in any event fall. (ii) In addition, on an *esto* basis, if the declarator did not succeed, ie if the court took the view that the path was indeed land to which public access rights applied, then the pursuers appealed against the s 14 notice. What they had done, ie blocking the path, was not for the 'purpose' of preventing or deterring the exercise of access rights.

And so battle was joined. How long the case lasted we do not know, but it must have been many days, with associated expense

The basis of the pursuers' first argument (access rights did not apply) lay in one of the key provisions of the 2003 Act, already mentioned, namely s 6(1)(b)(iv), which says that access rights do not apply to land which 'comprises, in relation to a house ... sufficient adjacent land to enable persons living there to have reasonable measures of privacy in that house ... and to ensure that their enjoyment of that house ... is not unreasonably disturbed'. In support of that argument the pursuers said that they had an autistic son who was disturbed by noise. Although evidence was led about this, the sheriff took the view that it was not relevant, since the 'section 6' question (what land is subject to access rights) is, like the 'section 14 purpose' question, to be determined objectively. As the sheriff said:[3]

> If the test were subjective, that would lead to the possibility of repeated applications being made depending on the particular views, concerns, family circumstances and even prejudices of any particular proprietor, which cannot be the purpose of the Act. I regard the test as an objective one, which factors in the particular characteristics of the property.... It would be wrong to base any decision on reasonable privacy on the very personal and individual circumstances of the pursuers' family in the present case. Looking objectively at all the circumstances, I am not satisfied that it has been established that a reasonable person living in a house of the type under consideration in the present case would regard the sound of people walking up or down the road on the other side of the two metre fence as unacceptable from the point of view of privacy in that house or their enjoyment of that house without unreasonable disturbance.

---

1 Paragraph 111. The period for the prescriptive constitution of a public right of way is 20 years: see s 3(3) of the Prescription and Limitation (Scotland) Act 1973.
2 Paragraph 1.
3 The two parts of this quotation are from paras 123 and 129.

The sheriff took the view that the house, with its gardens, had a reasonable degree of privacy because of walls and fencing. Moreover, the barrier was about 20 metres to the west, which she considered as being too far to be relevant. This seems reasonable in the context of the specific location, where there was a sort of pinch-point between, on the one side, the steep slope down to the river, and, on the other side, suburban streets. The decision does not lay down a general rule as to how near a property walkers can go, and indeed the position is strongly dependent on the situation on the ground. In the present case the sheriff made a site visit, and came to what seems a sensible conclusion.

In case the court was against them on the question of whether the path was subject to access rights, as in the event happened, the pursuers challenged the s 14 notice on the basis that obstruction of access rights had not been their 'purpose' in erecting the barrier. The core of this claim was that the path had been the locus of extensive antisocial behaviour, and that the motive for closing it was to shut down that behaviour. A great deal of evidence was led on this issue. The sheriff's conclusion was that the level of antisocial behaviour had been low, and accordingly that this was not an acceptable explanation of 'purpose': the purpose of erecting the barrier had indeed been in plain breach of s 14. Presumably, though this issue is not much explored in the case, had the level of antisocial behaviour been high, the pursuers might have won. But they lost on the facts.

There are some parallels between *Manson* and the earlier case of *Forbes v Fife Council*.[1] In that earlier case there was a path in Glenrothes that was not a public right of way. The residents, fed up with antisocial behaviour, erected gates at each end, with padlocks, so that only the residents would be able to use the path. The local authority served a s 14 notice, and the residents challenged it. As in *Manson*, they argued (a) that access rights did not cover the path, because of their privacy rights, and (b) *esto* they did cover the path, they were still entitled to close it to prevent irresponsible use. Sheriff Holligan came up with an interesting compromise. He held that access rights did apply, but he also accepted that there was indeed a problem with night-time antisocial behaviour. Accordingly, he allowed the gates to remain but ordered that they be left unlocked in the daytime. In *Manson* the local authority proposed precisely this approach, but the Mansons rejected it. But even apart from the fact that they were not prepared to accept any public access at all, even daytime access, given that on the facts (unlike *Forbes*) the court did not think that there had existed a serious problem of antisocial behaviour, the *Forbes* solution could not be adopted.

An appeal to the Sheriff Appeal Court was lodged. This no doubt explains why, when we made a site visit on 2 December 2018, the barrier, and associated notices, were still firmly in place. But we have since heard that the Mansons have abandoned the appeal and that the path is to be re-opened.[2] We look forward to making a future site visit.

---

1 2009 SLT (Sh Ct) 71 (*Conveyancing 2009* Case (47)).
2 See www.midlothian.gov.uk/info/200226/walking_and_cycling/441/outdoor_access_in_
   midlothian/2 (accessed 28 January 2019).

Human rights

The ECHR crops up quite often in these access cases, but its batting average has been zero. It was invoked in both *Renyana-Stahl Anstalt* and *Manson*. In the former it was argued that the s 14 procedure was in breach of article 6 (right to a fair trial). That failed, unsurprisingly, with very little discussion. In *Manson* it was argued that article 8 (right to family life) and article 1, Protocol 1 (right to property) had been breached. The argument failed, again unsurprisingly. The judgment in *Manson* has a useful discussion on the subject.[1]

Cove, Kolhe and creels

From time immemorial, fishermen have fished out of tiny Cove harbour on the southern outskirts of Aberdeen. Creel fishing is the main type. There is a pier. Above the highwater mark is an area where the boats, when not at sea, are, or were, drawn up, plus huts and winches used by the fishermen. The harbour is reached by a road, used by the fishermen but also by others:[2]

> Quite apart from creel fishing activities, I heard evidence of a wide variety of other activities carried on by members of the public at Cove harbour throughout living memory. Again, I heard evidence that a number of these activities have been carried on for generations. These activities include walking on the foreshore, the pier and the forelands, fishing from the pier and the forelands[3] using rod and line, or sometimes creels, swimming, kayaking and canoeing in the waters of the harbour, families enjoying picnics on the foreshore and at other points around the harbour and on the forelands, children playing in rock pools around the foreshore and amongst the rocks of the forelands at low tide and people scuba diving, kayaking, swimming and snorkelling within and outwith the harbour, sometimes launching boats from the harbour to support those activities.

In 2001 Pralhad Kolhe bought some land at Cove, his title including the pier, part of the land above the foreshore, and the *solum* of the access road. What happened between 2001 and 2014 we do not know, but in 2014 Mr Kolhe took action to keep people out. What was his motive? That is unclear.[4] In 2014 Mr Kolhe put up a sign saying 'COVE BAY HARBOUR – PRIVATE PROPERTY', and his solicitors wrote to the fishermen who beached their boats on his land that they were required to remove them. Then in 2015:[5]

> boulders were placed on the instructions of the pursuer along the Eastern and Western borders of the private road, thus preventing vehicular access from the private road to

---

1 Paragraphs 211–220.
2 *Kolhe v Robertson* [2018] SC ABE 43, 2018 GWD 25-324 at para 40 of the note of the sheriff, Andrew Miller.
3 The local name for the rocks at the seaward edge of the pier. Within the 'forelands' were the 'Inner Beattie', the 'Outer Beattie' and 'the Berryhillock', facts of no legal significance whatsoever, but which will be appreciated by connoisseurs of local toponymy.
4 Mr Kolhe did not give evidence in the case. The sheriff's note at para 51 ff has some material, which, however, does not help much with an explanation of motive. See also para 108.
5 Paragraphs 43 and 44.

any areas to the east or west of the road including the aforementioned areas used for parking,[1] the area on which the defenders' boats and winch huts are positioned and the foreshore. Similar boulders were also placed across the entrance to the pier, which prevented vehicular access onto the pier. At around the same time as the boulders were put in place, contractors acting on the instructions of the pursuer placed a bank of stones in a line approximately perpendicular to the private road on its western side, running immediately to the north of the area on which the defenders' boats and winch huts are positioned. The combined effect of the boulders and the bank of stones made it impossible to gain vehicular access from the private road to the area in which the boats and winch huts are stored.

These actions affected not only the fishermen but also the general public, who had hitherto often driven down the access road and on to the pier, where they had sometimes parked.[2]

Mr Kolhe raised the present action[3] seeking 'declarators that the defenders have no right or title to occupy and use the ground owned by him immediately to the north of the foreshore for the storage of their boats, vehicles and associated equipment and effects and orders requiring the defenders to remove their boats and associated equipment and effects from that ground'.[4] The defenders, who were the fishermen, not only resisted the pursuer's claim but also counterclaimed, seeking declarators that 'there exist public rights of way for pedestrians and vehicles from the public road at Balmoral Terrace, immediately to the north of the pursuer's title, on to the pier, to the foreshore and to the forelands at the harbour, interdicts to prevent the pursuer from interfering with the enjoyment of said rights of way by the defenders or other members of the public and orders requiring the pursuer to remove obstructions placed by him which, according to the defenders, prevent the defenders and other members of the public from using and enjoying said public rights of way'.[5]

Success was divided. It was held that (i) there was a public right of way for pedestrian use down the access road and thence on to the foreshore, and also (ii) there was a public right of way for both pedestrian and vehicular use down the access road and thence along the pier, to its end. But (iii) it was also held that there was no vehicular right of way to the foreshore.[6] Moreover, the defenders were ordered to flit and remove from the pursuer's ground, for they had no right to occupy land belonging to the pursuer.[7] But 'the parking of vehicles on the pier as a result of the exercise of the said public right of way for vehicles is a lawful activity'.[8] Thus not only was public vehicular access to the pier upheld,

---

1 This was parking at the edge of the access road.
2 This cannot have been particularly easy since the width of the pier was about 4 metres. Doubtless all drivers lived lives of exemplary sobriety.
3 *Kolhe v Robertson* [2018] SC ABE 43, 2018 GWD 25-324. For discussion, see M M Combe and D J Cusine, 'Public access to land in Scots law: two cases on the continuing place for public rights of way' 2019 *Juridical Review* 95.
4 Paragraph 8.
5 Paragraph 9.
6 Findings-in-fact-and-law, especially 4, 5, 6, 7 and 10.
7 Orders granted paras 1 ff.
8 Finding-in-law 8.

but also the right to park, as an ancillary right. This seems to be an innovative decision. There is an analogy with *Moncrieff v Jamieson*[1] where it was held that a right to park can be ancillary to a servitude right of way, though, despite the extensive citation of authority in *Kolhe*, the decision of the House of Lords in *Moncrieff* was not cited.

We hear on the grapevine that the fishermen are considering the possibility of setting up a community body to buy Mr Kolhe's land.

REAL BURDENS: INCITEMENT TO DRINK

The decision of the First Division in *King's Park Heritable Co Ltd v Royal Bank of Scotland*[2] raises a short, sharp point of some importance. The facts of the case are enjoyable. King's Park Heritable Co Ltd ('KPH') owned office premises in a late-Victorian building on the corner of Hope Street and Gordon Street in central Glasgow. J & G Oldfield Ltd ran an off-licence from a shop in the same building. Oldfield was not the owner but leased the shop from the Royal Bank of Scotland. In order to promote its business and to catch the eye of thirsty passengers emerging from nearby Central Station, Oldfield put up a panel on the shop's outside wall advertising *Long John* whisky. The sign was not easy to miss. It was 9 feet high, 38 feet long, and tastefully illuminated. It showed a man enjoying a glass of whisky.[3]

KPH did not like the sign. Perhaps it thought the sign in bad taste, or an incitement to drink and to drunkenness. Or perhaps it simply disturbed KPH's sensibilities; in the ensuing litigation KPH was to complain that the sign obscured the architectural features of the building.[4] Fortunately, a remedy for KPH appeared to be at hand. The building was subject to a deed of conditions which had been recorded in 1922. Article 10 of the deed provided as follows:

> To ensure harmony in the design and appearance externally of the front walls of the said buildings there shall not without the previous consent of a majority in number and representing at least 2/3 of the whole votes in respect of assessments in terms of Article 12 hereof … be allowed on the external walls of the buildings any painting affixing or exhibiting or any new form or style of signboard, name plate show case or the like than at presently existing.

Article 12 in turn set out a rather complex system of votes which required to be exercised at a meeting of the proprietors of the building.

In erecting the sign Oldfield had obtained the consent of RBS, Oldfield's landlord. But it did not seem to have occurred to either party to look at the titles to see whether further consents might be needed.

---

1   [2007] UKHL 42, 2008 SC (HL) 1: for discussion see *Conveyancing 2007* pp 106–17.
2   23 January 1963, First Division, Court of Session.
3   Long John whisky is named after 'Long John' Macdonald, who founded Ben Nevis distillery, near Fort William, in 1825.
4   Condescendence 6.

As KPH was quick to point out, the erection of the sign was a clear breach of article 10 of the deed of conditions. But in Oldfield's opinion and in that of RBS, it was a breach that could be swiftly mended. The consent that should have been obtained could be obtained just as well after the event as before. Accordingly, RBS wrote to all the proprietors in the building apologising for the inadvertent breach of article 10, and concluding:

> As the sign has already been erected and can be seen by the proprietors we do not propose to call a special meeting to give any further details, but we annex a form for voting for or against the retention of the sign.

The form said simply:

> I or we consent/do not consent to the erection of the above sign. Strike out whichever is inapplicable.

A sufficient number of proprietors struck out the words in the appropriate way for RBS and Oldfield to get their required majority. But KPH was not among them. Negotiations having broken down, KPH raised an action:

> To interdict the defenders from affixing, exhibiting or continuing to affix, exhibit or place on the external wall of the property situated at 86 and 88 Gordon Street, Glasgow, a large illuminated advertisement panel displaying the name 'Long John Whisky' with an individual drinking Long John Whisky and to ordain defenders to remove said advertisement panel so far as already affixed and to restore the section of the property to the condition in which it was previous to said interference and to find the defenders liable in expenses.

KPH was successful at first instance in the sheriff court[1] but lost on appeal to the sheriff principal.[2] The present stage of the litigation was the appeal from the sheriff principal to the Inner House of the Court of Session.

The Inner House gave judgment on 23 January 1963 and the decision attracted immediate attention in the legal press.[3] Yet, despite the case's evident importance, it has never been reported and was quickly forgotten about. It does not appear in any of the textbooks on conveyancing or property law and was quite unknown to us. The decision has come to light only because of Professor Roderick Paisley, who came across it in one his regular explorations of the National Records of Scotland. One wonders how many other decisions of note may lie there waiting to be discovered.

---

1 The decision, pronounced on 18 January 1962, was given by Sheriff Norman M L Walker.
2 'Sheriff principal' is the modern term. But this decision was given on 17 March 1962 and, in the language of the time, was a decision of the sheriff on appeal from the sheriff-substitute.
3 An unsigned article was published in the issue of the *Conveyancing Review*, a publication sadly long since defunct, for May 1963: see 'The case of the Long John sign' (1963) 3 *Conveyancing Review* 169.

A number of arguments were canvassed before the Inner House,[1] but in the end the decision turned on a single point. Article 10 of the deed of conditions required consent to be obtained *before* the sign was put up. Instead it was obtained *after* the thing had been done. That, said the Inner House, would not do at all. The burden was perfectly clear. And it had been breached. Hence KPH was entitled to insist on the sign being taken down. If Oldfield wanted to put it back up again, it would be necessary for Oldfield to go through the procedures set out in the deed of conditions.

At first sight this looks like a harsh decision founded on a pedantic and inflexible interpretation of the words used in the deed of conditions. But behind it lies a point of substance. In the words of Lord President Clyde:[2]

> It is one thing to ask proprietors whether they will consent to a sign, which has not yet been erected, being put up, but it is quite a different situation when they are told that the sign has been erected and when the erector apologises for having done so without asking the necessary consents and then seeks approval for its retention. Many people might say yes in the latter case who would have said no in the former. The issue in the second case accordingly is quite clearly not the same as in the first.

A vote for retention, in other words, is not the same as a vote for erection. From the point of view of KPH, it was not fair to substitute the one for the other. As Lord Guthrie emphasised, 'a person who holds his property under the protection of a real burden in his title should be enabled by the Court to enjoy that protection'.[3]

If flexibility is wanted, therefore, it has to be provided by the real burden itself and not by an appeal to the good nature of the court. As a matter of drafting, that is something which needs to be borne in mind. In the statutory Tenement Management Scheme, for example, proprietors are given power not only to approve acts of maintenance in advance but also to homologate those which were carried out without permission.[4] This sort of approach seems worth considering.

The thought is all the more important because, all too often, owners act without consulting the titles. No doubt, as a contemporary commentator noted, the decision of the First Division in *King's Park Heritable Co Ltd* was 'a salutary reminder to those who propose to effect alterations on their property that at the outset they should pay to the conveyancer who has laboured over their titles the modest tribute of looking at his handiwork'.[5] But for cases where they do not, the conveyancer's handiwork should perhaps include some means of escape.

---

1 The most important was an appeal to the equitable power of the court, derived from cases such as *Grahame v Magistrates of Kirkcaldy* (1882) 9 R (HL) 91, to decline to order the demolition of something which has already been erected and to award damages in its place. The main use of this power has been in encroachment cases: see in particular *Anderson v Brattisani's* 1978 SLT (Notes) 42. In *King's Park Heritable Co Ltd* the First Division was unwilling to use it to deprive the pursuer of a remedy to which, in the court's view, the pursuer was plainly entitled.
2 At p 6 of his judgment.
3 At p 8 of his judgment.
4 Tenements (Scotland) Act 2004 sch 1 r 3.1(a), (h). A previous act of maintenance which is approved in this way becomes a 'scheme cost' and so must be paid for by all the owners under r 4.
5 'The case of the Long John sign' 171.

FAMILIES, FEUDS, FRIENDS, FRAUDS AND FORGERIES

Introduction

Year after year, decade after decade, century after century, there are cases where lovers, friends and family who at one stage trusted each other fall out, *badly* fall out, about property issues, and end up suing each other. Sometimes these are divorce actions, in which case the specific rules of divorce law will generally provide answers. But often there are disputes between parties who are not married – relatives, ex-friends, ex-lovers – where divorce law cannot help, and even in disputes between spouses there can be basic property law issues for which divorce law in itself cannot provide answers.[1] Over the years we have covered many such cases. 2018 has yielded a good crop of these sometimes macabre disputes.

For the most part, and most of the time, clients tell the truth, or try to tell the truth, or something close to the truth. There are two particular areas of legal practice where that is notoriously not so: crime and divorce. And property disputes between relatives, ex-friends, and ex-lovers also share that quality of revealing that human beings are not always frank and honest.

One other characteristic of this area is that the stories are often bizarre, sometimes straining credulity, and the reader of these cases tends to be left with the suspicion, and sometimes the certainty, that much of what happened will never be known to any except the participants themselves.

Mother-in-law versus daughter-in-law

Catherine Cox and her husband were the public-sector tenants of 21 Easter Drylaw Bank, Edinburgh. In 2002 they exercised their right to buy. They borrowed the purchase price from Halifax plc. The loan was in fact serviced and finally fully repaid not by them but by their son Peter and his wife Karen.[2] There was an understanding that Peter and Karen would eventually inherit the property. Mr Cox senior passed away in 2009, whereafter Catherine was the sole owner, probably through the operation of a survivorship destination. She made a will leaving the property to Peter and Karen.

Over time she began to find getting upstairs difficult, and she decided to sell the property and buy another at 1 Almondside, Kirkliston, West Lothian, which would be more convenient for an older person, and which, moreover, would be nearer to her son and daughter-in-law. The Edinburgh property was sold, and the proceeds were paid, on her instructions, to Peter and Karen. Title to the Kirkliston property was taken in the name of Peter and Karen. The sale figure for the Edinburgh property was higher than the

---

1 An example from 2018 was *Chemcem Scotland Ltd v Beaton* [2018] SC FAL 32, 2018 SLT (Sh Ct) 371 which was at bottom a husband/wife dispute, though its outer form was that of a commercial claim.

2 Catherine claimed that she and her husband did make some contribution, but this claim was rejected by the court.

purchase figure for the Kirkliston property, and Peter and Karen retained the surplus, which amounted to £17,640. The sale and matching purchase took place in 2015.

Thus far, nothing surprising – an ordinary family story. But no sooner had Catherine moved in than things began to go wrong. She noticed that the council tax was in the name of Peter and Karen, and she said that she had been in some way deceived, and that the property should have been bought in her name, and not in the names of Peter and Karen. She also wanted the balance of the money from the sale of the Edinburgh property. Relations quickly soured. In the summer of 2016 Karen was charged with assaulting Catherine, and also assaulting one of Catherine's other children, Caroline Cox or Jones (ie Karen's sister-in-law). The result of Karen's trial in the sheriff court was acquittal. But the feud continued. Peter and Karen raised an action to have Catherine removed from the property. She moved out, and responded to the action by raising one of her own, the present action against Peter and Karen.[1]

In it she sought declarator that the defenders had acted as her agents, and that as a result of that fact they held the proceeds of sale of the Edinburgh property in trust for her, and that accordingly they had been bound to take title to the Kirkliston property in her name, and to pay her the free proceeds of the sale of the Edinburgh property. In the alternative she argued that the defenders had been unjustifiably enriched at her expense, in that the payment to them of the proceeds of sale of the Edinburgh property had been 'in error', and that they should pay her the whole sale figure for the Edinburgh property, under deduction of the contributions they had made to its purchase.[2]

A strong set of facts – a very strong set of facts – would have been needed to give any sort of plausibility to such arguments. But after the facts were examined at proof the Lord Ordinary[3] had no difficulty in concluding that the defenders had never acted as the pursuer's agents and that the payment to them of the proceeds of sale of the Edinburgh property had not been 'in error'. The evidence showed that when the pursuer signed the mandate, directing her solicitors to pay the proceeds of sale to the defenders, she had understood perfectly well what she was doing, and that she had indeed intended that the Kirkliston property would be acquired in the defenders' name not hers. She may later have thought better of it, but to regret choosing to do something is not the same as never having chosen to do it in the first place.

For completeness, we quote the mandate that the pursuer signed, which seems admirably clear:

> I, CATHERINE COX, authorise and instruct you to transfer the whole free proceeds from the sale of 21 EASTER DRYLAW BANK, EDINBURGH, EH4 2QL to the joint matter file of C0382.00006 in the name of Peter and Karen Cox whereupon the funds will be used for Peter and Karen Cox's purchase of 1 Almondside, Kirkliston. I

---

1 *Cox v Cox* [2018] CSOH 49, 2018 GWD 17-219.
2 This allowance for what the defenders had paid seems to have been absent from the pursuer's first, trust, argument.
3 Lord Pentland.

authorise you to pay to Peter and Karen Cox the balance of funds left over once the purchase price and associated fees and outlays have been paid.

A postscript. The judgment says: 'A complaint was made against Messrs Simpson & Marwick to the Scottish Legal Complaints Commission. This led to payment of the sum of £20,000 to the pursuer without admission of liability.'[1] No more is said. Given the findings of the Lord Ordinary, which do not indicate that Messrs Simpson & Marwick had acted in any way improperly, we find this puzzling.

Giving away the farm? (1): Cobairdy

Thomas Paterson owned land at Cobairdy, Aberdeenshire, where he had a dairy farm. In 2011 he sold some of his land to his son-in-law, George Wilson. Mr Paterson died in 2016.[2] Two of his daughters then raised the present action.[3] They claimed that the sale to Mr Wilson had been at 'gross undervalue',[4] and that it had been induced by fraud, or by undue influence, or by facility and circumvention. They concluded, not for reduction of the disposition, but for damages. The factual details of the case are not known in any detail, because the action was dismissed as irrelevant, without proof. But two snippets from the pleadings may be worth quoting, though it must be borne in mind that they were no more than averments. The first:[5]

> By 2011, the deceased was exhausted, vulnerable, weak and facile. The responsibility of running the estate and the said farming business was far in excess of the deceased's capacity as at that time even with the assistance of his late wife and the said contractors. By 2011 the deceased suffered from obvious anxiety and fatigue. He would frequently become tearful and emotional at family gatherings thereby demonstrating his obvious material vulnerability as there was no objective reason for such behaviour. In 2005/06 the deceased contracted very serious, ie painful shingles which left him with continuing material intermittent pain. He never recovered from this illness. By 2011, the deceased had poor eyesight, deficient hearing and he suffered from curvature of the spine. He was also illiterate.

The second snippet:[6]

> There were no missives. No advice was prepared by Fraser & Mulligan (or advice given to obtain advice) relative to capital gains and inheritance tax consequences or likely consequences should the disposition proceed. The disposition proceeded in the absence of any independent valuation from a suitable experienced chartered surveyor familiar with agricultural land in Aberdeenshire at the time.... [The deceased was] an established client of Burnett & Reid Solicitors in Aberdeen for approximately 50

---

1 Paragraph 31.
2 Or, in a puzzling adoption of English legal language, what happened in 2016 was Mr Paterson's 'demise': see para 5.
3 *Anderson v Wilson* [2018] CSOH 5, 2018 GWD 4-62.
4 Paragraph 24.
5 Paragraph 100.
6 Paragraphs 108–09.

years, *inter alia*, hav[ing] recognised expertise in agricultural, property and tax law. The deceased at that time also had an established tax accountant in Aberdeen, namely Ritson Smith. Neither were involved or instructed in the disposition.

The fraud case was that 'the defender deliberately, and without legal justification, arranged for the deceased to enter the said disposition at a price approximately one half of the subject's actual or likely market value'. Unsurprisingly, the Lord Ordinary[1] said: 'That averment ... is so lacking in specification as to be irrelevant.'[2]

But the argument based on facility and circumvention and the argument based on undue influence were both held to have been relevantly pled. In this connection the Lord Ordinary took the view that the non-involvement of the deceased's normal advisers fell to be regarded as 'irregular and unusual' and could be considered as a relevant element in putting forward a case of circumvention.[3]

Nevertheless, the action was dismissed, for two reasons. In the first place, it was held that the remedy for facility and circumvention, and for undue influence, is reduction. Damages cannot be claimed, only reduction. Secondly, even if the transaction could be attacked, it could not be attacked by the pursuers. In other words, the pursuers had no title to sue. 'They do not stand in a legal relation to the defender which gives them some right which the defender infringed.'[4] So who would have had title to sue? 'In the absence of the pursuers having a remedy that does not mean that no party had a remedy open to it for the alleged fraud. There was clearly a remedy open to the deceased and to his estate.'[5] We would respectfully agree.

Giving away the farm? (2): Bonnyton Moor

Mr Barr owned a farm, Bonnyton Moor Farm, in Eaglesham, Renfrewshire. The Barr family solicitor was James Cassels. 'He and the members of the Barr family were on very friendly terms and he was treated as a member of the family. He dined with them, socialised with them and was invited to weddings and birthday parties.'[6] In 2002/2003 Agnes Barr, the farmer's daughter, entered into a romantic relationship with Mr Cassels. This was by no means her first serious relationship. She had had husbands before. Mr Cassels had acted for her in her divorces.[7]

The land and the house

On 3 October 2003 Agnes Barr's father executed a gratuitous disposition in her favour of 1.42 hectares of his land at Bonnyton Moor Farm. The full circumstances

---

1 Lord Bannatyne.
2 Paragraph 70.
3 Paragraph 110.
4 Paragraph 95.
5 Paragraph 90.
6 *Barr v Cassels* [2018] CSOH 79, 2018 GWD 27-345 at para 72 per Lady Wolffe.
7 Paragraph 73.

are unclear. We know that later, when relations between Mr Barr and his daughter had deteriorated, Mr Barr had second thoughts and the possibility was considered of challenging the deed, though it seems that in the end no action was raised. This disposition was not, however, recorded, until 9 June 2006.[1] On the same day, 9 June 2006, another disposition of the same property was recorded, ostensibly signed by Ms Barr in favour of herself and Mr Cassels, equally between them, and to the survivor of them. This disposition, like the one from Mr Barr, seems to have been gratuitous.[2] The reason for the disposition was that Ms Barr and Mr Cassels had decided to build a house on the land and to live there together. The house, which was large, was completed in 2006, and Ms Barr moved in during October, Mr Cassels moving at the end of 2006 or the beginning of 2007.[3]

The conveyancing transaction

The conveyancing for the second transfer was carried out by Mr Cassels' firm, though not by him personally. Two letters during the transaction are worth quoting. The first was a letter of 14 April 2006 from the firm to Ms Barr: in her testimony she denied having received it.

Dear Ms Barr,

1.42 Hectares at Bonnyton Moor Farm Eaglesham

I have been instructed by James Cassels in connection with the transfer of title to the above area of ground, which is currently owned by yourself.

I am advised that you and Mr Cassels have agreed that the title should be transferred into YOUR JOINT NAMES AND TO THE SURVIVOR. This effectively means that on the first death the title to the ground 'automatically' passes to the survivor and in plain English if Mr Cassels were to die first then the title (ownership) automatically passes to you. It is also the case that if you were to die first that the title would pass to Mr Cassels. This is known ad [sic] 'a Destination' ie on the occurrence of a specific event (first Death) the titled [sic] is destined to pass to the survivor. It is also a contract that is entered into between you and in order to change the Destination then each party will require to consent.

It also means that each of you has a share in the title (ownership) and in the event of any dispute that cannot be resolved then the ultimate recourse to either of you would be to make an application to a Court of competent Jurisdiction seeking a decree of division and sale of the property. The court could order that the property be sold and the proceeds of sale divided between you.

---

1 It was recorded in the Register of Sasines. Under the law as it was before the Land Registration etc (Scotland) Act 2012, a gratuitous disposition of unregistered property did not trigger first registration. The delay in recording is surprising but the Lord Ordinary, Lady Wolffe, said (at para 144) that 'there is no basis for criticism arising from the gap in time between the signing of the 2003 disposition and its presentation for registration'.
2 The terms of the disposition are not quoted, but we infer that it was a 'love favour and affection' deed. But in the broader factual matrix it appears that Mr Cassels gave value: see below.
3 Most dates stated in evidence seem to be approximate. But the precise dates are probably not important from a legal standpoint.

The ownership of the buildings erected (or to be erected) on the land is also subject to the same rules and effectively the buildings become part of the land.

I have prepared a Disposition of the Land (and buildings) which is enclosed.

If it is your intention that that title (ownership) of the Land and buildings be transferred to your joint names and the survivor I would ask that you sign the deed at he [sic] place indicated by your pencilled initials and that you complete the date and place of signing. Your signature should be witnessed by an independent witness who should also sign and after their signature complete their personal details.

If you require any advice or instruction about signature please phone.

I MUST STRESS TO YOU THAT WHAT IS PROPOSED IS THE TRANSFER OF OWNERSHIP OF THE LAND AND BUILDINGS FROM YOUR SOLE NAME INTO THE JOINT NAMES OF YOURSELF AND MR CASSELS AND THE SURVIVOR.

You must appreciate that once done the title cannot then be transferred back without the consent of you both.

I would strongly urge that you take INDEPENDENT ADVICE as to the steps that you are about to take BEFORE SIGNING the Disposition.

In the vent [sic] that you are satisfied that you do not require that advice I would ask that you sign the enclosed letter and again have your signature witnessed in order that I can be sure of your receipt of this letter and your confirmation that you do not wish independent advice before signing.

Nothing in this letter is intended as advice to you other than to illustrate in broad terms the nature of the proposed transaction and it's [sic] effect. You should take independent advice if in any doubt.

The other letter was one prepared by the firm for her signature, allegedly sent to Ms Barr with the previous letter, and which was allegedly signed by her and returned, though in her testimony she denied having received it, let alone having signed it:

Dear Mr Findlay

1.42 Hectares at Bonnyton Moor Farm, Eaglesham

I refer to you [sic] letter of 14th April 2006 a copy of which is attached and I confirm that I have read and understand the terms thereof.

I have decided that I wish to proceed to execute the disposition in favour of myself and James M Cassels and to the survivor of us. I acknowledge that I have been advised to seek independent advice as to the nature and effect of granting the said disposition before signing but having had that advise [sic] I have declined to take independent advice.

The executed Disposition is attached hereto.

The action of division and sale

In or about 2007 the romantic relationship 'ended acrimoniously'.[1] What happened between 2007 and 2015 we do not know, but in the latter year Mr Cassels raised an action of division and sale in Paisley Sheriff Court and obtained

---

1 Paragraph 27. 2007 is the year the pursuer gave in evidence, but she also said in evidence (para 24) that she and Mr Cassels began to live together 'three or four months' after October 2006, and that thereafter they spent two Christmases together. It does not seem possible to reconcile these dates.

decree. Whether any attempt to enforce that decree was made prior to the raising of the present action is unclear, but at any rate by the time of the present action it had not been enforced

The action of reduction

To the decree against her in Paisley Sheriff Court Ms Barr responded by raising the present action in the Court of Session to have the second disposition reduced.[1] On what grounds? The question is simple, but no simple answer can be given. The Lord Ordinary[2] observed:[3]

It has not always been easy to discern the legal ground or grounds relied upon by the pursuer in this action of reduction. There is a degree of confusion in the pleadings (which refer to misrepresentation, negligent actings and breach of fiduciary duty). On the first morning of the proof, the pursuer's solicitor advocate endeavoured to clarify the pursuer's position and to focus matters by amendment to his first plea-in-law. In particular, he deleted the reference to 'negligent actings' and inserted instead the phrase 'breach of fiduciary duty'. The case was thereafter conducted on the understanding that this was the essential ground of challenge relied upon by the pursuer. Notwithstanding this, in [his] written submissions at the end of the proof he introduced the topic of undue influence and reintroduced the topic of negligence and undue influence, in addition to that of breach of fiduciary duty. When I asked him to confirm what grounds he relied upon, he identified breach of fiduciary duty, negligent misrepresentation and negligence.

Even on a benign reading of the pleadings, it is difficult to find relevant and specific averments or pleas-in-law for all of these. On a fair reading, the averments about misrepresentation are more apt to play a supporting role for the case of breach of fiduciary duty rather than to constitute a free-standing ground. They bear to relate to the circumstances by which the pursuer came to sign the disposition.

The pursuer's first plea-in-law, as amended, was:

The pursuer having been induced into executing the disposition condescended upon as a result of the Defender's misrepresentations, *et separatim* his actings including his breach of fiduciary duty, the disposition dated 10th May 2006[4] ought to be reduced.

The imperfectly-focused nature of the pleadings was not the only problem. The perhaps weary-sounding Lord Ordinary remarked: 'The matter called before me for a two-week proof. The pleadings in this case are extensive. The Closed Record extends to some 50 pages. There are averments of other matters not obviously or directly reflected to the conclusions.'[5]

---

1 *Barr v Cassels* [2018] CSOH 79, 2018 GWD 27-345. In her action against Mr Cassels Ms Barr was legally aided. 'Had [the full circumstances] been disclosed to or appreciated by the Scottish Legal Aid Board, it is questionable whether she would have received legal aid to raise these proceedings' was the Lord Ordinary's comment (para 166(4)).
2 Lady Wolffe.
3 Paragraph 126.
4 The identification of the disposition solely by date of execution without reference to date of recording will puzzle the property lawyer.
5 Paragraph 4. On account of the scale of the battle the Lord Ordinary's judgment runs to about 26,000 words.

At the heart of the pursuer's factual averments was the following.[1]

On or about 10th May 2006, the defender presented a document to the pursuer for her signature … It is a disposition of heritable property from the pursuer to the pursuer and the defender. The pursuer asked the defender what the document was for. She was told by the defender that the document would transfer her father's land to her. The pursuer did not read the document. The pursuer relied upon the defender's explanation of the purpose of the document in adhibiting her signature to it. At the time of adhibiting her signature, the pursuer was not aware of the earlier 2003 deed; nor aware of the true nature of the disposition to the disposition purportedly conveying title to the defender and herself … Morag Hill, the person allegedly having acted as witness to execution of the deed, was not personally present on the occasion that the pursuer's signature was adhibited to the document.

Where did the money come from?

Building the house cost a good deal of money. Where did it come from? In her written pleadings, the pursuer said: 'The Pursuer paid for the costs of construction. The defender, in receipt of State benefits, was not in any position to contribute towards its construction …'[2] This averment is surprising in that it emerged at proof that one of the parties was indeed on welfare, and the other not, but that the party who was on welfare was the pursuer, not the defender. The pursuer's testimony in court, as summarised by the Lord Ordinary, was remarkable, and not easy to reconcile with her written pleadings:[3]

She explained that the defender would give money for her to treat herself but she never touched this. She put it away. This was years before, when she and the defender had started dating and going to Chinese restaurants. He often gave her money in an envelope and, if it was not money, it was jewellery. This was every couple of weeks or months, and the amounts varied from £1,000, £5,000, to £10,000 at a time. Her position was that he had given her this money unconditionally, explaining to her that he could not use the money and she was to treat herself, but the pursuer never did. She used these monies to pay for the work on the house and to pay the men. She stated that in addition to the defender giving her a lot of money he had also given her his limited-edition Saab.

Also remarkable is what the defender said in his testimony:[4]

The defender confirmed he had funded the building of the house. It was funded in the following manner. He and the pursuer were in a close relationship and were going to build or buy a house. The defender had quite a lot of money and he gave the pursuer a lot of cash. He agreed with her evidence on this point. However, he gave her cash to hold. He did so because, he explained, he lived in a remote house whereas the Barr's farm had a safe and dogs and was a safer place for the cash.[5]

---

1 Paragraph 8(5).
2 Paragraph 8(4).
3 Paragraph 26.
4 Paragraph 74.
5 Why he kept substantial sums in cash seems never to have been explained.

There was agreement that he had made extensive gifts to her. 'The dispute between the parties is whether these were unqualified gifts (as the pursuer contends) or were provided to the pursuer to spend on materials and labour for the construction of the house' observed the Lord Ordinary.[1]

What did the pursuer sign? 'Property laws of the 14th century'?

In her testimony the pursuer denied having received the advice letter of 14 April 2006 and also denied having signed the 'waiver' letter enclosed with it, though she admitted that the signature appeared to be hers. Moreover she denied having signed the disposition, a striking claim in itself and doubly so given that in her written pleadings she had admitted signing it:[2]

> The pursuer was adamant she had only ever signed one document intending to have legal effect. This was the transfer of the parcel of land from her father to herself.[3] She maintained that that document began with a passage all about property laws of the 14th century.

She expressly denied that the disposition by herself to herself and Mr Cassels and the survivor had in fact been signed by her.

Evaluation of the evidence

Perhaps unsurprisingly, the Lord Ordinary, after hearing all the evidence, said that 'I find the pursuer to be a largely incredible and unreliable witness'.[4] She found that the pursuer had received the advice letter, and signed the waiver letter and the disposition. As to the costs of building the house, she found that the defender 'had contributed all or substantially all of the costs to the construction and fitting out of what became a two-storey five-bedroom modern house'.[5] She found that there had been no misrepresentations on the part of the defender.

Breach of fiduciary duty?

The defender was the pursuer's law agent. In acquiring a one-half share of the land was he in breach of his fiduciary duties to her? The Lord Ordinary invoked the Inner House case *Aitken v Campbell's Trs*,[6] where a Glasgow solicitor was extensively involved in property developments in association with one of his clients. What was held in that case was that the transactions must be subject to the 'strictest scrutiny' but that if in fact the transactions between the parties were 'fair and reasonable' they could not be challenged. Applying that test to the facts of the present case it was held that the defender had not been in breach of fiduciary duty.

1　Paragraph 146.
2　Paragraph 14.
3　A disposition is not, in the typical case, signed by the disponee. But this point seems not to be discussed in the decision. After all, the pursuer's case was weak enough already.
4　Paragraph 133.
5　Paragraph 147. What about the 'limited-edition Saab'? No finding-in-fact about that was, alas, made.
6　1909 SC 1217.

Result

The final outcome of the litigation was therefore decree in favour of the defender. It seems unfortunate that this action was ever raised, and it is surprising that it received what must have been extensive funding from the Scottish Legal Aid Board. And given that it was legally aided it seems likely that the defender, despite having been vindicated, will end up having to pay his own expenses.

The weirdest case of 2018?

Now for what is possibly the weirdest case of 2018: *Brooke v Kelly*.[1] Elizabeth Brooke owned a house. The location is not reported, but seems to have been in Glasgow. It was a former council house. Its value is not known, but a figure of £125,000 was suggested at one point.[2] It does not appear that there was any standard security over it. In 2012 Ms Brooke agreed to sell the house to Mary Kelly. The agreement was oral. What price was agreed is unclear. Ms Brooke said that the sum she actually received was £18,000. Ms Kelly said that the sum that she paid was a total of £45,000. One point on which there *was* agreement was that not a penny went through the hands of their law firms and not a penny was paid into the seller's bank account. The money was paid in cash. The payments were made *after* the transfer had already taken place, so that at that time Ms Brooke must have had confidence in Ms Kelly. That confidence was not to last.

Some 'sales on a handshake' never involve solicitors and never result in registration: money changes hands, and possession changes hands, but nothing else. Here, however, the parties to the handshake sale did go to their respective solicitors, and a disposition was drawn up, executed, and registered. Both law firms were told the same false story, namely that the transfer was by way of gift. Accordingly, the disposition that was drawn up bore to be gratuitous.[3]

Notwithstanding the transfer, Ms Brooke continued to live in the house. What the basis of the continuing occupation was, from her point of view, is unclear. But Ms Kelly claimed that it was by virtue of a tenancy, and she produced a document to that effect, the rent being stated as £520 per month, and bearing to have been signed by Ms Brooke. Ms Brooke denied that she had signed it. No rent was ever paid. After a couple of years Ms Kelly transferred the property to one of her sons.[4] She then raised an action in the sheriff court against Ms Brooke for eviction, presumably on the ground of non-payment of rent. This

---

1 [2018] CSOH 53, 2018 Hous LR 56. But such choices are subjective. Some judges on the panel of *Strictly Weird Cases 2018* will understandably prefer others, such as *Khan v Saddique* [2018] CSOH 41, 2018 GWD 16-212, or – another worthy contender – *Barr v Cassels* [2018] CSOH 79, 2018 GWD 27-345.

2 See para 38.

3 This being on its face a gratuitous transaction, Ms Brooke swore an affidavit of solvency, which, opined the Lord Ordinary, was probably false: see para 9.

4 Was this a sale or was it gratuitous? This is unclear but one would guess that it was gratuitous.

action is puzzling (like everything else) since it seems that Ms Kelly was, by the time of the action, no longer the owner of the property, having disponed to her son. This eviction action was eventually dismissed: we do not know on what ground, though lack of title to sue would be one possibility. Thereafter Ms Brooke raised the present action for reduction of the disposition that she had granted in favour of Ms Kelly.

We pause, at this point, to note that, since the property was in the ownership not of the defender but of one of her sons, it might be expected that the son would have been called as a co-defender. This important issue, however, seems not to have been raised.[1]

The basis of the action was that the disposition had been granted as a result of facility and circumvention. There was a proof, in which the Lord Ordinary[2] said of the sworn testimony of the parties: 'I place no reliance on the evidence of either the pursuer or the defender.'[3] But other evidence was available, and the conclusion was that the claim of facility and circumvention was without merit. The evidence showed that Ms Brooke's mental state was unimpaired; that she had fully understood what the transaction involved; that she had fully intended to go ahead with it; and indeed that it was she, not Ms Kelly, who had instigated it. Accordingly, the action failed.

What really went on between Ms Brooke and Ms Kelly is impossible to say, but the Lord Ordinary hazarded some suggestions. Ms Brooke was in financial difficulties and wished to hide the property from her creditors while at the same time being able to continue to live in it. Indeed she entered into a debt arrangement scheme shortly after the transfer. Payments by Ms Kelly to Ms Brooke were in cash so as to ensure that they would not pass through her bank account; indeed there was some evidence that she had rejected an offer to buy the house from another person on the basis that that person had said that he would pay by cheque.[4]

The full richness of this case – including its allegations of theft, of benefit fraud, of bribery, of forgery, and of witness intimidation – cannot be conveyed within the space that we have available, but we warmly recommend our readers to take a no doubt well-merited break by the fireside and enjoy half an hour of astonishing reading.

Forgery, yes, but by whom?

Khan v Saddique[5] is yet another factually strange – very strange – case from 2018. And, as so often, even after a full hearing in court the real truth of much of what happened remains utterly obscure.

In 1998 Muhammad Khan bought 78 Dixon Avenue, Glasgow. He rented it to a lady whose name does not appear but who was the wife of the defender,

---

1 The question of reduction in relation to third parties is discussed at pp 214–20 below.
2 Lady Wolffe.
3 Paragraph 11.
4 Paragraph 31(6).
5 [2018] CSOH 41, 2018 GWD 16-212.

Muhammad Saddique.[1] In 2002 a disposition was registered purportedly granted by Mr Khan in favour of Mr Saddique. Well over ten years later Mr Khan raised the present action seeking to have the disposition reduced as a forgery. Thus much is fairly clear. Little else is.

The main evidence in the proof came from Mr Khan, his wife, and from Mr Saddique. 'I did not regard the evidence of any of those three as entirely credible' was the politely-phrased comment of the Lord Ordinary.[2]

Mr Khan had bought the property in 1998 for £79,950, with a £75,000 loan from Abbey National plc, by means of an endowment mortgage. He never lived there; he lived chiefly in Pakistan.[3] Why did he buy it? That is unclear.[4] Why did he select the defender's wife as tenant? That is unclear.[5] Was there a written tenancy agreement? That is unclear. What was the rent? According to Mr Khan, 'there had been no fixed sum for rent of the property; he was interested only in obtaining enough to cover the mortgage payment'.[6] Why this was so was not explained. Mr Khan's statement that 'he was happy that the rent was never increased'[7] is not easy to understand. It seems that the rent was paid out of social security benefits received by Mr Saddique's wife. It went into an account in the name of Mr Khan out of which the mortgage payments were made.

Before getting on to the crucial issue, the alleged sale and disposition in 2002, we will mention, as illustrative of the unusual nature of the case, the standard security granted by Mr Khan when he bought the property in 1998. It bore to have been signed in Glasgow on 30 September 1998. At that time Mr Khan was in Pakistan. According to the testing clause it was witnessed by Mohammed Iqbal, but he denied having signed,[8] and a handwriting expert agreed that it was not his signature. The handwriting expert inclined to the view that the person who signed as witness to the 1998 standard security was in fact Mr Saddique,[9] and

---

1 Or possibly he rented it to Mr Saddique. No written lease was produced in evidence. Mr Khan and Mr Saddique between them seem to have conducted their affairs by ignoring Mrs Saddique, as if Mr Saddique was the tenant, but the social security department seems to have been told that Mrs Saddique was the tenant.

2 Lady Carmichael: see para 9.

3 Though the address Mr Khan gave to Lloyds Bank was one in Manchester, where he did not live. It was the address of unspecified 'relatives of his wife': see para 28. As with almost everything in this case, the use of an address where Mr Khan did not live was unexplained. For some comments by the Lord Ordinary, see para 120.

4 There is some material about this at para 23 but no answer emerges.

5 Mr Khan said that 'the defender was his friend' (para 34) but (para 89) the defender did not agree. There was evidently some sort of connection between them though its nature was never clarified. In one document they were described as brothers-in-law, though both denied this in court. The pursuer asserted (para 46) but the defender denied (para 107) that in 2009 they had had a meeting in Pakistan. As will be seen, the Lord Ordinary concluded that the defender had acted as a witness to the standard security granted by Mr Khan. There was some evidence that the defender had 'visited him [the pursuer] in Blackburn [Lancashire] to pay respects following the death of the pursuer's father' (para 43). One of the many mysterious aspects of the case is that Mr Khan's UK driving licence was kept by Mr Saddique.

6 Paragraph 44.

7 Paragraph 45.

8 Paragraph 111.

9 Paragraph 57.

this view was accepted by the Lord Ordinary,[1] despite Mr Saddique's denial.[2] Whatever the truth may have been, however, the standard security was not directly relevant to the point at issue in the case, namely the validity of the 2002 disposition. Mr Khan accepted that he had granted the standard security and the loan secured by it was later paid off, as will be seen shortly.

The ostensible sale in 2002 by Mr Khan to Mr Saddique had been handled by a sole practitioner named Anthony David Murphy, who was struck off a few years later.[3] He acted, or purported to act, for both sides. Donald Reid, giving evidence as an expert in conveyancing practice, reported to the court on the files of Mr Murphy.[4] The Lord Ordinary remarked, damningly:[5]

> The conveyancing files have the appearance of having been constructed to resemble in some superficial respects what records of a property transaction should look like. Given the extent of the irregular practices identified by Mr Reid, I have no confidence that I can place reliance on any part of their content as reflecting accurately any contact that might have taken place with either of the parties, or as being a record that such contact actually took place at all.

Mr Khan denied ever having instructed Mr Murphy. Mr Saddique said he did instruct him but indirectly, all his dealings having been done through a Mr Hassan. The price agreed or allegedly agreed was £80,000, which matched what was needed to pay off the Abbey National loan. The money was paid, the loan was paid off, and the standard security was discharged. Rent ceased to be paid. Mr Saddique financed the purchase in part through a loan, secured by a standard security.

Between 1998, the year of Mr Khan's purchase, and 2002, the year of the alleged sale, property prices tended to rise. Yet any such rise was not reflected in the price paid by Mr Saddique. Evidence was heard about the probable value of the house in 2002, but it proved inconclusive. The Lord Ordinary said that 'it is likely that this transaction was for less than full market value. I do not know why the pursuer agreed to sell the property for £80,000'.[6]

It might be supposed that Mr Khan, as landlord, would have noticed that rent had ceased to come in. Allegedly he did not. The Lord Ordinary observed:[7]

> The pursuer's account as to his not having consulted his bank statements after 2002 is … a very strange one.… There is a close coincidence in timing between the transaction [of 2002] and the point when the pursuer stopped looking at his

---

1 Paragraph 124.
2 Paragraph 91.
3 www.ssdt.org.uk/findings/complaints-of-professional-misconduct/law-society-v-anthony-david-murphy/. Mr Murphy was struck off in 2011. The decision of the Discipline Tribunal does not mention his handling of the property at 78 Dixon Avenue, Glasgow. Attempts were made to obtain his evidence in the proof, but without success. 'I was told that he was understood to be outwith Scotland' said the Lord Ordinary (para 5).
4 His evidence makes compelling reading: see paras 70 ff.
5 Paragraph 129.
6 Paragraph 133.
7 Paragraphs 118 and 119.

bank statements. The timing is simply too convenient to be credible. It is near to inconceivable that an educated person like the pursuer would have had no concern as to whether or not the mortgage and insurance payments associated with his property were being met. It is also close to inconceivable that he would have been content to take no active interest in maintaining the property if he had believed that it remained his own.

As for the disposition, the Lord Ordinary accepted the evidence of the handwriting expert that the signature was not the pursuer's.[1] She also accepted the expert evidence that it was not Mr Saddique who forged the signatures.[2]

Given that there were no missives, given that the law firm's conveyancing file was concocted, and given that the disposition was forged, there was not much evidence that there was a sale. Nevertheless, on the basis of the evidence the Lord Ordinary was able to say that 'I am satisfied on the balance of probabilities that the pursuer and the defender reached an agreement orally for the sale and purchase of the property'.[3] Whilst the defender was not himself the forger, was he aware that the deed had been forged? 'I am not satisfied that the evidence demonstrates that the defender was aware of the forgery at the time of registration in his favour', said the Lord Ordinary.'[4]

Of course, an oral agreement of sale could not suffice to save a disposition that had been proved a forgery. Nevertheless, the defender prevailed in the litigation on the basis of a plea of personal bar. Once again we quote the Lord Ordinary:[5]

> The pursuer knew that he personally had not signed any document transferring title to the property. He did not challenge the transaction until 2013. The words and conduct of the pursuer in agreeing to sell the property to the defender caused the defender to pay money to purchase the property, and also to believe that the pursuer intended title to pass to the defender in exchange for payment. The defender believed that the transaction had been effective in transferring title to him. The defender has continued to act to his prejudice in reliance on those words and conduct, in paying interest on his mortgage, and by carrying out improvements to the property. The pursuer is therefore personally barred from seeking reduction of the disposition.

One can certainly see the force of this conclusion. After all, (i) there had been an oral agreement to sell; (ii) the forgery of the disposition was not the defender's; (iii) in reliance on the transaction, the defender had expended considerable sums of money; and (iv) the pursuer had allowed all this to happen, doing nothing to challenge the transaction for more than ten years. There is, however, a difficulty. In a recent case, not cited to the court, the Inner House has held that where a

---

1 The pursuer's wife had also ostensibly signed, presumably in relation to the Matrimonial Homes (Family Protection) (Scotland) Act 1981, and it was also accepted that that signature too had been forged.
2 Paragraphs 56 and 115.
3 Paragraph 146.
4 Paragraph 144.
5 Paragraphs 146 and 147.

disposition is proved to be a forgery, an action to reduce it cannot be defeated by a plea of personal bar.[1]

Finally, one might ask: what on earth was going on? One possibility is that in 1998 Mr Saddique wished to buy the property but to do so through a nominee, and the nominee was Mr Khan. That hypothesis would explain many aspects of the case. For instance it would explain why the 'rent' matched the mortgage payments, it would explain Mr Khan's lack of interest in what was happening to the property, and it would explain why the price paid in 2002 matched the outstanding loan. But there is no obvious reason why Mr Saddique would have wished to buy through a nominee. And both parties in their testimony, albeit they disagreed on so many things, agreed that the lease had been a genuine lease. We are baffled.

Must a trust of heritable property be in writing?

In *Chemcem Scotland Ltd v Beaton*[2] the pursuer was a company whose shares were wholly owned by husband and wife, the latter being the defender in this action. It appears that they were also the company's directors. At some stage the relationships seem to have broken down, although the details are unclear.

The litigation concerned properties acquired by the defender from a third party. The company sought 'a declarator that the transfer to the defender of certain properties in High Street, Linlithgow, West Lothian, was a conveyance and transfer in trust for behoof of the pursuer and that the heritable properties are held by the defender in trust'.[3] From that it appears that the alleged trust was created through the dispositions, those dispositions being dispositions in trust. But elsewhere it is averred that the defender bought the properties using funds of the company, which would seem to suggest that (according to the company) what she held in trust was initially the money, and thereafter what was bought with the money, ie that this was a case where a trustee used trust funds to buy property from ordinary sellers. But this is to speculate. The facts of the case are unclear, and it is also unclear what position the respective parties were adopting in the litigation. Why and on what basis a trust was asserted, as opposed to some other type of claim against the defender, is unclear.

The interest of the case lies chiefly in the argument of the defender that a trust of heritable property cannot be constituted without writing. Given that there was no such writing here, the defender argued that the action was, as a consequence, irrelevant, and thus fell to be dismissed. In Wilson and Duncan's *Trusts, Trustees and Executors* it is said that trusts 'will require to be in writing ... if they relate in any way to an interest in land',[4] citing s 1(2)(b)

---

1 *Chalmers v Chalmers* [2014] CSOH 161, 2015 SCLR 299 rev [2015] CSIH 75, 2015 SLT 793, discussed in *Conveyancing 2014* pp 196 ff and *Conveyancing 2015* pp 200 ff.
2 [2018] SC FAL 32, 2018 SLT (Sh Ct) 371.
3 Paragraph 1.
4 W A Wilson and A G M Duncan, *Trusts, Trustees and Executors* (2nd edn, 1995) para 2–55.

of the Requirements of Writing (Scotland) Act 1995. Likewise, in Gordon and Wortley's *Scottish Land Law* it is said that 'where a real right in land is involved or the trust is testamentary the trust must be constituted in writing',[1] citing s 1(2)(b) and s 1(2)(c) of the 1995 Act. But the sheriff[2] did not agree. He observed that the 1995 Act's rule about heritable property is about the creation of real rights, and the right of a beneficiary in a trust is not a real right. Hence, he held, there is nothing in the 1995 Act to require that a trust of heritable property be in writing, at least in the normal case.[3] We incline to agree with the sheriff on this point.[4] However, we fear that there is much about the law of the constitution of trusts that is obscure. Obviously, no conveyancer would dream of setting up a trust without writing, and even on the basis that an unwritten trust is possible, it will in practice be very difficult to satisfy a court as to the existence of such a trust.

BEWARE: IS THIS A SALE AT UNDERVALUE?

On 24 July 2014 Carnbroe Estates Ltd concluded missives to buy a commercial property at 9 Stroud Road, East Kilbride, for £550,000, the seller being Grampian Maclennan's Distribution Services Ltd. The purchase was to be financed by a loan from Bank of Scotland plc in the sum of £600,000. But the bank had a concern. D M Hall had valued the property at £1.2 million on the open market, or £800,000 if a restricted 180-day marketing period were assumed. On 28 July 2014 the bank wrote to the Carnbroe Estates' solicitors to express concern at the apparent discrepancy between the open-market value and the purchase price. The bank explained that it feared that its standard security might be adversely affected if a liquidator of Grampian sought to challenge the transaction as a gratuitous alienation. The reply from the solicitors was that National Westminster, a major creditor of the seller, was on the point of enforcing its standard security over the property, and so there was simply no time for the property to be marketed in the usual way. In the circumstances the price was, it might be said, a reasonable one. The bank was satisfied with this reply.[5] On 15 August 2014 it released the £600,000, and on 18 August the transaction settled. So this was a quick, off-market below-value sale, a distress sale, or what is sometimes called a fire sale. The managing directors of the two companies were, it seems, old friends. As well as the debt owed to NatWest, Grampian Maclennan's Distribution Services Ltd had extensive other debts, especially to HMRC.

---

1 W M Gordon and S Wortley, *Scottish Land Law* (3rd edn, 2009) para 16–08.
2 Sheriff John Mundy.
3 An exception would be where the owner of heritable property declares that he holds the property henceforth in trust, in which case writing is required: see Requirements of Writing (Scotland) Act 1995 s 1(2)(a)(iii).
4 In its examination of the constitutions of trusts, the Scottish Law Commission appears to have taken the same view: see *Discussion Paper No 133 on the Nature and Constitution of Trusts* (2006) para 3.15.
5 It is unclear whether the bank used solicitors of its own.

Although the price was £550,000, what was actually paid was only £473,604.68. This was the sum that was owed by the seller to NatWest. It was paid over to NatWest, which as a result granted a discharge of its standard security.[1] The following month, September 2014, the seller went into insolvent liquidation, and the liquidators raised an action to reduce the disposition. Their case was straightforward. A 'gratuitous alienation' is a concept that covers not only its literal meaning – a transfer for no consideration – but also any transaction in which the net value of the debtor's patrimony is lessened, for example by a waiver of a debt, or a purchase at overvalue, or a sale at undervalue. The vulnerable period[2] is, subject to certain qualifications, two years back from the date of the liquidation.[3] Of course, gratuitous alienations by a person who is *solvent* cannot be challenged under this chapter of the law. But those who are insolvent should not be diminishing the net value of their estate.

The action of necessity involved evidence as to value. Both sides produced evidence from valuers, which turned out to be well below the £1.2 million figure produced originally by D M Hall. But both were well above the actual price of £550,000. The pursuers' expert valued the property at £820,000 while the defender's expert valued it at £740,000. 'Both of these were market values, which assumed a bargain between a willing seller and a willing buyer at arm's length with a proper marketing period and no element of compulsion.'[4]

The key question in the case was whether, in all the circumstances, the sale was indeed at undervalue. Just as the pursuer's argument was straightforward – that this had been a sale at undervalue, by an insolvent company, and thus unlawful – so the defence was straightforward, namely that this was a distress sale, and that the figure achieved was not unreasonable given that fact.

At first instance the defence was accepted.[5] The liquidators reclaimed, and the First Division reversed the decision and granted decree of reduction, the

---

1 Whether Bank of Scotland plc was told that the sum actually paid by the buyer to the seller was not £550,000 but only £473,604.68 is unclear. The balance was, in fact, eventually paid, but only after the seller had gone into liquidation. This remarkable and disturbing aspect of the transaction was not explored in this litigation.

2 This term, and another with the same meaning, the 'hardening period', is not much used in Scotland but is used quite commonly internationally. It means the period prior to the opening of insolvency during which transactions may be liable to subsequent challenge. For instance a disposition six years before sequestration would be outside the vulnerable period, whereas a disposition six weeks before sequestration would be within it. The rules are less than simple. The periods are: (i) in the case of a challenge on the ground that the transaction was a gratuitous alienation, the vulnerable period is either two years or five years depending on the circumstances, and (ii) in the case of a challenge on the ground that the transaction was an unfair preference, the vulnerable period is six months. See Bankruptcy (Scotland) Act 2016 ss 98 and 99 and, for companies, Insolvency Act 1986 ss 242 and 243. But this is a mere summary of a complex area of law. For floating charges the vulnerable period is two years: Insolvency Act 1986 s 245.

3 The governing provision for companies is s 242 of the Insolvency Act 1986. The position for natural persons and other entities such as partnerships is the same: see Bankruptcy (Scotland) Act 2016 s 98. The rules have a long history and ultimately derive from the *actio pauliana* of Roman law.

4 [2018] CSIH 7 at para 8.

5 *Joint Liquidators of Grampian Maclennan's Distribution Services Ltd v Carnbroe Estates Ltd* [2017] CSOH 8, 2017 GWD 3-37.

Opinion of the Court being given by Lord Drummond Young.[1] He said, in a careful and important analysis of the law, set in its commercial context:[2]

> Once a debtor appears to be insolvent, he is obliged to manage his assets in such a way as to protect the interests of his creditors, as a general body.... For this reason, we are of opinion that the courts should take a relatively strict view of the adequacy of consideration. Adequacy must be assessed objectively ... The need for a strict and objective approach is particularly important if the debtor's business has ended or is about to come to an end. In such a case, although a solvent winding up is possible, in many cases there is an obvious risk – frequently a likelihood – of insolvency. In that event the policy of protecting the interests of creditors operates with full force. Moreover, quite apart from the possibility of an insolvent winding up, once a business has ceased to operate the discipline of ordinary commercial relations goes with it. Normally those in business are constrained to act in a fair and reasonable way towards their suppliers, customers and other creditors because they want to do repeat business. On cessation of business this consideration no longer operates, as can be observed with insurance companies in run-off ... Furthermore, if the debtor's business is about to come to an end, the need for a forced sale to maintain the liquidity of the business and hence its continuation simply disappears.

So decree reducing the disposition was pronounced.

What about the standard security that the defender had granted to Bank of Scotland plc? That is unclear from the case as reported, but we understand that there was no conclusion seeking the reduction of the standard security, though the action was intimated to the bank.[3] The standard security, therefore, remains valid, and the effect of the reduction of the disposition will be that the property re-vests in the company in liquidation subject to the standard security granted by the buyer. It would still be possible for the liquidators to raise a separate action to reduce the standard security, a possibility discussed in the following section, but as to whether this might in fact happen we have no information.

Why is this case of interest to conveyancers? In the first place, it is a reminder of what has always been the law, though not always borne in mind, namely that even a sale can, depending on the circumstances, be reducible as a gratuitous alienation, if the price is clearly below fair market value. In the second place, and this was the legal issue in dispute, the fact that the sale is a distress sale (or fire sale), is no defence. Of course, distress sales, involving realisations at materially less than market values, may be perfectly valid. But if the seller is insolvent at the time, they may be open to attack. And all this is important not only in relation to advice given to a buyer, but also in relation to advice given to the buyer's lender. There are evidently issues of professional liability here.

---

1 *Joint Liquidators of Grampian Maclennan's Distribution Services Ltd v Carnbroe Estates Ltd* [2018] CSIH 7, 2018 SC 314, 2018 SLT 205, 2018 SCLR 532. But this is not the end of the story, for the defender has been granted leave to appeal to the Supreme Court. For what it is worth, our view is that the decision of the Inner House is sound.

2 Paragraphs 24 and 25. More could have been quoted, for the judgment is a valuable one, but for reasons of space we must be selective.

3 We thank James Lloyd of Messrs Harper Macleod for this information.

REDUCTION AND HERITABLE PROPERTY

This year there has been a crop of cases involving actions of reduction. They serve as a reminder that all is not clear in this area of law. Some of the problems seem to be subjective, in that those advising litigants may not always have had the law sufficiently in focus, while other problems seem to be objective in the sense that there are real uncertainties as to what the law is. The subject is large and here we can do no more than touch on certain points.

Void or voidable?

A distinction that is reasonably firmly established in modern law is the distinction between (i) void deeds and (ii) voidable deeds, which themselves will typically result, after registration, in (i) void titles or (ii) voidable titles.[1]

If a disposition[2] is void, then, following registration in the Land Register, the disponee's title is a nullity and ownership remains in the disponer.[3] One example would be where the disponer lacks capacity on account of dementia. Another would be forgery.

If a disposition is voidable, matters are different. A voidable disposition is valid unless or until it is reduced. Hence on registration the disponee does become owner. The disponer has an option to reacquire the property by means of an action of reduction, but only an option. If the option is not exercised, the disponee remains owner. Examples where a disposition is voidable would be where it has been induced by fraud, or by undue influence, or by facility and circumvention. In the case of an elderly person the distinction between a voidable deed and a void one can be a fine one, because it may depend on whether that person's mental state has crossed the line into incapacity. Still, the distinction is one that must be drawn. In practice, actions for reductions of deeds granted by elderly persons often plead, as alternatives, both that the granter was *incapax* and, *esto* that he or she was still *capax*, that there was facility and circumvention etc. So both voidness and voidability are often pled together.

An action of reduction is used both for void dispositions and also for those that are voidable. But its effect, if successful, is different in the two cases. In the case of a void disposition, the reduction does not alter any property rights. Its effect is declaratory. It takes away what was merely an *apparent* title. If Seraphina owns a property and Titania forges Seraphina's signature on a disposition in her own favour, the transfer is void, and ownership never vests in Titania. So the effect of the reduction is simply to make that fact manifest. But change the facts. Seraphina is induced by Titania's undue influence into signing a disposition. The disposition is valid if voidable, and Titania becomes owner. Her title is not merely an apparent one: it is an actual one. If Seraphina then exercises the option of

---

1 Whether this distinction was always so established in Scots law is another matter.
2 Or other deed, but for simplicity we consider dispositions, and in practice almost all actions to reduce heritable deeds concern dispositions.
3 Land Registration etc (Scotland) Act 2012 s 49(4). Registration does not cure the invalidity of the deed: there is no Midas touch under the 2012 Act.

reduction, the consequence will be that ownership will move back from Titania to Seraphina. So in the case of a voidable deed, unlike the case of a void deed, reduction results in a *change* of property rights and is not purely declaratory. So the two types of reduction are very different.

Though the issue did not arise in 2018, it may be worth noting, on the subject of reduction, that the rules about registering reductions were modified by the Land Registration etc (Scotland) Act 2012.[1] (i) Where a void deed is reduced, the consequence is a 'manifest inaccuracy' and the Keeper is then bound to rectify the Land Register.[2] (ii) Where a voidable deed is reduced, the decree of reduction is registrable, and 'does not have real effect until so registered'.[3] So reductions of void dispositions enter the Land Register by means of rectification, but reductions of voidable deeds enter the Land Register by means of registration.

Reduction and personal bar

An action to reduce a voidable disposition may fail on the ground that the pursuer is personally barred. That does not seem to be controversial. But what about an action to reduce a void disposition? Can such an action fail by reason of personal bar? This issue arose in 2018 in the Outer House decision of *Khan v Saddique*.[4] A disposition ostensibly signed by Mr Khan was registered in favour of Mr Saddique. Many years later Mr Khan raised an action to reduce the disposition on the ground that his signature had been forged. Evidence was led and the court concluded that the signature had indeed been forged, though the question of who was responsible could not be determined. Despite winning on the question of forgery, the pursuer lost the action, because the court took the view that the failure over many years of Mr Khan to challenge the deed resulted in personal bar against him.

In another recent case, *Chalmers v Chalmers*,[5] a disposition was forged and there was an action to reduce it. The Lord Ordinary held that, despite the fact of forgery, the action of reduction failed on account of personal bar. The pursuer reclaimed, and the Inner House reversed, holding that in such a case personal bar cannot be pled. This decision does not seem to have been cited to the court in *Khan v Saddique*. Standing the Inner House decision, *Khan v Saddique* would, with respect, appear to have been wrongly decided.

Third-party rights

Convening the third party as joint defender

One of the most difficult issues concerns the position of third-party rights. Suppose that the disponee has, since registration, granted rights to third parties.

---

1 For discussion, see K G C Reid and G L Gretton, *Land Registration* (2017) para 6.12.
2 LR(S)A 2012 s 80.
3 Conveyancing (Scotland) Act 1924 s 46A(1).
4 [2018] CSOH 41, 2018 GWD 16-212.
5 [2014] CSOH 161, 2015 SCLR 299 rev [2015] CSIH 75, 2015 SLT 793, discussed in *Conveyancing 2014* pp 196 ff and *Conveyancing 2015* pp 200 ff.

Registered grants fall into two categories: (i) dispositions and (ii) subordinate rights such as standard securities and servitudes. Such third-party rights are in practice common, and, naturally, they complicate matters. It is no longer simply a question of Seraphina versus Titania (we say 'simply' but of course even the two-party case may be far from simple). Instead a third party is also involved.

A third-party right can readily be discovered by a legal report, and if the legal report reveals such a right, the holder of that right can be called as a joint defender. That much may seem straightforward. Yet it seems sometimes not to happen in practice. In *Brooke v Kelly*[1] Ms Brooke sought reduction of a disposition to Ms Kelly. Yet before the action was raised Ms Kelly had already disponed to someone else, X. Nevertheless it seems that X was not convened as co-defender. Some case reports are simply silent as to third parties but that does not necessarily mean that there were no such parties; it may simply mean that they were ignored.[2]

Why are holders of third-party rights sometimes not called as joint defenders? We do not know. We suspect that when the matter goes to the law firm's (no doubt excellent) court department, expressions such as 'search' and 'legal report' may be less familiar than they are in the conveyancing department. What the court department has in its folder is the questionable disposition, plus precognitions and other material, and the matter proceeds as matters in court departments usually proceed: X versus Y. The other possibility is that the court department knows that there might be third-party rights, and possibly even knows that there actually are such rights, but it is not considered that the third-party right holder should be convened as a joint defender.

Why the issue matters

Suppose that the action goes ahead, without calling the third-party right-holder, and the action is successful. The disposition is reduced. Here matters become tricky. Does the reduction take away the third party's right, or not? This is, in and of itself, a procedural question, rather than the substantive question of what defence the third party might have, of which more below. In our view the answer to the procedural question is one that applies, in general (though there are some qualifications), right across civil procedure in private law, namely that a decree does not prejudice parties not called. To take an absurd but illustrative example. Suppose that Kenneth Reid and George Gretton both claim to own St Kilda. They quarrel. Reid raises against Gretton an action of declarator that he, Reid, is the owner of St Kilda. Gretton defends poorly (nobody will be surprised) and decree is granted. What is the effect of the decree as against the actual

---

1   [2018] CSOH 53, 2018 Hous LR 56.
2   One case where it is clear that the third party, a standard-security holder, was called is *Khan v Saddique* [2018] CSOH 41, 2018 GWD 16-212. In this case there was an interesting agreement between the pursuer and the standard-security holder (para 2): 'The pursuer and the second defender have agreed that in the event that reduction of the title of the first defender is granted as first concluded for, reduction of the standard security in favour of the second defenders shall only be granted when the sums due by the first defender to the second defenders have been repaid by the pursuer, that to a maximum sum of £70,000.'

owner of St Kilda, that most worthy institution the National Trust for Scotland? None. Why? Because the NTS was not convened, so the decree could not affect it. Actions between X and Y cannot (generally speaking) prejudice Z.

Suppose that X raises an action to reduce a disposition in favour of Y, and Y has already granted a standard security to Z, and Z is not convened in the action. If X wins, the decree, as such, will have effect against Y but not against Z. It may be (depending on the circumstances) that Z's standard security will not be able to withstand attack, but that is a separate point. The decree against Y does not touch the standard security. This is true not only if the disposition was reduced as voidable. It is even true if the disposition was reduced as being void. After all, it may be that, if Z had been convened, Z could have satisfied the court that the disposition was in fact valid. (At an extreme, the X/Y litigation could even have been collusive.)

Faced with a decree against Y but not against Z, the Keeper would in our view be bound to reinstate X's name in the Land Register, but would not be bound to delete the standard security. Indeed, the Keeper would be bound *not* to delete the standard security. If the standard security is to be deleted, that would require a new action,[1] against Z. It would have been more straightforward to have convened Z in the first action. Whether such an action would succeed depends on the substantive law applicable to Z's position, to which we now turn.

What are the conclusions of the action?

Another, and perhaps simpler, way of looking at the question is to consider what the conclusions are in an action of reduction. If X concludes for the reduction of the X/Y disposition, but does not have a conclusion for reduction of the Y/Z standard security, then the decree in X's favour will, to state the obvious, reduce only the disposition. The standard security will remain unreduced, and therefore will still encumber the property, even though Y will lose ownership of that property.[2] And as already said if there is a conclusion for reduction of the standard security, that would necessitate calling Z as a defender.

The substantive position of third parties

So much for the general question of the effect of a decree against a party not called. We turn now to the question of substantive property law, which will be determinative as and when Z is in fact called, ideally in the original action to reduce the disposition but also, in the alternative, in a separate action. The general principles here are not in doubt. The position varies according to whether the initial disposition from X to Y was void or voidable.

If the disposition was void, then the common-law rule is that all third-party rights granted by the disponee will also be void, even if the third parties were

---

1 We say 'require' but in many cases the X/Z issue would be resolved without litigation. Z would be unlikely to incur the expense of defending an undefendable action. Of course, it may not in all cases be undefendable: to this issue we turn shortly.
2 As an example, this appears to be the situation in *Joint Liquidators of Grampian Maclennan's Distribution Services Ltd v Carnbroe Estates Ltd* [2018] CSIH 7, 2018 SC 314, 2018 SLT 205, 2018 SCLR 532.

in good faith and gave value. In the immortal words of Ulpian, 'nemo plus juris ad alium transferre potest quam ipse haberet'.[1] But the Land Registration etc (Scotland) Act 2012 protects a third party who has acted in good faith in some, but not all, types of case due to the doctrine of realignment.[2] Most notably, if Z has taken a disposition from Y, then his title will usually be valid, notwithstanding that Y's title was void.[3] One type of case where the 2012 Act does not protect the third party, so that the common-law rule applies, is a standard security. So if there is a forged disposition by X to Y and Y grants a standard security to Z, who is in good faith, Z is not protected: the standard security is void, although Z will normally benefit from a different protection: the Keeper's warranty.[4]

The other case is where the disposition is voidable. Here too there is a common-law rule, which is that Z is protected if he has acted in good faith and for value, and this protection applies across the board, thus including standard securities.[5] The 2012 Act has no provision on the subject, being content to leave matters to the general law.

Where a disposition (or other deed) is voidable because of insolvency law, ie because it was a gratuitous alienation or an unfair preference, there are statutory rules that in effect reiterate the common law rule.[6]

Does the protection of the Y/Z transaction imply the protection of the X/Y transaction?

It is sometimes said that the existence of Z (holding a third-party right, obtained for value and in good faith) will prevent reduction of a voidable X/Y transaction. A typical example by a well-known scholar, D M Walker, is illustrative:[7]

A voidable contract[8] is no longer reducible if a third party has, in good faith, for value and without notice of the defect, acquired a real right of property in the subject-matter of the voidable contract, as where a thing sold under a voidable contract has been resold,[9] or pledged,[10] or land acquired by fraud has been resold,[11] or disponed in security.[12]

---

1 *Digesta* 50.17.54.
2 LR(S)A 2012 ss 86–90. Realignment is a large topic: for a full account, see Reid and Gretton, *Land Registration* ch 12.
3 LR(S)A 2012 s 86.
4 LR(S)A 2012 s 73.
5 See K G C Reid, *The Law of Property in Scotland* (1996) para 692.
6 Insolvency Act 1986 ss 242(4) and 243(5); Bankruptcy (Scotland) Act 2016 ss 98(7) and 99(7).
7 D M Walker, *Civil Remedies* (1974) p 161. The passage would seem to be loosely based on W M Gloag, *The Law of Contract* (2nd edn, 1929) pp 533–34.
8 The reference to 'contract' here is problematic, unless the term is taken in a broad sense. Contract and conveyance are different, and a title arises out of the latter rather than the former. Perhaps it was a slip of the pen – the section of the chapter in which the passage appears is headed 'Reduction of *deeds*: grounds for reduction' – or perhaps Professor Walker was thinking primarily about sale of goods, where there is no deed of conveyance.
9 Here Professor Walker cites the Sale of Goods Act 1893 s 23 (= Sale of Goods Act 1979 s 23).
10 Here Professor Walker cites *Price & Pierce Ltd v Bank of Scotland* 1910 SC 1095, 1912 SC (HL) 19.
11 Here Professor Walker cites Stair I.40.22; *Wilson v Elliott* (1826) 4 S 429, (1828) 3 W & S 60; *Fraser v Hankey* (1847) 9 D 415. (The reference to Stair is not accurate.)
12 Here Professor Walker footnotes *Williamson v Sharp* (1851) 14 D 415.

But this view of the law is not supported by the authorities which Professor Walker cites. Whilst a full discussion would be beyond the scope of the present note, it is submitted that the rule is that the Y/Z transaction[1] is protected, not the X/Y transaction. If the Y/Z transaction was a disposition, it comes to almost the same thing anyway.[2] The difference emerges where the Y/Z transaction was not a disposition but the grant of a subordinate right, such as, say, a servitude or a standard security. Take a straightforward case. There is a disposition by X to Y which is voidable. A year later a servitude is granted by Y to a neighbour Z. Z paid for the servitude and acted in good faith. A few months thereafter X decides to exercise his option to avoid the transfer. He raises an action to reduce the disposition. The existence of the servitude does not block that action. Decree of reduction will be pronounced and the extract decree will be registered in the Land Register. The servitude will be unaffected. X will have reacquired ownership, but the servitude will still stand. The same would be true if the third-party right were a standard security rather than a servitude.[3]

What if Y has not yet granted any third-party right, but X fears that he might do so after the action has been raised but before it has been heard and determined? The answer is to register a caveat in the Land Register.[4] That will not bar Y from granting a third-party right, but it will mean that anyone (ie a prospective Z) taking such a right does so in the knowledge of X's action, with the result that the shield of good faith is not available to him.

Reduction and discretion

One other area of difficulty remains to be discussed. We quote a passage from another 2018 case, *Barr v Cassels*,[5] concerning an allegedly voidable disposition:

> Both parties accepted that the remedy of reduction is an equitable remedy and that the court may take into account facts and circumstances not directly related to the merits or subject-matter giving rise to the parties' action. So, for example, the acquisition of rights by a third party in good faith and for value in the subjects (eg such as a heritable creditor), had this occurred, is likely to have been a relevant factor in the exercise of the court's discretion to grant or refuse reduction.

The question of judicial discretion in relation to the reduction of voidable deeds is a difficult one into which we will not attempt to enter here. No authority is cited for the view expressed, no doubt because it was a matter of concession by both sides. But we are aware of no authority saying that reduction is subject to judicial discretion.[6]

---

1 To recapitulate: the situation under consideration is where the X/Y transaction was voidable and Z has acquired a real right in good faith and for value.
2 The disposition is still reducible. But the reduction cannot have *proprietary* consequences since Y has (by the time that the action of reduction is raised) no proprietary right *anyway*.
3 In this latter case that would not involve X in personal liability for the secured loan.
4 LR(S)A 2012 s 67; see Reid and Gretton, *Land Registration* ch 18.
5 [2018] CSOH 79, 2018 GWD 27-345. The passage is to be found at para 165.
6 D M Walker in his extensive chapter on reduction in *Civil Remedies* (1974) makes no mention of judicial discretion.

Whatever the law on that point may be, we think, with respect, that the existence of a third-party right is not something which could engage any such discretion. As we have said, the existence of a third-party right held by Z is simply irrelevant to a reduction of the X/Y transaction.

PROPERTY FACTORS: TO REGISTER OR NOT TO REGISTER?

Introduction

The rising tide of registration has engulfed many of those involved in property management and letting, of whom letting agents are merely the most recent example.[1] Property factors were caught relatively early on. The Property Factors (Scotland) Act 2011 set up a Register of Property Factors[2] and required all property factors to register there.[3] Some 400 have now done so. On registration taking place, factors become subject to a Code of Conduct, prepared by the Scottish Government, which sets mandatory rules on a wide range of matters including the provision of information to clients, transparent pricing, dispute resolution, and so on.[4] Disgruntled homeowners can refer their complaints to the First-tier Tribunal.[5] The idea is to stamp out the abuses that, according to some, were a feature of the former unregulated system. Failure to register is a criminal offence, punishable by a fine or even by imprisonment.[6] It is therefore important to be clear who is and who is not a property factor, and hence who is and who is not under an obligation to seek registration.

A lengthy definition of 'property factor' is given in s 2 of the Act. An initial distinction is made between (i) local authorities and housing associations, and (ii) other persons and bodies who carry out property management. So far as the latter are concerned, two cases are identified by s 2. One is the typical factor who manages, but does not own, the common parts in a residential development.[7]

---

1 For registration of letting agents, see Housing (Scotland) Act 2014 Pt 4 (ss 29–62); Letting Agent Registration (Scotland) Regulations 2016, SSI 2016/432. An overview can be found in *Conveyancing 2017* pp 90–91.
2 Available at http://sedsh119.sedsh.gov.uk/propertyfactorregister/.
3 Property Factors (Scotland) Act 2011 ss 3–7. For an overview of the Act, see *Conveyancing 2011* pp 109–16.
4 PF(S)A 2011 s 14. See Property Factors (Code of Conduct) (Scotland) Order 2012, SSI 2012/217, and, for the Code of Conduct itself, www.scotland.gov.uk/Publications/2012/07/6791/0. Amendments are under consideration: see p 110 above.
5 PF(S)A 2011 s 17. For an example from 2018 which was appealed to the Upper Tribunal, see *Speirs Gumley Property Management v Lafferty* 2018 Hous LR 78. There is a steady stream of traffic to the First-tier Tribunal; the Tribunal's decisions can be found at www.housingandpropertychamber. scot/property-factors/property-factors-decisions.
6 PF(S)A 2011 s 12.
7 PF(S)A 2011 s 2(1)(a): 'a person who, in the course of that person's business, manages the common parts of land owned by two or more other persons and used to any extent for residential purposes'.

The other is a person who both owns and manages.[1] More precisely, the second case is:[2]

> a person who, in the course of that person's business, manages or maintains land which is available for use by the owners of any two or more adjoining or neighbouring residential properties (but only where the owners of those properties are required by the terms of the title deeds relating to the properties to pay for the cost of the management or maintenance of that land).[3]

The idea is to cover companies, such as those in the Greenbelt group, which take a conveyance of the common areas in a residential development and then charge the homeowners for the cost of maintenance by means of real burdens. But the net is spread more widely than that, and two recent cases have, for the first time, tested its full extent. In neither case had the property manager sought registration under the Act. The first case, *Procurator Fiscal, Oban v Melfort Pier Holidays Ltd*,[4] was a criminal prosecution for failure to register, indeed apparently the first prosecution to take place under the Act. The second, *Cullochgold Services Ltd v Blair*,[5] was a civil action by a property manager to recover arrears of service charge. In the first case, the absence of registration was the basis of the prosecution; in the second it was a defence on the part of the homeowner to the claim for payment.[6]

The definition in s 2(1)(c) of the 2011 Act, quoted above, sets three main requirements for an owner-manager to qualify as a property factor. In the first place, the person must manage or maintain land 'in the course of that person's business'. In the second place, the land must be 'available for use by the owners of any two or more adjoining or neighbouring residential properties'. Finally, the neighbouring owners must be required in terms of the title deeds to pay for the cost of management or maintenance. There is, in other words, to be a link between the right to use and the obligation to pay. The first of these three requirements was claimed to be lacking in *Melfort Pier Holidays*.[7] In *Cullochgold Services* the alleged shortcoming was in respect of the second requirement.

The first requirement: management in the course of a business

The arrangements in the development under scrutiny in *Melfort Pier Holidays* were non-standard but by no means unknown.[8] Melfort Pier Holidays Ltd ('MPH') had

---

1 For discussion of what are sometimes called 'land maintenance companies', see *Conveyancing 2011* pp 116–18.
2 PF(S)A 2011 s 2(1)(c).
3 It will be observed that there is no requirement that the property factor own the land; but cases in which the land is *not* owned by the property factor are already captured by s 2(1)(a).
4 13 September 2017, Oban Sheriff Court, unreported.
5 6 July 2018, Perth Sheriff Court, unreported. We are grateful to one of the parties, Mike Blair, for making the judgment available to us.
6 For other defences employed in this case, see pp 20–23 above.
7 In *Melfort Pier Holidays* it was also argued, albeit faintly, that the third requirement was not satisfied in respect that the homeowners were liable only for *part* of the cost of management and maintenance. The argument did not prosper.
8 One of the co-accused, Mr John C Christlieb, a director of MPH, gave the examples of Gleneagles and Cameron House.

created a development centred around Melfort pier and harbour at Kilmelford, near Oban. As part of the development, 18 houses were built. MPH retained ownership of 13 and let them out as holiday homes. The remaining five houses were sold. The development was subject to a deed of conditions. Among other topics, the deed made provision for a recreational area. Everyone was entitled to use the area, and everyone was bound to contribute to the cost of its maintenance. A management structure was put in place, and MPH was the first manager. A management fee could be levied but MPH had not so far done so.

A summary complaint was made against MPH by the Procurator Fiscal at Oban for failure to register as a property factor. MPH challenged its competency and relevancy.[1] In particular, MPH argued that MPH could not be a property factor in the sense of s 2(1)(c) of the 2011 Act because the statutory requirement that the management function be carried out 'in the course of that person's business' must be understood as meaning 'in the course of that person's business *as a property factor*'. MPH's business was the letting of holiday cottages. Admittedly, a literal interpretation of s 2(1)(c) would not allow the addition of the words suggested by MPH. But the provision, said MPH, must be interpreted purposively, and the purpose of the 2011 Act – as evidenced by statements in Parliament by the private member who promoted the legislation[2] – was to cure the lack of regulation in the property factoring industry. MPH, however, was not part of that industry. MPH was no more a property factor than was an advocate who chose to manage the common areas of the building in which he happened to live. An advocate's business was advocacy; MPH's was holiday cottages.

The sheriff[3] rejected this argument, surely correctly:[4]

> Why then did Parliament include the expression 'in the course of its business'? In my view the answer lies in the mischief that it sought to remedy. The mischief arose from unscrupulous factors seeking to exact unnecessary and excessive charges and fees from homeowners, presumably in order to maximise their own profit. Business is generally an activity carried on with the aim of profit, regardless of whether that aim is in fact achieved. If the maintenance of land is conducted by a for-profit body such as a business, then, regardless of whether the profit comes from management fees, there is potential scope for conflict between the business and homeowners whose interest in the common land is of an entirely different nature. By including this expression, Parliament sought to ensure that 'self-factoring' amateurs, such as the advocate in senior counsel's example above, would not fall under the Act – he or she would not be acting 'in the course of their business', so no potential conflict would arise from any desire to make profit.[5]

---

1 The account that follows relies on the Report by the trial sheriff, Sheriff Patrick Hughes, to the Sheriff Appeal Court following an appeal against the sheriff's decision on competency and relevancy given on 13 September 2017. We are grateful to Sir Crispin Agnew of Lochnaw QC, who acted for the defenders, for making this available to us. In the event, the appeal was not proceeded with and the case went to trial.
2 Patricia Ferguson MSP.
3 Sheriff Patrick Hughes.
4 At p 14 of the sheriff's Note.
5 One may speculate that the position would be different if the advocate charged a fee for his services. In that event, the advocate might be seen as engaged in two separate businesses (ie advocacy and property factoring), with registration being required in respect of the second.

At the trial itself,[1] the sheriff found that the management arrangements pre-dated the 2011 Act and that, on becoming aware of the legislation, MPH made inquiries of the Scottish Government as to the need for registration but did not receive a definite answer. While, therefore, MPH was mistaken to think it did not require to register as a factor, the reasons for the mistake were understandable. MPH and its two directors were acquitted accordingly.

The second requirement: land available for use

At issue in the other case, *Cullochgold Services Ltd v Blair*, was the requirement in s 2(1)(c) of the 2011 Act that the land which the manager owned must be 'available for use by the owners of any two or more adjoining or neighbouring residential properties'. Those who had to pay must have a right to use.

The facts in *Cullochgold* were that the claimant owned and operated a private sewerage system. The respondent owned one of the houses served by the system and, under a deed of conditions, had to pay a service charge for the privilege. Was the claimant a property factor and so bound, as the respondent contended, to register under the Act? As the case was taken under the simple procedure in the sheriff court, the sheriff[2] was reluctant to make a formal finding on the matter but indicated that, in her view, the claimant was not a property factor 'because the sewage works themselves are not available for use by the owners of property'.[3] What the owners used was the service and not the service's source.[4]

It seems worth adding that, where a right of use does exist, questions may arise as to its juridical nature. The right cannot derive from ownership because, in cases like this, the homeowners do not own the recreational or other area which they are taken bound to maintain. Nor is it likely to be attributable to lease or proper liferent because there can be few developments in which the homeowners are tenants of the recreational areas and, probably, none in which they are liferenters. With these types of right eliminated, the only type of real right remaining which is capable of conferring a right of use is servitude. It is true that, on a traditional view of things, servitude was not thought capable of including a right of recreational use, and certainly such a right is not among the fixed list of servitudes recognised at common law.[5] But the fixed list no longer applies to servitudes created, under the Title Conditions (Scotland) Act 2003, by registration,[6] and the recent decision of the Supreme Court in an English appeal, *Regency Villas Title Ltd v Diamond Resorts (Europe) Ltd*,[7] seems to open

---

1   This took place on 13 August 2018. The details that follow are taken from the *Press and Journal* of 14 August 2018.
2   Sheriff Gillian A Wade QC.
3   Paragraph 76.
4   In fact, the claimant also owned a grassy area which was made available for the owners to use, but the present litigation was concerned only with the sewerage works and the sheriff, rightly or wrongly, was disinclined to look to wider considerations.
5   D J Cusine and R R M Paisley, *Servitudes and Rights of Way* (1998) paras 2.50 and 3.71.
6   Title Conditions (Scotland) Act 2003 s 76.
7   [2018] UKSC 57, [2018] 3 WLR 1603.

up the prospect of servitudes for recreational use. *Regency Villas* is analysed elsewhere in this volume.[1]

Civil consequences for non-registration?

Failure to register is a criminal offence, as we have seen. But might there also be consequences in the civil law? In *Cullochgold*, one of the respondent's purposes in raising the absence of registration was to question the claimant's right to collect the service charge sued for. After all, a person who takes the trouble to register as a property factor but is later removed from the register is thereby deprived, by s 9 of the 2011 Act, of the right to recover fees and costs. Why then should fees and costs be recoverable by a person who failed to register in the first place?[2] Appealing though this logic is, however, it derives no support from the Act. The sanction for failure to register is, under s 12, a matter for the criminal law alone. Consequently, the sheriff in *Cullochgold* did not accept 'that a failure to register as a property factor necessarily vitiates the right to claim for services which have been rendered'.[3]

CRIMINAL PROPERTY LAW

HM Advocate v Younas[4] is the second case concerning a flat, 82 Polwarth Gardens, Edinburgh, belonging to a career criminal, Mohammed Younas. The first was the 2014 case of the same name.[5] The earlier case was in the High Court of Justiciary, and the second case in the Court of Session. The facts are puzzling, and some of the legal arguments are also puzzling. The applicable statute, the Proceeds of Crime Act 2002, is complex and obscure. Among its manifold deficiencies is its inadequate grasp of property law.

The High Court case

Mr Younas had a serious criminal record. In addition to his conviction in Glasgow High Court in 2012 for dealing in diamorphine (heroin), which was the conviction which triggered the confiscation proceedings, Mr Younas, as Lord Pentland explained, had other criminal convictions:[6]

> These include offences of theft by housebreaking, housebreaking with intent, attempted theft by housebreaking and fraud. On 11 March 1994 he was convicted at Edinburgh High Court of conspiracy to rob and of offences under the Carrying of Knives etc (Scotland) Act 1993 and the Bail etc (Scotland) Act 1980. He was sentenced to a total of 33 months imprisonment for these offences. On 27 September 2001 the respondent was convicted at Glasgow High Court of two offences of contravening

---

1 See pp 169–74 above.
2 Paragraph 48.
3 Paragraph 73.
4 [2018] CSOH 9, 2018 SLT 227 affd [2018] CSIH 75, 2018 SLT 1303.
5 *HM Advocate v Younas* [2014] HCJ 123, 2015 SCL 162 (*Conveyancing 2014*, Case (75)).
6 [2014] HCJ 123 at para 2.

section 4(3)(b) of the 1971 Act and was sentenced to 10 years imprisonment. The drugs involved in those offences were diamorphine and cocaine. For the offence which has given rise to the present proceedings the respondent was sentenced to 8 years and 11 months imprisonment.

In the 2014 case the Crown sought a confiscation order under the Proceeds of Crime Act 2002, in the amount of £126,000.[1]

One might suppose, given the word 'confiscation', that the proceedings were for the confiscation of the flat at 82 Polwarth Gardens. Not so. The word 'confiscation' in the legislation is used in a slightly odd sense. The order sought by the Crown in the 2014 case was for payment of money, not the seizure of some particular asset, and the calculation of how much money was to be 'confiscated' involved identifying and valuing Mr Younas's estate. So the question in the 2014 case was whether the flat was part of Mr Younas's estate. Given that he had bought the flat in 1990, completing title by recording the disposition in the Register of Sasines,[2] and given that at the time of the proceedings there had been no other entries in the Sasine (or Land) Register, this might appear to be a simple question with a simple answer: Mr Younas was and remained the heritable proprietor of the flat, and so it was part of his estate with the result that the sum to be 'confiscated' should be based on the value of the flat.

But there were complications. Mr Younas had been sequestrated in 1993. His trustee (who was the Accountant in Bankruptcy) did not complete title. In 2002 the trustee concluded missives to sell the flat to Mr Younas's sisters, Farzana Ashraf and Ruksana Ashraf.[3] The sisters paid the price, but they declined to accept a disposition. Why? That is unknown. This is probably how conveyancing is done in the outer fringes of the Andromeda Galaxy.

Though we have not seen a copy of the missives it seems that they did not have a supersession clause. So the missives remained in force.

In the 2014 case, both Mr Younas and the two sisters (who appeared in the case as minuters) argued that the flat should not be included in the assessment of Mr Younas's estate, on the basis that the sisters had a right to it under missives. It was argued that the missives made the sisters 'the true legal owners of the property'.[4] But since even a delivered disposition, before registration, does not make a buyer 'the true legal owner', this argument, based on mere missives, was remarkable. It was also argued 'that the effect of the respondent's sequestration was to divest him of his interest in the property and to confer upon the Accountant in Bankruptcy what was said to be an absolute title to it'.[5] This was equally without merit. Sequestration makes the trustee the unregistered holder (uninfeft proprietor, to use the older terminology) of the debtor's heritable property, but the real right remains in the debtor until either the trustee transfers title to a buyer or the trustee makes up title in his or her own name.

---

1 *HM Advocate v Younas* [2014] HCJ 123, 2015 SCL 162.
2 In 1990 Midlothian was not yet an 'operational' county in relation to the Land Register.
3 Why there was such a long delay, from 1993 to 2002, is not known to us.
4 [2014] HCJ 123 at para 44.
5 Paragraph 50.

Lord Pentland rejected the argument of the sisters and made an order in favour of the Crown for £126,000. Mr Younas, however, failed to comply: hence the second case.

The Court of Session case

It might be thought that if such an order is not complied with, then, since it is a debt, the Crown would enforce it like other debt, namely by diligence or by sequestration. But the Proceeds of Crime Act 2002, with its penchant for the complex, has its own special enforcement procedure, and in the second, 2018, case it invoked that procedure, appointing an 'enforcement administrator' with power to sell the property. At this point one of the sisters, Farzana Ashraf,[1] intervened once again, making an application under s 135(1) of the 2002 Act to have the property at 82 Polwarth Gardens excluded. In effect, she was seeking to relitigate the issue that had already been disposed of in 2014.[2] So the case was litigated once again, with the same outcome, first in the Outer House[3] and thereafter, also in 2018, in the Inner House.[4]

The 2002 Act says that the 'powers [of enforcement] must be exercised with a view to allowing a person other than the accused ... to retain or recover the value of any interest held by him'.[5] 'References to an interest, in relation to land in Scotland', the Act adds, 'are to any estate, interest, servitude or other heritable right in or over land including a heritable security.'[6] Farzana Ashraf argued that the missives meant that she was such a person and that the value of her 'interest' was the value of the flat. Accordingly what she was asking the court to do was to exclude the flat entirely. Her 'interest' in the flat was said to arise on the basis of (i) the missives with the trustee in sequestration, and (ii) the fact (which was averred, but which the Crown did not accept) that monthly mortgage payments to Nationwide Building Society in respect of a standard security granted over by the flat by Mr Younas at the time of his purchase in 1990 had been kept up by the two sisters.[7]

---

1 In the High Court case both sisters were involved but in the Court of Session only one was. The absence of the other was not explained at this stage, though when the case went to the Inner House Farzana Ashraf said that her sister had transferred her rights to her, although, as the Inner House commented laconically at para 3, 'this was not vouched'.

2 Might the doctrine of *res judicata* have been relevant? The case does not discuss the point other than to note that the Crown 'accepted that, notwithstanding that the interested party was heard in the High Court confiscation proceedings as a minuter, she was entitled also to be heard on her present application to vary the order': see [2018] CSOH 9 at para 3. When the case was in the Inner House it was accepted that Farzana Ashraf was entitled to be heard in the current proceedings, but it was suggested that she should not have had the right to be heard in the original proceedings in the High Court: see [2018] CSIH 75 at para 10.

3 *HM Advocate v Younas* [2018] CSOH 9, 2018 SLT 227. The Lord Ordinary was Lady Wise.

4 *HM Advocate v Younas* [2018] CSIH 75, 2018 SLT 1303.

5 Proceeds of Crime Act 2002 s 132(3)(a).

6 Proceeds of Crime Act 2002 s 150(2)(g).

7 Clearly the Nationwide, as standard security holder, would have had an 'interest' in the property and so would have been protected against the confiscation. This issue is not explored in the litigation. We would conjecture that by 2018 the whole debt had been paid off.

Evidence was heard as to whether the sisters had in fact been the persons who made the monthly payments. The court did not accept that they had, so this argument failed as a matter of fact. But we would suggest that it was unstateable even as a matter of law. If Adam pays Bertie's debt to Clara, the result is that Adam has a right to be reimbursed by Bertie. That is true regardless of whether the Bertie/Clara debt is secured or unsecured. So even if it had been proved (which it was not) that the sisters had been making the monthly mortgage payments, the result would have simply been an obligation due to them by Mr Younas. On any view of the 2002 Act, that would not amount to an 'interest' in the property.

The other line of argument was that the sisters had an 'interest' in the property because of the missives. This was rejected by the Lord Ordinary because of 'the decision taken by Ms Ashraf and her sister not to insist on taking title to the property during the whole period since [the missives] and Ms Ashraf's evasiveness in evidence in relation to the circumstances in which she has not previously pursued the matter of obtaining title to the property'.[1]

Ms Ashraf also argued that the flat should be excluded because of article 1 of the first Protocol of the European Convention on Human Rights.[2] This argument too was rejected by the Lord Ordinary. 'Having chosen not to convert her personal right under the missives into a proprietorial right that could be given protection, she has no stateable human rights claim.'[3] This was perhaps a rather innovative ground for rejecting an A1P1 argument.

Ms Ashraf reclaimed to the Inner House.[4] The focus was on the meaning of 'interest'. The Second Division took the view that 'the reclaimer does not have any heritable right in the property having only a personal right under the missives. The Lord Ordinary was correct to state that the reclaimer had no more than a personal, contractual interest in the missives, that her rights were no greater than those of an unsecured creditor'.[5] As for the A1P1 argument, the Inner House agreed with the Lord Ordinary's view, and added, seemingly as an additional reason, that 'the reclaimer has never enjoyed a right of possession in the property'.[6] This last point, however, may perhaps be questioned, as the missives had given the sisters a right of possession.

Some further reflections

Where does the 2018 decision leave the missives? It was said by the Lord Ordinary that 'the obligations due to her (and her sister) in terms of the missives are unaffected by the realisation of the property by the administrator'.[7] If that is right, the trustee in sequestration might be in an awkward position, since he

---

1 [2018] CSOH 9 at para 44.
2 The property protection provision, generally referred to as A1P1.
3 Paragraph 46.
4 *HM Advocate v Younas* [2018] CSIH 75, 2018 SLT 1303. The Opinion of the Court was given by Lady Dorrian.
5 Paragraph 15.
6 Paragraph 16.
7 [2018] CSOH 9 at para 44.

would not, after sale of the flat by the enforcement administrator, be in a position to dispone.[1] But the Lord Ordinary also said that 'Mr Younas is the person with an obligation to transfer property in terms of the missives'.[2] If that is right, any problem for the trustee would disappear: it would be Mr Younas on the hook of the now unimplementable missives, not the trustee. But is it right that the obligation was that of Mr Younas? No authority is cited and we can think of none. It is true that s 64(1) of the Bankruptcy (Scotland) Act 1985[3] imposes on the bankrupt an obligation, owed to the trustee, to sign documents when lawfully so requested by the trustee. But that is not the same as saying that the bankrupt is the party to contracts made by the trustee.

An attempt by the sisters to sue the trustee would encounter considerable difficulties. The trustee had been discharged, so a new trustee would have to be appointed. A decree ordering the trustee to dispone the property would not be possible given that the enforcement administrator would have sold the property. So any action would be for damages for failure to dispone. But the reason for non-disposition would be the fact that the sisters had refused to accept a disposition. Even if these difficulties could somehow be overcome, it is not easy to see how any decree for damages against the trustee could be enforced. Comparable problems would arise if the action were to be, not for damages, but for repayment of the price under the law of unjustified enrichment.

Three final thoughts. One is a question. Who actually occupied the property over the years, that is to say, from the sequestration in 1993 until now? That, like much else in this case, is unclear. Another thought is this. When the sequestration took place the trustee did not complete title. Had title been completed, presumably the property would not now be regarded as part of Mr Younas's estate. It is curious that a seemingly insignificant decision back in 1993 should later have such consequences; though it is equally true to say that if the sisters had not, inexplicably, refused to accept a disposition, the property would likewise have fallen outwith the confiscation net, so that in a sense there was a break in the chain of causation. The third thought connects with the second. It might seem unfair that the sisters, having bought the property from their brother's trustee, must now lose it. But they lose it by their own inexplicable decision to refuse to accept the disposition that they had paid for.

PROPERTY TAXES IN SCOTLAND[4]

Introduction

Changes announced in the 2017 Scottish Budget, particularly those affecting income tax rates (albeit with modifications following their announcement), have

---

1 The trustee had been discharged. But a new trustee can be appointed, and in fact the minuter said that she was seeking to have a new trustee appointed.
2 Paragraph 40.
3 The statute applicable to the sequestration of Mr Younas. The equivalent provision today is s 215(1) of the Bankruptcy (Scotland) Act 2016.
4 This part is contributed by Alan Barr of the University of Edinburgh and Brodies LLP.

been running throughout the 2018–19 tax year; and the 2018 Scottish Budget on 12 December 2018 continued the policy of divergence from policies affecting the rest of the UK. It was noted that once devolution (or assignment, in the case of 50% of VAT receipts raised on Scottish expenditure) comes into effect for all of the taxes for which legislative provision has now been made, the taxes concerned will make up nearly half of all of the expenditure for which the Scottish Parliament is responsible.[1]

The greatest overall economic impact will come from devolved income tax and, while the changes proposed for that are significant, the powers available to the Scottish Parliament are limited to rates and thresholds. In contrast, the fully devolved land and buildings transaction tax continues to develop, with new rates, rules and reliefs coming into effect in 2018 and 2019. That year also brought further tax tribunal decisions, including on substantive matters, as well as a further decision on all too prevalent penalties. It is of course this tax which affects all those dealing with Scottish land, whatever their taxpayer status.

Developments in 2018 again brought to prominence the lack of an annual Finance Act in the current Scottish tax landscape, which makes it difficult to introduce technical tax changes requiring primary legislation in any meaningful timescale. In its 2018 Programme for Government the Scottish Government committed itself to work closely with stakeholders to develop a new process for the planning, management and implementation of changes to the fully devolved taxes (ie land and buildings transaction tax and Scottish landfill tax). The 2018 Scottish Budget confirmed that a consultation will be launched in February 2019, and the new process itself will be announced in the Scottish Budget 2020–21.[2]

But whatever happens in the process for Scotland and indeed in relation to Europe, Scottish taxpayers and their advisers on land matters continue to need to be aware of the impact of at least two tax systems.

Land and buildings transaction tax (LBTT)

First-time buyer relief

The consequences of the lack of an annual Finance Act in Scotland, and in particular the lack of an ability to make immediate changes by Budget resolutions, are well illustrated by the introduction of first-time buyer relief in Scotland. Its 'rUK' equivalent was introduced with immediate effect in the November 2017 UK Budget. This gave rise to a zero-rate of SDLT for first-time buyers on properties with a consideration up to £300,000, and some measure

---

1 See *Scottish Budget:2019–20* (www2.gov.scot/Publications/2018/12/9450) p 27. It may be worth noting that the main document published by the Scottish Government immediately after the Scottish Budget speech lacks the word 'Draft', which formed part of the title of its predecessors. The change in title does not make implementation of the Budget any more certain for a government which lacks an absolute majority in the Scottish Parliament.

2 *Scottish Budget:2019–20* p 7.

of relief where the consideration did not exceed £500,000.[1] The limited Scottish response required consultation and legislation[2] before it could come into effect. This was not until 30 June 2018, for chargeable transactions with a settlement date on or after that date and for which the date of contract was on or after 9 February 2018.[3]

The guts of the relief are set out in the opening provisions of a new sch 4A to the Land and Buildings Transaction Tax (Scotland) Act 2013:

Eligibility for relief

1.—(1) Relief may be claimed in respect of any chargeable transaction if –
    (a) it is an acquisition of a major interest in land (see section 60),
    (b) the land consists entirely of residential property and includes a dwelling,
    (c) the buyer, or (if more than one) each of the buyers, is a first-time buyer who intends to occupy the dwelling as the buyer's only or main residence,
    (d) the transaction is not one of a number of linked transactions, and
    (e) the transaction is not one to which schedule 2A (additional amount: transactions relating to second homes etc) applies.

   . . . . . .

Meaning of first-time buyer

2. In this schedule 'first-time buyer' means a person who –
    (a) has not previously been a buyer in relation to an acquisition of a major interest in land which consisted of residential property including a dwelling, and
    (b) has not previously acquired an interest in a dwelling situated outside Scotland that is equivalent to the interest of a buyer referred to in sub-paragraph (a).

Relief from the tax

3.   The relief consists in the tax not being chargeable in respect of the first £175,000 of consideration payable in respect of any chargeable transaction.

So the maximum relief is £600, by the extension of the 0% band for LBTT from £145,000 to £175,000; and it marks a continuation of the slice system which is the basis of LBTT – paying at the lower rates up to a level and at the higher above that level – as opposed to the slab system which bites for additional dwelling supplement ('ADS'). It was anticipated that the relief would take more than 80% of first-time buyers outwith an LBTT charge.

Significant conditions attach to the relief, one of which serves to disqualify any transaction which is liable to ADS. This seems a little unfair and perhaps illogical – because of other restrictions it can only be relevant if the buyer is buying more than one dwelling in his or her first purchase (otherwise the person

---

1 See now Finance Act 2003 s 57A and sch 6ZA, inserted by Finance Act 2018 s 41.
2 Land and Buildings Transaction Tax (First-Time Buyer Relief) (Scotland) Order 2018, SSI 2018/221, inserting sch 4A into the Land and Buildings Transaction Tax (Scotland) Act 2013.
3 SSI 2018/221 art 6.

would not be a first-time buyer). In policy terms, there does not seem a reason to exclude such a buyer from this extension of the nil rate band for basic LBTT (ADS of course being a separate matter).

The most important condition is that the buyer must be a 'first-time buyer'. Here is what Revenue Scotland guidance has to say about this:[1]

> A first-time buyer means a person who does not own nor has previously owned a dwelling in Scotland, the rest of the UK or the rest of the world. All forms of ownership in the legal systems of the rest of the UK which are equivalent to ownership in Scotland are treated as ownership for the purposes of this relief. For instance, a dwelling for which an individual holds a tenant's interest under certain types of lease in the rest of the UK would count towards dwellings owned by an individual. Additionally, the prevailing Scottish concepts regarding ownership apply across the foreign legal systems and must be read in accordance with the prevailing law and practice of the country in which the dwelling is situated when determining whether an individual owns a dwelling outside of Scotland.

So there could be a bit of international private law to be applied in deciding whether 'owners' (or more importantly, former 'owners') of foreign property are excluded. But, of course, it goes further than that, in that, as the guidance notes, tenants may sometimes be excluded through being treated as owners.

Ownership of a share of any land leads to exclusion from the relief, and the offending ownership can come by gift or inheritance as well as by purchase. It seems more than possible that there will be many otherwise qualifying first-time buyers who have at some time owned a share of an inherited property, and may not have been aware of the disqualifying effect on the relief.

If it is the intention of a couple to buy together, but one of them has the taint of former ownership while the other does not, it would seem possible for the one who has never owned anything to buy with first-time buyer relief and then transfer a half-share to the partner. If that transfer is for no consideration, then of course that transfer would not attract LBTT. Of course, it may have other tax consequences, especially where the partners in question are not married or civil partners; and lending conditions may preclude this type of planning.

New non-residential rates

With effect from 25 January 2019, a new rate structure was introduced for non-residential purchases.[2] The lower rate of non-residential LBTT was reduced from 3% to 1%, the upper rate increased from 4.5% to 5%, and the starting threshold for the upper rate reduced from £350,000 to £250,000. The new rates are:

---

1 See Revenue Scotland, *First-time buyer relief* (LBTT 3048; www.revenue.scot/land-buildings-transaction-tax/guidance/lbtt-legislation-guidance/exemptions-reliefs/lbtt3010-3#overlay-context=node/946/revisions/2116/view).

2 Land and Buildings Transaction Tax (Tax Rates and Tax Bands Etc) (Scotland) Amendment Order 2018, SSI 2018/372, para 2.

Purchase price	LBTT rate
Up to £150,000	0%
Above £150,000 to £250,000	1%
Above £250,000	5%

This is claimed to make Scotland the most 'competitive' part of the UK for non-residential land transaction taxes – but the new top rate will have a greater effect than the reductions at the bottom end, as compared with current LBTT rates. It is to be noted that the Scottish Government anticipates a rise in receipts from non-residential LBTT as a result of these changes (as well as from those made to additional dwelling supplement).

Additional dwelling supplement

Before its introduction, ADS was forecast to raise some £23.5 million per year. In fact, the first year brought in £77.4 million net – more than three times the forecast. Year 2's net total was £98.3 million, and the first half of the present financial year indicates that we may be heading for a figure in excess of £100 million for 2018–19.

The number of transactions affected – or at least in which consideration has to be given as to whether ADS is an issue – was always and continues to be significant. That is running at about 2,000 transactions a month out of total residential LBTT returns of around 10,000 a month (although the latter figure is much more variable). So somewhere between a quarter and a fifth of all residential transactions are affected by ADS.[1]

This makes ADS a tempting target for tax increases. Despite this, it was still somewhat unexpected to find in the 2018 Scottish Budget an announcement that ADS was to increase from 3% to 4% from 25 January 2019.[2] Figures in the Scottish Budget documents indicate that, with the increase, ADS will account for more than a third of the amount raised by 'basic' LBTT.[3] And with the new 4% ADS, the top rate of LBTT will now be a staggering 16% on the amount of the consideration above £750,000. As the tax applies only to the land and buildings element of a transaction, a reasonable attribution of as much as possible to other things being bought will be all the more attractive. The £20,000 carpet looms again....

Perhaps this is the Scottish Government's response to the 1% SDLT surcharge proposed in the UK Budget for purchases of residential property by non-

---

1 On all of this see Revenue Scotland, *Land and Buildings Transaction Tax Statistics* (www.revenue. scot/about-us/publications/statistics/land-and-buildings-transaction-tax-statistics-0#overlay-context=about-us/publications/statistics).

2 SSI 2018/372 para 3.

3 *Scottish Budget:2019–20* p 31.

residents.[1] In effect, everyone will be treated as a non-resident for Scottish ADS purposes in terms of the rate they will pay, which removes what might have been a difficult and sensitive definitional problem.

Another ADS development illustrated the difficulties faced by a Scottish Government wishing to reform and improve its tax legislation. It was recognised that there was an anomaly in relation to certain 'family units' in respect of the relief from ADS which exists for buyers replacing their main residence. That relief prevents ADS applying where all that is happening is that a taxpayer is replacing one such residence with another, but may in that process come to own two residences at the time of the replacement, either permanently or on a temporary basis. However, the rules on counting ownership within 'economic units' (such as joint buyers, spouses and cohabitants) meant that, where only one member of such a unit was replacing a main residence, the relief did not apply. So for example a couple who each owned a dwelling purchasing a new one together would not qualify.

This anomaly was cured in part by secondary legislation in 2017, amending schedule 2A of the Land and Buildings Transaction Tax (Scotland) Act 2013.[2] This was always intended to be retrospective, but that could only be achieved by primary legislation, which had to wait until 2018.[3] This is aimed at ensuring that spouses, civil partners or cohabitants who jointly buy a main residence are considered to be replacing their main residence when their previous main residence is sold, but that residence was owned by only one of them. This applies to prevent tax being charged at the outset when what will now be deemed to be the couple's main residence has sold before the purchase; and to allow for repayment when that previous residence is sold after the purchase.[4]

But fairly typically, and as noted last year,[5] the revised relief is distinctly limited. Notably, it only applies if the property sold was the main residence of both the joint buyers. That this unwelcome view of things is correct was demonstrated by the first judgment on a substantive matter (as opposed to decisions on penalties) to be issued by the First-tier Tribunal for Scotland Tax Chamber. This was the *Goudie & Sheldon* case. Although the appeal began before the new relief came into effect, the Tribunal considered the position under the law as revised.

The *Goudie & Sheldon* case

Goudie & Sheldon v Revenue Scotland[6] involved two doctors, who became a couple. Dr Goudie had jointly owned a property in Edinburgh with his brother and

---

1 See *Budget 2018* (HC 1629, October 2018) para 3.40; HM Treasury/HMRC, *Stamp Duty Land Tax: non-UK resident surcharge consultation* (11 February 2019).
2 Land and Buildings Transaction Tax (Additional Amount–Second Homes Main Residence Relief) (Scotland) Order 2017, SSI 2017/233.
3 Land and Buildings Transaction Tax (Relief from Additional Amount) (Scotland) Act 2018.
4 Land and Buildings Transaction Tax (Scotland) Act 2013 sch 2A paras 8A, 9A; Revenue Scotland, *LBTT Technical Bulletin 3* (28 December 2017, www.revenue.scot/sites/default/files/LBTT%20Technical%20Update%20-%2028%20December%202017_1.pdf) para 4; Revenue Scotland, *Guidance on Additional Dwelling Supplement* para LBTT10062A and examples 47A, 48A and 73A.
5 *Conveyancing 2017* p 191.
6 [2018] FTSTC 3.

a friend, which they had purchased in October 2012 ('the first property'). Dr Sheldon had never lived there.

Dr Goudie lived at the first property until 31 July 2015 when he and Dr Sheldon moved into a rented flat where they lived until, on 29 April 2016, they purchased a property in Edinburgh in joint names for £382,000 ('the new property'). LBTT and ADS, amounting to some £23,000 in total, were paid in relation to the new property. On 28 June 2017, Dr Goudie disposed of his interest in the first property and then submitted a repayment claim for ADS (some £11,000) This was refused and that refusal was the subject of the appeal.

Essentially, the appellants' arguments were as follows:

(a) If Revenue Scotland's application of the legislation is correct, the scope of the legislation breaches and distorts the principles agreed by the Scottish Parliament.
(b) Revenue Scotland's application of the legislation is incorrect.
(c) If Revenue Scotland's application of the legislation is correct, the legislation is fundamentally defective.
(d) The legislation is unfair and discriminatory.

By email dated 17 April 2018 the appellants confirmed that the 'core of our argument' was that there must be something fundamentally wrong with either the legislation or Revenue Scotland's interpretation of it and therefore the latter's decision ran counter to ordinary notions of fairness and principle. This was later refined into an argument based on *Pepper v Hart*[1] and what must, in the view of the appellants, have been the intentions of the legislature.

The First-tier Tribunal, having considered the terms of the legislation, concluded that ADS was correctly payable. Given that Dr Sheldon had never resided in the property, at any stage, the revisals could not assist the taxpayers: Dr Sheldon was not replacing a main residence as she had never lived in the residence which had been disposed of. That meant that the appellants were forced back on the argument that the result was absurd and that, applying principles of statutory interpretation and *Pepper v Hart* to get at the underlying policy, there had been a drafting mistake. This argument also failed. The legislation was unambiguous and consistent with policy. There was no proper basis on which to resort to Parliamentary debates (and this would not, it seemed, have helped the appellants a great deal in any case). Furthermore, the Tribunal had no jurisdiction to consider either fairness or indeed the conduct of Revenue Scotland. Discrimination was not in issue; and it was irrelevant that the position might have been different elsewhere in the UK.

The *Clark* case

Fairness was also put forward unsuccessfully in the second substantive case on ADS to reach the First-tier Tribunal. *Clark v Revenue Scotland*[2] involved a claim for

---

1 [1993] 1 AC 593.
2 [2018] FTSTC 4.

repayment of ADS of some £15,000 (from total LBTT of £39,000) in a transaction that settled in November 2016. The repayment was on the basis that this was the replacement of a main residence, although in rather unusual circumstances.[1] Essentially what happened was that neighbours purchased the property next door to their house and knocked through, creating (although rather in their view restoring) one residence where previously there had been two, at 8 and 8B Mortonhall Road, Edinburgh. Once the project was complete, the Clarks claimed to have disposed of their former residence, essentially on the basis that it no longer existed, as such; and that the legislation should not adversely affect taxpayers doing what they had done.

Revenue Scotland's argument was simple and effective – the Clarks had not disposed of ownership of their previous dwelling, in any normal sense of that word. They concentrated on the legal meaning of ownership. They rejected (again) any notion that the Tribunal could consider alleged 'unfairness' of clear statutory provisions.

The Tribunal agreed with Revenue Scotland, drawing on normal dictionary definitions of 'dispose'. Even if there had been a disposal, this would have included in part the subjects which had been purchased in the transaction in question and that was sufficient to exclude repayment.[2] There was no possibility of the Tribunal being able to address any alleged unfairness. The appeal was dismissed.

Other LBTT matters

The Scottish Budget for 2019–20 confirmed that the residential rates and thresholds for basic land and buildings transaction tax would remain unchanged, as would the rates and thresholds for leases.[3] The Scottish Budget also contained an announcement that there would be two new LBTT reliefs, replicating the position in the rest of the UK, in relation to 'seeding' (the initial transfer) of properties into entities known as Property Authorised Investment Funds and Co-owned Authorised Contractual Schemes. There is also to be a relief when units in CoACSs are exchanged. There is to be further consultation on these reliefs once there is sufficient clarity on the terms of the UK's withdrawal from the EU; subject to that the intention is for the new reliefs to be introduced in the course of 2019.[4]

Earlier in 2018 a welcome change was introduced in relation to group relief. This corrected an anomaly in relation to share pledges, the existence of which could preclude the availability of group relief in circumstances where it would otherwise be available (and indeed where it would be available elsewhere in

---

1 The money actually went back and forth. The repayment was made, but then reclaimed when Revenue Scotland issued a closure notice.
2 See Land and Buildings Transaction Tax (Scotland) Act 2013 sch 2A para 8(1)(a), which excludes repayment where the disposal is of ownership of a dwelling which 'was or formed part of the subject-matter of the chargeable transaction'.
3 *Scottish Budget:2019–20* p 30.
4 *Scottish Budget:2019–20* p 30.

the UK).[1] Regulations have corrected the position;[2] their effect was explained by Revenue Scotland as follows:[3]

> The Land and Buildings Transaction Tax (Group Relief Modification) (Scotland) Order 2018 (the Order) amended the rules on group relief and the restrictions to its availability. Prior to the Order, where, for instance, a parent company transferred property to a subsidiary and the parent company granted security to a lender over the shares in the subsidiary, group relief was not available as the pledging of the shares constituted an 'arrangement' under which the lender could obtain control of the subsidiary but not the parent. The Order inserts a new paragraph 10A which, if it applies, means that group relief is no longer restricted in transactions where the effective date of the transaction is on or after 30 June 2018 and the qualifying conditions are met.

As with the modification to ADS in relation to the replacement of a main residence by one of a couple (discussed above), it was confirmed by the Finance Secretary that this change will be made retrospective in due course.

Three-yearly review returns for commercial leases

2018 brought the first batch of three-yearly review returns in relation to commercial leases.[4] Revenue Scotland issued reminders to tenants, one important point being that a review return must be submitted even if there have been no changes to the lease or if no additional tax is due. Although the first possible three-year anniversary for a lease attracting LBTT occurred on 1 April 2018, review returns are also due from tenants on the assignation or termination of an LBTT lease. Here is Revenue Scotland's initial guidance on the requirements:[5]

> On 1 April 2018 Revenue Scotland updated the Scottish Electronic Tax System (SETS) to enable tenants and their agents to submit a further LBTT tax return as part of the requirements set out in the Land and Buildings Transaction Tax (Scotland) Act 2013. Under the Act, leases subject to LBTT on or after 1 April 2015 must be reviewed on every third anniversary of the lease to ensure the correct amount of LBTT is paid. The Act also requires a further return to be submitted on assignation or termination of the lease (whether early, at the end of the envisaged term or otherwise). Any returns submitted after 30 days of the three-year anniversary of the lease will incur penalties for failure to file a return. Late payments will also incur interest and penalties for failure to pay tax.
>
> To help tenants understand their obligations and how to submit returns, Revenue Scotland created a new dedicated section on its website which includes new legislative and 'how to' guidance, worked examples, FAQs and an information leaflet. In addition, the paper LBTT return form was also updated and the tax calculator was

1 See *Conveyancing 2017* pp 192–93.
2 Land and Buildings Transaction Tax (Group Relief Modification) (Scotland) Order 2018, SSI 2018/222.
3 See Revenue Scotland, *LBTT Technical Bulletin 4* (10 August 2018; www.revenue.scot/sites/default/files/LBTT%20Technical%20Update%20-%2010%20August%202018.pdf) para 3.
4 Land and Buildings Transaction Tax (Scotland) Act 2013 sch 19 para 10.
5 Revenue Scotland, *LBTT Technical Bulletin 4* para 4. For further guidance and a number of worked examples, see Revenue Scotland, *LBTT Legislation Guidance* paras LBTT6014-LBTT6017.

amended to help leaseholders calculate the amount of LBTT due. Revenue Scotland has also published three new YouTube videos – one providing a general overview of the leases review and two videos providing guidance on submitting a return for taxpayers and agents.

Penalties

Mention of penalties (including those which apply for failure to make returns timeously, whether or not any tax is due) prompts reference to the range of decisions from the First-tier Tribunal for Scotland Tax Chamber. The first of these were dealt with in some detail last year.[1] There was a further appeal on penalties reported in 2018, *Emold Ltd v Revenue Scotland*.[2]

The appeal involved actual tax and a failure to pay it timeously, the penalties thus arising under ss 168 and 169 of the Land and Buildings Transaction Tax (Scotland) Act 2013. The total penalty was £1,527. This was in addition to an accepted liability of £100 for late submission of the return. The penalty was calculated on the basis of 5% of the LBTT and ADS due. The appellant accepted that payment was late, but maintained that the amount of the penalty was excessive in the circumstances. There was not much by way of further argument.

The Tribunal noted that:[3]

The Scottish Parliament has balanced the interest of the taxpayer with those of the Exchequer. A taxpayer may be spared a penalty if the taxpayer has an excuse, but the excuse must be a reasonable one. Similarly, if there are special circumstances that apply then the penalty can be remitted, suspended or compromised.

The onus of proof in regard to both reasonable excuse and special circumstances lies with the appellant. No excuse has been offered beyond insufficiency of funds. As can be seen from paragraph 178(3)(a) an insufficiency of funds is not a reasonable excuse unless attributable to events outside the taxpayer's control. Neither Revenue Scotland nor we have been furnished with any reason as to why the appellant did not have the funds on the date for payment. A simple insufficiency of funds cannot suffice.

Accordingly, we find that no reasonable excuse has been established.

The same reasoning in relation to insufficiency of funds was applied to the question of special circumstances. In that context the landfill tax penalty case of *Straid Farms Ltd v Revenue Scotland*[4] was considered, together with the earlier jurisprudence on that concept considered in that case. Special circumstances must operate in relation to the individual taxpayer and are distinguished from general matters. Having eliminated insufficiency of funds as a type of special circumstance, there was nothing left. The Tribunal held that the penalty was proportionate; underpinned by a clear policy objective; and did not offend against Article 1, Protocol 1 of the European Convention on Human Rights. The Tribunal concluded on the penalty regime in general:[5]

---

1 *Conveyancing 2017* pp 196–200.
2 [2018] FTSTC 2.
3 Paragraphs 13 and 14.
4 [2017] FTSTC 2.
5 Paragraph 32.

It is very clear, both from the Policy Memorandum and the explicit wording in RSTPA that, following consultation, the Scottish Parliament intended penalties to start at 5% of the outstanding tax, where tax was not paid on time, and thereafter to rise to a maximum of 15%. The compliance intention is very clearly to ensure that returns are filed on time and tax paid on time. The penalty calculated by reference to a percentage of the tax due is expressly pitched at a level to maximise compliance.

Scottish income tax

While this is not of specific relevance to the taxation of land, income from land is one of the categories of income of Scottish taxpayers which will be affected by the differing rates (and thresholds) applied to Scottish taxpayers.

The 2018 Scottish Budget followed some six weeks after the UK Budget, in which the headline announcements included raising the personal allowance to £12,500 and the combination of that allowance and the basic rate band to £50,000, both to take effect for the 2019–20 tax year.[1] As is becoming better known, the devolution of income tax to the Scottish Parliament is restricted to the rates and thresholds for the tax, as it applies to non-savings and non-dividend income (broadly: employment, pensions, self-employment and rental income) of Scottish taxpayers. For 2018–19, a structure involving five rates for Scottish taxpayers on that income has been in place.[2] The proposal for 2019–20[3] maintains both that structure and the rates but, for the first two rates, alters the thresholds up to which they apply. These thresholds increase with inflation; but the thresholds at which the Scottish higher rate and top rate cut in are to be frozen. This provides the following rates for different levels of affected income:

Bands	Band name	Rate
Over £12,500–£14,549*	Starter Rate	19%
Over £14,549–£24,944	Scottish Basic Rate	20%
Over £24,944–£43,430	Intermediate Rate	21%
Over £43,430–£150,000	Higher Rate	41%
Above £150,000**	Top Rate	46%

*Assumes individuals are in receipt of the Standard UK Personal Allowance.
**Those earning more than £100,000 will see their Personal Allowance reduced by £1 for every £2 earned over £100,000.

1 *Budget 2018* (HC 1629, October 2018) para 3.7.
2 See *Conveyancing 2017* pp 193–95 for details. See also the Scottish Rates of Income Tax (Consequential Amendments) Order 2018, SI 2018/459, which amended UK tax legislation to ensure that tax relief and other relevant legislation, in particular gift aid, the marriage allowance, and pension tax relief, operate in conjunction with the new Scottish rate structure.
3 *Scottish Budget:2019–20* pp 27–29, confirmed by the Scottish Rate Resolution, 19 February 2019.

The Scottish Government is not, therefore, proposing to replicate the increase in the higher rate threshold to £50,000 announced for the rest of the UK.

This has some important knock-on effects. National Insurance thresholds are tied to the UK higher rate threshold, meaning that, on these proposals, there will be a marginal rate of tax and NI totalling 53% on the slice of earned income between £43,430 and £50,000, as compared to 32% in the rest of the UK. The overall effect will vary depending on a taxpayer's individual position. We are told that '55% of income tax payers in Scotland will pay less tax than people earning the same wage in the rest of the UK', which presumably means that 45% will pay more or, in a few cases, the same. With the higher rate threshold frozen for a second year, the number of people paying more can only grow.

It should be stressed that these proposals may yet be amended; and it is to be hoped that any amendments may bring more rounded and arithmetically friendly thresholds at the two lowest levels.

Other Scottish property taxes

Scottish landfill tax

Rates of Scottish landfill tax for 2018–19 were set by the Scottish Landfill Tax (Standard Rate and Lower Rate) Order 2018[1] at £88.95 per tonne (standard rate) and £2.80 (lower rate). In the 2018 Scottish Budget, it was confirmed that the rates are to be increased to the planned UK rates for 2019–20, which are £91.35 (standard rate) and £2.90 (lower rate). The credit rate for the Scottish Landfill Communities Fund (SLCF) is to be maintained at 5.6%. Scottish landfill tax receipts are forecast to reduce over the next five years – very substantially from 2021–22 onwards – as more and more waste is diverted from landfill (which is after all the aim of the tax).[2] It remains to be seen what will be done to replace the revenue from this particular filling of holes in the ground.

Aggregates levy

Part of the answer to replacing revenue from filling holes may lie in the implementation of the devolution of a tax on making similar holes – aggregates levy. In a theme unchanged from last year's Scottish Budget, there are apparently ongoing legal issues in relation to the UK tax (in turn deriving from European considerations), which need to be resolved before the devolution of the tax can be completed. Research continues in anticipation of the tax being devolved; and further integration with waste and other environmental policies is specifically mentioned.[3]

Non-domestic (business) rates

Responsibility for non-domestic rates is fully devolved to Scotland, and the regime continues to diverge from the position in the rest of the UK. The amount

---

1   SSI 2018/87.
2   On all of this, see *Scottish Budget:2019–20* p 32.
3   *Scottish Budget:2019–20* p 35.

of non-domestic rates paid is the rateable value of the property (ie its open market rental) multiplied by the 'poundage'. Rateable values are set at periodic revaluations; the last one for Scottish property was in 2017.

In response to widespread calls from Scottish business, the Scottish Government proposes a below-inflation increase in the non-domestic rates poundage for 2019–20 to 49p, which caps the increase at 2.1%. This means that 90% of properties will pay a lower poundage than in the rest of the UK. The Large Business Supplement is set at 2.6p.

In addition there is to be an enhanced 100% fibre broadband relief for a ten-year period to 31 March 2029. Confirming previous announcements, there will be a continuation of the Small Business Bonus Scheme; the transitional relief for Aberdeen City and Shire offices; a relief for day nurseries; and relief for all but the largest hospitality properties across Scotland. The Scottish Government has shelved the idea of imposing a levy on out-of-town retailers, which will be a welcome announcement to some.

Work is still going on to implement the recommendations of the Barclay Review[1] and the Scottish Government confirms that legislation needed to implement some of the changes will be introduced in early 2019.[2]

UK taxes on land

Among the announcements with the most widespread effects was a negative one, in that the UK Government has decided not to proceed with legislation to demand shared occupancy for rent-a-room relief. However, the relief will continue to be available only for letting in a main or only residence.[3] The relief exempts from income tax a limited amount of rent from residential property.

In the opposite direction, from April 2020 the additional capital gains tax relief which extends principal private residence relief to cover certain lettings[4] will be restricted where there is shared occupancy between the owner and the tenant.[5] From the same time, the final period of ownership qualifying for relief irrespective of occupation[6] will be reduced from 18 to nine months.[7]

In relation to the annual tax on enveloped dwellings ('ATED'), the Autumn Budget announced an increase by CPI inflation (2.4%) in the amounts chargeable for 2019–20.[8]

The major reforms announced last year in relation to the taxation of capital gains on land owned by non-residents[9] are carried into effect by very extensive legislation,[10] which, among other things, replaces the whole of Part 1 of the

---

1 *Report of the Barclay Review of Non-Domestic Rates* (www.gov.scot/Publications/2017/08/3435).
2 On all of this, see *Scottish Budget:2019–20* pp 33–34.
3 *Budget 2018* (HC 1629, October 2018) para 3.10.
4 Taxation of Chargeable Gains Act 1992 s 223(4).
5 *Budget 2018* para 3.41.
6 Taxation of Chargeable Gains Act 1992 s 223(1).
7 TCGA 1992 s 223(1).
8 Annual Tax on Enveloped Dwellings (Indexation of Annual Chargeable Amounts) Order 2019, SI 2019/401.
9 See *Conveyancing 2017* p 200.
10 Finance Act 2019 ss 13 and 14, schs 1 and 2.

Taxation of Chargeable Gains Act 1992. Detailed reporting rules are included in the new legislation. Changes have been made following consultation to allow for reasonable estimates of valuations and apportionments; to remove non-UK properties from the rules; and to remove non-UK resident companies from the reporting requirement.

In the Budget, the Chancellor introduced a new capital allowances regime affecting investment in immoveable property – the structures and buildings allowance ('SBA'). SBA applies to capital expenditure on non-residential buildings under contracts entered into after 29 October 2018. It allows for a 2% straight-line writing-down allowance against construction or renovation costs for buildings or structures (such as bridges) used for a qualifying business purpose, including those used in oil and gas ring-fenced trades. Expenditure qualifying for capital allowances under other headings will not qualify for SBA. Expenditure qualifying for SBA will not be eligible for the annual investment allowance. Eligibility for allowances will transfer with the underlying property, and purchasers will simply inherit the remaining tax written-down amount of the initial spend. Additional rules will apply in cases where structures or buildings are destroyed, or substantially refurbished following significant damage.[1]

---

1   See *Budget 2018* (HC 1629, October 2018) para 3.23 and the Technical Note *Capital allowances for structures and buildings* (29 October 2018, https://assets.publishing.service.gov.uk/government/uploads/system/uploads/attachment_data/file/752092/Capital_allowances_for_structures_and_buildings_technical_note.pdf). The basic legislative provision is Finance Act 2019 s 30.

⚜ PART V ⚜
TABLES

TABLES

CUMULATIVE TABLE OF DECISIONS ON VARIATION OR DISCHARGE OF TITLE CONDITIONS

This table lists all opposed applications under the Title Conditions (Scotland) Act 2003 for variation or discharge of title conditions. Decisions on expenses are omitted. Note that the full opinions in Lands Tribunal cases are usually available at http://www.lands-tribunal-scotland.org.uk/.

Restriction on building

Name of case	Burden	Applicant's project in breach of burden	Application granted or refused
Ord v Mashford 2006 SLT (Lands Tr) 15; *Lawrie v Mashford*, 21 December 2007	1938. No building.	Erection of single-storey house and garage.	Granted. Claim for compensation refused.
Daly v Bryce 2006 GWD 25-565	1961 feu charter. No further building.	Replace existing house with 2 houses.	Granted.
J & L Leisure Ltd v Shaw 2007 GWD 28-489	1958 disposition. No new buildings higher than 15 feet 6 inches.	Replace derelict building with 2-storey housing.	Granted subject to compensation of £5,600.
West Coast Property Developments Ltd v Clarke 2007 GWD 29-511	1875 feu contract. Terraced houses. No further building.	Erection of second, 2-storey house.	Granted. Claim for compensation refused.
Smith v Prior 2007 GWD 30-523	1934 feu charter. No building.	Erection of modest rear extension.	Granted.
Anderson v McKinnon 2007 GWD 29-513	1993 deed of conditions in modern housing estate.	Erection of rear extension.	Granted.
Smith v Elrick 2007 GWD 29-515	1996 feu disposition. No new house. The feu had been subdivided.	Conversion of barn into a house.	Granted.

Name of case	Burden	Applicant's project in breach of burden	Application granted or refused
Brown v Richardson 2007 GWD 28-490	1888 feu charter. No alterations/new buildings.	Erection of rear extension.	Granted. This was an application for renewal, following service of a notice of termination.
Gallacher v Wood 2008 SLT (Lands Tr) 31	1933 feu contract. No alterations/new buildings.	Erection of rear extension, including extension at roof level which went beyond bungalow's footprint.	Granted. Claim for compensation refused.
Jarron v Stuart 23 March and 5 May 2011	1992 deed of conditions. No external alteration and additions.	Erection of rear extension.	Granted. Claim for compensation refused.
Blackman v Best 2008 GWD 11-214	1934 disposition. No building other than a greenhouse.	Erection of a double garage.	Granted.
McClumpha v Bradie 2009 GWD 31-519	1984 disposition allowing the erection of only one house.	Erection of 4 further houses.	Granted but restricted to 4 houses.
McGregor v Collins-Taylor 14 May 2009	1988 disposition prohibiting the erection of dwellinghouses without consent.	Erection of 4 further houses.	Granted but restricted to 4 houses.
Faeley v Clark 2006 GWD 28-626	1967 disposition. No further building.	Erection of second house.	Refused.
Cattanach v Vine-Hall	1996 deed of conditions in favour of neighbouring property. No building within 7 metres of that property.	Erection of substantial house within 2 metres.	Refused, subject to the possibility of the applicants bringing a revised proposal.
Hamilton v Robertson, 10 January 2008	1984 deed of conditions affecting 5-house development. No further building.	Erection of second house on site, but no firm plans.	Refused, although possibility of later success once plans firmed up was not excluded.
Cocozza v Rutherford 2008 SLT (Lands Tr) 6	1977 deed of conditions. No alterations.	Substantial alterations which would more than double the footprint of the house.	Refused.

Name of case	Burden	Applicant's project in breach of burden	Application granted or refused
Scott v Teasdale 22 December 2009	1962 feu disposition. No building.	New house in garden.	Refused.
Rennie v Cullen House Gardens Ltd 29 June 2012	2005 deed of conditions. No new building or external extension.	Extension of building forming part of historic house.	Refused.
Hollinshead v Gilchrist 7 December 2009	1990 disposition and 1997 feu disposition. No building or alterations.	Internal alterations.	Granted.
Tower Hotel (Troon) Ltd v McCann 4 March 2010	1965 feu disposition. No building. Existing building to be used as a hotel or dwellinghouse.	No firm plan though one possibility was the building of flats.	Granted.
Corstorphine v Fleming 2 July 2010	1965 feu disposition. No alterations, one house only.	A substantial extension plus a new house.	Granted.
Corry v MacLachlan 9 July 2010	1984 disposition of part of garden. Obligation to build a single-storey house.	Addition of an extra storey.	Refused.
Watt v Garden 4 November 2011	1995 disposition. Use as garden only.	Additional 2-bedroom bungalow.	Granted but with compensation.
Fyfe v Benson 26 July 2011	1966 deed of conditions. No building or subdivision.	Additional 3-bedroom house.	Refused.
MacDonald v Murdoch 7 August 2012	1997 disposition. No building in garden.	Erection of 1½-storey house.	Refused.
Trigstone Ltd v Mackenzie 16 February 2012	1949 charter of novodamus. No building in garden.	Erection of 4-storey block of flats. Parking of 2 cars.	Refused.
McCulloch v Reid 3 April 2012	2011 disposition. No parking in rear courtyard.	Erection of 2 houses.	Refused.
Franklin v Lawson 2013 SLT (Lands Tr) 81	1980 feu disposition. No alterations to house.	Erection of 2-storey extension.	Granted.
Trustees of John Raeside & Son v Chalmers 2014 GWD 35-660	1989 disposition. Agricultural purposes only.	Erection of mews house in back garden.	Granted.

Name of case	Burden	Applicant's project in breach of burden	Application granted or refused
Sinton v Lloyd 11 June 2014	Instrument of sasine of 1813 prohibiting building.	Erection of new house and extension of existing house.	Granted.
MacKay v McGowan 2015 SLT (Lands Tr) 6	Feu disposition prohibiting building.	Erection of 2-storey extension.	Granted.
Ferguson v Gunby 2015 SLT (Lands Tr) 6	1972 deed of conditions preventing alterations.		Granted.
O'Donnell v Craig 2 May 2018	1985 deed of conditions preventing building.	Erection of 4 houses in garden.	Granted.
Martin v Turnbull 26 June 2018	Deeds of 1980 and 1982 preventing building.	Erection of second house in garden.	Refused.
Cadman v Cook 2018 Hous LR 64	1874 feu disposition preventing building.	Erection of 21-unit building for sheltered housing.	Refused.
Crolla v Reid 18 April 2018	1978 deed of conditions prohibiting subdivision of flats.	Subdivision of a flat.	Granted.
Chan v Sanderson-Tolsma 29 November 2018	2003 deed of conditions.	Erection of second house.	Granted.
Rubislaw Quarry Aberdeen Ltd v Hill of Rubislaw (Q Seven) Ltd 5 January 2018	2003 deed of conditions.	Erection of a heritage centre.	Refused.

Other restrictions on use

Name of case	Burden	Applicant's project in breach of burden	Application granted or refused
Church of Scotland General Trs v McLaren 2006 SLT (Lands Tr) 27	Use as a church.	Possible development for flats.	Granted.
Wilson v McNamee 16 September 2007	Use for religious purposes.	Use for a children's nursery.	Granted.
Verrico v Tomlinson 2008 SLT (Lands Tr) 2	1950 disposition. Use as a private residence for the occupation of one family.	Separation of mews cottage from ground floor flat.	Granted.

Name of case	Burden	Applicant's project in breach of burden	Application granted or refused
Whitelaw v Acheson 29 February and 29 September 2012	1883 feu charter. Use as a single dwelling; no further building.	Change of use to therapy and wellbeing centre; erection of extension.	Granted subject to some restrictions.
Matnic Ltd v Armstrong 2010 SLT (Lands Tr) 7	2004 deed of conditions. Use for the sale of alcohol.	Use of units in a largely residential estate for retail purposes.	Granted but restricted to small units and no sale of alcohol after 8 pm.
Clarke v Grantham 2009 GWD 38-645	2004 disposition. No parking on an area of courtyard.	A desire to park (though other areas were available).	Granted.
Hollinshead v Gilchrist 7 December 2009	1990 disposition and 1997 feu disposition. No caravans, commercial or other vehicles to be parked in front of the building line.	Parking of cars.	Granted and claim for compensation refused.
Perth & Kinross Council v Chapman 13 August 2009	1945 disposition. Plot to be used only for outdoor recreational purposes.	Sale for redevelopment.	Granted.
Davenport v Julian Hodge Bank Ltd 23 June 2011	2010 deed of conditions. No external painting without permission.	Paint the external walls sky blue.	Refused.
Duffus v McWhirter 2014 GWD 34-647	2005 disposition prohibiting commercial use.	Commercial equestrian use.	Refused.

Flatted property

Name of case	Burden	Applicant's project in breach of burden	Application granted or refused
Regan v Mullen 2006 GWD 25-564	1989. No subdivision of flat.	Subdivision of flat.	Granted.
Kennedy v Abbey Lane Properties 29 March 2010	2004. Maindoor flat liable for a share of maintenance of common passages and stairs.	None.	Refused.

Name of case	Burden	Applicant's project in breach of burden	Application granted or refused
Patterson v Drouet 20 January 2011	Liability for maintenance in accordance with gross annual value.	None, but, since the freezing of valuations in 1989, ground floor flats had reverted to residential use.	Variation of liability of ground floor flats granted in principle subject to issues of competency.
Melville v Crabbe 19 January 2009	1880 feu disposition. No additional flat.	Creation of a flat in the basement.	Refused.

Sheltered and retirement housing

Name of case	Burden	Applicant's project in breach of burden	Application granted or refused
At.Home Nationwide Ltd v Morris 2007 GWD 31-535	1993 deed of conditions. On sale, must satisfy superior that flat will continue to be used for the elderly.	No project: just removal of an inconvenient restriction.	Burden held to be void. Otherwise application would have been refused.

Miscellaneous

Name of case	Burden	Applicant's project in breach of burden	Application granted or refused
McPherson v Mackie 2006 GWD 27-606 rev [2007] CSIH 7, 2007 SCLR 351	1990. Housing estate: maintenance of house.	Demolition of house to allow the building of a road for access to proposed new development.	Discharged by agreement on 25 April 2007.

Applications for renewal of real burdens following service of a notice of termination

Name of case	Burden	Respondent's project in breach of burden	Application granted or refused
Brown v Richardson 2007 GWD 28-490	1888 feu charter. No buildings	Substantial rear extension.	Refused.
Council for Music in Hospitals v Trs for Richard Gerald Associates 2008 SLT (Lands Tr) 17	1838 instrument of sasine. No building in garden.	None.	Refused.

Name of case	Burden	Applicant's project in breach of burden	Application granted or refused
Gibson v Anderson 3 May 2012	1898 disposition. No building other than 1-storey outbuildings.	2-storey house.	Refused; burden varied to allow limited building.
Macneil v Bradonwood Ltd 2013 SLT (Lands Tr) 41	Mid-Victorian feus limited building at foot of garden to 1 storey.	1.5-storey houses.	Refused; burden varied to allow the proposed houses.
Cook v Cadman 2014 SLT (Lands Tr) 13	1876 feu prevented building.	4 additional houses.	Refused; burden varied to allow the proposed houses.

Applications for preservation of community burdens following deeds of variation or discharge under s 33 or s 35

Name of case	Burden	Respondent's project in breach of burden	Application granted or refused
Fleeman v Lyon 2009 GWD 32-539	1982 deed of conditions. No building, trade, livestock etc.	Erection of a second house.	Granted.

Applications for variation of community burdens (s 91)

Name of case	Burden	Applicant's project in breach of burden	Application granted or refused
Fenwick v National Trust for Scotland 2009 GWD 32-538	1989 deed of conditions.	None. The application was for the complete discharge of the deed with the idea that a new deed would eventually be drawn up.	Refused.
Patterson v Drouet 2013 GWD 3-99	1948 deed of conditions apportioned liability for maintenance in a tenement on the basis of annual value.	Substitution of floor area for annual value.	Granted: compensation refused.
Gilfin Property Holdings Ltd v Beech 2013 SLT (Lands Tr) 17	1986 deed of conditions apportioned liability for maintenance in a tenement on a percentage basis rooted in rateable value.	Substitution of a more equitable apportionment.	Granted.

Name of case	Burden	Applicant's project in breach of burden	Application granted or refused
Stewart v Sherwood 7 June 2013	1986 deed of conditions.	Addition of a prohibition on letting.	Granted except in one respect.
Scott v Applin 16 May 2013	2005 deed of conditions.	Removal of requirement that the full-time manager should be resident.	Granted.
McCabe v Killcross 2013 SLT (Lands Tr) 48	Feu dispositions from 1976.	Altering apportionment of liability for maintenance following division of one of the flats.	Granted except in one respect.
Bennett v Skene 11 May 2018	Deeds of 1950 and 1961 apportioned liability for maintenance in a tenement on the basis of assessed rental.	Substitution of floor area for assessed rental.	Granted.

Personal real burdens

Name of case	Burden	Applicant's project in breach of burden	Application granted or refused
Grant v National Trust for Scotland 8 August 2014	Conservation agreement from 1962 prohibited non-agricultural use.	Building of houses.	Granted in part.

Servitudes

Name of case	Servitude	Applicant's project in breach of burden	Application granted or refused
George Wimpey East Scotland Ltd v Fleming 2006 SLT (Lands Tr) 2 and 59	1988 disposition. Right of way.	Diversion of right of way to allow major development for residential houses.	Granted (opposed). Claim for compensation for temporary disturbance refused.
Ventureline Ltd 2 August 2006	1972 disposition. 'Right to use' certain ground.	Possible redevelopment.	Granted (unopposed).

Name of case	Burden	Applicant's project in breach of burden	Application granted or refused
Graham v Parker 2007 GWD 30-524	1990 feu disposition. Right of way from mid-terraced house over garden of end-terraced house to the street.	Small re-routing of right of way, away from the burdened owner's rear wall, so as to allow an extension to be built.	Granted (opposed).
MacNab v McDowall, 24 October 2007	1994 feu disposition reserved a servitude of way from the back garden to the front street in favour of two neighbouring house.	Small re-rerouting, on to the land of one of the neighbours, to allow a rear extension to be built.	Granted (opposed).
Jensen v Tyler 2008 SLT (Lands Tr) 39	1985 feu disposition granted a servitude of way.	Re-routing of part of the road in order to allow (unspecified) development of steading.	Granted (opposed).
Gibb v Kerr 2009 GWD 38-646	1981 feu disposition granted a servitude of way.	Re-routing to homologate what had already taken place as a result of the building of a conservatory.	Granted (opposed).
Parkin v Kennedy 23 March 2010	1934 feu charter. Right of way from mid-terraced house over garden of end-terraced house.	Re-routing to allow extension to be built, which would require a restriction to pedestrian access.	Refused (opposed).
Adams v Trs for the Linton Village Hall 24 October 2011	Dispositions of 1968 and 1970 reserved a servitude of access.	Re-routing to a route more convenient for the applicant.	Granted (opposed).
Brown v Kitchen 28 October 2011	1976 feu disposition reserved a servitude of pedestrian access.	Re-routing to the edge of the garden.	Granted in principle (opposed) subject to agreement as to the widening of the substitute route.
Hossack v Robertson 29 June 2012	1944 disposition reserved a servitude of pedestrian access.	Re-routing to end of garden to allow building of conservatory.	Granted (opposed).
Cope v X 2013 SLT (Lands Tr) 20	Servitude of access.	Substitute road.	Granted (opposed).

Name of case	Burden	Applicant's project in breach of burden	Application granted or refused
ATD Developments Ltd v Weir 14 September 2010	2002 disposition granted a servitude right of way.	Narrowing the servitude so as to allow gardens for proposed new houses.	Granted (unopposed).
Stirling v Thorley 12 October 2012	1994 and 1995 dispositions granted a servitude of vehicular access.	Building a house on half of an area set aside for turning vehicles.	Refused (opposed).
Colecliffe v Thompson 2010 SLT (Lands Tr) 15	1997 disposition granted a servitude of way.	None. But the owners of the benefited property had since acquired a more convenient access, secured by a new servitude.	Granted (opposed).
G v A 26 November 2009	1974 disposition granted a servitude of way.	None. But the owners of the benefited property had since acquired a more convenient access (although not to his garage).	Granted (opposed) but on the basis that the respondent should apply for compensation.
Graham v Lee 18 June 2009	2001 disposition granted (a) a servitude of way and (b) of drainage.	None.	(a) was granted provided the applicants discharged a reciprocal servitude of their own, and compensation was considered. (b) was refused.
McNab v Smith 15 June 2012	1981 disposition granted a servitude of vehicular access for agricultural purposes.	None. But the owner of the benefited property could access the property in a different way.	Granted (opposed) but, because works would be needed to improve the alternative access, on the basis of payment of compensation.
Stephenson v Thomas 21 November 2012	1990 disposition granted a servitude of vehicular access.	None. But the owner of the benefited property could access the property in a different way.	Refused (opposed) on the basis that there were safety concerns about the alternative route and the benefited proprietors were proposing to revert to the original route.

Name of case	Burden	Applicant's project in breach of burden	Application granted or refused
McKenzie v Scott 19 May 2009	Dispositions from 1944 and 1957 granted a servitude of bleaching and drying clothes.	None. But the servitude had not in practice been exercised for many years.	Granted (opposed).
Chisholm v Crawford 17 June 2010	A driveway divided two properties. A 1996 feu disposition of one of the properties granted a servitude of access over the driveway.	None. But the applicant was aggrieved that no matching servitude appeared in the neighbour's title.	Refused.
Branziet Investments v Anderson 2013 GWD 31-629	1968 disposition granted a servitude of vehicular access.	Narrowing the servitude to 5 metres so as to allow rear gardens for new houses.	Granted (opposed) except that at either end the width was to be larger.
Mackay v Bain 2013 SLT (Lands Tr) 37	Servitude of pedestrian access over the front garden of applicant's property (1989).	None.	Refused (opposed). The servitude was the only means of access to the respondents' front door.
Pollacchi v Campbell 2014 SLT (Lands Tr) 55	Servitude of vehicular access.	Re-routing to allow creation of garden.	Refused.
Yule v Tobert 2015 GWD 39-620	Servitude of vehicular access over yard (1984).	None, but dominant proprietor wished to use access to allow teachers at his nursery to park.	Refused application to restrict servitude to residential purposes.
United Investment Co Ltd v Charlie Reid Ltd 2016 GWD 1-13	Servitude of vehicular access (1963).	Major redevelopment of site.	Granted (opposed) but subject to the possibility of compensation if loss in value to the benefited property could be shown.

CUMULATIVE TABLE OF APPEALS

A table at the end of *Conveyancing 2008* listed all cases digested in *Conveyancing 1999* and subsequent annual volumes in respect of which an appeal was subsequently heard, and gave the result of the appeal. This table is a continuation of the earlier table, beginning with appeals heard during 2009.

Aberdeen City Council v Stewart Milne Group Ltd
[2009] CSOH 80, 2009 GWD 26-417, 2009 Case (6) *affd* [2010] CSIH 81, 2010 GWD 37-755, 2010 Case (9) *affd* [2011] UKSC 56, 2011 Case (13)

Alexander v West Bromwich Mortgage Co Ltd
[2015] EWHC 135 (Comm), [2015] 2 All ER (Comm) 224, 2015 Case (71) *rev* [2016] EWCA Civ 496, 2016 Case (60)

AMA (New Town) Ltd v Finlay
2010 GWD 32-658, Sh Ct, 2010 Case (8) *rev* 2011 SLT (Sh Ct) 73, 2011 Case (1)

Argyll & Bute Council v Gordon
2016 SLT (Sh Ct) 196, 2016 SCLR 192, 2016 Case (78) *affd* [2017] SAC (Civ) 6, 2017 SLT (Sh Ct) 53, 2017 Case (73)

AWG Business Centres Ltd v Regus Caledonia Ltd
[2016] CSOH 99, 2016 GWD 22-407, 2016 Case (40) *affd* [2017] CSIH 22, 2017 GWD 9-131, 2017 Case (43)

Blemain Finance Ltd v Balfour & Manson LLP
[2011] CSOH 157, 2012 SLT 672, 2011 Case (69) *affd* [2012] CSIH 66, [2013] PNLR 3, 2012 GWD 30-609, 2012 Case (70)

British Waterways Board v Arjo Wiggins Ltd
12 May 2016, Fort William Sheriff Court, 2016 Case (15) *affd* [2017] SAC (Civ) 15, 2017 GWD 15-240, 2017 Case (17)

Brown v Stonegale Ltd
[2013] CSOH 189, 2014 GWD 2-27, 2013 Case (71) *affd* [2015] CSIH 12, 2015 SCLR 619, 2015 Case (85) *affd* [2016] UKSC 30, 2016 GWD 20-359, 2016 Case (73)

Caven v Irvine Housing Association
2016 GWD 38-682, 2016 Case (36) *affd* [2018] CSIH 23, 2018 Case (54)

Chalmers v Chalmers
[2014] CSOH 161, 2015 SCLR 299, 2014 Case (22) *rev* [2015] CSIH 75, 2015 SLT 793, 2015 Hous LR 82, 2016 SC 158, 2015 Case (27)

Cheshire Mortgage Corporation Ltd v Grandison; Blemain Finance Ltd v Balfour & Manson LLP

[2011] CSOH 157, 2012 SLT 672, 2011 Case (69) *affd* [2012] CSIH 66, [2013] PNLR 3, 2012 GWD 30-609, 2012 Case (69)

Christie Owen & Davies plc v Campbell

2007 GWD 24-397, Sh Ct, 2007 Case (53) *affd* 18 Dec 2007, Glasgow Sheriff Court, 2007 Case (53) *rev* [2009] CSIH 26, 2009 SLT 518, 2009 Case (82)

Collins v Sweeney

2013 GWD 11-230, Sh Ct, 2013 Case (3) *affd* 2014 GWD 12-214, Sh Ct, 2014 Case (4)

Compugraphics International Ltd v Nikolic

[2009] CSOH 54, 2009 GWD 19-311, 2009 Cases (22) and (90) *rev* [2011] CSIH 34, 2011 SLT 955, 2011 Cases (21) and (74)

Co-operative Group Ltd v Propinvest Paisley LP

17 September 2010, Lands Tribunal, 2010 Case (36) *rev* [2011] CSIH 41, 2012 SC 51, 2011 SLT 987, 2011 Hous LR 32, 2011 Case (38)

Cramaso LLP v Viscount Reidhaven's Trs

[2010] CSOH 62, 2010 GWD 20-403, 2010 Case (58) *affd* [2011] CSIH 81, 2011 Case (57) *rev* [2014] UKSC 9, 2014 SC (UKSC) 121, 2014 SLT 521, 2014 SCLR 484, 2014 Case (31)

EDI Central Ltd v National Car Parks Ltd

[2010] CSOH 141, 2011 SLT 75, 2010 Case (5) *affd* [2012] CSIH 6, 2012 SLT 421, 2012 Case (4)

ELB Securities Ltd v Love

2014 GWD 28-562, 2014 Case (38) *affd* [2015] CSIH 67, 2015 SLT 721, 2015 Hous LR 88, 2015 Case (66)

Euring David Ayre of Kilmarnock, Baron of Kilmarnock Ptr

[2008] CSOH 35, 2008 Case (82) *rev* [2009] CSIH 61, 2009 SLT 759, 2009 Case (93)

JAL Fish Ltd Small Self-Administered Pension Scheme Trs v Robertson Construction Eastern Ltd

[2017] CSOH 70, 2017 SLT 577, 2-17 Case (1) *affd* sub nom *Law v Robertson Construction Eastern Ltd* [2018] CSIH 24, 2018 SC 428, 2018 SLT 377, 2018 Case (1)

Fortune's Tr v Medwin Investments Ltd

[2015] CSOH 139, 2015 GWD 34-552, 2015 Case (87) *affd* [2016] CSIH 49, 2016 SLT 923, 2016 Case (75)

Frank Houlgate Investment Co Ltd v Biggart Baillie LLP

[2013] CSOH 80, 2013 SLT 993, 2013 Case (61) *affd* [2014] CSIH 79, 2014 SLT 1001, 2015 SC 187, 2014 Case (65)

Fraser v McDonald

18 July 2017, Perth Sheriff Court, 2017 Case (13) *rev* [2018] SAC (Civ) 8, 2018 Case (21)

Martin Stephen James Goldstraw of Whitecairns Ptr

[2008] CSOH 34, 2008 Case (81) *rev* [2009] CSIH 61, 2009 SLT 759, 2009 Case (93)

Gordon v Campbell Riddell Breeze Paterson LLP

[2015] CSOH 31, 2015 GWD 12-216, 2015 Case (74) *affd* [2016] CSIH 16, 2016 SC 548, 2016 SLT 580, 2016 Case (63) *affd* [2017] UKSC 75, 2017 SLT 1287, 2017 Case (65)

Gray v MacNeil's Exr

2016 SLT (Sh Ct) 250, 2016 Case (37) *rev* [2017] SAC (Civ) 9, 2017 SLT (Sh Ct) 83, 2017 SCLR 666, 2017 Hous LR 47, 2017 Case (42)

Gyle Shopping Centre General Partners Ltd v Marks and Spencer plc

[2015] CSOH 14, 2015 GWD 6-127, 2015 Case (56) *rev* [2016] CSIH 19, 2016 GWD 10-205, 2016 Case (38)

Hamilton v Dumfries & Galloway Council

[2008] CSOH 65, 2008 SLT 531, 2008 Case (37) *rev* [2009] CSIH 13, 2009 SC 277, 2009 SLT 337, 2009 SCLR 392, 2009 Case (50)

Hamilton v Nairn

[2009] CSOH 163, 2010 SLT 399, 2009 Case (51) *affd* [2010] CSIH 77, 2010 SLT 1155, 2010 Case (44)

Hill of Rubislaw (Q Seven) Ltd v Rubislaw Quarry Aberdeen Ltd

[2013] CSOH 131, 2013 GWD 27-545, 2014 Case (11) *affd* [2014] CSIH 105, 2015 SC 339, 2014 Case (10)

Hoblyn v Barclays Bank plc

[2013] CSOH 104, 2013 GWD 26-533, 10313 Case (51) *affd* [2014] CSIH 52, 2014 GWD 30-376, 2014 HousLR 26, 2015 SCLR 85, 2014 Case (60)

Holms v Ashford Estates Ltd

2006 SLT (Sh Ct) 70, 2006 Case (40) *affd* 2006 SLT (Sh Ct) 161, 2006 Case (40) *rev* [2009] CSIH 28, 2009 SLT 389, 2009 SCLR 428, 2009 Cases (19) and (52)

Hunter v Tindale

2011 SLT (Sh Ct) 11, 2010 Case (16) *rev* 2011 GWD 25-570, Sh Ct, 2011 Case (19)

Iftikhar v CIP Property (AIPT) Ltd

[2017] CSOH 148, 2017 GWD 40-609, 2017 Case (4) *rev* [2018] CSIH 44, 2018 GWD 24-301, 2018 Case (2)

Jack v Jack

[2015] CSOH 91, 2015 Fam LR 95, 2015 Case (94) *affd* [2016] CSIH 75, 2016 Fam LR 177, 2016 Case (77)

K2 Restaurants Ltd v Glasgow City Council

[2011] CSOH 171, 2011 Hous LR 171, 2011 Case (20) *affd* [2013] CSIH 49, 2013 GWD 21-420, 2013 Case (5)

Kennedy v Dickie & More Holdings Ltd

[2015] CSOH 103, 2015 GWD 25-436, 2015 Case (3) *rev* [2016] CSIH 37, 2016 GWD 18-325, 2016 Case (4)

Kenwright v Stuart Milne Group Ltd

[2015] CSOH 86, 2015 GWD 22-389, 2015 Case (11) *rev* [2016] CSIH 45, 2016 GWD 20-351, 2016 Case (5)

Kerr of Ardgowan, Ptr

[2008] CSOH 36, 2008 SLT 251, 2008 Case (80) *rev* [2009] CSIH 61, 2009 SLT 759, 2009 Case (93)

Khosrowpour v Mackay

[2014] CSOH 175, 2015 GWD 1-8, 2014 Case (17) *rev* [2016] CSIH 50, 2016 Case (17)

L Batley Pet Products Ltd v North Lanarkshire Council

[2011] CSOH 209, 2012 GWD 4-73, 2011 Case (62) *rev* [2012] CSIH 83, 2012 GWD 37-745, 2012 Case (43) *rev* [2014] UKSC 27, 2014 SC (UKSC) 174, 2014 SLT 593, 2014 Case (39)

Lamont (J H & W) of Heathfield Farm v Chattisham Ltd

[2017] CSOH 119, 2017 GWD 30-470, *Conveyancing 2017* Case (60) *affd* [2018] CSIH 33, 2018 SC 440, 2018 SLT 511, 2018 Case (70)

Liquidator of Letham Grange Development Co Ltd v Foxworth Investments Ltd

[2011] CSOH 66, 2011 SLT 1152, 2011 Case (64) *rev* [2013] CSIH 13, 2013 SLT 445, 2013 Case (47) *rev* [2014] UKSC 41, 2014 SC (UKSC) 203, 2014 SLT 775, 2014 Case (70)

Livingstone of Bachuil v Paine

[2012] CSOH 161, 2012 GWD 35-707, 2012 Case (12) *rev* [2013] CSIH 110, 2013 Case (9)

Loch Lomond and Trossachs National Park Authority v Renyana-Stahl Anstalt
[2017] SAC (Civ) 11, 2017 SLT (Sh Ct) 128, 2017 Case (18) *affd* [2018] CSIH 22, 2018 SC 406, 2018 SLT 331, 2018 SCLR, 2018 Case (35)

Luminar Lava Ignite Ltd v Mama Group plc
[2009] CSOH 68, 2009 GWD 19-305, 2009 Case (91) *rev* [2010] CSIH 1, 2010 SC 310, 2010 SLT 147, 2010 Case (77)

McCallum v City of Edinburgh Council
2016 GWD 24-450, 2016 Case (34) *affd* [2017] CSIH 24, 2017 SLT 466, 2017 Hous LR 42, 2017 Case (37)

McGraddie v McGraddie
[2009] CSOH 142, 2009 GWD 38-633, 2009 Case (60), [2010] CSOH 60, 2010 GWD 21-404, 2000 Case (48) *rev* [2012] CSIH 23, 2012 GWD 15-310, 2012 Case (38) *rev* [2013] UKSC 58, 2013 SLT 1212, 2013 Case (32)

MacQueen v MacPherson
3 October 2014, Oban Sheriff Court, 2014 Case (2) *rev* [2015] CSIH 60, 2015 GWD 26-449, 2015 Case (4)

McSorley v Drennan
May 2011, Ayr Sheriff Court, 2011 Case (14) *rev* [2012] CSIH 59, 2012 GWD 25-506, 2012 Case (6)

Mehrabadi v Haugh
June 2009, Aberdeen Sheriff Court, 2009 Case (17) *affd* 11 January 2010, Aberdeen Sheriff Court, 2010 Case (15)

Mirza v Salim
[2013] CSOH 73, 2013 GWD 17-348, 2013 Case (65) *rev* [2014] CSIH 51, 2015 SC 31, 2014 SLT 875, 2014 SCLR 764, 2014 Case (67)

Moderator of the General Assembly of the Free Church of Scotland v Interim Moderator of the Congregation of Strath Free Church of Scotland (Continuing)
[2009] CSOH 113, 2009 SLT 973, 2009 Case (96) *affd* [2011] CSIH 52, 2011 SLT 1213, 2012 SC 79, 2011 Case (77)

Morris v Rae
[2011] CSIH 30, 2011 SC 654, 2011 SLT 701, 2011 SCLR 428, 2011 Case (39) *rev* [2012] UKSC 50, 2013 SC (UKSC) 106, 2013 SLT 88, 2013 SCLR 80, 2012 Case (41)

Multi-link Leisure Developments Ltd v North Lanarkshire Council

[2009] CSOH 114, 2009 SLT 1170, 2009 Case (70) *rev* [2009] CSIH 96, 2010 SC 302, 2010 SLT 57, 2010 SCLR 306, 2009 Case (70) *affd* [2010] UKSC 47, [2011] 1 All ER 175, 2010 Case (52)

NRAM plc v Steel

[2014] CSOH 172, 2015 GWD 1-34, 2014 Case (63) *rev* [2016] CSIH 11, 2016 SC 474, 2016 SLT 285, 2016 SCLR 736, 2016 Case (62) *rev* [2018] UKSC 13, 2018 SC (UKSC) 141, 2018 SLT 835, 2018 Case (73)

Orkney Housing Association Ltd v Atkinson

15 October 2010, Kirkwall Sheriff Court, 2010 Case (21) *rev* 2011 GWD 30-652, 2011 Cases (22) and (41)

Pocock's Tr v Skene Investments (Aberdeen) Ltd

[2011] CSOH 144, 2011 GWD 30-654, 2011 Case (40) *rev* [2012] CSIH 61, 2012 GWD 27-562, 2012 Case (36)

R M Prow (Motors) Ltd Directors Pension Fund Trustees v Argyll and Bute Council

[2012] CSOH 77, 2012 GWD 21-438, 2012 Case (44) *affd* [2013] CSIH 23, 2013 GWD 12-260, 2013 Case (44)

R & D Construction Group Ltd v Hallam Land Management Ltd

[2009] CSOH 128, 2009 Case (8) *affd* [2010] CSIH 96, 2010 Case (4)

Regency Villas Title Ltd v Diamond Resorts (Europe) Ltd

[2017] EWCA Civ 238, [2017] 3 WLR 644, 2017 Case (15) *affd* [2018] UKSC 57, [2018] 3 WLR 1603, 2018 Case (25)

Regus (Maxim) Ltd v Bank of Scotland plc

[2011] CSOH 129, 2011 GWD 27-600, 2011 Case (52) *affd* [2013] CSIH 12, 2013 SC 331, 2013 SLT 477, 2013 Case (43)

Rivendale v Keeper of the Registers of Scotland

30 October 2013, Lands Tribunal, 2013 Case (35) *affd* [2015] CSIH 27, 2015 SC 558, 2015 Case (29) and (84)

Royal Bank of Scotland plc v Carlyle

[2010] CSOH 3, 2010 GWD 13-235, 2010 Case (67) *rev* [2013] CSIH 75, 2014 SC 188, 2014 SCLR 167, 2013 Case (75) *rev* [2015] UKSC 13, 2015 SC (UKSC) 93, 2015 SLT 206, 2015 Case (91)

Royal Bank of Scotland v O'Donnell

[2013] CSOH 78, 2013 GWD 19-388, 2013 Case (59) *affd* [2014] CSIH 84, 2014 GWD 33-641, 2014 Case (54)

Royal Bank of Scotland plc v Wilson

2008 GWD 2-35, Sh Ct, 2008 Case (61) *rev* 2009 CSIH 36, 2009 SLT 729, 2009 Case (75) *rev* [2010] UKSC 50, 2011 SC (UKSC) 66, 2010 SLT 1227, 2010 Hous LR 88, 2010 Case (66)

Salvesen v Riddell

[2012] CSIH 26, 2012 SLT 633, 2012 SCLR 403, 2012 HousLR 30, 2012 Case (51) *rev* [2013] UKSC 22, 2013 SC (UKSC) 236, 2013 SLT 863, 2013 Case (50)

Schubert Murphy v The Law Society of England and Wales

[2014] EWHC 4561 (QB), [2015] PNLR 15, 2015 Case (78) *affd* [2017] EWCA Civ 1295, [2017] 4 WLR 200, 2017 Case (65)

Scottish Coal Company Ltd v Danish Forestry Co Ltd

[2009] CSOH 171, 2009 GWD 5-79, 2009 Case (9) *affd* [2010] CSIH 56, 2010 GWD 27-529, 2010 Case (3)

Sheltered Housing Management Ltd v Bon Accord Bonding Co Ltd

2007 GWD 32-533, 2006 Cases (24) and (35), 11 October 2007, Lands Tribunal, 2007 Case (21) *rev* [2010] CSIH 42, 2010 SC 516, 2010 SLT 662, 2010 Case (25)

@Sipp (Pension Trustees) Ltd v Insight Travel Services Ltd

[2014] CSOH 137, 2014 Hous LR 54, 2014 Case (42) *rev* [2015] CSIH 91, 2016 SLT 131, 2016 Hous LR 20, 2015 Case (51)

Smith v Stuart

2009 GWD 8-140, Sh Ct, 2009 Case (2) *affd* [2010] CSIH 29, 2010 SC 490, 2010 SLT 1249, 2010 Case (10)

STV Central Ltd v Semple Fraser LLP

[2014] CSOH 82, 2014 GWD 16-299, 2014 Case (61) *affd* [2015] CSIH 35, 2015 SLT 313, 2015 Case (59)

Tenzin v Russell

2014 Hous LR 17, Sh Ct, 2014 Case (51) *affd* [2015] CSIH 8A, 2015 Hous LR 11, 2015 Case (43)

Thomson v Mooney

[2012] CSOH 177, 2012 GWD 39-769, 2012 Case (63) *rev* [2013] CSIH 115, 2014 GWD 14-263, 2013 Case (74)

Tuley v Highland Council

2007 SLT (Sh Ct) 97, 2007 Case (24) *rev* [2009] CSIH 31A, 2009 SC 456, 2009 SLT 616, 2009 Case (48)

Van Lynden v Gilchrist

[2015] CSOH 147, 2015 SLT 864, 2015 Case (65) *rev* [2016] CSIH 72, 2016 SLT 1187, 2017 SCLR 351, 2016 Case (47)

Wright v Shoreline Management Ltd

Oct 2008, Arbroath Sheriff Court, 2008 Case (60) *rev* 2009 SLT (Sh Ct) 83, 2009 Case (74)